Of Two Minds:
An Anthropologist Looks at American Psychiatry

WHEN GOD TALKS BACK

WHEN GOD
TALKS BACK

UNDERSTANDING THE AMERICAN
EVANGELICAL RELATIONSHIP
WITH GOD

T. M. Luhrmann

ALFRED A. KNOPF · NEW YORK

2012

THIS IS A BORZOI BOOK
PUBLISHED BY ALFRED A. KNOPF

Knopf, Borzoi Books, and the colophon are
registered trademarks of Random House, Inc.

Owing to limitations of space, all acknowledgments for permission to
reprint previously published material may be found following the index.

Library of Congress Cataloging-in-Publication Data
Luhrmann, T. M. (Tanya M.), [date]
When God talks back : understanding the American evangelical
relationship with God / by T. M. Luhrmann. — 1st ed.
p.   cm.
Includes bibliographical references and index.
ISBN 978-0-307-26479-4
1. Vineyard Christian Fellowship—Case studies.
2. Evangelicalism—Psychology—Case studies.
3. Psychology, Religious—United States—Case studies. I. Title.
BX8785.L84 2012
277.3'083—dc23   2011040116

Jacket photograph by Don Hammond/Aurora Photos
Jacket design by Jason Booher

Manufactured in the United States of America

First Edition

for Richard

CONTENTS

A NOTE ON QUOTATIONS

I have had hundreds of conversations with evangelicals. I have many notebooks scrawled with journal entries, and a stack, about six feet high, of notes and transcripts (not to mention another twelve feet, or thirteen thousand pages in files, of transcript material from the experiment I ran). I adhere closely to the transcripts in my quotations, but my quotations are often not exact. When we speak out loud, we use language differently from the way we do when we write, and the written form of spoken speech—the "transcriptese" that types out the grunts, verbal gestures, and conversational hedges of ordinary talk—can make people sound more foolish and more hesitant than they are. Linguistic anthropologists are of course intensely interested in these verbal infelicities, and to them I apologize. I believe I have retained the sense of the speakers' words. This is an example of the way I have made the quotations more reader-palatable:

> THE ORIGINAL: "I will retreat, like go into the bedroom, close the door and sit on my bed for like an hour and just see what happens and like commune with God. My husband will be like on the other side of the house and won't interrupt me or anything like that."

> THE WAY THE QUOTATION APPEARS IN THE BOOK: "I will retreat into the bedroom, close the door, and sit on my bed for like an hour and just see what happens, commune with God. My husband won't interrupt me."

Biblical quotations are usually from the New Revised Standard Edition or the New International Version, but sometimes from the glorious King James.

PREFACE

This book begins with a few simple questions. How does God become real for people? How are sensible people able to believe in an invisible being who has a demonstrable effect on their lives? And how can they sustain that belief in the face of what skeptical observers think must be inevitable disconfirmation? This book answers these questions by taking an outsider's perspective into the heart of faith through an anthropological exploration of American evangelical Christianity.

It ought to be difficult to believe in God. God is invisible. You cannot shake God's hand, look God in the eye, or hear what God says with your ears. God gives none of the ordinary signs of existence. The sacred books are full of impossible contradictions, apparently absurd beliefs—invisible fathers, talking snakes, a dead man who comes to life and flies up to heaven.

And yet of course people do believe in God. According to a Gallup poll, roughly 95 percent of Americans say that they believe in the existence of "God or a higher power," a percentage that has remained steady since Gallup began polling on the eve of the Second World War. In 2008 the Pew Foundation conducted a quite extensive representative survey. In its sample, two-thirds of Americans completely or mostly agreed that angels and demons are active in the world today, and nearly one-fifth said that they receive a direct answer to a specific prayer request at least once a week.[1] Many Americans not only believe in God in some general way but experience God directly and report repeated contact with the supernatural.

People who do not believe in God look at these statistics and conclude that if so many people believe in something for which there is no evidence, something about the belief process must be hardwired and belief must have arisen because it serves some other, more useful end. The new field of evolutionary psychology argues that many of the building blocks of our psyche were formed through a slow evolutionary process to adapt us to a dangerous, unpredictable world. When we hear a noise in the next room, we immediately wonder about an intruder even when we know the door is locked. That's to our advantage: the cost of worrying when no one is there is nothing compared to the cost of not worrying when someone is. As a result, we are primed to be alert for presence, whether anyone is present or not.

Faced with these findings, some are tempted to argue that the reason people believe in supernatural beings is that our evolved intuitions lead us to overinterpret the presence of intentional agents, and those quick, effortless intuitions are so powerful that they become, in effect, our default interpretation of the world. From this perspective, the idea of God arises out of this evolved tendency to attribute intention to an inanimate world. Religious belief would then be an accidental by-product of the way our minds have evolved. That, in a nutshell, is what a flood of books on religion argue—*Breaking the Spell, Religion Explained, Faces in the Clouds*—and those reading them sometimes conclude that anyone with logical training and a good education should be an atheist.[2]

That conclusion is shortsighted. Evolutionary psychology looks only at part of the puzzle. It describes the way our intuitions evolved and explains why claims about invisible agents seem plausible, and why certain ideas about God are found more often in the world than others.[3] But evolutionary psychology does not explain how God *remains* real for modern doubters. This takes faith, which is often the outcome of great intellectual struggle.

Faith asks people to consider that the evidence of their senses is wrong. In various ways, and in varying degrees, faith asks that people believe that their minds are not always private; that persons are not always visible; that invisible presences should alter their emotions and direct their behavior; that reality is good and justice triumphant. These are fantastic claims, and the fact of their improbability is not lost on those who accept them—particularly in a pluralistic, self-aware society like twenty-first-century America. Many Christians come to their religious commitments slowly, carefully, and deliberatively, as if the attitude they take toward life itself depends upon their judgment. And they doubt. They find it hard to believe in an invisible being—let alone an invisible being who is entirely good and overwhelmingly powerful. Many Christians struggle, at one point or another, with the despair that it all might be a sham.[4]

They have always struggled. In earlier centuries, before atheism became a real cultural possibility, they may have struggled more about the nature of the supernatural than about whether the supernatural existed at all, but they struggled. Augustine agonized. Anselm despaired. The long tradition of spiritual literature is full of intense uncertainty about the true nature of a being that can be neither seen nor heard in the ordinary way. And whether or not people ever voice the fear that God himself is an empty fantasy, whether or not they tussle with theology, Christians of all ages have wrestled with the difficulty of believing that God is real for them in particular, for their own lives and every day, as if the promise of joy were true for other people—but not for themselves. That is why one of the oldest stories in the Hebrew Bible has become iconic for the process of coming to commitment.

> So Jacob was left alone, and a man wrestled with him till daybreak. When the man saw that he could not overpower him, he touched the socket of Jacob's hip so that his hip was wrenched as he wrestled with the man. Then the man said, "Let me go, for it is daybreak." But Jacob replied, "I will not let you go unless you bless me." The man asked him, "What is your name?" "Jacob," he answered. Then the man said, "Your name will no longer be Jacob, but Israel, because you have struggled with God and with humans and have overcome." Jacob said, "Please tell me your name." But he replied, "Why do you ask my name?" Then he blessed him there.[5]

The idea of believers struggling with doubt can be disconcerting to skeptics, who tend to imagine belief as an either-or choice, and who imagine that a good Christian has a straightforward commitment to God's reality. But when you are willing to take seriously the importance of doubt, you can see it everywhere in Christianity. The Gospels themselves expect doubt. "Do you still not see or understand?" Christ sadly asks his followers. "Are your hearts hardened?" Jesus was after all executed because people did not believe that he was the son of God, and even the disciples themselves were often painfully confused about who Christ was and what he asked of them. "But they still did not understand what he was saying and were afraid to ask him." When a father brings his small boy to Jesus for healing because he is terribly ill, Jesus tells him sternly that he will heal only those who believe. "Lord, I believe," the father implores him. But then he adds, "Help my unbelief."[6]

Faith is hard because it is a decision to live as if a set of claims are real, even when one doubts: in the Christian case, that the world is good; that love endures; that you should live your life as if the promise of joy were at least a possibility. These are not intellectual judgments on the same order as deciding how many apples you should buy at the market. They are ways of experiencing life, attitudes we take toward living in the world. The Gospels clearly present the commitment to faith as a choice in the face of the uncertainty of human knowledge. Indeed, most Christians believe quite explicitly that what humans understand about God is obscured by the deep stuff of their humanness, and that their humanness—the way their minds and emotions have adapted to their social world—has shaped their interpretation of the divine. For that matter, so did the early Christians. The men and women who met in small, secret house groups to worship their god believed that the divine was inherently unknowable by human beings, whose human eyes and ears and hands are made to sense a mundane world. They took for granted that what they perceived was profoundly limited. This is the point of Paul's famous caution, in the stately translation that has echoed down the centuries:

For now we know in part, and we prophesy in part.
But when that which is perfect is come, then that which is in part
  shall be done away.
When I was a child, I spake as a child, I understood as a child; but
  when I became a man, I put away childish things.
For now we see through a glass, darkly, but then face to face: now
  I know in part, but then shall I know even as also I am known.[7]

We will not see God clearly, Paul says, until we no longer see with human eyes.[8] This is why Kierkegaard could describe the decision to believe as a leap in the dark, as a choice founded not on evidence but on the way we choose to live in the face of inadequate evidence. The fact of human uncertainty about the ultimate, and the stakes of our decision in the face of that uncertainty, are also why one can argue that no one is an adult until he or she has seriously considered the question of God.[9]

Let me be clear: This book does not answer the question of whether

God exists, or for that matter the question of whether God is truly present when someone experiences God as present. I am a social scientist, and I do not believe that social science—the study of the social life of humans—can answer those questions. I wrote this book because I think I can explain to nonbelievers how people come to experience God as real.

This is an important story because the rift between believers and nonbelievers has grown so wide that it can be difficult for one side to respect the other. Since evangelical Christianity emerged as a force in American culture, and especially since the younger George Bush rode a Christian wave into office, nonevangelical observers have been transfixed by the change in the American religious landscape. Many have been horrified by what they take to be naïve and unthinking false beliefs, and alarmed by the nature of this modern God.

It is indeed a striking God, this modern God imagined by so many American evangelicals. Each generation meets God in its own manner. Over the last few decades, this generation of Americans has sought out an intensely personal God, a God who not only cares about your welfare but worries with you about whether to paint the kitchen table. These Americans call themselves evangelical to assert that they are part of the conservative Christian tradition that understands the Bible to be literally or near literally true and that describes the relationship with Jesus as personal, and as being born again. But the feature that most deeply characterizes them is that the God they seek is more personally intimate, and more intimately experienced, than the God most Americans grew up with. These evangelicals have sought out and cultivated concrete experiences of God's realness. They have strained to hear the voice of God speaking outside their heads. They have yearned to feel God clasp their hands and to sense the weight of his hands push against their shoulders. They have wanted the hot presence of the Holy Spirit to brush their cheeks and knock them sideways.

While these longings for God's realness are not novel in our religious history, what is new is that the experiences and practices we associate with medieval monks or impoverished snake-handlers have now become white, middle-class, and mainstream. Ordinary Americans are now embracing a spirituality that mid-twentieth-century generations had regarded as vulgar, overemotional, or even psychotic. This suspension of disbelief and embrace of the irrational makes skeptics deeply uneasy. But in fact, evangelical Christians are sharply aware of the logical contradictions that nonevangelical observers see so clearly. What enables them to sustain their commitment is a learning process that changes their experience of mind.

This book explains how this new use of the mind allows God to come alive for people. It explains what people learn, how deep the learning goes, and how powerful it is. My goal is to help nonbelievers understand this learning process. This will not turn the skeptic into a believer, but it will help to explain how a reasonable person could choose to become and remain this kind of Christian. Perhaps that will serve as a bridge across the divide, and help us to respect one another.

Let us begin by turning the skeptic's question on its head. If you could believe in God, why wouldn't you? There is good evidence that those who believe in a loving God have happier lives. Loneliness is bad for people in many different ways—it diminishes immune function, increases blood pressure, and depresses cognitive function—and we know that people who believe in God are less lonely. We know that God is experienced in the brain as a social relationship. (Put someone in the scanner and ask them about God, and the same region of the brain lights up as when you ask them about a friend.) We know that those who go to church live longer and in greater health.[10]

So why wouldn't you believe? Particularly in this God. The major shift in American spirituality over the past half century has been toward a God who is not only vividly present but deeply kind. He is no longer the benign but distant sovereign of the old mainstream church; nor is he the harsh tyrant of the Hebrew Bible. He is personal and intimate. This new, modern God is eager for the tiniest details of a worshipper's life. He welcomes prayers about the nation, of course, but he also wants prayers about what outfit to wear in the morning. He may be grand and mighty, but he is also as closely held and precious as a child's first puppy. This God loves unconditionally; he forgives freely; he brings joy. Why would one not believe?

But the deep puzzle of faith is not why someone should believe in God. The puzzle is how: how sensible, reasonable people, living in more or less the same evidential world as the skeptic, are able to experience themselves as having good evidence for the presence of a powerful invisible being who has a demonstrable effect on their lives and are able to sustain a belief in that presence despite their inevitable doubts.

It is a problem all Christians face, although it is magnified in a secular society in which many people do not take God seriously. The problem for ordinary Christians—often surrounded by other Christians, often having grown up among good, committed Christians—is how to maintain their belief despite their skepticism: not the puzzle of why we all believe to some extent in the supernatural when we are thinking quickly, automatically, superstitiously, but the problem of how to commit to what the Bible says is true in the face of the contradictions they experience in their world. They believe—or want to believe—that the world is fundamentally good or was at least created by a fundamentally good power that is still present and responsive. Yet they see around themselves a world of great injustice. They believe, or they think that they should believe, that God loves them—and yet they don't really experience themselves, in their heart of hearts, as loved and lovable. Or they know that God wants them to love their spouse, but they can't seem to behave in a loving way. Or they sit down to pray, but they cannot persuade themselves that anyone is listening. Or they believe in God, but what they interpret as God's will has just been flatly contradicted by someone they know and trust, and now they are bewildered and confused. They believe in some abstract, absolute sense that God exists, but they struggle to experience God as real in the everyday world. They want to know *how* to hang on to their convictions in the face of so much evidence to the contrary, and it is sometimes very difficult for them to do so.

At its heart, this is the dilemma of all human knowledge. We reach out to grasp a world we know to be more complex than our capacity to understand it, and we choose and act despite our awareness that what we take to be true may be an illusion, a wispy misperception. Plato captured this uncertainty in a famous allegory. Humans live, he suggested, as if chained within a cave with their backs to the entrance, able to see no more than the wall before them, forced to infer the nature of the real objects in the world from the flickering shadows those objects cast as they pass before a fire at the entrance of the cave.

Divinity poses a special sort of problem in epistemology. You cannot kick a stone and refute the argument from skepticism, as Samuel Johnson did when confronted with Bishop Berkeley's doubts that the world existed. There is no stone to kick. It is the essential nature of divinity that divinity is nonmaterial. There is nothing physical that a Christian can pick up and show to a non-Christian as irrevocable material proof of the existence of the Christian God; nor is there irrevocable physical evidence against that God's reality. Even if a believer is prepared to accept the existence of divinity without question, the knowledge that our humanness limits our understanding of God's real nature means that each believer is constantly making judgments about whom to trust about the specifics.

This is the problem of presence: that the evidence for divinity does not come directly from the senses. It usually comes indirectly, from other, more unreliable, sources.[11]

Those who say they know God are legion, and their testimony includes the earliest written texts to have survived the harshness of the Egyptian desert and last week's telephone call from your great-aunt Mildred. Any one person who has faith must believe that at least some of those who claim to know God are simply wrong. Few people who have faith are, I believe, willing to say that all those mistakes are malicious or mad. Most people, whatever their religious persuasion, assume that there are decent human beings with good intentions who have interpreted the evidence differently and are wrong. Most people who attend church disagree with some people in their churches at some times, sometimes even with their pastors or their friends, over the interpretation of a biblical text, over the decision about what kind of spiritual education their children need, over their conviction that a particular political judgment follows from a particular understanding of God. Those who have faith are acutely aware that all humans look out at the world from behind lenses that distort what is there to be seen.

So how, in the face of doubt and uncertainty, does God become real for someone? Particularly in our modern—or postmodern or late modern—American society, with all its exposure to scientific explanation, where the supernatural is often treated as entertaining fantasy, how does someone become confident that there is a supernatural God present in the everyday world? How does a living God become real to modern people?

I am an anthropologist, and in all likelihood I chose my profession because I have lived these questions. I have three cousins, sons of my mother's sisters. Each of them is a deeply conservative Christian, of the sort my secular friends would call fundamentalist. My mother's father was a Baptist minister, but my mother rebelled. My father's father was a Christian Scientist, but my father, too, rebelled—he became a doctor—and when I was a child, we went to a Unitarian church. Neither of them was willing to give up on church, but for neither of them did God really exist as a being in the world. When we met for larger family holidays, the conversations flowed around and past one another as my grandparents prayed, and my parents bowed their heads politely, and my cousins played in a world I did not understand. When I entered grade school, our family moved to a suburban town in New Jersey. The little girl in the house behind our garden was an Orthodox Jew, and on Friday evenings I would go over for dinner and turn the electricity on and off for them, a task that their religion forbade them to do. There is a name for such a helpful Gentile in Jewish households—a *shabbas goy*—but the apparent fiddle with the rules made my mother uneasy.

I grew up among all these good people whom I loved, and I saw that some of them took there to be something in the world that the others did not see, and their mutual incomprehension seemed deeper and more powerful than just knowing different information about the world. Later on, when I became a professor and taught a seminar on divinity and spirituality, I saw again the blank incomprehension that had startled me when I was young—decent, smart, empathic people who seemed to stare at each other across an abyss. The skeptics did not understand the believers, and the believers did not understand the skeptics. They did not even know how to get from here to there.

I set out many years ago to understand how God becomes real for modern people. I chose an example of the style of Christianity that would seem to make the cognitive burden of belief most difficult: the evangelical Christianity in which God is thought to be present as a person in someone's everyday life, and in which God's supernatural power is thought to be immediately accessible by that person. The Vineyard Christian Fellowship is a new denomination, a few decades old, and it represents this shift in the American imagination of God. These Christians speak as if God interacts with them like a friend. He speaks to them. He listens to them. He acts when they pray to him about little mundane things, because he cares. This kind of Christianity seems almost absurdly vivid to someone who grew up in a mainstream Protestant church; when I first encountered it, I imagined that people thought of God as if he were a supernatural buddy with a thunderbolt.

The Americans in this church are ordinary Americans. They are typically middle class, but one finds very wealthy and very poor people in the congregations. They are typically white, but the congregations include many minorities. Most participants are college-educated. The church took form in California, but there are now more than six hundred churches across the country and as many as fifteen hundred around the world. The Vineyard is arguably the most successful example of what one sociologist has called *new paradigm* Protestantism, the infusion of a more intensely expressive spirituality into white, middle-class Christianity.[12] This style of spirituality has also been called *neo-Pentecostal* because it represents the adoption of a Pentecostal ethos, and its flamboyant emphasis on the direct experience of God, into a form acceptable to the white mainstream. Another name is *renewalist.* According to a recent survey, nearly one-quarter of all Americans embrace a Christian spirituality in which congregants experience God immediately, directly, and personally.[13] The Vineyard typifies this powerful new impulse in American spirituality.

For over two years, I went to weekly services at a Vineyard in Chicago, attended local conferences and special worship sessions, joined a weekly house group for a year, and formally interviewed more than thirty members of the church about their experience of God. That is the anthropological method: we anthropologists learn, or at least we try to learn, from the inside out. We observe, we participate, and we converse, for hours and hours on end. After several years in Chicago, I moved to California and found another Vineyard to join. Again I joined a small group that met weekly, and again I went to conferences and retreats, and I interviewed congregants willing to talk to me about God. I was there for over two years. Members of these churches became my friends and confidants. I liked them. I thought they liked me. They knew I was an anthropologist, and as they came to know me, they became comfortable talking with me at length about God. I have sought to understand what they said.

What I have to offer is an account of how you get from here to there. The tool of an anthropologist's trade is careful observation—participant observation, a kind of naturalist's craft in which one watches what people do and listens to what they say and infers from that how they come to see and know their world. I am, more precisely, a psychological anthropologist: I add to my toolkit the experimental method of the psychologist, which I use to explore the constraints on the way people make meaning. At one point I ran a psychological experiment, to test whether my hunch that spiritual practice had an impact on the mind's process was true. (It was.) But mostly I watched and I listened, and I tried to understand as an outsider how an insider to this evangelical world was able to experience God as real.

It didn't have much to do with belief per se. Skeptics sometimes imagine that becoming a religious believer means acquiring a belief the way you acquire a new piece of furniture. You decide you need a table for the living room, so you purchase it and get it delivered and then you have to rearrange everything, but once it's done, it's done. I did not find that being or becoming a Christian was very much like that. The propositional commitment that there is a God—the belief itself—is of course important. In some ways it changes everything, and the furniture of the mind is indeed distinctively rearranged. But for the people I spent time with, learning to know God as real was a slow process, stumbling and gradual, like learning to speak a foreign language in an unfamiliar country, with new and different social cues.

In fact, what I saw was that coming to a committed belief in God was more like learning *to do* something than *to think* something. I would describe what I saw as a theory of attentional learning—that the way you learn to pay attention determines your experience of God. More precisely, I will argue that people learn specific ways of attending to their minds and their emotions to find evidence of God, and that both what they attend to and how they attend changes their experience of their minds, and that as a result, they begin to experience a real, external, interacting living presence.

In effect, people train the mind in such a way that they experience part of their mind as the presence of God. They learn to reinterpret the familiar experiences of their own minds and bodies as not being their own at all—but God's. They learn to identify some thoughts as God's voice, some images as God's suggestions, some sensations as God's touch or the response to his nearness. They construct God's interactions out of these personal mental events, mapping the abstract concept "God" out of their mental awareness into a being they imagine and reimagine in ways shaped by the Bible and encouraged by their church community. They learn to shift the way they scan their worlds, always searching for a mark of God's presence, chastening the unruly mind if it stubbornly insists that there is nothing there. Then they turn around and allow this sense of God—an external being they find internally in their minds—to discipline their thoughts and emotions. They allow the God they learn to experience in their minds to persuade them that an external God looks after them and loves them unconditionally.

To do this, they need to develop a new theory of mind. That phrase—

theory of mind—has been used to describe the way a child learns to understand that other people have different beliefs and goals and intentions. The child learns that people have minds, and that not everything the child knows in his or her mind is known by other people. Christians must also learn new things about their minds. After all, to become a committed Christian one must learn to override three basic features of human psychology: that minds are private, that persons are visible, and that love is conditional and contingent upon right behavior. These psychological expectations are fundamental. To override them without going mad, people must develop a way of being in the world that is able to sustain the violations in relation to God—but not other humans. They do it by paying attention to their minds in new ways. They imagine their minds differently, and they give significance to thoughts and feelings in new ways.

These practices work. They change people. That is, they change mental experience, and those changes help people to experience God as more real. The practices don't work for everyone, and they do not work for each person to the same extent, but there are real skills involved here, skills that develop a psychological capacity called *absorption* that perhaps evolved for unrelated reasons, but that helps the Christian to experience that which is not materially present. These skills and practices make what is absent to the senses present in the mind.

To say this is not to say that God is an illusion. I am pointing out the obvious: that the supernatural has no natural body to see, hear, or smell. To know God, these Christians school their minds and senses so that they are able to experience the supernatural in ways that give them more confidence that what their sacred books say is really true.

It is a fragile process, because what they are doing is so hard, because it violates so much of what we take for granted. It takes an enormous amount of work. People must learn to see differently, and think differently, and above all feel differently, because for most people it will be a lifelong challenge to believe—to really feel as if they know in their heart of hearts—that God loves them as they are. When people build their understanding of God out of their own experience, they shape what they know of God's love out of the way they have experienced their mother's and father's love. But sometimes parents are not so loving, and always the love of a parent falls short of unconditional acceptance. The challenge of Christianity is being able to remap your own interior world from the way in which you learn to imagine God—and if it is hard to learn to experience yourself as truly in relationship with an invisible presence, it is harder still to experience yourself as feeling the love, tolerance, kindness, and forbearance you would feel if you truly, deeply, genuinely felt loved by the creator of the universe. Even when Christians succeed, they may grasp the moment—and then it may be gone.

Uncertainty remains at the heart of this process, as it has always done. Way back in the spring of 54 Anno Domini, Paul wrote from Ephesus to a church on the other side of the Aegean in the city of Corinth. He had founded the church some years previously in one of his evangelizing journeys around the Mediterranean, and it was now in trouble. Its members were squabbling about whether they could share meals with non-Christians, how they should settle disputes, whether marriage was appropriate for them—in short, about what it meant to be a Christian. Paul was a keenly pragmatic man who imagined believers as they could be but created a form for them as they were, ordinary folk who aspire, who stumble, and who often fall. But while he could solve the problem of whether people should marry and where they should take their conflicts, the church at Corinth had other troubles that Paul could not settle so easily.

In their passionate discovery of what they took to be the one true God, the Corinthians sought out moments when they thought that the supernatural divine broke into this mundane world. Those moments no doubt demonstrated to them that their god was real and lived among them still. Some of them spoke in tongues, giving voice in languagelike speech the speaker does not understand and believes to be divine. They seem to have paid excited attention to dreams, visions, and ecstatic transports. And they were arguing about how to interpret these experiences, how accurate they were, and what authority to give to those who experienced them. They were arguing, in short, about the most difficult problem that confronts anyone who believes or wants to believe in God: not whether God exists, in some abstract, in-principle, out-in-the-universe way, but how to find God in the everyday world and how to know that what you have found is God, and not someone else's deluded fantasy or your own selfish wish. For the Christians I met, the problem at the center of their faith is identifying the divine in ordinary life and distinguishing it from madness, evil, and simple human folly.

The story I tell in this book is how they solve this problem. It is a kind of detective story. I set out to pick up and piece together clues about the way ordinary people living in a pluralistic, scientific society come to experience—to some extent—a God that is as present to them as Christ was to Mary Magdalene when she came to tend him in his tomb. Like all stories, it is told from a particular point of view.

I call this point of view the anthropological attitude. Anthropologists are taught as students to seek to understand before we judge. We want to understand how people interpret their world before passing judgment on whether their interpretation is right or wrong. And so I will not presume to know ultimate reality. I will not judge whether God is or is not present to the people I came to know. Yet I believe that if God speaks, God's voice is heard through human minds constrained by their biology and shaped by their social community, and I believe that as a psychologically trained anthropologist, I can say something about those constraints and their social shaping. The person who hears a voice when alone has a sensory perception without a material cause, whether its immaterial origin is the divine presence or the empty night. Only some religious communities encourage people to pay attention to their subjective states with the suggestion that God may speak back to them in prayer. I will ask how a church teaches people to attend to their inner awareness and what training in prayer and practice they provide—and I can answer that question. Only some people have those startling, unusual experiences (although more people, it happens, than most of us imagine). I will ask whether some people are more likely to have those experiences than others, and whether there are differences in temperament or training that might set those who are able to have such experiences apart from those who don't—and again, I can answer that question.

But the anthropological attitude demands humility, and there are questions I cannot answer. In Michelangelo's *Genesis,* man reaches out for God, and God for man, and their fingers do not quite touch. An anthropologist can describe only the human side of that relationship, the way humans reach for God. I can describe the way a church can teach congregants to pay attention and learn to use their minds to help them make their experience of God real and concrete; I can describe the practices they develop, and the way they learn those practices and teach them to each other. I can describe what we know of the psychological mechanisms through which the mind can sense the presence of something for which there is no ordinary sensory evidence and the way those mechanisms are different from psychiatric illness. But my methods cannot distinguish between sensory deception and the moments when God may be reaching back to communicate through an ordinary human mind.

We see through a glass darkly. There is much we do not know, even now, about spiritual experience. I can take up Paul's problem about knowing when God is truly present, but I cannot solve it. The goal of this book is simply to help readers understand the problem of presence more deeply, to understand why it is a problem—why it can be hard for Christians to know when God has spoken—and to explain how, in this day and age, people are nonetheless able to identify that presence and to experience it as real.

WHEN GOD TALKS BACK

CHAPTER ONE

The Invitation

Make a joyful noise to the Lord
All the earth
Worship the Lord with
Gladness
Come into his presence with
Singing.

Psalm 100:1–2

A real God for a real people

Vineyard T-shirt slogan

I FOUND THE CHURCH in my own backyard, a few blocks from where I lived in Chicago, meeting in the neighborhood club between the pancake breakfasts and the local basketball games. These days the church meets in the stately Lutheran chapel down the street, visible evidence that its style of spirituality is replacing the old mainstream, but back then I found the congregation because they'd hung a purple banner out front announcing the "Vineyard Christian Fellowship." I went in looking for a nondenominational church that taught people to hear God speak back, but I didn't go back for months after my first visit because nobody did anything to suggest they were much different from the people in the liberal mainstream churches I'd known as a child. Nobody spoke in tongues or fell over in spiritual bliss. The pastor—a modest man in his thirties—explained a book of the Bible chapter by chapter, as if he were lecturing to an undergraduate class. In fact, the service even looked like an undergraduate class. People were taking notes. Many of them had their Bibles out, and they were staring at the text as if they were trying to analyze a difficult poem.

I finally went back for a second visit because I had done enough reading to figure out that this was in fact exactly the kind of church in which

God was not a distant, abstract, principle but a person among persons. I stayed for two years.

On a Sunday, the service in this church begins with music. A mainstream Protestant church distributes hymns throughout a service like raisins in morning cereal. There, hymns aren't so much individual prayers as collective assertions in which the congregation stands up as a group to affirm to each other that they are there. But at a church like the Vineyard, music is prayer. The church sets aside a full thirty minutes for the music at the beginning of the service, and they call this section of the service "worship." There are no hymnals, just PowerPoint-projected lyrics of songs people know so well that many sing them with their eyes shut. Worship is intensely individual, even when everyone sings together. "During worship," reads the bulletin, "feel free to sit or stand, sing or pray. Some people raise their hands as a sign of surrender to God, or dance in celebration. Please worship in the way you feel comfortable." The techies dim the lights. Some people stand, eyes closed, palms out and upward, swaying slightly, their cheeks sometimes wet with tears. Some sit and rest their foreheads on clasped hands. Some kneel in prayer. Occasionally someone lies prostrate or dances in the open space to the side of the seating area. I have seen people speak intently but silently during the worship period, mouth moving, eyes focused on something no one else can see. I have heard people bawling with great, gulping sobs. Meanwhile, latecomers wander in for coffee and doughnuts at the back, hugging friends and settling into their seats. It is intense and casual all at once. Someone once described this negligent arrival to me as "Vineyard time," as if congregants dribbled in because they were relaxed, tardy people, but a more accurate read is that the worship time is understood to be private, personal, a time to commune with God alone while in the presence of others. Church in the old-fashioned sense begins when worship time ends.

Once I noticed this personal, intimate connection, I began to listen to the music. Contemporary Christian music is instantly recognizable. When you pull out of the airport in a new city, flicking through radio stations in a rental car, it takes only a bar or two to spot it. I used to let it wash over me without paying much attention. Now I listened. Here in these songs, the remarkable God of this kind of church shines forth. Rarely do you hear of his judgment; always you are aware of his love; never, ever, does a song suggest you fear his anger. He is a person:

lover, father, of course, but more remarkably, friend. Best friend. One song begins with breathless amazement that God pays attention to the singer, that he hears the singer, thinks of the singer, loves him or her. Then the chorus, clean, simple and repetitive, as these songs tend to be. "I am a friend of God / He calls me friend" ("Friend of God"). Some songs are rousing, and people punch at the air with their hands: "Blessed be the name of the Lord!" or "Shout to the earth his name!" There are songs to drive with and dance with and clean the house with. But mostly these are songs to cry with: songs about perfect, idyllic friendship in a most imperfect world. "Now I've gone and let you in . . . will you please still be my friend?" ("The Real Me").

This God is intensely human in this music, and the singer wants him so badly that the lyrics sound like a teenage fan's crazed longing for a teen idol she can touch. Unlike older church hymns, you do not sing *about* God but *to* God, directly to him in the second person, and with unbridled yearning. "I long for your embrace / Every single day" ("Here with Me"). "Oh, to be a friend of God is all I desire" ("All I Want").

But this God is also a supernatural substance. These worship songs suggest that you, the singer, feel him in your body, like bones in your thighs and blood in your arteries. He is in you, but he is also apart from you, someone whom you love and who loves and cuddles you. In "Breathe," God is the substance in your lungs. Then the song goes on to describe your feelings for God as unchecked passion for a person who can go missing: "And I'm *desperate* for you / And I'm *lost* without you." There is a yearning for something so intimate it is part of you but is somehow also missing, something that you really, really want but do not quite yet have. "We Are Hungry" says it bluntly: "Lord, I want more of you . . . Lord, I need more of you." Some songs are almost sexual, with a touch so light that the suggestion could slip past. Here is the megahit "Dwell": "Dwell in the midst of us / Come and have your way."

The music is also an invocation. More responsively human and more supernaturally present than the God most of us grew up with, this God is asked to walk into church on Sunday morning with the music, and people speak as if they come because he is there. On Sunday mornings the band would pause after a few songs and the leader would pray softly into the silence. "God, we love you so much. Help us to hear you clearly today. Come into our midst . . . Come, Holy Spirit, come . . . Come . . ." And people waited (even the coffee drinkers) to let God come. People talk about this as if they mean it literally. They say things like "God really showed up today," and they distinguish between times when they felt that God was present and times when they did not feel his presence, although then they add quickly that he is always there.

This is a God people talk about as being somewhere as well as everywhere; being present at a particular time as well as always. God is of course understood as eternal, omnipresent, and everywhere. If you ask congregants where God is in church, they will look confused. But still they speak as if God has a particular presence and a specific voice. The church behaves as if God will be tangibly present after he has been invited to come.

We waited in reverent stillness until the band softly picked up again. Sometimes during that next song, a congregant would come up to the microphone and read out the scriptural passage God had nudged him or her to remember in that quiet time, or announce that God wanted us to pray for someone with a particular problem. People expected God to "nudge." When we took communion, there were no lines of people swept from their seats by watchful attendants and returned in file. During the communion worship song, people went forward at a time of their own choosing to pick up a broken matzo and a small cup of grape juice, and then they walked back with it to their seat, to consume when it felt right.

The reason people have their notebooks out during sermons isn't because the sermon is *about* God, the way a college lecture is about the American Revolution or the poems of Emily Dickinson. Rather, the pastor's sermon teaches the congregation to *use* the Bible to relate to God, both as a God of power and as a best friend. Church is a class in which you learn how to hear what God has to say. The pastor teaches that when you are intimate and personal with a supernatural being, God speaks to you. Not all the time and usually not audibly, but in as real and as practical a way as if you were sitting down to coffee with a puzzle you had to solve.

As the pastor recounts the story, he founded this church because God told him to. Arnold is an unassuming man, slender and bearded, calmer than many urban Chicagoans. He grew up in southern California, in the white upper-middle-class world of Newport Beach. As a teen, he worked as a beach lifeguard and wore flip-flops to class. His mother was deeply religious, but his father was a hardworking, fun-loving, fast-living real estate developer with little time for church. They divorced when Arnold was in junior high. By the time he got to high school, he still went to church, but he wanted to be successful, like his dad.

Like many evangelicals, Arnold tells the story of a crisis, a sharp confrontation with humiliation or despair, and a turning point at which he consciously chose Christ. These stories are told again and again in evangelical churches, and often they acquire a local sameness, so that any church seems dense with the same kinds of personal struggles. For a while I attended an evangelical church in southern California in which everyone told conversion stories of self-destructive addiction. Here is an example of the genre:

> [Meth] was my drug of choice. Did it for breakfast, lunch, and dinner for almost four years. Other than that, I basically did everything. I've never abused needles, but I've smoked heroin. A lot, a lot of acid, and a lot of Ecstasy and shrooms . . . Dropped in weight to ninety-something pounds . . . I blew up my Dad's apartment in a great fire into this huge mushroom cloud and it blew me up against the wall and blew off the sliding glass door onto the balcony . . .
>
> I know God was trying to tell me I was going the wrong way.

A woman of insight, I remember thinking as I listened to her story. But we are all blind to the bars on our own cage.

By contrast, Arnold's conversion story seemed positively Augustinian. (In his *Confessions*, Augustine reports as an example of his sin that he stole some pears from a neighbor's garden with the wanton thoughtlessness of a teenage boy. A modern reader familiar with the addiction narrative feels that Augustine was not exactly hitting bottom.) In his final year of high school, Arnold sneaked into the house of a girl to invite her to a party, and her astonished father caught him crawling across the floor and collared him. Then Arnold's water polo team lost the championship match. A few weekends later, at the age of eighteen, confused, scared, and embarrassed, he began to pray intensely. He felt that God confronted him and asked him to choose—and he chose Christ. At the church Arnold founded, people don't tell devastation-and-redemption narratives of conversion, stories of leaving methamphetamine for God. They talk about deciding that it was time to choose Christ.[1]

Arnold was in a secular university in southern California when he heard God call him to the ministry. The moment took place at a Vineyard

Christian Fellowship meeting in an empty warehouse that the church rented each Sunday morning. Arnold wasn't even sure if he liked the church at the time. People were dancing in their seats to the music and raising their hands to praise God, and Arnold felt a little awkward and out of place. Then "all of a sudden, it was like a whole sentence spoken into my heart. I felt that God said, 'Arnold, I've called you into ministry.' I'd been doubting. I was always kind of insecure about whether I should go into ministry. I walked out of that service and never doubted it again."

Arnold went to seminary in Chicago. On Sundays he went to a Vineyard church. (There were seven of them in the area.) One day, in passing, he heard the pastor mention that the Vineyard wanted to plant a church down in one of the city neighborhoods. The name of the neighborhood intrigued him and stuck in his memory, though he had never seen the area. He prayed that God would give him a supernatural sign to see whether he should explore it. A couple of weeks passed, and nothing happened. Then he sat at the information table one Sunday—it was the only Sunday he ever sat there—and again he prayed to God about whether he should explore the neighborhood. That morning some college students walked up to him and said that they wanted to talk to someone about having a pastor move to that very neighborhood and start a Vineyard there. That caught Arnold's attention. "But was it a sign from God? I was unsure. So I said, 'God, give me another sign.'"

At the time, he had a man living with him who'd recently been released from prison. Arnold did this kind of thing routinely. He would say that he had "a heart" for the poor. Even when he was in college, he did ministry work in inner city neighborhoods, and he would invite homeless men to sleep in his apartment. He told himself that it was safe because he didn't have anything worth stealing. Now, looking back, he is startled by his temerity. It so happened that the mother of the man released from prison lived in the neighborhood the college kids had mentioned. When the man came back after visiting her, Arnold asked him what the place was like without mentioning his interest in it. "The first thing he says after throwing himself dramatically on the couch was, 'That area, man, you would love that neighborhood.' He said, 'Actually you were *made* for that neighborhood.'" Arnold paused and looked at me. "Well, that was pretty stunning."

People tell stories like this in the church with the rhythm of dawning discovery—and *then,* and *then,* and *then,* as if God had to work *so hard* to get them to see. They love these stories, because they are the enactment of a relationship between a creature and his creator, between a dull, cautious, skeptical human and a loving, patient, persistent God. By this point Arnold was intrigued but not persuaded. It is risky to start a church, because the judgment people make in coming to a church is always in part about the person of the pastor. To fail is painful. Arnold felt uncertain about whether a Chicago neighborhood filled with intellectuals would really trust a young, unmarried guy from southern California. He also felt uneasy about whether a Vineyard church would take off in an urban, racially mixed neighborhood. Most Vineyard churches are suburban. Most of their congregants are white.

Yet the guy from prison was right. Arnold loved the neighborhood. For years the place had been an intellectual island within the inner city. As the nineteenth century moved into the twentieth, the area grew up just outside the city, with gracious mansions built in the austere style of Prairie architecture and Arts and Crafts design. By the 1950s, however, that part of Chicago had become a ghetto. You could go for blocks without seeing a white face—until you came to the college neighborhood. Over the next few decades the area grew seedy and dangerous. The mansions fell into disrepair, and drug dealers moved into the abandoned buildings. Still, there was a thriving jazz scene, and it was one of the few middle-class neighborhoods where interracial couples felt welcome. By the end of the twentieth century, the ghetto's edge had receded, the mansions were being renovated, and real estate values had shot up, but the neighborhood retained both its fierce intellectualism and its racial diversity. This was when Arnold saw it, and as he might say, it spoke to him. He badly wanted to build a racially diverse church, and here was a community that might welcome a young pastor with an intellectual bent and a commitment to social justice.

The first worship gathering was small, fewer than twenty people, almost all of them college students. That was in 1998. By 2005, around two hundred people showed up at the church on any Sunday morning. Young people still predominated, but most were no longer undergraduates (although there were still plenty of them). Instead, the congregants were mostly young adults in their early and mid-twenties. One autumn during the time I attended, fourteen women were pregnant—one in seven of the women in church on a Sunday morning—and toddlers wandered the aisles. About a quarter of the congregation was African American. There were elderly congregants and Korean and Chinese congregants, people who worked clerical jobs and postdoctoral fellows in the medical school. And there were many poor people, some of whom slept in the park. You could go to an evening gathering mostly comprised of graduate students and medical school students, and find yourself praying with someone who was hoping to be accepted into the military because otherwise she risked going to jail.

This was not without awkwardness. When I decided to do ethnographic work in the church, I joined one of the house groups—small groups that met weekly to worship and discuss the Bible. About half the church belonged to one of them. My group was formed by Elaine, who stood up in church one Sunday, announced that she was creating it, and invited anyone who was interested to show up. We were a motley group: a young white stock trader and his wife; a white social work student and her Filipino boyfriend, still working on his GED; an African American librarian; two graduate students, one Asian, one white, one in sociology, the other a biochemist; two African American medical students; and our American-born Korean leader. Most people were in their twenties except for the librarian and myself, both mid-forties. We were very different kinds of people. As one woman said drily, "We'd *never* all be friends if it weren't for this group."

For a while, we invited some of the church people who slept in the park. They would leave their shopping carts downstairs in the entryway with an apologetic note pinned on top and come upstairs. It shifted the tenor of the evening. People found it hard to ask other people to pray that they would pass their sociology exam after we had prayed for a homeless man to find work and housing. Elaine invited Mary, one of the homeless women, to live with her, and the church paid the woman's rent for months while she worked in the local coffee shop. The woman didn't really like living with Elaine, who was then filled with earnest Christian zeal and refused to allow Mary not only to drink alcohol inside the apartment but to watch *Law and Order* and other godless programs. After a while, Mary moved on, and the rest of the homeless drifted on with her. (They kept coming to church.) We returned to praying for each other's success in exams and job interviews.

The spring I arrived, in 2003, the church met in the gym of the neighborhood association building. The association had painted the walls with crude pictures of children playing games. An oversize stuffed bear sat high up on a corner pillar, gathering dust. The air ducts whined and rattled with the wind. Each Sunday morning, the setup crew pulled out folding chairs and arranged them in rows before a cloth backdrop and a wooden cross. Next to most rows they put out a few Bibles and a cupful of pens. The technical setup was more elaborate. The service—both the teaching and the worship songs—were done with PowerPoint, so there had to be a screen and an LCD projector. There was a band, usually with at least one guitar and often a synthesizer; sometimes someone crooned behind with a violin. So there were microphones and amplifiers and a sound system. At least two harried young men sat in the technical booth during services, one to manage the sound board and the other to work the PowerPoint. The band sang as the spirit moved them, repeating stanzas and lyrics as they chose, and the young men would shuffle frantically through PowerPoint screens to keep up. After the worship music, there was a break for coffee and doughnuts, and then people returned to their seats, Styrofoam cups in hand. First there were announcements, as in any church. The expectant mothers were forming a support group, or there was a class or a movie or a conference. Then someone, usually the pastor, stood up to deliver the teaching.

The teaching in a church like this focuses squarely on the Bible, and it is as different from the sermons in a mainstream Protestant church as contemporary Christian music is different from the mainstream's hymns. A mainstream minister often uses a scriptural text as the launching point to reflect on human experience—the difficulty of marriage, say, or stress during the Christmas season. At churches like the Vineyard, the pastor understands himself to use everyday human experience to illuminate the biblical text. And while the music presumes that you are close to and intimate with God, the teaching presumes that you do not know how to have this intimacy, that you must be taught, and that your learning depends on using the Bible and learning to pray. When people call a church like this "Bible-based," they mean not only that the Bible is taken more or less literally but that the pastor speaks to help you to understand the Bible— not to help you understand yourself, or to feel more comfortable, or to give you political direction, though all these might be thought to be consequences of deepening that biblical understanding. Rather, you listen to the pastor to learn what God is saying to you through his book. This is also why this portion of the service is called a "teaching" rather than a "sermon." A "sermon" implies that the speaker himself is important; that it is his insights you have come to hear. To call it "teaching" is to emphasize that the teacher is less important than his subject. God is speaking; the teaching begins to teach you how to listen.

The emphasis is upon reading the text for what it says, as if you can read it straight, for its truth. There is no sense that texts from the past hide from us behind authorial intentions we can no longer understand, or that they were written for a social and economic community we do not live in now. On Sunday mornings and in house group, we would read the most obscure and historical texts—Judges, for example—as if they were written for *us*, to help us understand how God wanted us to be with him. This is a common style of reading in evangelical churches.[2]

After the teaching, there is usually a final worship song, and in the silence of the final bars, someone will stand and say, "If you need prayer, do not leave until you get prayer." Here prayer channels the supernatural. In a church like the Vineyard, people often talk about the Holy Spirit as if it is substance, as if it flows through the body like water through a chute or accumulates in the room like a heavy gas. They speak as if spirit collects up front around the worship band during church, dense on the floor, and does not dissipate until well after the service has ended. Some people told me that I should come to the second of the two Sunday-morning services because more Holy Spirit builds up the longer people pray. God comes when his spirit is called—if he chooses—and his power strengthens through the worship as if the singing itself were bringing the power into presence, the way Aslan sang the beasts of the new Narnia into life. In this atmosphere, prayer by a trained person is imagined as a vehicle to draw that supernatural presence to the person in need.

Some people come to the service specifically for the prayer. At the close of the service, six or so members of what is called the prayer team line up against one wall of the gym. (You have to be trained to be on the prayer team, and you can be dismissed if the pastor thinks you shouldn't participate.) They wear little tags to identify themselves as on the prayer team. While other congregants shrug on their coats and chat, the prayer team members lay hands on the shoulders of those who want prayer and then pray aloud over them, their faces focused with intense concentration, the supplicants often choking back sobs. Above the muffled voices, the pastor calls out softly to those who are leaving, "Go with God, you guys."

. . .

The God of this evangelical church illustrates the dominant shift in American spirituality of the last forty years, toward a more intimate, personal, and supernaturally present divine. To be sure, God is imagined in many different ways in America. The sociologist Peter Berger memorably described American spirituality as a sacred canopy, but Christian Smith, a sociologist who has done as much as anyone to track down the empirical data about American evangelicalism, describes it as more like a collection of umbrellas.[3]

The term *evangelical* is hard to define precisely. It is typically understood as implying three commitments: belief in the literal or near-literal truth of the Bible; belief that one can be saved only by choosing a personal relationship with Christ, or being "born again"; and belief that one should, to some extent, evangelize and share the good news of salvation with others. But evangelicals comprise an enormous range of people whose views and practices and spiritual imaginations veer wildly. They include snake-handlers and home-schooling militia members and people in mainstream congregations. They include Pentecostals, members of a spirituality that emphasizes the direct experience of God through speaking in tongues, languagelike sounds thought to be an expression of the Holy Spirit moving through the body. They include conservative Baptists, for whom tongues are an anathema. They include most of the Moral Majority, and they include left-wing activists. About 40 percent of Americans describe themselves as born again or evangelical; about a third of those who call themselves born again are pro-choice; only 60 percent of those who call themselves evangelical believe that the Bible should be taken word-for-word as the literal word of God.[4]

In general, however, people seem to call themselves evangelical to signal something about their own sense of spirituality and their commitment to using it to change the world around them.[5] They are asserting that they want Jesus to be as real in their lives as the Gospels say that he was real in the lives of the disciples, and they want to know the Gospels not as literature or poetry but as history. For many of them (but admittedly not all of them), this involves an intense desire to experience personally a God who is as present now as when Christ walked among his followers in Galilee.[6]

Like the term *evangelical,* this reach for a personal experience of God has many forms. The most dramatic include tongues; supernatural healing, where a pastor calls down the Holy Spirit to cure a painful back; being slain in the spirit, when the Holy Spirit moves down a room like a force and knocks someone over; and prophecy, when someone utters truths about the future that have come from a supernatural source. These phenomena are what Paul, in the first letter to the Corinthians, called the "gifts" of the Holy Spirit: healing, miraculous powers, prophecy, tongues, and other "signs and wonders." Churches that encourage the use of spiritual gifts are often called charismatic.[7] Many of the most famous (or infamous) American evangelical pastors have been charismatically oriented, like Jimmy Swaggart, Pat Robertson, and Benny Hinn. Jerry Falwell was at least sympathetic to explicitly charismatic churches—he ran Jimmy and Tammy Fay Bakker's PTL (Praise the Lord) ministry for a while—as was Billy Graham. Less dramatic forms involve the encouragement to experience God interacting with you in daily life, the kind of personal experience described in *The Purpose Driven Life,* by evangelical pastor Rick Warren, which may have sold more copies in the United States than any book other than the Bible.[8]

The evangelical interest in the direct personal experience of God exploded in the 1960s. Americans have always been religious, but every so often our religious enthusiasm seems to crest. Historians have called these periods of religious excitement "great awakenings." They appear (more or less) from 1730 to 1760, 1800 to 1840, 1890 to 1930, and 1965 to the present.[9] During these decades, Americans were more likely to have had unusual spiritual experiences in which they fainted, spoke in tongues, saw visions, and so forth, and they were more likely to seek out and publicly celebrate these changes in consciousness as proof of God's living presence in their lives. These are not, of course, the only times when God has inflamed the American senses. Throughout the twentieth century, there were American churches that encouraged and even relied on unusual spiritual phenomena. Pentecostalism was born in Los Angeles in the early twentieth century and continued to grow over the decades. Southern Baptist churches encouraged richly spiritual experience well before the late twentieth century. Nevertheless, America does seem to have periods when great spiritual passion enters many humble homes. We are, scholars suggest, in such a period now.[10]

The demographic shift in American religion since the 1960s is remarkable. Two-thirds of the generation we call the baby boomers stopped going to churches and temples as adults. Half of them have now returned to religious practice, but not to the mainstream, hour-long services of their childhood. They have joined churches, temples, and odd little groups that put intense and personal spiritual experience at the center of what it is to believe in the divine.[11] Wade Clark Roof famously called them "a generation of seekers."[12] By 1996, a whopping 39 percent of Americans said that they were born again, and for most of them evangelical piety meant having a direct, personal, and vividly felt relationship with their Creator.[13] Many different kinds of data converge to suggest that at least a quarter of all Americans follow a faith in which the Christian god is understood to be intimately and personally present.[14]

Arnold's church represents a common post-1960s expression of this experiential spirituality: the new paradigm Protestant Christian churches.[15] These churches that treat God like a cozy confidant and call a near-tangible Holy Spirit into their presence on Sunday morning exist in great numbers in the United States. Alongside the more than six hundred Vineyard churches in the United States, there are hundreds and hundreds of Calvary Chapels, Horizon Christian Fellowships, Hope Chapels, Bethel Churches, and other nondenominational churches that share their general style. The new paradigm congregations are more likely to meet in gyms than in actual church buildings. Their members wear shorts and sneakers, not starched dresses and formal suits. They are more likely to have a rock band than a choir. They call themselves Bible-based, by which they mean that the Bible is taken to be literally or near-literally true, and they embrace a spirituality in which they seek God in the everyday. In many ways, these churches take the spiritual innovations of Pentecostalism and render them palatable for white, educated, middle-class congregations. This is a far cry from the mainline American church fifty years ago: an hour-long service attended in your stiff Sunday clothes, a short sermon, some dutiful prayers, a little mingling in the courtyard, and you were done.

Where then did this intimate, personal, supernaturally present God come from, this happy companion with thunderbolts? The story goes back to the 1960s. The quest for a closer, more personal God emerged around the country in many different ways. Folk songs and guitars crept into Sunday services around the time that Catholics took Latin out of the mass and instructed their priests to wear laymen's clothes. But the most dramatic and iconic agents of the change were the hippies themselves and their vision of the early disciples as the first great radical revolutionaries. One of the greatest paradoxes of a movement many people think of as a right-wing threat is that it was fueled by the most countercultural left-wing movement our country has ever seen.[16]

It was 1967, the Summer of Love. As many as a hundred thousand young people found their way to San Francisco, many indeed wearing flowers in their hair. They came for what one flyer called a "holy pilgrimage" to create a new way of being human. They thought that they were leaving behind a corrupt world of hypocritical elders and joining a revolution that would change the world. They were reading *Walden* and the Beat poets, and they wanted to shake loose reality as they had known it. That January, at the Golden Gate Be-in, Timothy Leary had urged people to "turn on, tune in, and drop out." "If it feels good, do it" became a slogan.

Many Americans were aghast at the hippies and bewildered by their choices. Ronald Reagan's quip became famous: "A hippie is someone who dresses like Tarzan, has hair like Jane, and smells like Cheetah." But some evangelicals—including Billy Graham, then at the zenith of his fame—understood and even approved of the search for meaning (if not of the LSD). They wanted to help, and soon it was clear that hippies needed help. As thousands of people descended on San Francisco, city services collapsed. A group called the Diggers had issued a manifesto offering free food to those who came to join the revolution, but they were soon overwhelmed. People kept coming, and many simply slept on the street at night, hungry and unwashed. Women may have had the hardest time. Even before that famous summer, a hippie broadsheet remarked that "rape is as common as bullshit on Haight Street."[17] When a young Baptist pastor, Kent Philpott, ventured into the Haight in April 1967, he was deeply shocked. He began to pick up runaways, contact their parents, and send them home. Grateful parents sent money. Around the same time, some hippies began to attend the First Baptist Church in Mill Valley. The pastor, John MacDonald, began to realize that there was a need the mainstream church was not addressing. By the late summer of 1967, a concerned, mostly Baptist group had rented a store in the Haight they called the Living Room. They painted scripture verses on the walls with psychedelic suns and got food and coffee donated from a local grocer. As many as twenty thousand people came through their doors in two years.

One of them was Lonnie Frisbee. Lean and handsome, with big brown eyes, curly dark shoulder-length hair, and a beard, Lonnie knew he looked like a kitchen calendar image of Jesus. He deliberately wore the faux shepherd shirts you could find back then (when new cheap imports from India were sold alongside bongs and incense and other paraphernalia for the spiritual tourist) along with love beads and bell bottoms, the kind with daisies embroidered on the side.

Lonnie had the kind of adolescence that was becoming common in the early 1960s. In high school, he ran away from his home in Costa Mesa, California, to find himself. In the sweet lazy drawl on the great documentary footage that remains the richest source of knowledge about his life, he lists the way stations of the journey: "Edgar Cayce, flying saucers, drugs, marijuana and LSD, metaphysical meditation, hypnosis." Christianity was initially just one of those psychedelic stopping points. He had a vision in which God came to him and told him that his role was to bring a sea of people to Christ, and he saw an ocean as large as the Pacific, filled with human beings holding out their arms for grace. It was, he later said, a trip like any other, "except this one lasted. It was real and it was solid and it changed my life."[18]

At first, Jesus was a complement to the acid, not a replacement. A high school friend remembered:

We hiked up to Tahquitz Falls [near Palm Springs]. Lonnie wanted to go to the very top fall, and once we got there he spread his backpack, and he spread out—I remembered LSD, and he had marijuana, and he had all of his oil paints, and I remember that he proceeded to paint a picture of Jesus on the rock, a full-size picture on the rock. Then he got kind of into a yoga position, and he pulled out his Bible, and he said, 'We're gonna read the Bible now.' He was reading about John the Baptist and how John the Baptist baptized, and he baptized us up at Tahquitz Falls. Even though we were all on drugs.

Among the early hippie Christians, that's what people did. Another friend recalled, "I took my LSD and lay down on the floor for a few hours, and when I got up I was a Christian. It was really that simple."

In retrospect the resonance between hippie culture and Christianity makes sense. The historian Preston Shires points out that hippies were in large measure raised in liberal Christian households with weekly Sunday school lessons on love and brotherhood in the era of the civil rights struggle and the entry into war. Love was the message of the hippie revolution—the Be-In was announced as "a renaissance of compassion, awareness and love"—and the revolution was needed because the elders had failed to follow through.[19] On top of that, the early Christian disciples were compelling figures because they seemed like—and with that long hair, even *looked* like—hippies. The early Christian disciples, after all, were young radicals who believed in a love that their elders preached but did not follow, and they fought against the corruption and war of Rome with a new vision of the way humans should live and relate to each other, more or less the way hippies were fighting against the establishment and the Vietnam War.

Lonnie ended up in the Living Room because someone found him preaching the gospel on a street corner while high on LSD. They took him in and soon sent him out to one of the first of the hippie Christian communes, the House of Acts (or as they often called it, the Big House) up in Marin County. Out at the Big House, people lived together in the way they imagined the early disciples had done. Acts 2:44–45: "Now all who believed were together, and had all things in common. And they sold their possessions and goods and divided them among all, as anyone had need." In Lonnie's commune, they gave away personal possessions, ate together, and read the Bible. The commune seems to have made Lonnie's Christianity more orthodox: at any rate, he seems to have stopped taking drugs at this point.

There is no record of how Lonnie discovered Pentecostalism, but by that point, he spoke in tongues. He began to baptize his new friends in what he called the "Holy Spirit," egging them on to speak in tongues and to feel the power of God course through them. "He said," one man remembered, "'Well, have you been baptized in the Holy Spirit?' I go, 'I don't *think* so. I don't even know what it is.' He said, 'Well, let me tell you more about it . . .' I felt the spirit of God come down upon me in such a powerful way, and Lonnie was kind of encouraging me to start speaking in this—this unknown prayer language."

Within a few years, Lonnie's story had repeated itself across the country. Worried evangelists reached out with resources to hippies they saw in trouble; young revolutionaries refocused their rebellion around a countercultural icon, the long-haired sandal-footed son of Mary. And note that they reached out for Jesus—not for the church that Paul founded, not for Paul's theology, not for Christianity. They wanted the person: the radical rebel who loved. A popular poster appeared:

WANTED: JESUS CHRIST

Wanted for sedition, criminal anarchy, vagrancy and conspiring to overthrow the established government.

Dresses poorly. *Said* to be a carpenter by trade, ill-nourished, has visionary ideas. Associates with common working people, the unemployed, and bums.

Alien—believed to be a Jew

Alias—"Prince of peace," "King of the Jews," "Son of Man," "Light of the World," etc.

Professional agitator

Red beard, marks on hands and feet—the result of injuries inflicted by an Angry mob led by Respectable Citizens and Legal Authorities.[20]

Thousands of coffeehouses and communes sprouted up. In a dissertation that is still the richest history of this largely untold tale, Larry Eskridge drew maps with little dots to represent churches or coffeehouses he came across that had existed in the early 1970s (there must have been many he did not find) associated with the Jesus People. Around the country, the map is thick with dots.

By 1971, these young Christians had a name and a social mythology. Outsiders called them Jesus Freaks; insiders called them the Jesus People. They landed on the covers of *Look, Life,* and *Time* that spring, with psychedelic haloed images of Jesus and grainy photojournalism shots of mass baptisms in the oceans. In the *Time* essay: "Jesus is alive and well and living in the radiant spiritual fervor of a growing number of young Americans . . . If any one mark clearly identifies them, it is their total belief in an awesome, supernatural Jesus Christ, not just a marvelous man who lived two thousand years ago, but a living God."[21] The Jesus People movement is one of the most significant American religious phenomena of the postwar period, and one of the least studied. Eskridge calls this "scholarly amnesia."[22]

As the counterculture accepted Jesus, they made him their own. They had a come-just-as-you-are-to-worship ethos (that phrase would appear verbatim in a Vineyard worship song), and to the horror of more sedate congregants, they showed up for service with ripped and unwashed jeans. They abandoned the measured world of hymnal music and instead wrote rock and folk songs about Jesus. Reading the lyrics of that music now, at the stretch of many decades, one feels a shock akin to the startled discovery that Narnia and Middle-earth have Christian plots: "Spirit in the Sky." "He Ain't Heavy, He's My Brother." "Bridge over Troubled Water." "The Wedding Song (There Is Love)." Many of the top chart songs of the era were spiritual; some were overtly Christian.

As the Jesus movement grew, so did a kind of rock music that was explicitly theirs. It began with Larry Norman's "Only Visiting This Planet"— a striking title—and by the mid-1970s would be an established genre of the marketplace.[23] Meanwhile, *Jesus Christ Superstar* and *Godspell* came out as the decade of the 1960s ended, and their reception reflected the complicated feelings around the movement itself. Some middle-class, middle-aged adults were profoundly moved to see the ancient passion story retold for a new and different generation. Some were repelled that the scriptures should be treated with such disrespect. In *Godspell,* Jesus wears bright suspenders, a Superman T-shirt, and fluffy orange bedroom slippers. He prances around in a junkyard, and he daubs paint on the faces of his flower children as he tells them stories. It is easier to notice that most of the dialogue comes from the Gospel of Matthew if you turn on the movie's English subtitles.

And just as their generation spoke of a revolution that loved, and just as they sang songs like "Kumbaya, my Lord," and "All we are saying is give peace a chance," this Jesus was a Jesus of love. For sure, he strode into the temple and overthrew the money changers—but you were there by his side, a countercultural revolutionary. He did not thunder at *you.* You and he stood together, challenging *them.* And when you were not in the temple together, he was a peaceful, happy, zany Godspell God, infinitely patient, infinitely accepting, a God of endless love. The coffeehouses and the communes did not offer an institutional Jesus. They offered a personal relationship with a God who loved without restraint and without reservation. He was a God who, in the words of the historian Stephen Prothero, would hold your hand, wipe your brow, and get you through a bad trip.[24]

In 2008 I met Sally, an old Jesus People person, someone who had danced with Jesus and who let the electric excitement of the Holy Spirit take the place of drugs. In her twenties Sally had found herself in a conventional upper-middle-class Washington suburb, married to a conventional upper-middle-class lawyer, with a conventional martini-drinking life—with the exception of the over-the-top drugs she did on the weekends. She liked the freedom of the drugs and the sense they gave her of rejecting bourgeois complacency, but she didn't feel safe when she was high, and she didn't much like the person that her husband became.

Okay, Friday night comes. We go over to somebody's house. We smoke a bunch of joints. We cook shrimp with marijuana wrapped into it. We do the—you know, you take the laundry bags, the plastic laundry bags, and you braid them and you put a bottle of—a bowl of water underneath it. You light it on fire, and you watch—it's a light show. You listen to music. You take the baby and you put her on a pillow in the corner of the room and you tell her to go to sleep. And she does, because she's used to it. And you wake up at three o'clock in the morning, and it feels like the Russian Army's walked through your mouth and you feel like shit and you're not sure whether you're going to throw up. And somebody's getting laid on the couch, and you decide to ignore them, and then you think, Oh, let's go home. You pick up the baby, you drive home, you eat two Oreos and drink a gallon of water and go to sleep. And you wake up the next morning and you watch Bullwinkle. And then you watch a Dallas Cowboys game, and by about three o'clock in the afternoon, you feel all right again.

She saw one of her friends snap on LSD and end up hospitalized. She saw another so wasted that he peed on the couch. "We were marching against the war, we were involved in the civil rights movement, we were burning bras, we were having lie-ins where we'd all sort of sit around and make out. Yeah, it was political. But when it got to this other level, it was not political. It was kinky, bad, self-destructive, and scary, and I didn't like it."

But she didn't know how to get out of it. She'd had a spiritual experience when high on marijuana—the Vietnam War was well under way, and she had a vision of Moses handing her a body bag and saying "This is the body of Christ"—but she didn't know what to make of the vision or how to respond. One evening, one of her neighbors invited her to church. For Sally, church was not, at this point, about God. "Going to church was not a religious experience. It was a social experience." She didn't particularly want to go to this extra evening service, but she went. And it was different.

> People in their jeans. Hippies. I think, *This is sort of neat.* And then this guy gets up and starts talking. I can see that he believes something. He really believes something, and then—like he's orgasmically on fire. And I'm thinking, *Ooh, this isn't following the rules.* You know, we're not sitting in the pews. But it's not wild. It's not threatening. It's fun. He gave a sermon, but it was more like a talk, because he didn't stand in the pulpit, he wandered around. He talked about making manifest the "gift that is within thee." And I thought, *That sounds pretty good,* and—and then he started talking about love and knowing the love of God and so forth, and I'm sitting there and I'm looking at him like, *You mean you're supposed to go to a church and love and be loved? That's novel!* You really didn't hear that in church. You know, in church you heard about sin and debt and going through the routine—actually, you didn't hear anything. It was like dry sex, you know, it just didn't work. And that night, in that room, this guy was just on fire. You knew he had a passion, you knew he loved, you knew he was offering something different. His words were alive.
>
> He looked me sort of right in the eye, and he said, "Would you like to be whole?" And I said, "Whole, oh, that sounds really good." Love, whole, gift within you, you know? I said, "All that sounds really, really good." He said, "Can I pray for you?" By this point, I've lost everybody in the room. I have now become so clued in to this man and what's going on between us, and feeling a little excited, but a little bit awkward. And it was like—I just lost awareness. And now all of a sudden, all of these hands are on me, I don't know where they came from. But they're not just his hands, but they're a bunch of hands. And then I hear people singing and talking in tongues. And that's when I go, *Oh my God, this is spooky.* And I clam up. It was too much. But then I sort of stood up and turned around, and

that's when I saw the world as it is, the world as I now know it, and the world as it might be, should be, could be.

That was it. For the next ten years, she was one of the hippie Christians, and her life revolved around the Bible. It really was, she said, like living in *Godspell.* "All love and little or no judgment. No rules. Very little structure. Tons of humor. It was *sooo* seductive."

The Jesus people also made their Jesus their own by reading him straight out of the Gospels, with no expert interpretation. These newcomers to committed Christianity read the text bare, as if they could see it for what it was without scholarly training or knowledge of the historical context. They came at the text the same way, years later, that some of their generation would come to the Constitution—as if it were written for them, as if it were straightforwardly true, and as if all they needed to do to understand what the writer had meant was to read it. As the anthropologist Vincent Crapanzano points out in a provocative book, *Serving the Word,* this was a remarkable perspective, and it was new. Few Christians in the 1950s read the Bible as if it were a contemporary document.[25] Even the theologically conservative Christians who defended the Bible's literalism treated the book with historical distance. Jesus had of course performed miracles, and those miracles were real, but such supernatural acts had taken place in his age, not in ours. The name for this interpretive approach is *dispensationalism.* The idea was that God had different plans and relationships—different historical "dispensations"—with human society in different ages. Until the hippie Christians, dispensationalism dominated the conservative reading of the Bible, and it explained why the miraculous, supernatural acts done by Christ and his disciples did not happen now.[26]

Teens finding Jesus while high on acid, while the Beatles were discovering Maharishi Mahesh Yogi, did not think that the supernatural was safely in the past. In the Gospel of John, Jesus says that "the one who believes in me will also do the works that I do, and in fact, will do greater works than these." The hippies took that work to include the supernatural miracles. They seem to have modeled themselves on the disciples early in the Book of Acts. As Acts opens, the disciples are still in Jerusalem, waiting in their upper room, constantly in prayer. They have already seen Jesus alive after his death, and he has told them that they must wait in Jerusalem to receive power through something he calls the "Holy Spirit." Then the text describes what happened when that power descended: "Suddenly from heaven there came a sound like the rush of a violent wind."[27] Acts is the story of the supernatural miracles—"signs and wonders"—that the disciples do with this power as they wait for Christ to return and claim his kingdom. This seems to have been the way the hippies imagined themselves: a small, close, communal band of followers, with Jesus giving them instructions and the supernatural power of the Holy Spirit at their command.

The most visible expression of this Holy Spirit supernaturalism was speaking in tongues. "Tongues" are a flow of speechlike utterances that sound more or less as if someone is speaking in a language you do not understand. It is a skill—people talk about learning to speak in tongues and teaching others to speak in tongues—but it also has an uncontrolled, dissociative quality. Indeed, contemporary brain-imaging studies find that those who speak in tongues have less conscious control than when they sing.[28] Tongues are usually interpreted by those who use them as spiritual speech that can be understood only by God (or, depending on the church, by someone with the spiritual gift of interpreting tongues), but they are sometimes understood as the actual sudden acquisition of a language the speaker has never spoken before. The interpretive ambiguity comes straight out of Acts. The text moves from the violent rush of fire from heaven, when "divided tongues, as of fire, appeared among them, and a tongue rested on each of them," to the crowd (which gathered to hear them) commenting with amazement that "we hear, each of us, in our own native language . . . in our own languages we hear them speaking about God's deeds of power."[29]

In the late nineteenth century, a Kansas minister, Charles Parham, became fascinated by Acts and convinced that if the disciples had spoken in tongues, all who followed Christ should also speak in tongues. Parham recalls his awe when he entered the room where twelve of his followers sat one evening, bathed as he thought in the "sheen of white light" and speaking in at least six different languages. "Right then there came a slight twist in my throat, a glory fell over me, and I began to worship God in the Sweedish [sic] tongue, which later changed to other languages and continued so until the morning."[30]

. . .

When Parham's followers began to speak in tongues, they assumed that they were speaking in new human languages. They were not. The linguistic anthropologist William Samarin, in a wonderful book, describes tongue-speaking as human utterance that is phonologically structured—that is, the sounds are not random noise but are drawn from the speaker's language—but without systematic resemblance to any language, living or dead. They have neither grammar nor syntax. (One pastor told me with a wry laugh that you could pass as speaking in tongues if you say quickly and repeatedly "She bought a Honda.") But language or not, the person who speaks in tongues often feels great: refreshed, buoyant, and alive.

Astonishingly, Charles Parham and his followers appear to have been among the first to speak in tongues since the early Christians.[31] With Parham, the practice became part of twentieth-century Christianity, although its explosion and the emergence of a style of worship based on tongues—Pentecostalism—is primarily due to the talented young African American pastor William Seymour, who sat outside the door of Parham's classroom to learn from him in Jim Crow Topeka, where he was not allowed inside. Seymour later went out to Los Angeles to preach and held a revival meeting in a run-down hired church in Azusa Street in April 1906. The revival started slowly, with perhaps twelve people or so in attendance in those early days, but the devastation reported from the earthquake up north seemed to give the call an urgency and intensity. By September, there were crowds, the place was open twenty-four hours a day, and soon the practice of speaking in tongues spread throughout the country. Many onlookers were horrified. On April 18 the front-page story on the *Los Angeles Times* ran: "Weird babel of tongues, new sect of fanatics is breaking loose, wild scene last night on Azusa Street, gurgle of wordless talk by a sister." Even Parham demurred at the intensity of worship: he later called Pentecostalism "holy-rolling-dancing-jumping, shaking, jabbering, wind-sucking and giving vent to meaningless sounds and noise."[32] But while Pentecostalism grew steadily if not meteorically through the course of the twentieth century, until the Jesus People it seemed a small ripple in the larger Christian stream, an odd and embarrassing eddy in a swift and powerful modernizing current.

To be sure, Pentecostalism was becoming more visible even before the counterculture discovered it. David Wilkerson's account of Pentecostal ministry to young New York drug addicts, *The Cross and the Switchblade*, became a surprise best seller in 1963. The book arguably provided the first opportunity for middle-class Americans to learn in their own homes about this stigmatized, déclassé kind of Christianity from someone who believed in its power. And at least some of the early evangelists who wandered through Haight Ashbury seem to have accepted a this-worldly reality of the supernatural. Kent Philpotts's diary from the autumn of 1968 includes this entry: "A girl named Space, actually demon-possessed, we found in a trance right out of the street . . . a young beautiful girl had her whole body painted in weird designs. She was staring at an older grey-haired cat who was controlling the trance."[33]

But the hippies made the supernatural fun. When they discovered tongues, they took to them with delight. Speaking in tongues was the spiritual equivalent of long hair and bare feet, and the practice became, as the author of the contemporary mass-market *The Jesus Kids* put it, "the very heart of the Jesus People movement."[34] They didn't believe that speaking in tongues was an obligatory sign of "baptism in the spirit," as traditional Pentecostals held; they believed that if you chose Jesus, you had this special, miraculous, wonderful gift that might make flowers grow in a junkyard and turn something tarnished into something electric and alive.

The joy was infectious. In 1970 *The Late Great Planet Earth* came out. A prophetic account of the end times, it explained that Christianity was more powerful and more accurate than astrology, mystic vibrations, psychic clairvoyance, and Zen. It began, "It was a perfect night for a party," and ran through an astonishing array of gleefully oddball predictions about the coming global catastrophe that presaged the return of Jesus. An example: "One of the chief minerals in the Dead Sea is potash, which is a potent fertilizer. When the population explosion begins to bring famine, potash will become extremely valuable for food production."[35] *The Late Great Planet Earth* sold more than fifteen million copies. *The New York Times* called it "the number-one nonfiction bestseller of the decade."

The Christianity of the middle class did not change until pastors began to adapt their services to attract the hippies and found that the new style drew more people. Chuck Smith may have been the most successful of these spiritual entrepreneurs, and his experiment would ultimately give birth to the churches that I followed for two years in Chicago and then again in California.

Chuck Smith turned forty in 1967, old for a generation that said you couldn't trust anyone over thirty. He was the new straight-edged pastor at an undistinguished nondenominational church in Costa Mesa called Calvary Chapel, home to some two dozen members. The local beaches had hippies living on them—bead-wearing, draft-avoiding young people full flush into the radical social experiments of the day. Smith was troubled by them. "Dirty hippies. Why don't they take a bath?" But they also fascinated him. He urged his daughters to introduce him to one of them. "One evening around five o'clock our doorbell rang. There stood . . . a real, honest-to-goodness hippie—long hair, beard, flowers in his hair, bells on the cuffs of his pants." That was Lonnie Frisbee, who had drifted south from San Francisco, preaching on the beaches. Chuck and Lonnie liked each other immediately. Chuck later said, "I wasn't prepared for the love that came forth from the kid."[36] People said things like that about Lonnie. They said that when he asked the Holy Spirit to be present, it flowed through him as if he were a faucet. "When the anointing hit," someone recalled, "it was like walking with an apostle."

The beach-dwelling kids came first in twos and threes and then in a steady rain. At the beginning, they camped out in Smith's house. Then he rented a house for them—they called it the House of Miracles—and then another. Smith thought the kids on the beach were hungry for God but couldn't find God in the mainstream church life they knew. So he changed his church. Services became completely casual. Older church members, appalled at the sight of dirty feet on new carpet, hung up a sign that read, "No bare feet allowed." Smith yelled at the board and threatened to tear out the carpet. He took the pulpit on Sunday, but he gave Wednesday evening to Lonnie, and in that service Lonnie spoke as he was: long hair, beard, bells on his pants. He became known as "the hippie preacher." "The doors blew open at that point," a congregant recalls in the documentary made about Lonnie's life. Chuck Smith invited the hippie bands to play their music, and he invited back the bands that the audience liked. No one apart from the beach kids had ever heard Christian music like that before, and now the music became its own draw, a mixture of folksy yearning and upbeat rock that moved people lulled to somnolence by hundred-year-old hymns.

The Jesus who presided over these sessions was the hippie and countercultural Jesus: personally attentive, unconditionally loving, a Jesus with a great big bear hug of acceptance. Smith believed in that Jesus. When he and Lonnie spoke about Jesus, "it was as if they were swapping stories about an old college friend." "It was different," recalled a man who discovered Smith's sermons at Calvary and became a Christian. "He wasn't like reading a portion from the Bible and then saying a bunch of words . . . he was telling me about his personal friend."[37] In the documentary, one man remembers Lonnie as a tall skinny kid with long hair who got up on a bench at the beach and bellowed, "Hey!! God loves you! Come to God!" And "all these kids got off their towels, and they were weeping."

When the doors blew open, people streamed in and kept coming. They ran out of space at the original church, rented another, and outgrew that, too. They purchased a school and built a new chapel with three hundred seats and ran out of space the first Sunday. They purchased eleven acres and put up a circus tent to hold sixteen hundred folding chairs and planned two services. That night, before the first tent service, Smith recalled, "I looked out on that sea of folding chairs. I had never seen so many folding chairs in my life! I turned to Duane [a volunteer] and I asked, 'How long do you think it will take the Lord to fill this place?' He looked at his watch and said, 'I'd say just about eleven hours.'"[38] Duane was right. In 1974 they built a permanent sanctuary that could seat twenty-three hundred, and within three weeks they were holding triple services.

In the early days, Smith encouraged the intense personal experience of God. In the large circus tent, the biblical teachings were followed by "afterglow" services in which people would speak in tongues and tremble and sway as the Holy Spirit touched them. Lonnie often led these. He would pray for people, and they would collapse, shaking and crying and laughing through their tears, and they loved it. But things sometimes got out of hand. At a Vineyard conference, I met a woman who remembered those days under the big tent. People used to get there early, to get a seat, she said, and by the time church started, they became as hard to handle as fans at a rock concert.

Chuck Smith grew wary. He had grown up Pentecostal, and he remembered how he cringed when friends from outside his church joined him for a service.

Many times as I was seated with my unsaved friends that I had brought to church, Mrs. Newman would start breathing funny. I had learned that this was her prelude to speaking in tongues, so I would quickly pray, "Oh God, please don't speak in tongues today; my friends won't understand." Either God wasn't hearing me or Mrs. Newman wasn't listening to God, because she would stand up, shaking all over, and deliver God's message for the day in a loud, high-pitched voice. I would die inside as my friends giggled beside me.[39]

Smith didn't want people to snicker at God. Nor did he want people to come for the intense experience for its own sake, as if it were a drug. The apostle Paul had warned the Corinthians about the dangers of intense spiritual experience.

Not all the new converts at Calvary Chapel were bell-bottom radicals. Soon Chuck Smith no longer needed an emphasis on spiritual gifts—so dangerously seductive—in order to draw people in to the church. He wanted people there for the Bible, and he wanted the Bible to be the draw; when he shifted the emphasis to Bible teaching, people continued to flow in. He told Lonnie that if people fell down when he prayed for them, Lonnie would have to leave. Lonnie left. Then he came back, and Smith put the former hippie in a three-piece suit and gave him a job as an assistant pastor. Thus, as the great sociologist Max Weber argued, does the hot excitement of charisma cool down into routine.

But not everyone was ready for a cooldown. John Wimber, who would eventually found the Vineyard, was a portly man with a great smile who had started out as a musician—he was one of the early members of the Righteous Brothers—and became a Christian when he hit bottom on the then-not-uncommon journey through drugs, alcohol, and near divorce.[40] He joined a Quaker church in Yorba Linda, California, in 1963 and soon founded a small house group to study the Bible. Then there was another house group, and another—apparently eleven in total—and those participants joined the Quaker church. Wimber become copastor of the church in 1970, and under his tenure the church grew from two hundred to eight hundred, becoming the largest church in its denomination. But John Wimber was discontented. He left the pastorate to attend school and studied and worked for a while at Fuller Theological Seminary. It was around this time, in the middle 1970s, that he and his wife seem to have discovered tongues and to have yearned for the supernatural presence of God. There was another house group that began to teach musical worship as an end in itself, rather than a prelude to teaching, and it was interspersed with speaking in tongues. There was teaching, of course, but the music became a way for people to lose themselves in God. When Wimber began to lead the group, it swelled to fifty and then to a hundred. Then the Quaker church asked him and his wife to leave.

By that point John Wimber had discovered Calvary, with its afterglows and hippie freedom. He and Chuck Smith took to each other, and they agreed that Wimber's nascent church should become one of the satellite Calvary churches. As it grew, Wimber built the small group structure into the core of the organization, creating what they called "kinships": small house groups that met during the week to talk about God. Like the Jesus People, he focused on the Gospel story of this person, Jesus, and his supernatural encounters.[41] It was 1977.

As Wimber tells the story, when he taught the word of the Bible, he wondered why the miracles described in the scriptures no longer took place. He began to pray for healing in his services, doing an altar call for those who were sick. "It was humiliating," his biographer recounts. "The people doing the praying caught the illnesses of those they were praying for, even the headaches!"[42] For ten months, nothing happened. No one got healed. And then early one morning in 1978, Wimber prayed a dispirited prayer for a newcomer to the church, sick in bed with the flu. As he turned around to her husband to explain that prayer doesn't always work, she got out of bed and began combing her hair. She was completely well. "As he stumbled out the door, jubilation suddenly filled him and he shouted, 'We got one!'"[43]

Now the Holy Spirit seemed to come in buckets. The next month Wimber began a new house group. When he taught on the filling of the Holy Spirit, people asked him to pray that they, too, would be filled with the Holy Spirit. "As he [went around the room praying for them,] he felt spiritual power come out of his hands like electricity, and people fell over."[44] The excitement in the writings from this period is palpable. People seemed to feel that God was alive for them in a way God had never been before.

Still, what most people remember as the "watershed moment" did not take place for another two years. It happened through Lonnie. By this point John Wimber's church had grown to seven hundred people. Lonnie was still employed by the main Calvary church in Costa Mesa, under Chuck Smith's leadership, but he was uneasy in that suit. He would show up at Wimber's church and pray for people. On Mother's Day in 1980, Lonnie gave the Sunday-morning teaching at Wimber's church for the first time. This is the way John Wimber's wife, Carol, remembered it.

The young man shared his testimony, which was beautiful and stirring, then asked for all people under the age of twenty five (two thirds of the congregation, which now numbered over seven hundred) to come forward. None of us had a clue as to what was going to happen next. When they got to the front the speaker said, "For years now the Holy Spirit has been grieved by the church, but he's getting over it. Come, Holy Spirit."

And he came . . .

One fellow, Tim, started bouncing. His arms flung out and he fell over, but one of his hands accidentally hit a mike stand and he took it down with him. He was tangled up in the cord with the mike next to his mouth. Then he began speaking in tongues, so the sound went throughout the gymnasium (by now we were meeting in a high school). We had never considered ourselves charismatics and certainly had never placed emphasis on the gift of tongues. We had seen a few people tremble and fall over before and we had seen many healings, but this was different. The majority of young people were shaking and falling over. At one point it looked like a battlefield scene—bodies everywhere, people weeping, wailing and speaking in tongues, much shouting and loud behavior. And there was Tim in the middle of it all, babbling into the microphone.[45]

John Wimber said he spent that night awake, reading and rereading the scriptures, searching for the words "Come, Holy Spirit" in vain.[46] But he also read Jonathan Edwards and Charles Finney, the great American revivalist preachers, and by the morning, he had decided that these phenomena were in fact experiences of God. They kept happening. Soon the church discovered demons. One evening "a woman slid off her chair, causing a loud commotion, engulfed in a classic hissing demonic manifestation." They decided that she had an in-dwelling demon. Demonic exorcism became routine. Church membership jumped to two thousand. Carol Wimber called these the "glory years." John called it "doin' the stuff."[47]

Wimber and his followers thought that this was what the early church had been like—perpetual encounters with the spirit of God to demonstrate God's presence, to win converts, and even more to be present with his people as if he were walking by their side. By now this was the early 1980s. The hippies were gone. Church members dressed with the casual sobriety of the decade. And still the way they imagined Jesus, their sense of who they were by his side, was remarkably similar to the way the hippie Christians had imagined him. They loved the idea of a band of ardent disciples, in touch with God in a new and vital way, almost drunkenly in love with the divine. They repeatedly compared their own experience to those of scriptural times, particularly the Gospels and the Book of Acts. They spoke about the scriptures not as texts of an ancient people, but as if the events had just happened, as if John the Baptist were a family friend.

John Wimber began to behave as if Jesus stood by the podium and whispered to him when he had something to say. In her memoir, his wife remarked: "During this time, at the beginning, God started speaking to John so clearly about what he wanted to do in the meetings that it became distracting for him and he would lose his train of thought . . . [he would] stop in the middle of his lecture, turn his head to the side a little as if listening to an off stage coach."[48] Being committed to the supernatural in the face of the commonsensical became a point of pride. "If there is ever a choice between the smart thing to do and the move of the Holy Spirit," Wimber wrote, "I will always land on the side of the Spirit."[49]

Chuck Smith was not so sure that it was the Holy Spirit. In 1982 Calvary Chapel asked John Wimber to change the affiliation of his church. On the surface, the disagreement seemed minor. Even today the two denominations seem very much alike. Both Chuck Smith and John Wimber talked about the dull emptiness of mainstream churches, and both saw the liberal church as abandoning God. Both believed that the "dead orthodoxy" of many churches could be renewed through the experience of the Holy Spirit.[50] But to Chuck Smith, John Wimber crossed the line with demon possession. Smith framed his objections theologically: to be a Christian is to be saved, and he who is saved is safe from demons.[51] It is hard not to wonder if the more important problem was the cringe at what Carol Wimber called "all the shakin' going on."[52]

John Wimber now affiliated his church with a nascent organization called the Vineyard. This was a group that had also started as a Bible study, led by a couple called Ken and Joanie Gulliksen. Like Wimber's group, this one emphasized worship music and the Holy Spirit, and like Wimber's, it soon outgrew any one house. In the mid-1970s, the group met for a year on the beach in Santa Monica. Gulliksen remembered that he had the tannest church in the country. They called themselves the Vineyard because one day Gulliksen was reading in Isaiah, and this verse jumped out at him: "A Vineyard of wine, sing of it! I, the Lord, am its keeper; I water it every moment, lest anyone damage it, I guard it night and day." Gulliksen thought the Holy Spirit told him that his group was that Vineyard. The group became one church, and then three, and they became loosely connected to Calvary—one gets a sense, in this story, of the fluid quality of these church relationships—and when Chuck Smith became uneasy with Wimber's church, he suggested that Wimber define his church as a Vineyard. The Vineyard came to stand for a more spirit-focused church practice.

In 1982 Wimber's church became the Vineyard Christian Fellowship at Anaheim. It began to grow. Lonnie came on staff. John would speak; Lonnie would minister. They were, one congregant recalled, "the dynamic duo." Like Calvary before it, the Vineyard exploded in membership. Indeed, soon thirty Calvary churches would also change their affiliation. Perhaps they just reached the people whom Calvary's shift had left behind; perhaps—as Lonnie's friends would tell the story—when Lonnie called, the Holy Spirit came and drew believers to his church and others like moths to flame. "Lonnie would wave his leather coat [he had a leather cape on which he had painted the figure of Jesus] and call on the power of God, and people would be falling all over these old pews of the Baptist church. Lonnie would crawl over the pews to pray for people. He'd say 'speak in tongues, speak in tongues.' Then he'd touch them on the forehead and they would instantly begin to speak in tongues." Whatever drew people, they came. More than twenty-five years later, the Vineyard is still expanding.[53]

But Lonnie is no longer there. In the mid-1980s, a young male congregant came in to see an assistant pastor at Calvary and tearfully begged forgiveness for the six-month affair he said he'd had with Lonnie. Shortly afterward someone at Calvary asked John and Carol Wimber over dinner whether they were able to deal with Lonnie's homosexuality with compassion. The next day Lonnie was fired from visible ministry. (To be fair, Lonnie was also married at the time. Pastors are not supposed to be having affairs.) Within months, he left the church and was more or less expunged from the historical accounts of both Calvary and the Vineyard. In the early 1990s, Lonnie Frisbee died of AIDS.

By 2003, when I encountered the Vineyard, its charismatic intensity had somewhat abated. John Wimber had died of a massive heart attack in 1997. People who were there in the beginning, in the 1980s, talk about the wonder of the "glory years," when you felt that Jesus was moving by your side like a mighty wind, and when the wall between the eternal supernatural and the mundane was tissue thin. It doesn't feel that way anymore, they say. But the basic impulse of the church movement, as I encountered it in the decade after Wimber's death, is still recognizable as the one Wimber founded, and under the cover of its middle-class conventions, its Jesus and its God are still recognizable as those of the God that emerged out of the hot forge that was the counterculture. This God is the God of most of the experientially oriented evangelical churches—the new paradigm churches, the renewalist churches, and many others with more conservative pastors whose congregants read *The Purpose Driven Life, Celebration of Discipline,* and *Experiencing God.*

Their Jesus is deeply human and playfully, magically supernatural. You can see these features in the two musicals of the countercultural era: the hesitant, insecure Jesus of *Jesus Christ Superstar,* so close a friend of Judas that Judas cannot understand why the human man he loves does such unmanlike things; and the laughing, dancing Jesus of *Godspell,* not so much supernatural as magical, as playful as a child. The one tells a story of profound human friendship, troubled because Judas cannot allow himself to believe in the goodness that Jesus promises. The other is a tale of madcap joy.

Was it really new? These aspects of Jesus, and of God, have been present before in American society, but they have rarely been so sharply drawn. God is called "friend" in the aftermath of the Civil War—but it is Jesus the son, rather than God the father, who is described in this way.[54] Henry Ward Beecher's *Life of Jesus, the Christ* (1871) gives a feel for what the historian Stephen Prothero calls this American Everyman: a kind, good, domestic man; a dear friend.

Jesus was a citizen. He knew the fatigue of labor, the trials which beset poverty, the temptations arising from the practical conduct of business. He lived among men in all the innocent experiences of society life, a cheerful, companionable, and most winning nature. There was no gayety in his demeanour, but much cheerfulness.[55]

The post–Civil War Jesus is divine, but barely, and he is no madcap magician breaking loose. He doesn't giggle. He doesn't tease. And no barely contained supernatural force strains at his edges. In fact, this Jesus becomes the Jesus of the liberal Christian church: a kind man of great love who taught wisely and who may or may not have been divine. There are references to friendship with God and with Jesus in the Bible, but this friendship is not the free and easy companionship of two boys swinging their feet on a bridge over a stream.[56]

The remarkable shift in the understanding of God and of Jesus in the new paradigm churches of modern American Christianity is the shift that the counterculture made: toward a deeply human, even vulnerable God who loves us unconditionally and wants nothing more than to be our friend, our best friend, as loving and personal and responsive as a best friend in America should be; and toward a God who is so supernaturally present, it is as if he does magic and as if our friendship with him gives us magic, too. God retains his holy majesty, but he has become a companion, even a buddy to play with, and the most ordinary man can go to the corner church and learn how to hear him speak. What we have seen in the last four or five decades is the democratization of God—*I and thou* into *you and me*—and the democratization of intense spiritual experience, arguably more deeply than ever before in our country's history.[57]

That God seems implausible to those raised within the more conventional mainstream. But this Jesus is recognizable, even if he has been transformed like the statue of Glaucus by the saltwater tides of our time. He is—to some extent—the Jesus of the Gospel of Mark, the first Gospel that was ever written.

I find the Gospel of Mark profoundly moving. It has a craggy, jagged quality, as if it were hewn out of granite, as if the author simply put down the unpolished truth. In the text, John the Baptist shows up unexplained, as does Jesus, who is given no birth narrative, no parents, no genealogy. The author is telling this story to an audience already familiar with the tale. John simply says that he himself baptizes with water but the one who comes after will baptize with the Holy Spirit, and then he baptizes Jesus and the heavens are torn apart. The Gospel ends just as abruptly, at least in its original form. Mark 16:9–20 is a late addition. In those late verses, Jesus rises and returns to his disciples, upbraids them for their lack of faith, and says that those who believe will cast out demons, speak in tongues, pick up snakes with their hands, and drink deadly poison without harm. There are still Christian churches, tucked into the mountains of the American South, whose congregants thrust their hands into a box of rattlesnakes and drink strychnine from mason jars. In a beautiful, unnerving book, *Salvation on Sand Mountain,* a young southern writer went to explore these churches like an anthropologist, a sympathetic traveler in distant lands. One hundred fifty-plus pages into his book, he finds himself up at the front of the church with a snake writhing in his outstretched arms, alone in a blaze of white, still light. Yet the oldest ending of Mark is in some ways stranger. The women go to the tomb. They see that a stone has been rolled back, and a young man in white sits at its side and tells them that Christ is risen and has gone ahead. The young man tells them to tell this to the other disciples. But the women run away and say nothing, for they are afraid.

Mark's Jesus is deeply human (although not much of a pal). He gets hungry. He gets angry at being misunderstood, even though he is constantly forbidding those who recognize him (the demons) and those he has cured (for example, the leper) to explain who he is. His own parents think he has gone mad and try to restrain him. His own townspeople, from the place he grew up, take offense at him and he can do no acts of power among them. He is amazed at their unbelief. Above all, he is anguished at the prospect of his own ordeal, "grieved even unto death." On the cross, he cries out with great poignancy, "My God, my God, why have you forsaken me?"[58]

That line—it is a quotation from one of the psalms—will also appear in Matthew's version of the passion, but Matthew shows Jesus in far less agony in the garden. Matthew's Jesus is a teacher, and in the garden, he teaches: "The spirit is willing, but the flesh is weak." Luke's Jesus keeps his equanimity until the end. Luke's Jesus is a prophet like the prophets of old, and he retains the distance and the dignity of a prophet upon the cross. Luke gives him a line from a different psalm: "Forgive them, for they know not what they have done." John's Jesus is in some ways the most human in all the Gospels. Jesus gets thirsty. He becomes tired. It is in John's Gospel that Mary and Martha are presented as his real human friends. But John's Jesus is fully in control at his death. Flogged, bleeding, and humiliated as he has been, he has sufficient gravitas to assign someone to look after his mother, and when he dies, he refers back to the process that has led him to that point: "It is finished." John's Jesus has no agony in Gethsemane. Only Mark's Jesus is petrified at the thought of his coming death on the cross, and he is as lonely as we might be ourselves if the noose of an unjust law pulled tight.

Mark's Jesus is also more of a magician than the Jesus in the other Gospels, and the narrative is the story of a young man learning to understand and control a power so big it is nearly uncontrollable, the story of a boy learning to ride a stallion. In the early chapters, it is as if the supernatural healing is an accident. Jesus teaches in the synagogue; he is there to teach, and it happens by chance that a man comes in with a demon and is healed by him. He seems terribly cautious about what he can do. People begin to seek him out, and he heals them, but again and again he cautions them not to tell. Power leaks out of him when he is touched. People follow him to lay a finger on the fringe of his cloak, and when they do so they are cured. And it is tangible stuff, this power. When the woman with hemorrhages touches his robe, Jesus actually feels the power leave his body as it heals her. That is why he turns and asks, "Who touched me?" The other Gospels tell the story differently. She asks; he responds. They work through words. In Mark, the power heals before Jesus knows that it has gone. Then Mark shows that Jesus has mastery of this leaping power. In a scene so much like the work of a traveling magician that the other Gospel writers will not use it, a blind man asks Jesus to make him see. Jesus spits on his hands and touches the man's eyes until his world grows clear.[59]

This combination of Jesus's intensely human nature and his tangible supernaturalism creates a mystery, and that mystery and the burden of discipleship that it demands are the heartbeat of the Gospel's narrative. In 1901 the great German scholar William Wrede argued that the Gospel writer imported these characteristics into the text to explain why Jesus seems so unlike a messiah in his historical life. In the other Gospels, Jesus brings the "mystery of the kingdom" or the "mystery of the word." In Mark, Jesus brings simply "the mystery," and as Luke Timothy Johnson points out, the mystery is Jesus himself: not so much what he says or even what he does but simply who he is. In Mark, only the demons—and at the end, his human executioner—know that this man is the son of God.[60] Humans, on the other hand, are constantly amazed by him. He attracts. He says "Follow me," and people do. But he also repels. His parables are confusing. He says directly that he wants them to confound. His call to discipleship is hard: "Sell all you have, and follow me." And his disciples do not get it. "Who is this," they ask, "that even the wind and the sea obey him?" They do not understand what he says, and they are afraid to ask. Jesus says something straightforward; the disciples think it is a metaphor. He gives them a metaphor; they take it literally. He tells them, literally and metaphorically, "Keep awake!" Yet three times during his despairing watch in the garden, they fall asleep.[61]

In the Gospel of Mark, Jesus is a mystery, and when he dies, the story ends. We, the readers of the gospel, know that the story continues, but we are in the presence of a great unknown, although as humans we realize we share the weakness and the wrongheadedness of the disciples who fled.

That old, old mystery—how little we understand, how much it confuses us, how drawn we are to the promise, and how repelled we are by its irrationality—is at the heart of this new imagining of God. God is always a mystery, of course. But the Jesus that the Gospel writer presents in Mark is remarkable in being both utterly straightforward and quite unexplained. This new American Christ is just as raw, both concretely present and curiously untheologized. His churches emphasize intimacy, not historical understanding. They care that people know Jesus, not that they know and memorize the scriptural text, and they want their congregants to feel as if church is meeting in that upper room in Jerusalem, with Jesus at the table.

That is the invitation: to experience God as if he were real in the flesh and standing by your side, with love. The challenge is to learn how to do that.

🌿

CHAPTER TWO

Is That You, God?

When he has brought out all his own,
he goes on ahead of them,
and his sheep follow him because
they know his voice.

John 10:4

God, you're always present,
but it's cool when we know it.

Worship leader at the Vineyard,
December 2008

ONE OF THE FIRST THINGS a person must master at a church like the Vineyard is to recognize when God is present and when he responds. This can seem odd to someone raised in a mainstream church, where God is usually not imagined as a person with whom you have back-and-forth conversation throughout the day. At the Vineyard, people speak about recognizing God's "voice." They talk about things God has "said" to them about very specific topics—where they should go to school and whether they should volunteer in a day care—and newcomers are often confused by what they mean. Newcomers soon learn that God is understood to speak to congregants inside their own minds. They learn that someone who worships God at the Vineyard must develop the ability to recognize thoughts in their own mind that are not in fact their thoughts, but God's. They learn that this is a skill they should master. At the beginning, they usually find both the skill and the very idea of the skill perplexing.

The basic presumption that the mind is separate from the world is one of the most definitive achievements of childhood development. By the age of three, more or less—there's a good deal of controversy—toddlers understand that mental states can explain behavior. The classic experiment is the False Belief task. A child and the child's mother watch an experimenter hide a toy dinosaur under a pillow. Then the mother leaves the room, and the experimenter moves the toy to a new hiding place. When the mother returns, the experimenter asks the child where the mother thinks the dinosaur will be. Very young children point to the second hiding place, because that is where the dinosaur actually is. Older children understand that the mother does not know that the toy has been moved, and so they point to the pillow. They have developed what psychologists call "theory of mind." They understand that what people think may be different from what has happened in the world. They understand that people hold different ideas, and that these different ideas may explain what they do. And they know that their own thoughts cannot be known by other people unless they tell them. They no longer act, as very young children do, as if other people cannot see them when they shut their own eyes.

The task of becoming a Christian—at least this kind of Christian, an experientially oriented or "renewalist" evangelical—demands that one set out deliberately to overcome this fundamental human awareness that our minds are private. In little ways, of course, all of us act as if our minds and the world ooze into each other. We hit the golf ball and then lean in the direction we want the ball to travel. We say a quiet, earnest "please" when we click on an e-mail that matters. But it is one thing to hope fleetingly that a thought in your mind is heard by and responded to by something external; it is another thing to experience that moment as an actual conversation.

In effect, these Christians are asked to develop a new theory of mind. It is not radically different from the basic theory that toddlers acquire in every culture that we know: that humans act on the basis of what they hold in their minds, and those minds are in some deep sense separate from the world. (On this level, even chimpanzees exhibit classic theory of mind.) This new Christian theory of mind—we could call it a "participatory" theory of mind—asks congregants to experience the mind-world barrier as porous, in a specific, limited way. Humans are usually keenly aware of the difference between mental events generated within the mind (we call them thoughts) and those generated from an external source (which are usually called perceptions). In general, we know that when we hear the phone ring, the sound originated from outside of us, and we know this simply, straightforwardly, automatically. We know that when we think we would like a peanut butter sandwich, that thought comes from our minds, and again, this knowing feels simple and straightforward. To be sure, we sometimes get confused: Did I see it on television, or maybe it was a dream? But the confusions are relatively infrequent. We are constantly distinguishing between sounds and sights in the world and thoughts and images in our mind, and we do this so effortlessly that it rarely seems like a puzzle worth fretting about, this miracle that we are able to identify the source of the events in our minds.

When you attend a church like the Vineyard, you are presented with a theory of mind in which that distinction is all of a sudden no longer straightforward. You are asked to experience some of your thoughts as being more like perceptions. In a church like the Vineyard, God participates in your mind, and you "hear" what he says as if it were external speech. The general model is clear enough, although no one actually presented it to me as a bullet-point list. God wants to be your friend; you develop that relationship through prayer; prayer is hard work and requires effort and training; and when you develop that relationship, God will answer back, through thoughts and mental images he places in your mind, and through sensations he causes in your body. You still experience those thoughts and images and sensations, for the most part, as if they were your own, generated from within your own mind and body. You have to learn to experience those you have identified as God's as different.

These evangelical Christians, then, not only have to accept the basic idea that they can experience God directly; they must develop the interpretive tools to do so in a way that they can authentically experience what feels like inner thought as God-generated. They have to pick out the thoughts that count as God's and learn to trust that they really are God's, not their own, and they have to do so in a way that does not violate the realistic demands of the everyday world. The theory they develop to help them do so is partly provided by the sermons and the books and the social chatter, and partly by something they infer from the ways they learn to practice. To an observer, what is striking is how hard people work to feel confident that the God who speaks to them in their mind is also the real external God who led the Jews out from slavery and died upon the cross.

I met Sarah at the Vineyard church in California. A short Asian woman, slightly plump, with a short chin and expressive eyes, she recognized me as a newcomer immediately and came over to make me feel welcome. When she learned that I was an anthropologist, she cheerfully began to explain how she had come to know God.

Sarah had found the Vineyard through an ad in the local paper. She wasn't quite sure what she wanted out of a church, but she liked the sound of "scripture-based teaching in a casual setting." She was just turning fifty, and she was at one of those life crossroads, full of doubt about her job, her marriage, the choices she'd made. Up to that point, religion had been a social obligation for her. She'd spent her youth in a nondescript fifty-minutes-and-you're-out Methodist church, and converted to Catholicism, her husband's faith, when they married. She was never, she said, a good Catholic. She believed in God in an abstract, distant sort of way, but the rituals didn't move her. Yet the first morning Sarah attended a Vineyard service, she wept uncontrollably. She told me that she cried because for the first time in her life she was singing directly *to* God, not *about* God, a love song to a living person—a man, even—who loved her openly and unconditionally, and it made her sob. For the first three months, she cried in every service.

That first morning the pastor came over at the end of the service—bounded over, she said, as if he saw that she needed him. So she stayed. She took a course designed for newcomers to the church, and she kept coming on Sunday mornings. She joined a prayer group, and they taught her how to pray, and she became one of the active members of what they called the "prayer team." Eventually she became the church administrator and something of a backbone for a young church in which she was one of the oldest members. We will follow her closely in this book, because her journey has much to teach us.

At the beginning is the yearning. Individuals give many different reasons for their arrival at the Vineyard. Sometimes they speak as if sheer happenstance brought them into the church, and when the original reason for being there evaporated, they stayed anyway. Robert, for example, was a middle-aged realtor with little interest in God before he began to attend church with a new girlfriend. "How did I become a Christian?" Robert mused out loud when we met in his tidy office. "I was dating someone. It was very important for her to have whoever she was involved with share her faith. The relationship didn't work out, but for me the timing was perfect. I just never had a desire to get near to Christianity until I met her." People often come with a vague, uneasy discontent. Maybe they talk about purpose, maybe meaning; almost always they talk about wanting "more," as if the volume control of their life is set too low and the sound is weak and tinny. The vague yearning is understood to be the start of what is often described as a journey, and it is imagined as a desire, something you want to believe in rather than something you believe already: a mustard seed. The church bulletin put it this way:

> Many people go to church because they are looking for God. Perhaps this is why you have come [here]. You feel that there is something missing from your life. The famous French mathematician, Pascal, said that inside every person is a God-shaped void meant only for Him. God desires to have a relationship with you and to fill the emptiness you feel inside.

People often spoke about the emptiness as "hunger," and some said that they had not known what they were hungry for. That's the way Sarah put it. "The hunger was so strong. The word *drive* makes it sound too worldly, but that's what it's like, you know. You're just not gonna stop until you find exactly what you are looking for without knowing what it was you were looking for."

Sarah grew up in a small town in Arizona, where church was a social thing—church camps, church teas, church suppers, church fairs. It didn't have much to do with God. She was in her early twenties when she moved from her father's house into her husband's house. She converted to Catholicism to please his family, and that was fine. She had three children and a job, and life seemed busy. By her late forties, however, the children were more or less gone. The house felt quieter. She had more time. And something felt wrong, although it was hard for her to say exactly what that was. Then she and her husband went off on a vacation to celebrate turning fifty. A wonderful vacation, she said, the trip of a lifetime: they snorkled and swam, the food was fabulous, and everything was perfect— and then on the plane back, she thought, *This is so empty.* She did not think that she was depressed.

Sarah could point to the way she *wanted* to feel. She was then teaching high school equivalency (GED) classes to adults in southside San Francisco, many of them black and some of them homeless. Many were Christians, and Sarah thought that despite their poverty, they seemed to have something she sought. She called it "peace." She began to read her Bible, and when one student couldn't make her scheduled class, she offered to tutor him in math if he would read the Bible with her in exchange. Then another student invited her to a gospel service that celebrated his graduation, and as she sat there listening to the music—"heaven came down and filled my soul"—she felt suddenly alive as she had never felt before, as if someone had thrown a switch and turned her on. She walked out of the service and walked for miles, brimming with joy. She said that she didn't know what to do with feeling so good. The feeling faded, as such feelings do, and she began to look for a church. When she came to the Vineyard, she saw what she wanted again. "Not just happy smiles. Joy. Joy in the Lord. Peace for no good reason." She saw it on people's faces, and she wanted it.

But she did not know how to get it. She began to get up before dawn as her husband slept, to read the Bible and to meditate: "Thinking is your own thought and meditating is like focusing on something and sort of clearing space for something else to come in." She didn't really know what was coming in. In fact, she didn't really understand that anything was *supposed* to come in. "Now I know that the something is God, God's voice. But I didn't have the words to describe it at that time. I didn't understand. It was very confusing."

Sarah knew from the pastor's teaching and from her reading that God wanted to be in relationship with her, but at the beginning she felt that these were just so many words. "It seemed really wacky to me. At that point, I didn't feel connected to him." Part of her, she said, was simply afraid. "Part of me wanted it, but part of me was [saying] that it's crossing a line into total goofiness. I didn't want to cross that line." But part of the uncertainty was a genuine ignorance about how on earth she was supposed to get into a personal relationship with an invisible force whose face she could not see, whose voice she could not hear, whose hand she could not shake, but with whom she was supposed to have an intimate and ongoing dialogue about the small details of everyday life.

The process is not straightforward. In the middle of C. S. Lewis's *Mere Christianity*, a text written to invite skeptics and newcomers to the faith but read—as Lewis knew it would be—by those who have been Christians for many years, he says:

I want to start by saying something I would like everyone to notice carefully. It is this. If this chapter means nothing to you, if it seems to be answering questions you never asked, drop it at once. Do not bother about it at all. There are certain things in Christianity that can be understood from the outside, before you have become a Christian. But there are a great many things that cannot be understood until after you have gone a certain distance along the Christian road . . . Whenever you find any statement in Christian writings which you can make nothing of, do not worry. Leave it alone. There will come a day, perhaps years later, when you suddenly see what it meant.[1]

Lewis presumes that much of what he says about faith is opaque to those who are not Christian. A skeptic might interpret this as a preemptive defense against skepticism. A better way to make sense of it is to consider that believing in this God involves complex learning in which learners override basic intuitions as they learn. This kind of learning suggests that what people are doing is not only learning but unlearning. They are like students in a physics class who begin with their intuitions and then turn them upside down.[2]

In fact, the learning does begin with an insistence on unlearning. Most serious life changes are preceded by an inchoate yearning, but evangelical conversion stories emphasize the unease and build it into a kind of achievement, as if telling people to abandon their preconceptions makes it possible for the real learning to proceed, clearing the cognitive underbrush to build a road through a tricky bit of forest. At the very time that new Christians (or newly committing Christians) are attending church, reading the Bible, and hearing endless accounts of God's nature, they are also told that God is not who they thought he was. "God's appointment book doesn't read anything like: M/W/F 10:07–10:22 a.m., talking to Sarah from Pasadena."[3] As the author of *The Beginner's Guide to Hearing God* writes: "It's like God uses a radio when He speaks to us. God has not quit speaking to you. He has just turned the knob over to a different channel that you are not used to hearing Him on."[4] You are told, in short, that you should expect to feel confused.

So how do you even begin to identify the thoughts that are really God, or to pull out what is God from the ordinary static in your mind? I picked up *Dialogue with God* in a Vineyard-sponsored course one weekend (the course was called "The Art of Hearing God"). The author begins by saying that he yearned to hear God speak to him the way God spoke to people in the Hebrew Bible, but that God never spoke to him like that, so he could hear God with his ears. Then he realized—it was a revelation, he reported—that if God rarely speaks out loud, God's voice must be mingled with the flow of his own stream of consciousness. God is always speaking to you, he explains to his reader. The Christian just needs to learn how to listen. That means learning to pay attention to our own awareness in order to hear what he says. "God's voice normally sounds like a flow of spontaneous thoughts, rather than an audible voice. I have since discovered certain characteristics of God's interjected thoughts which help me to recognize them."[5] You just need to pay attention.

But attention to which moments? Congregants seem to learn to identify God's voice in their own mind the way we humans learn most abstract concepts, at least our everyday abstract concepts like "time." We give content to those abstract terms by, in effect, cognitively mapping that content out from everyday familiar experience. Lera Boroditsky was a young cognitive psychologist when she decided to explore this observation. She came up with an ambiguous question: "Next Wednesday's meeting has been moved forward two days. What day is the meeting?" If you imagine time as coming toward you, that day is Monday. But if you imagine yourself moving forward in time, then that day would be Friday. Boroditsky reasoned that people would draw on their most recent experience of moving through space to map out what it means to move through time, and so she sent students to the local airport to interview strangers. And indeed, those who had just flown in were more likely to say that the meeting was on Friday than those who were waiting to pick someone up. People on the train who were just about to get off were more likely to pick Friday than people in the middle of their journey. And standing in the lunch line for food in the Thai café in the basement of the psychology building, people who were closer to their food (and thus had traveled forward the long length of the line) were more likely to pick Friday than those who had just joined the line. People did indeed behave as if they mapped an abstract and disembodied time from their most recent experience of moving through space.[6]

This is the way people come to recognize an invisible God that the prayer books tell them is even more undefined and unexpected than they thought. They map this abstract God from their own particular lives. They use their own experience of how conversation happens and how they relate to trusted friends to pick out the thoughts and images in their minds that are like those ordinary moments, but different in certain ways.

But they don't talk about mapping. They talk about listening. And they say that the listening happens in prayer.

"Prayer" is the act of talking with God. In this evangelical world, prayer is treated as a skill. "Prayer is an unnatural activity," begins the how-to prayer manual written by Bill Hybels, pastor of Willow Creek, one of the largest evangelical churches in the country. In some crude sense, of course, he is wrong. Many people pray, or at least tell survey researchers that they pray. Eighty-eight percent of Americans say that they pray to God; 76 percent say that prayer is an important part of their daily lives.[7] What that means in practice ranges widely, particularly for evangelicals. I met people for whom prayer consisted of a few muttered sentences as they rode the escalator to work, people who would set aside more than an hour on Saturday morning to dance around their living room to worship songs, people who treated reading their Bible as a form of prayer, people who would put aside an evening to talk with God, and people who met for "prayer walks," where they would stroll together down particular city blocks and pray out loud for the people living in the buildings on the street.

What Hybels means when he talks about prayer as an unnatural activity is that whatever people do when they pray, they must learn to treat some inner mental phenomena as heard by an external presence, and other mental phenomena as not their own but as emanating from that presence. In the beginning, most people find it difficult. Sam was a business major in college when we met, several years after he had committed himself to Christ. "When I was starting to be a Christian," Sam recalled, "people would be like, 'So what's God saying to you?' And I'm like, 'Heck, *I* don't know.'"

The manuals and sermons establish the idea of a conversation between friends as the central model of prayer. "It seems unrealistic that we can bypass celestial voicemail and chat personally with the Creator of the universe, but that's exactly what the Bible says we can do."[8] Thus begins *Bruce and Stan's Pocket Guide to Talking with God*. There are hundreds of books available to the Christian who seeks to learn how to pray. *Bruce and Stan's Pocket Guide* is particularly just-plain-folks in style. It has lists and shadow boxes and little megaphones to mark big ideas. It sets out to teach you how to have a natural, unscripted conversation with God. "There are many ways to communicate with someone, but the best and most effective is talking face to face in normal everyday language, with no pretense, no hidden agendas and no formality. The same goes for God."[9] For the most part, the book sets out to dispel disbelief in the very possibility of having the conversation. "It's really important to understand that God is not an impersonal force. Even though He is invisible, God is personal and He has all the characteristics of a person. He *knows*, he *hears*, he *feels* and he *speaks*."[10]

So congregants begin to search for God's voice by holding conversations with him in their heads, modeled on the kinds of conversations they have with friends. If you are going to have a conversation, the manuals continue, you need to get quiet enough to listen for God's response. *Dialogue with God* recommends a "prayer closet," a place where you can go, unplug the phone, and be fully undistracted. I met people who had the equivalent of closets, quiet rooms where they could go at certain hours and shut the door. I even met people who used a closet. In theory (that is, according to the pastor and the prayerbooks) this "quiet time" is the most important form of prayer, some period of time (ideally, thirty minutes) that people deliberately set aside in their day for God. People are supposed to spend that time holding a conversation with God.

That indeed is the way these Christians talk about it. They speak about "getting to know" God, learning who he is, talking to him about their day. They describe God and Jesus as people you need to meet personally, as if you were out for coffee and had to figure out what the person across the table from you really meant. As one congregant said, "It's just like any relationship. If I had a best friend and we never hung out, where would our friendship be?"

After she married, Hannah, a young woman at the Vineyard just out of college, would create quiet time by explicitly telling her husband not to bother her, and then going into a room to be by herself with God: "I will retreat into the bedroom, close the door, and sit on my bed for like an hour and just see what happens, commune with God. My husband won't interrupt me." A woman came one Sunday to speak to us in a weekly evening meeting succinctly entitled "More." She implored us to spend quiet time with God because it would change our lives. She trembled with anxiety to speak in front of such a big group, but then she shut her eyes to talk to God (she apologized to us, but said that she needed to take a moment to talk to God), and when she opened them, she was calm. She said that we needed to feel about quiet time the way we felt about brushing our teeth: that we couldn't stand to go through a day without it.

And yet I never heard anyone say that they realized that God had spoken to them for the first time in quiet time, probably because in the beginning the conversation seems too forced, too much like silly pretend. In practice, the prayers that really persuaded people that God was speaking to them in their minds were prayers for other people, in which the ordinary thoughts that floated into their mind during the prayer seemed uncannily appropriate for the person about whom they prayed. Then the thoughts could be identified as extraordinary. When that happened— when there was some apparent external confirmation that an inner thought came from an external source—people got visibly excited and happy as they recounted their discovery.

People pray for each other in many different ways. In "prayer ministry," the person for whom one is praying is physically present. One stands before the person and puts one's hand on their arm or shoulder, or—if praying in a large group—on the arm or shoulder of someone who is touching them, or at least with one's hands out and facing them. (In general, men are supposed to pray for men and women for women.) This is the most visible form of prayer, because it takes place at the end of the service every Sunday. In "intercessory prayer," people pray, often out loud, for other people who are not present. People meet in small groups to pray for those who are ill—or for the church conference, or the Sunday service, or the distant war. People who are thought to be gifted in prayer acquire a list of people they have to pray over every day. By the time I met her, Sarah had so many people she felt that she had to pray over that it took her more than an hour to get through. She wrote their names down in her notebooks to make sure she prayed for every one in turn. She told me that the list had become so long that God had recently "released" some people from it. She was thankful for this.

The church requires those who would be part of the official prayer team that stands in front of the church on Sunday morning to take an actual class. These two-to-three-hour classes explain the way prayer works and how to do it. The classes teach that when you pray, you have mental events (not that those teaching use that phrase) that are the presence of

God in your mind. Your job is to pay attention to these events and follow where God "leads." This means that when you are praying, you should speak out loud in describing the images, thoughts, or impressions (often scriptural verses) that come spontaneously to mind, elaborating them as you understand them, paying careful attention to what is appearing in your mind and at the same time carefully paying attention to the emotions of the person being prayed over. The implicit theory is that God will speak to the person praying in ways that lead the person being prayed for to be emotionally moved. "Pray, listen and watch," advised the handout we got in the prayer ministry training class. "Listen for the leading of the Holy Spirit. Look for indications of the presence of the Holy Spirit (crying, peace, warmth, tingling, muscle spasms)." The idea is that you make yourself "available" for the Holy Spirit to work through, and the Holy Spirit will enter the other person through your prayer and (often) make them cry. People sometimes talk about this as being a "conduit." "I feel almost like a tube," Sarah once said to me, "that the Holy Spirit is feeding through me and into another person."

Even to Christians this sometimes sounds like psychotherapy, and indeed most sophisticated pray-ers speak, when they are praying, like empathic psychotherapists. Yet the language of the church attributes the empathy to the Holy Spirit so emphatically that sometimes the teachers make the process sound like the kind of mind-reading games children play on sleepover parties. Once a minister from another Vineyard, eagerly teaching us to hear God's voice, held up her key chain and announced that she was going to tell the Holy Spirit which key she was thinking about and that we were to ask the Holy Spirit to tell us which key she'd chosen. I went to a conference where we did another exercise: we put a member of our group in the center of our circle and prayed for her silently. The instructor told us to write down the images we felt we had received in that prayer so that other people's remarks would not "contaminate" what we said, and then we went around the circle in turn to share what had "happened." Many of us mentioned yellow or orange items: yellow foxgloves, a yellow canoe, an orange Chevy Convertible. The subject beamed and said that it was so cool to know that God knew her favorite color.

When I told these stories to members of the Vineyard, many cringed. And yet people often talked as if uncanny coincidence had enabled them to recognize a thought as a perception of God for the first time. They usually told some story about realizing that what they experienced as a random thought—or image, or a particular scriptural reference, maybe with a sudden rush of warmth—was in fact unusually relevant to the person they were praying over, and they felt that only an external God who had access to both minds could have planted a thought so relevant to the person who needed the prayer in the mind of the person who was doing the praying. Aisha was an intense, eager Christian who found her way to the Vineyard because she loved the idea of an intimate relationship with God, but she remembered being terrified the first time she prayed for a stranger as a member of the church's prayer team. "I didn't know what to say. I was really scared. And then, I remember, I saw something. It wasn't a vivid picture. It was more like my words *described* the picture than I *saw* clearly what the picture was. When I described it to the person I was praying for, he just started to cry. Then he explained why he was crying, and with that information, I was able to pray for him more. It was the most powerful thing."

In the first prayer training class I attended, our teacher told us that one of her first experiences in prayer ministry had made her realize that God was talking to her in her mind. She was then, she said, quite inexperienced and quite uncertain about what she was doing. In prayer training, she had been told never to give concrete advice in prayer and never to prophesy about birth, death, or marriage. A skeptic might see this rule as a hedge—don't predict anything that can be falsified—but the church sees it as a caution because the humans who interpret God's voice are so fallible. Soon afterward, she found herself praying as a member of the prayer team for a woman, a stranger to her, and as she prayed, she began to get images of a child. "Do you have children?" she asked the woman, and the woman said no. Nor had she nieces or nephews. Our teacher continued to pray, she said, but her images of children were so powerful and persistent that finally she blurted out (as she told the story) that "a child will come into your life." She felt awful afterward, she said, not only because she'd broken one of the cardinal rules but because she felt like a fool, making a prediction she was sure would come wrong. But a month later the woman came back to church and came up to her and thanked her, because she'd been pregnant when she had prayed for her and she hadn't known it. That was when our teacher knew that the image had come directly from God.

The church nudges people to interpret these uncannily coincidental thoughts as the presence of God by insisting that when God speaks to them in this way even when they are not praying, he wants them to pray for the people whom the thoughts or images represent. People spoke as if, in effect, one agreed to take on this responsibility when one became this kind of Christian. It was common for someone to report that the face of someone else had "popped" into their mind, and conclude, from this, that God wanted them to pray about that person. They often used the verb *pop* to describe this kind of experience, because *pop* implies that the image was spontaneous, and because it wasn't something they were already thinking about, so it was reasonable to suspect that God had deliberately placed it in their minds and for a reason. Alice was a matter-of-fact engineering student when I met her at church, and she was somewhat skeptical of spiritual drama. But she had no trouble with the idea that spontaneous thoughts come from God. "One day," Alice explained, "I read this book about Christian dating. For some reason, the name of a friend from high school popped into my head, every time I picked up the book. So I just randomly e-mailed her. I wrote, 'Well, I don't know what's going on, but I think God wants you to read this book.' She e-mailed back, 'Oh my goodness, this is amazing.' It turns out that she and her boyfriend were having problems. She was like, *wow*." "You have to be careful," Alice added quickly. "You have to think, is this coming from me or from God, and how will they react?" Then she added, "But if a person's name pops into my head and I don't e-mail them, and then something happens, I'm like, *God, you really told me to e-mail that person. You told me to e-mail, and I'm sorry.*"

Indeed, the failure to recognize God's voice—or even worse, in recognizing him, the failure to respond—is understood to carry real-world consequences. In one of the large sessions at a regional meeting—part conference, part retreat, part revival—one of the leaders explained that when she was an associate pastor, she had had a dream about someone in the church who was trying to become pregnant. She didn't know the woman terribly well, but it was a mildly troubling dream. She reported it to the pastor and thought she'd done her job. But then she learned that the woman had in fact been pregnant at the time of the dream—and that she had lost the baby. The woman telling the story said that she was devastated, and she spoke to us as if God let the baby die because she hadn't prayed. To me it was a disturbing idea, that this God—the perfectly tolerant source of unconditional love—would hang the balance of a child's life on a near-stranger's prayer. Later, one of the congregants who was in the seminar with me said that he didn't really understand why God acted like that, but he thought that God behaved with his worshippers the way a parent works with a child to help the child grow into adulthood. If a father is at the beach with his son, he said, he can make a sand castle, and it would be a more beautiful and perfect sand castle if he made it by himself. But no father does that. A father puts up with the messiness and does it with his son. His relationship with his son, the man went on, is much more important than a sand castle, which after all the waves will wash away.

Sarah didn't know how to pray at first. She did a lot of Bible reading and didn't consider it praying. She was trying to listen for God, but she didn't really know what that meant. "It was often unclear to me what were my own thoughts, what were thoughts that God was putting in my head, what were distractions." Now, looking back, she can see that God was speaking to her long before she recognized his voice. She'd get ideas about the people she saw on the street—that this man would develop a back problem he'd have to deal with today, that the kid with the skateboard had trouble brewing at home. "I think now that those were prayers being born."

Sarah said that it took her six to nine months before she felt that she understood how to develop a personal relationship with God. One Sunday, a few months after her first time at the church, someone said that they were forming a group for intercessory prayer and needed a place to meet. Sarah volunteered her apartment and said that she could wait outside. The group leader insisted she join them: "I think that God wants you in this group." When the group met, Sarah realized that people were planning to pray out loud in turn. She panicked. Then someone suggested that they pray all together, each praying the prayers they thought they should each at the same time, a soothing babble of praise and supplication. They never did it again, but she said that it gave her confidence. She began to pray in earnest.

Then came the moment when "it broke through"—a Vineyard phrase for the way people experience the supernatural in everyday life.[11] What "broke through" was the first real experience of having thoughts and images arise in her mind, while she was praying for someone else, and feeling sure that these thoughts and images came directly from God. This is the story that Sarah told:

It was the first year that I was with the church and the first year I was really praying for the church. The Vineyard Association was having their national meeting in California, and they asked for intercessors to be praying regularly for that. I took it very seriously, and I prayed every morning. And one morning I was just sitting in my prayer chair, I had just finished and I was thinking about a picture. I thought my mind was wandering. I kept on seeing these boats. And I was thinking about that, and the phone rang, and it was the pastor. He was at the meeting, and he was calling about something completely different—and it was really silly for him to be calling. And after we went through with that, I just waited, and then I felt moved to say, "Why did you call me?" And he said, "I don't know. I just felt like I was supposed to call you." And it clicked then, that the picture I had seen *wasn't* a distraction from my prayers but was *connected* to my prayers. I told him about this picture that I'd gotten. And he told me when he came back that several people had gotten the same picture, and that it was about Jesus with his hands on the wheel of a ship! It sounds like lunacy, you know. And yet that's how it works.

People told me that when you are learning to hear God, it really helps to write down your prayers. This is particularly striking to an anthropologist because some anthropologists and historians have argued that it was literacy and eventually print culture that enabled science to emerge by creating a source of truth and memory outside the fallible human mind. Writing a claim down makes it easier to check the claim for accuracy and so writing makes science possible.[12] But evangelical Christians encourage the use of writing because writing can make the supernatural more real. If you want someone to learn to experience the burbling stream of their thoughts as containing an external presence, writing things down is a useful tool because it actually externalizes the words of that presence. Vineyard congregants wrote out their prayers, and they did so, I thought, as a means to make their inner prayer process more tangible and not of the self.

Most people whom I met at the Vineyard seemed to have a "prayer journal." They'd write down their prayers, either before or after they prayed them, sometimes praying through the act of writing. They would check back from time to time to see what prayers God had answered. "I like looking back in my prayer journal and seeing what God has done for me after I've prayed," said one congregant. "It makes me feel so good." But writing down prayer requests was not just about confirming that the prayer produced results. They did not just write down what they said. They wrote down what God had replied in turn.

In the prayer group I joined, we each brought a journal and we left time in the evening to write down what we thought God was saying to us and how we responded to his words or images. When I started out in the prayer group, my spiritual adviser told me that it would be helpful for my prayer life if I wrote down my prayer as a dialogue: what I said to God, followed by what he said to me. That was what she had done, she said, when she started at a church like the Vineyard and yearned to hear God speak. She still journaled every day. Many congregants did. Sarah had filled twenty-five journals (presumably short ones) in the four years since she became a Christian.

Jane was a busy lawyer with a new job when I met her at the Chicago Vineyard. But she wrote in her prayer journal for thirty minutes before she fell asleep. She called this writing letters to God: "Like I might start with 'Dear God,' and then the things I'm thinking about." She starts out and then, she said, God takes over. "In the beginning I'm busy asking questions. I sort of run out of myself after a couple of pages. It's like I have lots of questions and God is sort of answering those questions." How can she tell it is God? "The tone is different." People often spoke of God "taking over," as if God controlled their hands, as in the automatic writing one finds among people who understand themselves to channel spirits.

Not everyone would go so far, but the insistence that you should write down your prayer to help you to hear God talk back runs throughout the manuals. *Dialogue with God* explains that the "four keys" to experiencing dialogue are: learning how to recognize God's voice in your everyday thought; learning to go to a quiet place and be still; attending to dreams and visions; and writing down the dialogue so that you remember it and it becomes real for you. In *Too Busy Not to Pray*, Bill Hybels says that you should mean what you say; pray from the heart; pray specifically; pray with adoration, confession, thanksgiving, and supplication; and then you should write it down.

I write out my prayers every day; I have not been able to grow in my prayer life any other way. Experiment and see what works best for you. Try writing out your prayers once a week at first. If you find it helpful, do it more often. If it cramps your style and makes you uncomfortable, find another way that is effective for you.

All you really need to do, he says, is to make your prayers regular, private, sincere, and specific. But it really helps, he says, to write them down.[13]

The manuals describe this writing-down as a hands-on involvement. It does involve the writer; it also externalizes and concretizes an inner, subjective experience, and blurs the boundary between what is within and without. "Don't just *read* this book," insists *The Purpose Driven Life* (more than twenty-five million copies sold). "*Interact with it.* Underline it. Write your own thoughts in the margins. Make it *your* book. Personalize it! The books that have helped me the most are the ones I have reacted to, not just read."[14] *The Purpose Driven Life* advises people to write down their responses to the daily readings in a journal, which is advice many evangelical Christians also take about their Bible. In other religious traditions, sacred texts are treated reverentially. The Torah is written on a sacred scroll and kept in a special cabinet, and its removal and reading are the central acts of the Sabbath service. Once while attending an Orthodox service, I dropped the Artscroll printed copy of the Tanakh (the Hebrew name for the Torah, the prophets and the writings; what Christians call—when slightly reorganized—the Old Testament). The woman next to me stooped down to pick it up before I did and kissed it before she handed it back. By contrast, evangelical Bibles are scrawled on, highlighted, underlined, starred, stuffed with notes and Post-its, and personalized with the possessive aggression of an urban boy spraying graffiti on a wall. *Mine.*

In addition to active prayer, there are more mundane ways to identify God as speaking to you, although the basic principle remains the same: the supernatural breaks through into the everyday, and if you know how to pay attention, you will be able to see it happen. Congregants would say, for example, that God spoke to them through circumstances. By this they meant that when events took place that skeptical observers might see as coincidences, they could recognize that the event was something God was using to speak to them about their lives. "Patterns and coincidences are not random," explained Stacy, a social worker, when I asked her how she heard God's voice. "A huge part of hearing God, for me, is just being able to recognize patterns."

Madeline was a gazellelike woman with exquisite taste, enough of an artist to have stenciled literary quotations on to the walls of her home and romantic enough to be writing on nineteenth-century English novels. But she did not want to appear fanciful. When I asked her to explain the way God spoke to her, she began reluctantly, with an eye on her husband, because "it's just goofy, it sounds just off the wall . . .

Well, a few years ago, we both really wanted kids. I really wanted to have a baby. But it just wasn't happening, and for me this became a deeper spiritual crisis. It wasn't just about having a baby anymore. I had this overall sense of, *Where are you, God?* I *really* wanted God to speak. I knew he was out there, but he didn't feel very close . . . I remember walking along the lake and telling him, *I want to hear from you, answer me!!* Maybe in a way I've never done before, like almost yelling. Like, *I'm desperate here. . . .* So I'm walking along the lake and I told him, *I need an answer.* And as I go around the corner, I see a full moon, the biggest moon I've ever seen. And it was just there in front of me. Immediately I knew it was God's answer. It wasn't words, it wasn't yes or no or this or that, but I knew it was the answer, and all of a sudden I felt totally peaceful. I knew that in that moment, God had responded. I still had months of ups and downs, but after that point, things were different.

It was several months later one Friday, and I was scheduled for a fertility test on Monday. But I had to take a pregnancy test first. I took the test, and it was positive. At first I was excited, and then I got completely dejected because I had been on this medication, so I thought in my head that it was just the medication giving me this positive result and I'm not really pregnant. I felt completely dejected and then I thought, *Now I have to go through this whole weekend of not knowing.* I went into the kitchen to wash my hands, and we just had this tiny little window in the kitchen, a tiny little triangle of space, and in that little triangle of space, I saw an enormous full moon. And I knew that I was pregnant. I just knew. I just started laughing, God's really funny. I mean, we have full moons every month. But I knew. I knew that God had answered me. And it was true. I was pregnant.

One encounters this kind of foundational certainty often in these Christian lives. The technical term for it is *noetic:* a sense of knowing somehow deeper than everyday knowledge, bedrock rather than topsoil. And the story of the absolute knowing is often told in this way: I knew it was true, and then I found out that it was. For those who tell these stories, the evidential confirmation—Madeline *was* pregnant—stands as testimony to the real point of the story, which is that the sense of certainty preceded its confirmation. Madeline said that she didn't need any more answered prayers: "Moments like that become rocks in your life. I will remember that moment when I spoke to God, when I prayed, and God responded."

Of course, if Madeline had not been pregnant, the moment would have lost its meaning. That is why, as Madeline told the story, her husband began to fidget. He didn't want me to think that faith depended on so flimsy a thing as circumstance. "There's a significant danger with experience being the basis for anyone's faith," he explained. "If our Christian walk is just simply us asking and him replying, then he becomes like Santa Claus. Like, what's the point of that?" And yet he too told me, when we first met, about an uncanny coincidence and how much it had meant to him, how it had confirmed his sense of God's active presence in his life.

People also said that they heard God speak through scripture. And certainly people read their scripture. Sometimes Bibles hold so many scrawled notes and Post-its that they are zipped in sealed pouches to help them stay intact. Most people seem to read the Bible daily, or at least said guiltily that they should. One member of my house group had read the entire text three times. Many began the days with reading, often in Psalms. Sam told me that two years into being a Christian, reading the Bible in the morning had begun to feel like taking a shower—you just didn't feel clean until you'd done it. In part, they seemed to get out of the Bible what other people got out of novels—a sense of how to live in the world, become an adult, and deal with unexpected things. "It's always very fascinating," Jane said, "to see that things I struggle with now, people struggled with in scripture."

But when evangelicals say that God speaks to them through the Bible, they mean that when they are reading, they will have a physical, emotional response to a passage: the passage "grabbed their heart," "wouldn't let them go," "stuck in their minds." Jane explained: "I was reading in Judges and I don't even know why I was reading it. There's a part where

God talks about raising up elders in the church to pray for the church. And I remember, it just stuck in my head and I knew that the verse was really important and that it was applicable to me. I didn't know why. It was one of those, let me put it in my pocket and figure it out later." How, I asked, did she know that it was important? "Because I just felt it. I just felt like it really spoke to me. I don't really know why. And a couple of days later a friend asked me to be on the prayer team, and it was like, wow, that's what it was."

"God is always talking to you," Sam told me. "You just have to learn to listen. He always talks to you through the Bible. When you read his word, something will grab your heart." That process turns the act of reading a text into a two-way conversation. The literary critic Stanley Fish has argued that there are no texts, only readers, because each time you read a book, it is in effect new for you; each time you read, you bring to the text a new perspective, and you are, to some extent, a new person. When he made the argument, Fish was thinking only of the reader's responses. Vineyard congregants read their Bibles in a conversation with God as if both they *and* the Bible were changing—not the words on the page but the way the words intentionally lead them to respond. They describe reading as if they were conversing: they look for the way God answers, inspires, consoles, enlightens by changing the way that the text reads. God is understood to be communicating when, as one congregant put it, "a verse just jumps out at me," or when you have a powerful bodily feeling—you feel peace, or intense joy, or suddenly you feel very tired, as if a burden has been lifted and now you can sleep.

Congregants also said that God speaks to them through their dreams, although in my experience dreams entered an account of the way people hear from God in the Vineyard less often than other avenues. Sometimes these are "prophetic" dreams, where the dream foretells what will happen. Sometimes dreams are treated as instructions to pray. Hannah commented, "Earlier during the summer I had a dream about a couple of people I know, and I woke up that morning and I was like that was a weird dream. Then I heard later in the day about the bombings in London and those two people are in London during the summer. And so it was like, whoa, I should have been *praying* for them."

In evangelical circles, as in societies around the world where the supernatural is thought to enter into the everyday, dreams are understood as conduits and vehicles.[15] "This dreaming stuff," said one conference leader.

"Do you think it's from God? Churches pretty much throw 'em out, the dreams. But if you read the scriptures, a lot of revelation comes through dreams. So why are we throwing them out?" Then she cited scripture: "In the last days, in Acts, God says, 'I will prop my spirit on all people. Your sons and daughters will prophesy. Your young men will see visions. Your old men will dream dreams.'"

Hearing God's voice is a complex process. It is not a simple identification skill, like learning to spot a red-tailed hawk, nor a basic mastery task, like learning to tie your shoes. People clearly thought that an experienced Christian should be more adept than a naïve one, but they also clearly thought that distinguishing God's voice was a richly layered skill. They seemed to think about sensing God more or less the way we think about sophisticated expertise in any field: that repeated exposure and attention, coupled with specific training, helps the expert to see things that are really present but that the raw observer just cannot, and that some experts are more expert than others. A sonogram technician looks at the wavy gray blur on the screen and sees a healthy boy. This is not a matter of taste or aesthetic judgment: there is, or is not, a boy in the woman's womb, and the technician can see evidence for the fact in a picture that leaves the expectant mother bewildered. And a very good technician sees details that a merely competent one cannot.[16]

This is the richest part of the new participatory theory of mind, and the part that congregants worry about, debate about, and come to different conclusions about. They believe not only that inner speech and imagery can be God, but that there are subtle rules that allow someone to identify God and that with experience one can become more expert in applying the rules and discerning the divine presence. There is no standard, agreed-upon list of these rules, the way there is a standard list of the books in the New Testament. There are guidelines, picked up somewhat catch-as-catch-can from books and sermons and other congregants, and individual congregants take those guidelines and apply them to their own mental experience in their own way. As they do so, again and again and again, they begin to develop their own pattern recognition. They speak as if they had literally developed a sophisticated map of their own mental life and become able to recognize God's presence in what they had previously experienced as a fuzzy mental blur.

I remember the first time I made a distinction between kinds of wine.

I knew, of course, that some wines are better than other wines, and that there are different kinds of wines, but this was pretty abstract knowledge. To me, it was mostly strong juice. Then I was invited to a wine tasting and drank wines against each other, and for the first time I could really taste the peppery spice of syrah. I still remember the moment, the sudden recognition of difference.

When you begin to learn about wine, you learn to distinguish the taste of the grapes. You learn to recognize the fruit, the spice, and the vanillins created when the wine is aged in oak barrels, and the tannins that coat your tongue and give the wine what experts call its "structure." There is a great deal of flowery foolishness in wine talk, pretension and performance. Some people learn the words but completely fail to identify the wine. Many, even some experienced wine tasters, can't even tell the difference between red and white wine in a blind tasting. Learning to taste wine is all about training perception. It is an olfactory training: and olfaction depends heavily on expectation. But it is not entirely expectation. Wine is made from a particular grape, grown in a particular place, and aged in a particular way. Most people, given enough training, get good enough to identify the grape. They do so by developing a discrimination system that allows them to draw contrasts between tastes: peppery versus smooth, cherry versus peach, flabby versus taut. Each expert's system is different. One taster's "angular" is another's "masculine." The critics use categories so specific and yet so vague they can make a novice laugh: "bacon fat" "incisive" "flinty." But the categories work. Some experts can identify the grape, the vintner, and the vintage from wine poured from a bottle wrapped in a paper bag. It is also true that developing the expertise to taste and to identify is not the same skill as the expertise to put those discriminations into words. Once I sat with two skilled tasters drinking a wine that Robert Parker had rated at 100 points—his highest rating. How would you describe it? I asked a man noted for his eloquence. He closed his eyes and sighed. "It's *good.*"

Learning to recognize God at a church like the Vineyard is not so very different. For these Christians, there is a fact: God has or has not spoken, and if he has spoken, he has said something in particular. Just as in tasting wine, there are categories and rules that help the Christian to sort out what is God from what is not. These are not nearly so precise as or precisely known as the rules for chess; they are more like guidelines. Still, with time and experience, Christians are expected to use the rules to develop recognition patterns that will help them to recognize the specific ways in which God speaks, and it is expected that each Christian will develop a discrimination system that is entirely his or her own.

But unlike wine, God has no label that can be examined when one pulls the bottle from the paper bag. One cannot go off by oneself and order in a case of God's comments to work through. As a result, the social community of the church—the large, loose aggregation of manual authors, pastors, friends, and fellow churchgoers who surround the person learning how to hear God's voice—play an even more important role than does the social community of the wine connoisseur. The community does not stand in for the truth; nor, in my experience, does the group presume to know the real truth of whether God has spoken to any particular person and if so, what God had said. But they gossip, and the gossip is important, as it always is when rules and meanings are ambiguous. Gossip circles around people who think they have heard God and—according to the gossipers—have not. People would say that so-and-so believed that God was telling her to serve the poor in Africa but really she just wanted to get out of the country on an adventure. That so-and-so thought she received deep insights from God in prayer but that in fact she was a bit self-important. That so-and-so felt that God intended her for this particular man, but they didn't think God's desires were the ones in play. One Sunday I was listening to an ardent young woman explaining to the congregation why they should send her on a missionary trip to Mexico when the man next to me leaned over with a little smile. "God sure seems to need a lot of work done in Puerto Vallarta," he whispered.

The name for the developing expertise of the congregant is *discernment*. Discernment is an old concept in the Christian tradition. It has carried a different meaning depending on the theology of the day. In the medieval era, when few (if any) doubted the reality of spirits and the supernatural pressed in upon the everyday like a damp, low cloud, *discernment of spirits* meant the ability to distinguish godly spirits from demonic ones. Individuals suffered the presence of beings who haunted their dreams and invaded their bodies. The salient question was not whether the vision was supernaturally inspired but what kind of supernatural activity had inspired it—and thus whether it was trustworthy, reliable, sound. Joan of Arc, for instance, was burned not because people doubted that she had had contact with supernatural forces but because people doubted that these supernatural forces were divine. This ability to discern the difference between divine and demonic spirits seems to be the sense in which Paul uses the term in his first letter to the Corinthians (the only time the term *discernment* is found in the Bible), when he speaks of the different "gifts" that humans have and lists among them the discernment of spirits.[17]

At the Vineyard, most people used the word *discernment* in a manner that was closer to the way Jonathan Edwards used the term. Edwards was the towering American who presided over the great spiritual revival in the American colonies in the middle of the eighteenth century. Historians call it our First Great Awakening. God, Edwards felt, came upon him unaware. He had been born into an era in which God spoke only through the Bible—not through the mind, not to ordinary men and women. But as Edwards approached his manhood, his congregants began to fall around him in his services, shaken by dramatic fits and visions. For him, the problem of discernment was not so much the challenge of telling good spirits from bad as the problem of figuring out whether the supernatural or human make-believe had caused his congregants to weep and groan. So he set out to establish guidelines to help to distinguish the presence of God from human dross. In 1741 he preached a famous sermon, "Distinguishing Marks of a Work of the Spirit of God." He began with a lengthy argument against those who would dismiss swooning and ecstasy as mere theater. "That there are some counterfeits is no argument that nothing is true." Then he went on to describe signs of the presence of the spirit of God: that someone thought more highly of Jesus; that he found himself more opposed to sin; that he was more confident of the truth of the scriptures; that he felt more love of God and humans. They are vague rules, perhaps, but they were rules. The experience is inherently ambiguous, and the skeptic's temptation is to dismiss the experience as so much human gunk. Jonathan Edwards believed that it was possible to distinguish between the gunk and God.

No one at the Vineyard ever laid out rules of discernment for me like a train schedule. I never heard a sermon that set them out in a list. But the rules existed within the community the way teenagers know the local expectations of how to dress and date. Congregants called them "tests." When I asked people how they knew that God has spoken to them, four tests came up again and again.

The first test was whether what you had heard or imagined was the kind of thing you would say or imagine anyway: if it was, the thought was probably yours. If not, it could be God. Spontaneous or unexpected thoughts were more likely to be attributed to God.[18] Elaine, who led my house group, explained to me how she heard God speak to her in her mind. "It is kind of like someone was talking to me. That's how real it is. I get responses." How do you know? I asked. "God speaks to me," she replied. What do you mean by that? I asked. You can hear him with your ears, outside your head? No, she responded. "For some people God speaks with a distinct voice, so you'd turn around because you think the person's right there. For me it hasn't happened like that. Well, I mean kinda, there has been kind of that sense, but not like you'd turn your head because someone was there." Can you say more about those God experiences? I prompted. She explained that she did not hear the voice like it really was another voice, but it was more than a passing thought. It was clearly, she felt, not her thought. She went on to give an example. "When people were praying over me and I'm just receiving it [meaning the prayer], all of a sudden I hear, 'Go to Kansas.' Because I was debating whether to go to Kansas, but I hadn't been thinking about it within a twenty-four hour period." That's what made it distinctive to her: she wasn't thinking about it, it wasn't something she would have thought about right then. "It makes you want to say," she continued, "'Where did that come from?'"

The second test was whether it was the kind of thing that God would say or imply. This was often articulated as making sure that what you thought God had said did not contradict God's word in the Bible. This caution was explicitly expressed in all the written material and nearly every casual conversation on the topic. *Dialogue with God,* for instance, states clearly (and repeatedly) that "if the revelation violates either the letter of the Word or the spirit of the Word, it is to be rejected immediately."[19] God is a loving God; a revelation that tells you to hurt yourself or someone else, people said, came from something other than God. "You need discernment," the pastor said. "There's a letter written from Paul when he says, 'Don't put out the fires of the spirit but test everything, and hold on to what is good.' We don't expect that God would want someone to cut themselves, or tell them to jump off a bridge. That is not God." Notice that this would not apply to Abraham and Isaac or the other points in the Hebrew Bible when God acts, as the biblical scholar Jack Miles puts it when writing about the Book of Job, like a fiend. When people talked about making sure that what you heard did not contradict the Bible, they really meant that it should be in keeping with the understanding of God's character as taught within this church: unconditionally loving, eternally forgiving. The God at the Vineyard was not a fiend.[20]

The third test was whether the revelation could be confirmed through circumstances or through other people's prayers. People would check with each other to see whether they had "gotten" similar images in prayer. They asked people to pray for them, and sometimes followed up to see what those prayers had revealed. In the summer of 2004 Elaine's roommate moved out of their studio apartment. Elaine had never lived alone and wasn't really sure if she wanted to, and the total rent of the place was about what she earned each month. She began to pray to God to see if he wanted her to move out or to take a roommate. She thought that he wanted her to stay. That made her uneasy. So she began to ask other people to pray for her as well, and to tell her what sort of messages and images they saw. "It's a lot more money than I was paying before. So my human intellect was saying, 'Live with someone.' There's scripture about being in community, having a roommate. But there's a sense"—a sense that arose from her experience in prayer—"that I should really be living by myself. A friend of mine was praying, and she saw me in a studio by myself. I'm like, okay. I respect how she sees. She's been sensing God and the Holy Spirit for longer than I have. So I need to take that into account. It doesn't mean that I'm deliberately going to stay there because of that but I need to test that. You test prophecy. You ask God for more confirmation. That [the confirmation] could be God really saying it to me clearly. It could be someone else having a word or something." Then one of her friends had an image, in prayer, that Elaine thought was a sign. "One person had an image for me about being on the second floor, and studying, and being by the window with light shining in. That was kind of—okay, I remember that. I'm just kind of waiting [for something to happen]. A lot of it is waiting."

The final test was the feeling of peace. Prayer and God's voice are thought to give you peace and comfort. If what you heard (or saw) did not, it did not come from God. Jacob was a young professional who joined the Chicago Vineyard because, he felt, God told him to do so. One Sunday, standing in the congregation in another state, he knew God was telling him that he and his wife should move down to the neighborhood where the new church was being "planted."

I really just felt really clearly that God put [that neighborhood] into my head. I didn't know the church at all. I knew there was a Vineyard there because I'd heard about it in another church, around the time the church was planting, but I didn't know anything about it. I didn't spend any time in the neighborhood. I was like this is really weird but I couldn't shake it. The rest of the service I just prayed over it and God just confirmed it. There was this total peace that would be present when I would think about the neighborhood and the Vineyard there. I can't explain it any other way.

Stanley and Trish struggled when Trish, a medical student, was assigned for residency to a city that had not been her first choice. Stanley had a great job in a specialty law firm in Chicago, and there was no comparable job for him in the other city. (There were many medical students in the church, and as was often the case, the residency match took many of them to their third, fourth, and even fifth choices.) For Stanley and Trish, this meant separation for at least a year while their daughter was still a toddler. They did not know what to do and were not sure whether God intended Trish to abandon medicine altogether. They prayed and prayed. The pastor held a prayer meeting at their house so that people could pray over them. Their house group prayed over them. People prayed with them in church. Eventually, in part because of what they thought, felt, and experienced in prayer, they decided to accept Trish's assignment. And as they did so, they began to feel peace: a sense of settled acceptance that they took as a sign that they had correctly interpreted God's words to them.

These rules are learned in tandem with more private patterns of recognition. People learn to recognize God's voice through rules that are socially taught and collectively shared, but also in ways that are private, individual, and unique. Augusta, who was an accomplished prayer expert, described "goosebumps and just warm all over and just very peaceful, and I know that he's there." The goosebumps drew her focus to what she was thinking of at the time; it was God's way of saying "pay attention." Stacy said, "I can actually feel him, talking to him throughout the day, either out loud or in my head. I usually feel the security that goes with his presence." Gareth, a solemn undergraduate with his sights on seminary, described "a really deep warmth in my heart, sometimes just bubbling over into laughter." Some people talked about images. Some spoke about tugs. Hannah talked about different cues in different settings:

> If all of a sudden I feel peaceful and I'm not moving, I don't feel a sense to move, then I know God's doing something in me, building that relationship. If I am praying for someone and I can't stand still, then I know that God is giving me some words to share. If I'm at home reading my Bible and I'm able to concentrate really well—not drifting off into my to-do list—then I know that my relationship is being built.

It was acknowledged in the church that each person would experience God in his or her own way, and would develop individual patterns of learning to recognize him. "I get a lot of images," someone will say. And someone else: "I rarely see images. When I pray for people, I get sensations that I can in turn translate into words . . . Like more than seeing the bird, you feel the flight of the bird."

To the anthropologist, the central principle was identifying the "not-me" experience: a thought, or image or sensation that one felt was not one's own. If a thought felt spontaneous and unsought, it was more likely to be identified as God's. God's words "popped" into the mind. If a thought felt stronger or different from other thoughts, it was more likely to be identified as God's. Congregants sometimes spoke of God's words as "loud" to indicate that they felt stronger or different from their own, as does this middle-aged woman when she explained why she knew that God wanted her to go to a retreat early to pray: "There's a very small group of us, that get together—frequently on Wednesday mornings—just to pray. Just before the women's retreat, it was pretty loud and clear that I needed to be there a couple days early. More than a thought. It was something I was supposed to do." And if a thought was more emotionally potent, it was more likely to be God's.

These principles guide many of us, whether evangelical Christians or not. We are more likely to treat thoughts that we experience as spontaneous, stronger, or more emotional as more meaningful; as containing hidden, important knowledge we should attend to. That is why people take dreams seriously, even when they talk dismissively about "mere" dreams, or why we can be shaken by sudden insights.[21] Evangelical Christians take the common tendency and elaborate it into a deliberate practice. They also set out to teach people to pay attention only when their thoughts seem to be good or helpful: the thoughts of God. Otherwise, you are instructed to ignore them.

Over time, despite the fact that God's voice came muffled by uncertainty and doubt, people became able to experience a sense that God spoke back and that they recognized his voice. That is a remarkable achievement, and it seems to make those who achieve it confident and relaxed.

When I first met Elaine, she was wondering whether she should invite a homeless woman to move in with her. She had asked God, she told me, and he had said no. "What does that mean?" I asked her, puzzled. She looked at me as if I were a little slow and said, "God puts the word into your mind. He just says no." It was as if the word just appeared in her mind, and she knew—she just *knew*—that it wasn't her own but came from God. She was very clear that one had to learn to recognize his voice, and that she had done so. People talked about learning to recognize God's voice the way they recognized a person's voice on the phone: "It's a different sort of voice. I mean, I know my own voice. If I thought of your voice I would think of how your voice sounds, and if I think of my voice I think of how it sounds, even if I'm not hearing anything. It's a different tone of voice." Or: "It's like recognizing someone—it's like, how do you recognize your mom?" They were insistent that you could learn to identify God: "It gets to a point you just *know* it's God's voice. It's very snappy and comes with constant prayer just nonstop."

They also agreed that this took practice and persistence. Kate, married to Jacob, remembered that she was in high school when her church—one of the many Vineyard churches in Chicago—went through a revival. "There was this really high expectation that God wanted to step into your life and heal and give you gifts and give you words. It had happened in the Bible and it was happening with people I knew—and I thought, *This is what the relationship with God is supposed to be like.*" But it wasn't so easy. She did feel like she'd heard God speak to her once, when she was thirteen and her parents were divorcing. She ran out of the house one evening and slammed the door and shouted that she couldn't take it anymore. She ran down to a park and sat on a bench, crying. She remembered telling God how angry she was that he let her family fall apart. And then "I felt like God just spoke to my heart, I don't know how else to put it."

It wasn't really a voice, she said, more "kind of remembering the words on a page." God told her that even though everything else in her life was changing, he—God—was still the same. And she felt an overwhelming sense of peace. It was a vivid, powerful moment. But it never happened again, not like that.

> Throughout high school, I was really trying to figure out, what does God's voice sound like? [And they said] it takes practice. Because it's not an audible thing. And that kind of made sense. But there were times when I sat back, and I was like, *Okay guys, I don't hear anything.* I used—kind of like the scientific method, but I didn't know what I was listening for. I'm like, *That's not very helpful.* I asked God to speak to me and to speak clearly, and I'd ask other people to pray for me that I would hear God's voice. Sometimes I realized that I was kind of going at it like how you would practice throwing a ball because I didn't know what else to do.
>
> Then I started to realize that I expected to hear back from God, that I had faith that he would want to say something to me. A small, still voice sounds vague—but it's a good description. Kind of like the impression words make on a page. It's easy to confuse it with things I'm thinking in my head. But I began to realize that God answers questions you were asking him later on, when you'd be having a conversation with someone and they'd say something, and you'd feel a kind of click in your heart, like that's the answer. Or I'd be reading scripture, or there'd be a song, and at a line or passage, I'm like, *That's it.* Sometimes I can feel it in my heart, or spirit, like there's this part of me that feels completed. Sometimes it's sort of a feeling, sometimes it's something more specific, like a phrase or a sentence. Usually, it's either an image or an impression of an idea. It's not like a real physical thing, but it feels deeper than a physical emotion. Sometimes it's immediate. Sometimes it's not.

These days Kate experiences prayer as a conversation. She talks; God listens and responds. She says that sometimes she thinks he's guiding her thoughts. Sometimes she thinks prayer becomes a way to practice her ideas on someone. She says that she feels very free in the conversation, although she occasionally wonders whether she should be more reverent. "I mean, I just leave my stuff in front of God. I say, 'Okay God, I just don't know what to do. I'm sorry, I know it's wrong for me to feel this way, but this is what I'm feeling and what should I do?'" She gets angry at him and even yells at him when things go wrong—when she organizes a trip for the church and the bus company is flaky or it rains: "'Okay God, I'm trying to have faith here.'" Sometimes, she says, she laughs out loud when she's praying. She says he's her best friend.

For all the practice, hearing God's voice remains a complicated discrimination task for these congregants. Many of them clearly experience themselves as getting better at picking out God's voice from the everyday flow of inner speech, but they also clearly experience the process as inherently ambiguous, and they hesitate to assume that their interpretations are accurate. That was the conference speaker's point about dreams: that we *should* take dreams seriously, and most of us *don't*. Congregants were acutely aware that dreams, thoughts, images—even scriptural associations—were likely the products of their all-too-human minds. As one congregant with many years of practice explained: "I can choose to believe this is from God, or I can think this is just from me, and the reality is that it could be either, and I know that. There is always a choice to believe what it is." Or in the words of another, "Sometimes when we think it's the spirit moving, it's just our burrito from lunch."

This is an important point, sometimes hard to grasp from the outside. The more you believe that it is possible to experience God directly, the more uncertainty you invite about any particular claim to God's presence. If you allow the possibility that God speaks to humans, you believe that he speaks to human minds and human hearts, and inevitably, you question the accuracy of those human reporters more deeply than you question the accuracy of the scriptural text. In theologically conservative Christianity, the Bible is God's book, and as a congregant you probably feel that the Bible is literally, or near literally, true, even if it is shaped by human hands. (John Wimber said cheerfully, in a remark illustrating this cast of mind, "God's got a book out!") You do not feel that way when the person in the seat next to you happens to say that God has spoken to them. By the time a congregation expects every congregant to have personal conversations with God, that congregation expects many of those supposed conversations to be self-interested fantasies. After all, they know these people. They are likely to be cautious and skeptical about other people's claims concerning what God has said to them, particularly if those claims have concrete consequences (for example, if someone reports a "word from God" about which pastor to hire). In this way uncertainty and ambiguity are inevitable correlates of intimacy.

And so already, in this first step, the congregant who seeks to experience God directly and immediately begins to tolerate uncertainty. He or she may never voice doubts about whether God exists. He or she may be quite clear the Bible is literally true, every word taken down in dictation from a supernatural God. But any congregant who hears God speak necessarily hesitates. Already, experiencing God is in a different category from experiencing one's human spouse. It may be better, but it is different. And this first step is not enough. Just learning how to point to these signs of God's presence, how to fish moments out of everyday awareness like so many trout, is not sufficient to create what God is said to offer: a personal, intimate relationship. To develop that relationship—and moreover, to feel truly comfortable in experiencing moments in the mind as conversations with an external being—one needs to experience God as personlike. As the congregant becomes willing to take this next step, as God does indeed become more personlike, the difference between knowing God and knowing persons will become more marked.

🌿

CHAPTER THREE

Let's Pretend

Sing to Him a new song
Play skillfully, and shout for joy

Psalm 33:3

The woman smiled at me.
"Jesus is the perfect playmate,"
she said.

Field notes, spring 2008

I F THE FIRST TASK in becoming able to experience God as an intimate friend is learning to recognize God in the privacy of one's mind, the second task is learning to relate to God as a person. But God is not very much like human persons, despite our anthropomorphism. We do—when thinking quickly, automatically, intuitively—see faces in the clouds, and we hear people in the bushes, and that impulse undoubtedly makes the idea of a person who cannot be seen more plausible. Yet it is quite a different matter to sustain that impulse into an enduring sense that the cloud (or something behind it) talks, listens, and responds. These are the characteristics of persons, and our willingness to attribute personhood to things usually depends on whether those things react like humans in ways we can see or hear. That is a high demand.

Human interaction—real human interaction, with two people together in a room—is remarkably dense. We move, touch, gesture, mimic. The face alone is so complex that its forty-three muscles convey in combination as many as three thousand distinct expressions.[1] We scan people's faces intently as we talk, and what we see in their faces affects what we say. Confronted with a masklike face that we cannot interpret, we can become tongue-tied and confused. Talking to someone whose face is empathic and noncritical, we say things we never meant to share.

But God has no face. You cannot look him in the eye and judge that he hears you speak. He does not make the little phatic grunts we make to each other on the phone, to show we're still listening. Even when people learn to pick mental events out of their mind that they attribute to God, it can be difficult for them to shake their doubts without that more fibrous quality of the human back-and-forth.

To deal with this problem, the churches like the Vineyard invite congregants to *pretend* that God is present and to make believe that he is talking back like the very best of buddies. It is a suggestion straight out of C. S. Lewis. In *Mere Christianity*, Lewis entitles a chapter "Let's Pretend." If you have read this far, he writes, you probably pray, and whatever else you pray, you probably say the Lord's Prayer. *Our Father, who are in heaven . . .* "Do you now see what those words say? They mean quite frankly, that you are putting yourself in the place of a son of God. To put it bluntly, *you are dressing up as Christ*." We are, Lewis points out, human bundles of self-centered fears, wants, and small-mindedness. But in speaking this prayer, one plays at being a child of the divine. Lewis approves of this: he thinks that if you pretend that you are with God, God will become more real for you. "Let us pretend in order to make the pretence into a reality."[2]

Let us pretend in order to make the pretense into a reality. This is a modern sentiment, remarkably self-aware, directed at a reader who wants to believe that something is true but is not yet able to accept it. The idea of imitating Christ is an old one: as Paul says, "Be imitators of me, just as I also am of Christ."[3] The great fifteenth-century mystical text of Thomas à Kempis, *The Imitation of Christ*, instructs the reader to strive to become Christ-like: "Lord Jesus, because your way is narrow and despised by the world, grant that I may despise the world and imitate you." But *to imitate* is not the same as *to pretend*. *To imitate* is to behave in reality. If you imitate someone who is waving her hand, you do, in fact, wave your hand. A boy who imitates the distress signals of a ship at sea is still sending Morse code signals, even if he is not at sea. *To pretend* carries the implicit understanding that the pretender is not what he imitates. The boy pretends to be on a sinking vessel even though he is standing on his own front lawn. To imitate is to act. To pretend is to suspend disbelief. We think of pretending (at least in adults) as a denial of what we know to be true: she pretended that her husband hadn't cheated on her, even though she knew he had. Lewis uses the word *pretend* as if pretense makes possible our denial of what we know to be false but cannot quite reject. In *The God Delusion,* the scientist Richard Dawkins states bluntly that we cannot choose to believe.[4] C. S. Lewis thought that this was exactly what pretending enabled us to do.

To be sure, evangelicals rarely use words like *pretend* and *make-believe.* At the Chicago Vineyard, our pastor, Arnold, explicitly encouraged us to experience God as a friend, without uttering the word *imaginary.* But he invited us to behave with God the way children behave with imaginary friends. He encouraged us to set out a second cup of coffee for God in the morning—to pour God an actual cup of steaming coffee, to place it on an actual table, and to sit down at that table with our own mug to talk to God about the things on our minds. He held Sunday-morning sessions in which he asked people to talk out loud about their human best friends, and then told us to think of God as like that, but better. He explained that many of us thought of God as distant and magnificent, but that God wanted to be intimate with each of us, as if he were a buddy. He explained that we should be familiar with God: that we should hang out with God, tease God, ask God's advice about small things ("God, which of these muffin recipes should I choose?"), and rake God down when we thought he was out of line. If we truly allowed God to break into our lives in that way, Arnold said, we'd really relax with him, and we could trust him in a way most of us, he said, did not. In my field notes from Sunday-morning gatherings, as I listened to his teachings, I scrawled GOD IS YOUR BEST FRIEND in capital letters.

The "let's pretend" invitation is found in much of the evangelical world. *Experiencing God* (more than four million sold) is one of those best-selling manuals used in one house group after another. We used it in ours. The book sets out to teach the reader to create a real, practical, and personal relationship with God, who is described (in part) as a person like any other. "A person cannot love without another 'someone' to love. A love relationship with God takes place between two real beings."[5] Then it provides some practical exercises to help the reader experience God that way. This is the exercise entitled "Experiencing God today":

Adam and Eve walked with God in the cool of the day. Take some time today to "walk with God" and cultivate a more intimate relationship with Him today or this week. If your location, physical condition and weather permit, find a place outside to walk. Use this time to get out of your routine. You may even want to plan a special trip for part of a day just to be alone with God. The place could be:

—your neighborhood   —a wooded area in the country
—a city park   —a sandy beach
—a garden   —a mountain road
—a lakeshore   —anywhere

Spend the time walking and talking with God. If the location permits, you may even want to talk out loud. Focus your thoughts on your love of your heavenly father. Praise Him for his love and mercy. Thank Him for expressions of His love to you. Be specific. Express to God your love for Him. Take time to worship Him and adore Him. Then just spend time with Him. Talk to Him about your concerns, and listen to what He may want to say to you.[6]

Modern evangelical literature is full of this imaginative informality. In *The Shack,* by William Young, which spent weeks on the *New York Times* best-seller list, God (or rather, the Trinity) shows up as a large black woman, a Middle Eastern laborer, and an Asian gardener. They cook chicken for supper and make a mess with the saucepans.

I knew only one person in the Chicago Vineyard who really poured that second cup of coffee. But I knew people who talked about setting an extra dinner plate for God or pulling out a chair for him to sit on while they poured out their troubles. When they said those things, they often remarked that they didn't go as far as other people did. They were a little embarrassed by what they'd done. "There was a time," Stacy, the social worker, recalled, "when I was like, I'm gonna have dinner with Jesus because I was really stressed out about my life. I'm gonna have dinner with Jesus, just him and me. But it wasn't like there was an actual chair for God. I had a friend who like actually set out a chair and told God everything." Still, many people spoke casually about chatting easily, comfortably, and openly with God about whatever came into their head. (They often used "God" and "Jesus" interchangeably in this context.) They talked about giggling with God as they walked down the street. They talked about catching themselves speaking out loud, or suddenly laughing out loud because of something God had said or done. When I was doing this research, one of my colleagues sent me a Facebook posting from a student that captures the vivid, silly intimacy that people described, like an escapist daydream that it was okay to dream.

> Jesus is turning my world upside down! I used to think that being a Christian meant going to church, trying to squeeze in 30 minutes of "quiet time" or "Jesus time" a day, and claiming his name so that I can say, "Yeah, I'm a Christian." But Jesus didn't die for that. He didn't die so that we could be religious. He died so that religion would die—so that false worship would die! He didn't die so that I could spend 30 minutes a day with him—he died so that I could spend 24 hours a day with him. He died so that I could wake up thinking about him—so that I could dance with him in the shower in the morning—so that I can be in his presence when I eat my cheese grits—so that I can ask him what brand of shampoo I should buy—so that I can turn the volume off of my cell phone so that I can talk aloud to him on the bus without anyone noticing that I'm talking to an invisible man—so that I can watch my James Bond movies with him—so that we can play practical jokes together—so that I can go to sleep thinking about him—so that I can enjoy the silly, funny times as well as the intense moments of life with him—so that I am NEVER alone. He didn't die so that I could pray how I am told to pray, and stand in church when I am told to stand, and raise my hands when everyone else did. That all has its place, but he didn't die for that. He died so that I can scream at the enemy in the middle of worship—so that I can jump up or down or lie on my face—so that I can do laps around the room or do the worm down the middle of the chapel if I so please! He didn't die so that we could be religious. He died so that we could rebuke religion and embrace relationship! This is what I want! THIS is what I love!

You do not talk this way about God by happenstance. Congregants make a deliberate, conscious choice to hang out with God in the hair products aisle. They *decide* to treat the almighty like a girlfriend. Madeline, who had seen her pregnancy in the moon, recalled: "I remember being in high school and kind of struggling, wondering [whether I should talk to God about] things that I knew were petty. I don't do that anymore. I just kind of throw everything out there."

I used to ask people whether they prayed to God about their haircuts.

(I was looking for something that seemed trivial but not as commonplace as parking. Even atheists pray about parking.) Some people quickly said that it would be unseemly to pray about a haircut. "Not usually on that level," explained Gareth, the future seminary student. "Usually it's more on the level of, what I should be doing in the coming year, or something like that." Others tumbled over themselves to tell a story. "I actually do," said Stacy, chuckling.

> I get my hair cut downtown, at this place where the students give free haircuts. You know, they're learning. The last time I was there, I was watching this one girl who was cutting, and I could see that she was having problems on what should have been a pretty easy cut. So I thought, *Why don't I just pray?* I just said a really quick prayer, like "God, I just pray that this will be a good experience. I need a good haircut. You know, it's probably my last haircut before I go to graduate school. I don't have a lot of money to like make corrections with a bad haircut." And I ended up getting the teacher's pet, and [when he was done, he said,] "That's the best haircut I've ever given!"

When people admitted to praying about things like haircuts, they would go on to explain that they talked to God about little things because that's what you do in relationships. Helen, still a sophomore, put it this way: "God's just like a friend. Like my friends, I go to them with every little thing. Prayer isn't just, 'Thank you for this and please do that.' It's like a *personal* friendship, a personal relationship."

In short, the congregants set out, at the church's invitation, to treat God like an imaginary friend. When I asked people whether they experienced God as an imaginary friend, they usually rejected the word *imaginary*—and then accepted the comparison. This was the way Sam, the business major, put it:

> It *is* like having an imaginary friend, in a sense. I mean I talk to him all the time like he's always next to me. The only way it differs is that you *know* that he's there. I mean that sounds crazy, the fact that there is somebody *in* you. But you have a sense of security, you have a sense of not being alone, like there's somebody there for you, and you feel that you're talking to him. You just know beyond a shadow of a doubt that somebody is there with you. I'm walking down the

street talking to God like out loud. People must think that I'm so wacky.

The comparison felt right to them because they did experience this God as an invisible companion. "Yes, in the sense that there's always someone to talk to," Madeline responded. People spoke with God when they were walking down the street, danced with God in their living rooms, and fretted sometimes out loud with God about the trivial small concerns in their everyday lives. But they never quite treated these interactions as equivalent to human interactions. That's true of imaginary companions, too.

The classic definition of an imaginary companion was published in 1934: "an invisible character, named and referred to in conversations with other persons or played with directly for a period of time, at least several months, having an air of reality for the child but no apparent objective basis."[7] Children with imaginary companions behave as if this being can act in the world, and they respond to them more or less as if they were alive. The author Margaret Svendsen gave this example:

> Shortly before her second birthday Mary [began to refer] to "Tagar," her imaginary companion. She led Tagar around on an imaginary string. Food was kept for it under the radiator where it also slept; she always fed it on the floor. It was particularly fond of ice cream, as she was. "Berrie and Auntie" followed Tagar, appearing when she was about 3½ years of age. They were two persons, but lived together. Mary would set places for them at the family table. Although dishes and silver were laid and Mary would ask as if they had enough, real food was never offered them. On other occasions, she would seize the opportunity at meal-time to tell her father all the things which they had done. Mary might be punished but they never were, and never did anything wrong. Berrie and Auntie frequently accompanied her and her parents on outings, and on several occasions she attempted to draw her real companions into play with them, by insisting that she talk with them on the telephone.[8]

Children often play with stuffed animals in similar ways. In the comic strip *Calvin and Hobbes,* Calvin's parents see Hobbes as a small, stuffed tiger. To Calvin, Hobbes looms over him, directing his play, commenting on his parents, more sophisticated and self-aware than them all. If you include these stuffed animals, imaginary companions are quite common. Two different studies found that over 60 percent of children had an imaginary companion at some point by the age of six.[9]

Imaginary friends seem to be most common in the toddler years, which is one reason many adults do not remember having them, but in fact they can be found at all ages, even in adulthood.[10] They also come and go over a child's life. They can be terribly important for a year, and then be casually dropped. In the Peter, Paul and Mary song "Puff, the Magic Dragon," when Jackie Paper ends his relationship with Puff, it is the magic dragon who slips unconsoled into his cave. And they seem to serve many different purposes for those who create them. While some of the children who create them are shy or lonely, many of them seem to be quite social.[11]

For years, the psychologist Marjorie Taylor has interviewed children and their parents about imaginary companions in her lab at the University of Oregon. (The university is located in Eugene; one of the imaginary companions, when drawn, turned out to be tie-dyed.) She has found that adults who had imaginary companions as children are less neurotic, more self-confident, and more sociable than those who did not.[12] And children's imaginary companions—which are remarkably varied—seem to serve different purposes for them. They keep loneliness at bay. They listen, as did this doll, recalled by an adult: "She gave me her undivided attention as I poured out all my hurts, all my betrayals, all my goodness and my badness. She never told. She never scolded me."[13] And they are fun. As Taylor comments: "Who could be a better partner in play than an imaginary friend? Unlike real children, they can be depended upon to play the game of the child's choice, go along with the child's spontaneous rules, and let the child win."[14]

Children do not confuse these imaginary companions with real people. It is true that children sometimes refuse to allow their mothers to "suffocate" the objectively filthy plush bunny in the washing machine. They can insist that an extra place be laid at the table for their invisible friend. Mothers do sometimes worry that their child does not know the difference between the fantastic and the real. But the children do not treat imaginary companions as real all the time. On Monday they may talk to the plush bunny and squeeze him tight, but then ignore him until Friday. They may insist that a place be set at the table, but not insist that real food be placed on the plate. They continue to treat their invisible friends as alive even after a clueless adult sits down on top of them. Imaginary companions are in a special epistemological category.

For members of the church, the informal God experiences in which God was the best of friends also seemed to be in a different epistemological category than an encounter with an actual human or, for that matter, than whatever the Bible said about God. People clearly took the encounters seriously. They delighted in the time they spent chatting with God, the time singing with God in the shower. But they seemed to treat those moments in a different way than they treated, say, a plan to have coffee with a human person or the decision to repair the brakes on the car.

That was particularly striking in the way people spoke about "date night" with God. *Date night* was a term only women used. (Men would talk about evenings for "quiet time" with God.) The women would set aside the night, and they imagined it romantically: it was a "date." They might pick up dinner or set out a plate at the table, and they imagined their way through the evening talking to God, cuddling with God, and basking in God's attention. They never confused date night with dates with their human husbands, and they were never bothered by God's failure to munch down on a taco. They behaved as if they believed that their experience of God took place only in their minds. But they also spoke as if it were more real, in some ways, than their everyday reality.

Hannah was an intense, wiry young woman with long dark hair and brown eyes. She seemed to be at every event I went to at the Vineyard, but she had attended a mainstream church until she had arrived in college and wandered into the Vineyard on a whim. "When I first came to the Vineyard, I was a baby Christian," she told me. "I'd been a Christian since I was eight, but I hadn't really grown much since then. Before I came I never—like, I always saw prayer as talking to God, but I didn't realize he was also gonna talk to me and I needed to sit there and listen." It took her some time to figure out how to pray, but by the time we met, she experienced herself as hearing from God. For example, when she was troubled about something, she would have a vivid mental image that would make things clear, in the sense that the mental image would emotionally settle her down and give her guidance. "Last summer I was trying to figure out whether I should date this guy or not. Like, what's God's plan for me? In church I had this image of the cross, with rivers coming out of it in different colors, and the rivers were around me and washing me, and I ended up at the foot of the cross, looking up at Jesus. Then I felt like it didn't matter so much whether I dated that person or not, that I didn't need to be so worried about what I was doing."

She soon became an active member of the prayer team. On good days, when she was praying for someone and it was going "well," she was able to speak out loud to her prayer subject the words that God gave her for that person—while at the same time talking to God in her mind about what to do next, as if she were simultaneously conducting two conversations, playing two simultaneous games of chess. She got more words than images. That was good, she thought, because she felt that she could convey words more easily to someone else. Praying for friends became part of what it meant to be a friend. She and her friends, like many in the Vineyard, would pray for each other and then report back afterward the thoughts and images that "came up" in their minds. "The words will just come out that I need to pray for them, and I can go back the next day and be like, 'You know, I was praying for you yesterday and this is what I got.'"

The ability to hear God speak had become far more vivid for her as she had learned to imagine God as a person by her side. She admitted it had taken practice: "Like an infant learning how to put sentences together, and then to actually have a conversation—not to be talking the whole time or listening the whole time. To learn how to speak and listen and respond. It's sort of like, the more you do something, the better you get at it. Like when you play a piano piece, and you play it over and over, and finally you get it." By the time I met her she was talking to God casually and easily throughout the day, asking him about what she should do, telling him what she had been thinking. She thought that the relationship was a lot like the relationship with an imaginary friend, except in being real. "It's definitely similar. Sometimes I imagine he's walking right alongside me, that there's a physical person there and he's going along with me and we're having a great conversation." He was certainly person-like. She got mad at him—not because he allowed genocide in Darfur, but because little things happened in her life that she did not like: "I was upset with him for making me a dorm counselor." She laughed at what she took to be his jokes. "I'll trip and fall, and I'll be like, *Thanks, God.*" She lit candles when she prayed, and—perhaps unknowingly following an ancient tradition—she imagined that her prayers went up to him as an aroma and that he could literally smell her prayers.[15] She thought that she saw the effect of those prayers in her life: "My belief in God has dramatic effects for me now."

But Hannah did not treat her relationship with God as a relationship with a human. Despite all the books she had read and the prayer courses she had taken, despite her firm and committed belief in God, despite her enthusiastic description of her close and chatty relationship with God, she did not act as if God was a person who was actually present. She had to remind herself deliberately that he was always there to hear. For example, she told me that just the previous summer she'd realized something "silly." "I moved to the outskirts of the city and I'm still coming in every day. And so I'm seeing these different people on the bus and the train, and awesome things are happening. I was getting prophetic words for them, and I'd intercede in prayer for these people and for the city in my mind. And I was like, *How do I know whether I'm supposed to tell someone these things?* Then I went to a conference, and I asked a pastor there these questions: 'What should I do with these things?' He was just like, 'Just ask God.'" She shook her head in astonishment. "Why didn't I think of that?" She had simply forgotten that God was there by her side as her closest and most trusted companion.

And it is why date night mattered. She began date night when she was single and kept calling it that even when she had a serious boyfriend: "I told him, 'I'm going on a date tonight,' and he's like, 'You're joking, right?' I told him no." And she giggled. She liked to infuse the heavenly relationship with the qualities of the everyday because it made that otherwise ethereal relationship more visceral. "I'd ask him how such and such was going for Dale. How such and such was going with Madeline. Then he'd get on to his relationship with me. 'How are we doing with this, how are you doing with that?'" She'd go off by herself and pick up a sandwich at the local Subway (just one sandwich), and then walk down to the lake, where she would sit on one of the benches. Then she would imagine that God was sitting next to her with his arm around her, or sitting at eye level across from her, and she would talk with him and write down what he said in her journal. She knew that this was artifice. She pointed out that she didn't even have a mental image of God when he sat there with her. But she did it because imagining her relationship with God as like her relationship with a boyfriend cut through the awkwardness and difficulty of understanding who or what God was in the first place. "Since I know that God dwells inside me, I *know* I don't need a space for him to sit

beside me. I'm asking my unconscious—which is really the Holy Spirit—
'What do you think about this idea?' And I recognize that it's not me,
but God inside me, that I'm having a conversation with. Which makes
this relationship way more complicated. Human relationships are always
outside of you, you know. But that's often how I think of him. Trying to
imagine some real but not-real figure outside of my own self."

There is an entire stream of thought in evangelical Christianity that
encourages this light, fanciful, not-real-but-more-real-than-real quality
to the experience of God. Another one of the popular books about the
experience of God begins by inviting readers *not* to be reliable, responsible adults: "Our inner story is most audible in the morning, or sometimes
in the middle of the night when the inner editor that tells us how we
'should' respond to the world has gone off duty." That inner story, they
explain, is our yearning for God. The authors tell us that it is our "life's
enchantment"—it is a romance. Indeed, Brent Curtis and John Eldredge
entitled their book *The Sacred Romance*. The point of calling something
a romance, of course, is that it is not quite true because it is better than
true.

> I first remember the Romance calling to me when I was a boy of six
> or seven, just past dusk on a summer evening, when the hotter and
> dustier work of the farm had given way to another song. Something
> warm and alive and poignantly haunting would call to me from the
> mysterious borders of the farm that was my world . . . I remember
> being in that place until the music of life would fill me with the
> knowledge of some Romance to be lived; an assurance that there
> was reason to joust against dragons with wooden swords; a reason to
> wear not one but two pearl-handled revolvers in the cowboy stories
> I weaved and lived out each day . . . The magic assured me of loves
> and lovers and adventures to be joined and mystery to be pursued.[16]

We are a long way from, say, the ontological proof for the existence of
God. In this passage God is not an explanation for anything. He is more
like a state of mind.

That state of mind is a lot like being engrossed in good magical fiction
of the Harry Potter kind. *The Sacred Romance* compares the scriptures,
approvingly, to Tolkien's Middle-earth and to C. S. Lewis's Narnia. The
authors refer to the Gospels as a "fairy tale," and they say that this is their

"wonderful strength"—and the only difference from fairy tales is that the Gospel happens to be true. They explain that our refusal to believe in the miraculous because it is childlike and irrational is the true danger that besets the average Christian. "The crisis of hope that afflicts the church today is a crisis of *imagination*."[17]

Then the authors explain how to circumvent the danger: to ignore the theological, explanatory purpose of the idea of God and instead to enjoy God as a person just like you. "If we try to relate to God as Author"—e.g., the being who is ultimately responsible for the misery and unfairness we see in our world—"we will go mad or despair." Instead, they say, you have to see God as a *character,* a hero in the story he has written. Even more, they want you to know a God who is as affected by you, the human reader, as much as you are affected by him: "When we see God as the Hero of the story and consider what he wants for us, we know one thing for certain: we affect Him. We impact the members of the Trinity as truly as they do each other."[18] This is a remarkable claim. God is eternal, almighty, and unchanging, but he gets hurt when you don't come out to play.

One consequence of this vivid "let's pretend" is that heresy fades to unimportance. The authors of *The Sacred Romance* or of *Experiencing God* express not one shred of concern that someone will imagine God falsely or inappropriately. They worry that someone will not experience God at all. "You will never be satisfied just to know about God. Really knowing God only comes through experience as He reveals Himself to you."[19] Nor did Arnold, the Chicago pastor, worry much about the risk that someone would invite God to dinner and get God wrong. Arnold worried about disbelief and about the leaden dullness of some church services. He called that state "church-wounded": that people's prior experience in a church might lead them away from Christianity. I was a little tentative when I first told him that I thought the church was more eager to have people experience God than it was worried about the risk that they would confuse God's voice with the rumblings of their stomachs. But he was delighted. He thought I had grasped something important about the church. "Faith," he told me, "is about taking risks."

By this, Arnold meant that faith demands that you have the expectation that God will act even if that expectation violates common sense. In one of his teachings, he quoted a Vineyard author as saying that "taking risks in faith is like jumping off a ten meter platform over an empty pool and expecting God to fill it while you are in mid-air." This was not, of course, anything he would actually do. Like most Vineyard congregants, he warned against doing something dangerous (like walking into traffic) just to "test" God, to see if God would save you. Nor for that matter was it anything that the author had recommended. The author had described the idea as a fantasy, a "daydream," in which he and God were chatting about what it means to trust God. In the daydream, he explained, God told him to jump off the suicidally high board. "This is the way it works," God said in the daydream. "You leave the board, *then* I fill the pool with water."[20]

The quotation appeared in a book entitled *Naturally Supernatural*. The book is sold to Vineyard congregants as a kind of training manual for experiencing God, one of many such manuals available to experientially oriented evangelical Christians (among them, *Experiencing God, Hearing God, Dialogue with God,* and so forth). The book serves, as the author writes, as a "call not just to hear the Word, but to put it into practice." By this he means learning to experience the immediacy of what he calls "God's kingdom" today. "Many, myself included, have somehow mistakenly understood that eternal life is something that happens at the end of our earthly lives." Instead, you should know that eternal life happens now. In the book, God is explicitly depicted as supernatural, and Christians are explicitly expected to have supernatural experiences as enactments of their relationship with God: "We are a natural people who have been invited and called to an amazing supernatural task." Equally striking is that the author explains that he wrote the book to help "everyone to play."[21] The cover of the book sports a toddler in a superman outfit several sizes to big for him, proudly pretending that he is a superhero.

What does it mean that everyone should "play"? When people at the Vineyard said this, they often meant that what you set out to do supernaturally might not happen, but you should act as if it would: you should "play." Arnold liked the quotation about the diving board because it evoked for him just how foolhardy belief could seem, even to the believer. In the teaching during which he put the quotation up in PowerPoint, he said that a faithful person should pray for healing in the expectation that God will heal, and that if he does not expect the prayer to work, God will not act. But he should also know that the healing might not happen. A faithful person should believe that God will give her insights into other people or tell her specific things to pray for on behalf of other people— insights that in general people call "prophecy." She should share those words with those for whom God had intended them, and she should know that she will not experience prophecy without faith. But she should also know that what she experiences as prophecy might be mere fantasy. You need, Arnold said, to run the risk that you are wrong in your experience of God in order to have that experience of God in the first place. You must allow yourself to live as though God's supernatural power is real, accessible, and reliable—and yet at the same time know that it might not show up. Then he went on to instruct us to listen for God with our senses, to anticipate that God would "speak" to us in our prayers, and to use what God said as specific, clear expressions of what He wanted us to do. He told us we would have to work at it and practice. But he wanted us to try: "Take a moment and listen to the voice of God this afternoon. Try it out today . . . see if God has something for you."

Try it out today. That phrase—spoken, we should note, to people who really believe in God and who would show up in any polling data as theologically conservative evangelical Christians—says something about just how hard Arnold thought it was to experience God as really present, and about his assumption that his congregants also found it difficult. *Try,* after all, implies the possibility of failure. The insistence that more is required from us runs throughout the Gospels. But this particular insistence had to do with the real challenge of accepting the reality of an invisible interlocutor, and that challenge has grown more salient in our secular world. In churches like the Vineyard, taking God seriously is presumed to be a problem even for long-term church-convicted Christians. These churches presume the congregant struggles with disbelief—even when he or she believes. They presume they need to get their congregants over their hesitation to believe anything so apparently nonsecular, nonmaterial, nonworldly, and nonrational. That's why they entice them into "let's pretend" play.

Does it work? The scholar who pointed out that "let's pretend" play can make play real was an idiosyncratic psychoanalyst called D. W. Winnicott. Donald Wood Winnicott was raised in a large, comfortable Devonshire house with a clutch of sisters and cousins and a rambling garden with space for everyone. He grew up, with no doubt that he was loved, in the precious decades just before the First World War, when the sun never set upon the British Empire and the world seemed safe and good. After the

First World War and the loss of many of his boyhood friends, Winnicott became a psychoanalyst and focused his attention on play.

Winnicott's deepest insight was that play occurs in the boundary between the mind and the world, in what he called, with characteristic simplicity, the "intermediate area of experiencing." This intermediate area exists between an external reality, which wishing will not change, and the child's inner reality of hope and fear. Winnicott coined the term *transitional object* for the toy that often becomes so special to a child around the toddler years—the bunny that cannot be left behind, the blanket that cannot be washed. He argued that these objects stand for what is good and emotionally real within the relationship with the mother in a concrete form that is neither the child nor the mother. Yet he pointed out that to call the transitional object a "symbol" was not quite right from the point of view of the child. Teddy is real to the child, not a symbol of something else, the way the inscribed wooden block on my desk is a symbol of a happy sabbatical year at a center for advanced study. Transitional objects can become so real to the child that in some ways they become more important than the parent. Mother goes off to work. Teddy is always there, and Teddy evokes some of the same feelings associated with the mother but without the cost of her absence. If by chance Teddy is left behind on a picnic table, the child can be devastated in a manner that seems out of kilter for something made of cloth and stuffing. That the object survives the child's attacks—Teddy is suddenly walloped against the wall, then hugged—makes that reality more sweet.

The crude interpretation of these transitional objects is that they enable the child to master the real, external absence of the mother by creating a measure of control over an object that represents the mother (or to put it still more crudely and psychoanalytically, the "breast"). Winnicott does give us this interpretation, after a manner: "It is true that the piece of blanket (or *whatever* it is) is symbolic of [something] such as the breast." Because the child controls Teddy, the child can experience a sense of control over the mother. But what really matters, Winnicott says, is that Teddy allows the child to hold what is good about the mother when the mother is not there. "The point of [the transitional object] is not its symbolic value so much as its actuality. Its not being the breast (or the mother), although real, is as important as the fact that it stands for the breast (or the mother)."[22] Because the stuffed bear is but is not the mother—and because the bear is not the child—the bear becomes a way for the child to hold, physically, the trust and good feeling about the mother in the mother's absence.

It turns out that just asking a child to care for a stuffed animal may be enough to improve their health. During the second Israel-Lebanon war in July and August 2006, as many as half a million Israelis were relocated out of the danger zone to large tent camps on the edge of the desert. Half of them were children. Most of them had heard explosions and alarms; most had seen the aftermath of bombing; and many of them had nightmares, insomnia, excessive crying, and other signs of stress. Two days before the war ended, several Israeli psychologists gave some of the younger children plush Huggy-Puppies. They were told that the stuffed dogs were sad because they were far from home and lonely, and they were asked if they could care for the puppies and take them to bed with them at night. Three weeks later these children had significantly fewer stress symptoms than they had when they began, and fewer symptoms than children in a matched comparison group, who had no Huggy-Puppies to take to bed at night.[23]

Winnicott thought that this intermediate area of experiencing was the place of the human experience of God, because God is fundamentally an emotional commitment that the world is good in the face of the apparent absence of that goodness. It is an insight that seems appropriate to the shadow of the trenches: that God is the capacity to hold on to what is good about the world when all seems bleak. Winnicott thought that an adult's capacity to believe in a good world was not so different from a toddler's capacity to believe that a mother who was absent could return, and he thought that the concept of God served much the same function as the straw-stuffed bear and became emotionally real in more or less the same way. He believed that because God is invisible to the senses, each individual must make him anew out of their own private emotional experience of the good; but that God could not be God unless God was experienced as standing apart from the self. Winnicott thought that a God who was emotionally real for someone was like a teddy bear: more real than a daydream because anchored in the external world of plush and buttons, but meaningless—inert plush—without that inner world.

The surprising thing is that a large portion of the evangelical church seems to have come to the same conclusion about how to make God come alive for congregants. Books like *The Sacred Romance* assert that the church on its own terms will fail, at least in this pluralistic, scientific world. So they encourage the reader to imagine God as present—theological precision be damned. "We must be careful," *The Sacred Romance* says at one point, "or these will be only religious words."[24]

Those who created the immensely popular and widespread practice of Inductive Bible Study have made the same bet, and they accept the same light touch around what is real and true. This can be startling to an outsider. After all, theologically conservative Christians are supposed to believe that the Bible is literally true, and they do. Most of the congregants I knew would say that the Bible was true and accurate in everything it affirmed, everything that mattered. Some might concede that the age of the earth was a mistake, the kind of error made by a scribe of the time. They would still insist that the stories were true, that the events were historical, that the miracles had actually taken place, and that everything that Jesus was said to have done was real. Some would say that the Bible was true word for word.

Yet when people in many evangelical Bible studies—like those sponsored by the evangelical college organization InterVarsity, for example—set out to learn about the Bible, they are explicitly invited to use their imaginations to fill in the gaps in the text so that the Bible becomes their own private story. The form of Bible study that dominates small house groups in most evangelical churches and in campus ministry is a method that turns a sometimes obscure text into a story that is personally specific to the reader. In this method, you take a passage—for example, Luke 15:11–32, the story of the prodigal son—and you talk about what the passage says, what it means, and how it applies to your life. This is not about scholarship. You do not, in this method, learn about when the scripture was written or which other scriptures it cites—not that there would be anything wrong with that, but it simply isn't the goal of the method. The method asks you to put yourself in the story and then to make the story true for your own life. "What's God thinking here? What's he feeling? What is he saying to you?" Elaine asked us when we read the prodigal son together. "Your objective," as a leading Inductive Bible Study website states (they call themselves the Godsquad), "is to learn to read the Bible as if God were personally speaking to you."[25] That's what people say. "It's a love story," someone gushed to me once, "and it's written for *me*."[26]

The first time my house group met, Elaine handed out Matthew 13:31–33, the parable of the mustard seed.

Another parable He put forth to them, saying: "The kingdom of heaven is like a mustard seed, which a man took and sowed in his field, which indeed is the least of all the seeds; but when it is grown it is greater than the herbs and becomes a tree, so that the birds of the air come and nest in its branches." Another parable he spoke to them: "the kingdom of heaven is like leaven, which a woman took and hid in three measures of meal till it was all leavened."

The first thing she asked us to do was to draw a picture of what the passage said. We showed off our pictures to each other, mostly lopsided sketches of what looked like ceiling cracks. Then we talked about what a mustard seed was and decided that its most important feature was that it was tiny. "He chose such simple things to describe heaven," someone said with a sigh. We talked about leaven (yeast) and what leaven did to bread. (I began to appreciate the point of this concreteness when, later on, one of the college students, apparently not yet a cook, said innocently, "What's vinegar?") Then the discussion began to drift into the contemporary world. We decided that examples of leaven were the civil rights movement, the YMCA, the Founding Fathers. And then we turned to our own lives. What, Elaine asked, are the mustard seeds in your life? What could we do to nurture them? And what about the kingdom of God seems small to you?

Elaine would ask us to go into the minds of the characters in the Bible stories we read. She'd ask us to imagine being in the scene, one of the crowd, and ask us what we noticed, there on the road in the swell of rough-robed people around our master. She would ask us to choose a character in the story, like the lawyer who asks Jesus how he could get eternal life (Luke 10:25), and to imagine what that character thought and felt. At the beginning I always seemed to be asking the wrong question. One evening, for example, we read Jeremiah 1:11–19, the passage in which Jeremiah announces that calamity will break forth across the land from the north: "Then the Lord said to me, 'Out of the north calamity shall break forth on all the inhabitants of the land. For behold, I am calling all the families of the kingdoms of the north . . . Therefore prepare yourself and arise.'"

It is a horrific passage, describing a terrible conflagration and a harsh attack that lands Jeremiah in prison. I wanted to know who these families actually were, when this event took place, and why the author of

Jeremiah had placed the testing of the prophet at the beginning of the passage. In other words I wanted to know about the text, its history, and its construction—scholars' questions. No one else was interested. Elaine explained to me that the word *families* referred to us. She wanted us to talk about what the passage told us about God's character, the kind of person he was. She took it for granted that God had a human character. We decided that God was a planner; that he used people to fulfill his aims; and that he was funny. God's humor is perhaps not an obvious inference from this passage about holy vengeance, but the group member who talked about this said, "He's saying, okay, just pull yourself together here, no dawdling." Someone else in the group remarked that God knew that his people would disobey Jeremiah and still, with all God's power, he let them disobey. "I wonder," she said, "whether God sees all the foolish things I do, and lets me do them anyway." People immediately reassured her that he did.

People spoke like this in the house group. They took these sentences written hundreds and hundreds of years ago and turned them into admonishments or encouragements about what had happened to them that afternoon. When we read the parable of the Good Samaritan, Nancy burst out that the priest and the Levite who didn't help the beaten man weren't compassionate, and neither was she herself. Nancy was a middle-aged woman with a modest apartment that she worked hard to support. A woman at her workplace needed a place to live. Nancy didn't really want to offer her a place in her own home. She thought that the story was telling her that she should be more compassionate; and indeed, she then offered the woman her living room. When we talked about Exodus, Jacob, Kate's husband, commented, "When God brings the Israelites into the desert, at one point he allows the Israelites who did not know or follow God to die, so that new generations could inherit the land. I think there have been times when God's done that pruning in my life."

Once, in another group, I pointed out that in the Gospel of Mark, the disciples are portrayed as really stupid. I was excited because I thought I was learning something about the way the author of the Gospel had put the text together. The leader of the group gently redirected my attention back to my own life. "Yes," she said, "that's what it is like to be human and to follow Jesus." Another group member chimed in, eager to help me to get it right, "I would have said it this way: I am really stupid. The disciples remind me of how stupid I am." Nobody talked about why the author of

Mark's Gospel, writing in the aftermath of the brutal destruction of the second temple, chose to depict the disciples as obtuse. They wanted to use the passage to remind themselves of how little they understood about God. Yet for all my irrepressible scholarliness and my outsiderly comments, only once did someone actually tell me that I had misinterpreted a verse, and even then she did so in private; when I told that story to others, they roared with laughter at the person who had done it. People just did not worry about heresy. They worried about making God come alive for them. As Alice, the engineering student, once said, "Words, words, words. It's the relationship that counts."[27]

People may have said that every word of the Bible was literally true, but it was also true that nobody cared which translation anyone used.[28] Pastors switched between translations from sermon to sermon, choosing the translation of the passage that seemed more compelling or that made their point more clearly. In the group I joined when I moved to California, the leader gave us three different translations of a passage we were supposed to pray with during the week. She did not concern herself with which translation was authentic or accurate. She wanted us to use the translation that spoke to us or moved us, or that made the story more meaningful for us. She wanted us to enter the passage as participants and to imagine that we were there as the story unfolded. She told us that Jesus was a storyteller, and she thought that what mattered was that his stories became so real for us, it was as if they had happened in our own lives.

It seemed to me that the play did work for people. The great achievement of all this playlike activity—imagining what God is feeling when the elder brother rebels, trying to hear God's voice in prophecy, pretending that you and God are drinking coffee together at your table—is to enable someone to treat God as a person, not a packet of rules and propositions, and to draw inferences about what God thinks and wants that are directly relevant to that person's life. When pretend play ascribes personlike qualities to an inanimate or invisible object, that object evokes for the person playing a host of implicit assumptions we humans bring to bear about other humans, but not about tables and chairs. We attribute intentions and we infer emotional responses, so long as we remain within the play frame.

Even very young children can manage the complicated epistemological task that is playing. If you put a bear-shaped object stuffed with sawdust in a shoebox, turn an imaginary faucet, and announce that you are washing Teddy with a block of wood as if it were soap, a two-year-old child not only accepts that you are giving Teddy a bath but enters into the activity as if it were the bath of a breathing, thinking, desiring, personlike being. The child can draw out the causal relationships that follow from these "let's pretend" stipulations. A two-year-old can take Teddy out of the shoebox and announce that "Teddy's all wet" because Teddy has been in a pretend bathtub full of pretend water. The child can add new stipulations and draw out more causal chains. That two-year-old can take a paper towel and "dry Teddy off" even though the paper towel is not a cloth towel and even though the stuffed bear is not actually wet; and after the stuffed bear's "bath," the child may announce that it is time for Teddy's story if—in the child's experience—baths lead to stories that lead to bed. Play is a human activity that allows a child (or adult) to attribute these personlike qualities to nonpersonlike objects.[29]

Playing together helps. People said that when they read the Bible together and talked about what God was thinking, it made the external reality of a living, interacting God just that much more real. Hearing about the way other people have experienced God's voice makes it easier to feel that there really is a voice to hear. Imagining other people's conversations makes it easier to infer what God must be saying to you. In house group, we sat around one evening talking about how the group was helpful in what people called their "walk" with God. One man explained how much his experience of God had changed since coming to the Vineyard. "God's voice is like a fuzzy radio station, 95.2, 94.9, that needs more tuning. You're picking up the song, and it's not so clear sometimes. It's clearer to me now." Reading the Bible with your imagination could have the same effect. Hannah explained, "I relate to [the apostle] Paul a lot because I can see him writing these words, or dictating these words to someone else who's writing them, and imagining this church way off that he's writing to and him recollecting his interactions with them that he's writing about." Hannah was sharply aware that she did not see God directly, that as a human she was limited in what she could perceive. Conversations with friends about their experiences with God "help me see how they saw God, and then I get a better picture of how I might see God." It was as if people did all this work with their imaginations to help their God-concept stand separate from themselves, and the community stood around them to help hold the concept out there, separate from their minds.

At the same time, it also seemed to me that those playing never quite forgot that some of what they were doing was self-generated, as if going for a walk with God carried a memory-trace of choosing to pretend. These "let's pretend" play practices did seem to make God more real—more emotionally compelling, more present, more everyday—to those who could become engrossed in them. But as those who could play with God grew more confident that God interacted with them from a place that was truly external to their own private minds, they became quite comfortable with the idea that any one of these small playlike interactions was a product of their own imagination. In fact, they often behaved as if their specific experiences of God could well be just make-believe.

Elaine told me that she was trying to hear God speak in the little things, so that she could hear his voice when it really counted. She began to ask him what she should wear every morning. The Sunday we spoke, God told her—as she experienced it—to wear the blue shirt. But when she put it on, her bra showed, so she took off the blue shirt and put on a black one. When she arrived at church, she was standing around with the worship team. The pastor walked by, smiled, and said (she reported), "I see you are all wearing blue today." Elaine told me this story to illustrate how mortified she was at having not taken God seriously. The real point, of course, was that Elaine—a deeply committed Christian who had repeatedly explained to me that every word of the Bible was accurate—did not, as she stared at her closet, treat her inference about what God was thinking ("wear the blue shirt") as an actual insight into divine intention. She thought she had just imagined it.

After Elaine told me this story, I began to ask other people whether they asked God to tell them what they should wear in the morning. Rachael, a young college student, said yes: "I definitely do that. When I can't decide what to wear. Like, God, what should I wear?" Then she laughed. "And you know, then I kind of forget about the fact that I asked God. I think God cares about really, really little things in my life. I mean I know God cares, but I don't expect him to tell me what to wear. I'm like, 'Oh, I think I'll wear that and forget I even asked God!'" And still she thought it was important to ask: "But I also believe in looking for God in little things." People spoke to me about how badly they felt when they fell asleep talking to God—but they still fell asleep. They said that they were embarrassed to feel that they should study in addition to praying that they would pass their exam—but they still studied.

There was a sense of in-betweenness in these experiences of God. These congregants were clear that God was real, but they were not always clear that God was present in specific playlike practices the way they were pretending that he was. When I asked Stacy whether she believed that God was truly present when she imagined him in front of her, she said, "I can sit here and have a conversation with God as if he's in that chair. I know that I experience God. I know that I hear him. But how do I know that it's different than, you know, my imaginary friend Harold? I don't." The ambiguity simply became part of the nature of God. Sometimes when someone asked a question in house group, someone else would shrug and say, "It's God stuff"—meaning, as Alice put it, "It's a mystery, it's still not clear."

Even after she had grasped that God was speaking to her in her mind, Sarah worried that she wasn't experiencing God: "For a while I tried to have a relationship and just hear him and speak to him." But it didn't really work, because she could not shake the uneasy sense that it was all in her mind. She told me that at one point she just decided deliberately to act as if what she imagined she heard from God really was God. That is, she decided to act as if the words and images that cropped up in her mind that she thought might be God were in fact God—and that she should act on them. (Admittedly, most of this "action" was deciding to pray about someone specific.) "I finally realized that it was as if he said, 'I'm not gonna tell you what to do, or what my role is, unless you're gonna do it.'" She decided to imagine, in other words, that the God she imagined in her mind was real and was personlike, in that he cared directly about her and spoke directly to her. She pretended in order to believe.

When she did that, God became real in her life as a person. "When I understood that he was alive today, that he was speaking today, that he was working through people today, I really felt like, *permission.* It really felt like relief to have a conversation with him." The permission was to break free of the restrictive, formal bonds imposed by what she had understood about the proper relationship between a distant, holy God and his worshipful subject. By "relief" she meant that the relationship could be natural and relaxed, that she didn't have to crouch in humility, shielding her eyes from his glory, focused only on what she thought he wanted her to say. She could just be herself, and as herself she daydreamed a lovely, funny, warm relationship between them into being. This new God teased her, with a wicked sense of humor.

> One Sunday I went out for lunch with people after church . . . I could see people being blessed by just the people that were there, and I felt like I was a blessing to people. As I was walking back to my car, I was just all sort of full of myself and this wonderful experience—and a bird pooped right on me. I had a new shirt on, and just this big glob of really ugly bird poop, not nice white poop. It was just hysterical. It was awful, and it was so funny. I just knew it was God, you know, it was just like, "I hear you and I see you and here we go, get right back in your place," but just in a real gentle and in a sweet and intimate kind of way. He does stuff like that to me all the time, very often when pride is rearing its ugly head. But when you're disciplined in a sweet and a loving way like that, it goes a long way with anybody, but humor especially for me makes a big difference. I just love that side of him.

She found herself chattering away to God about whatever mattered, however trivial. It wasn't that she really felt that they were best friends. "I feel extremely close and extremely far away at the same time." She said that when they got too "buddy buddy," he would remind her that he was God. Notice that he did so, in the above case, like a schoolboy. He made the bird poop. The very silliness made her feel even more intimate. He didn't send an archangel when she stepped out of line. He played a ridiculous private joke. He chastised her, in a way that made it clear that he was paying the most scrupulous and loving attention to everything she thought, and then he did something to make things right.

> It was pretty early on in my relationship with him. I was just all full of myself one morning. I just had wonderful devotions and worships and just felt so close and just went out, and it was the most god awful day out. It was like icy rain and gray and cold, and it was sleety, and I'm just all full of joy of the Lord and saying, "God, I praise you that it was just not snowing and it's not accumulating and the streets aren't icy." I went around the corner and hit a patch of ice and just about went down. I just burst out laughing out loud.

It was just so funny that he would just put me in my place in such a slapstick personal kind of way. But then he just graced the rest of my morning when the bus showed up right away, which it never does. I was reading, and I missed my stop to get off at the train, and I heard him say [audibly,] "Get off the bus," and looked up and hollered out, and the bus driver actually stopped like half a block away and let me get out. I just felt that intimacy all morning. Like when you go from holding a new boyfriend's hand to kissing him good night.

A good part of what made "let's pretend" work for Sarah was that she took it seriously enough to violate her own strongly held sense of right religious behavior. Sarah said that it was when she was able to become screamingly furious at God that he became a person for her, as if she walloped him against the wall of her skepticism and discovered that he survived. At first, she told me, she tried to hold anger back, shocked at what she was thinking. "It would just annoy me no end when I'd feel like he was telling me to do something and I didn't at all know how to do it, I didn't know how it could possibly work out, I just didn't understand." She began to tell him the way she felt. Then she yelled. Then she even swore. "When I finally heard myself saying some really bad words to God, I knew I had a real relationship with him. And those things kind of went a long way to sort of, you know, making it more intimate, making it realer." He became more personlike when she did that, of course. When she explained why this mattered to her, she said that she became more confident that he would not leave, as if in becoming more personlike, he had also become more likely to abandon her when she got mad at him and yet he did not. "It has to do with [knowing] that he would love me even if I was swearing at him. So I began to trust him enough to be able to express that, to be able to lay that down."

Not-real-but-more-than-real. By the time I met her, Sarah was willing to tell me that when she was praying and she felt God's presence moving through her body or in her mind, she felt extremely close. "When I'm ministering to someone and I know that the words that are coming out of me aren't mine, and I know that the pictures that I'm seeing aren't mine, there's a real intense closeness and oneness that you feel." At the same time, when she didn't feel his presence, she felt in some ways even closer because then she felt that she didn't need some kind of evidence that he was there. She was able to say to me, when I asked her how she was able to relate to a being she could not see with her eyes, that she did feel as if she "saw" him.

> I feel like I do see him and I do see his face and I see his hand on what's going on around me. That's a part of the experiential thing or things that before I would have identified as coincidence or just a fluke or something, but things that are so specific it couldn't be anything but God. They're so personal, they're so intimate that it couldn't be anything but God.

She had become able to integrate her cognitive capacity to recognize God's presence in specific moments—her capacity to interpret God's response to her through circumstance, through reading scripture, through identifying circumstances and thoughts and sensations as from God—into an internal imaginative representation of a person.

This had made God more real for Sarah. She described moving from a period where she experienced God directly and often—a period that was terribly exciting—into a period in which she experienced God directly less often, but her confidence in his presence had become even stronger.

> In the beginning I would like pray and I would get immediate feedback that that was right on, or I'd just find out in another way that something I've been praying about had actually happened. God would give me that kind of confirmation and affirmation. I don't get that [immediate confirmation] as much anymore, but when I get it, it's bigger and it's enough to carry me from time to time.

In other words, she talked as if she had progressed from a childlike discovery of an externally existing God into a stage in which she carried an internal representation of God's love that sustained her in the absence of specific moments of recognizing God's presence.

Sarah seemed, at this point, to have learned not only to create an internal representation of God but to interact with that representation in a way that felt to her like an actual human interaction: real when he was present, convinced when he was absent that he would return. And then she played with him. She teased him, she giggled with him, she felt that she played pranks with him. And it didn't really matter whether he was really there when she thought he was: "It's still hard for me to tell." She thought of her uncertainty as just part of the human limitation of those who strive to know God.

> Sometimes when I pray, I see his glory. There's what I call the throne room, and depending on what I'm praying about and what I'm doing, I'm like in different positions in the same room. Very often I'm at the back, but sometimes there's something where I'm up in front. It's just like, I mean this is gonna sound a little wacky, but it's just like light. It's like a throne and robes. Some of the images are like in Revelations, light that you can't really get right up to and you don't want to. You can't really exactly see, but it's being in the presence of the Lord. And that's where you hear the prayers. Sometimes I feel like I'm hearing the prayers that have gone before and the prayers that are going on now and the prayers that are to come, and I just sort of join in that chorus.

This is play, but it is a serious play: a play that cultivates the imagination for a serious end, precisely because congregants presume the basic claim of Christianity to be unbelievable, even foolish, in a modern, secular society. And the function of the emphasis on play is to make the player's commitment to the serious truth claims embedded in the play more profound.

The point about play is that it is distinct from nonplay: a "free activity," as the historian Johan Huizinga defined it in *Homo Ludens,* "standing quite consciously outside 'ordinary' life in being 'not serious' but at the same time absorbing the player intensely and utterly."[30] When dogs play, they sometimes signal to each other with a distinctive play-crouch, and they infer from the crouch that their snarling intensity is not to be taken as aggression. The anthropologist Gregory Bateson talked about this as a layering of epistemological frames. There is a "play frame" and a "reality frame," and when we play, we act within the play frame. We bathe the teddy bear in invisible water, and we dry him off with a towel of air, and we are not confused when our hands do not get wet.

But when evangelicals go on "date night" with God, the play frame is also a reality frame. They know that they are pretending to talk to God, and much in the way they talk about date night signals that they know that this is not really God. That, after all, is why someone can ask God what shirt she should wear—and forget to wait for the answer. At the same time, date night with God is not just "let's pretend." It is, as congregants insist, a way of encountering God. The crucial part of play in a Christian context is that the play claim that God is an imaginary companion is also a real claim about the nature of the world, a claim about the objective reality of the Holy Spirit and God's supernatural presence. It is play but not play, the place where—as Huizinga said of sacred play in general—"the distinction between belief and make-believe breaks down."[31] In other words, the playlike behavior is not seen as play (I know that when I speak to God, he will answer), and yet the framing claim "this is play" does not quite disappear (I don't treat the thought *Wear the blue shirt* as a real word from God). I thought of this as a kind of epistemological double register: real but not real, not real but more than real, absolutely real for all time but just not real in that moment.

And so this playfulness enhances the complexity of the belief commitment that these Christians make. Just as the belief that God speaks directly to each of us demands skepticism about whether any particular identification of God's voice is really God ("Sometimes when we think it's the spirit moving, it's just our burrito from lunch"), the faith practice of encouraging people to ask God what shirt they should wear demands that they have to tolerate ambiguity about how seriously they take any imagined interaction with God. When you sit on a park bench and imagine God's arm around your shoulders, God is real in a different way than either the park bench or a daydream. Congregants certainly say that God is real. But they are practicing experiencing God as real in a distinctive way.

CHAPTER FOUR

Developing Your Heart

*May the God of hope fill you with all joy
and peace as you trust in him, so that you
may overflow with hope by
the power of the Holy Spirit.*

Romans 15:13

[God] looks at you and grins.

Enjoying God

I F YOU CAN RECOGNIZE GOD, and you have learned to relate to him as existing in the world—if this God is real to you—you should feel the feelings that should come from such a relationship. You should feel that you are deeply loved, and your own heart should grow in the warmth and acceptance of that love, and you in turn should become more loving, forgiving, understanding, and patient. "From love, with love, and for love" was the way my prayer group described the way we should experience our relationship with God. So too in *The Purpose Driven Life:* "Because God is love, the most important lesson he wants you to learn on earth is how to love."[1] In a church like the Vineyard, Christians are supposed to experience themselves as unconditionally loved. This, the third task, is quite difficult for human beings, whether or not the lover is invisible.

So again there are specific faith practices to help them learn. These practices share a good deal with psychotherapy, and they have a great side benefit. They enable churches like the Vineyard to deliver emotionally to their congregants—to make their congregants feel better about themselves—even when the faith of those congregants is weak. These emotional practices can make it worth your while to go to church even if you don't quite yet believe, completely and entirely, in this God.

. . .

It is a big promise to claim that any Christian will be able to feel unconditionally loved by God. The promise combines Luther's assertion that
we are saved by faith alone with the idea that salvation will happen *right
now* and you will know because you will feel differently. The first part of
the promise—that you are saved because you believe, not because you
are good—is hard enough to parse as a moral vision.[2] The second seems
ridiculous. It is almost laughably obvious that you can't just announce
that you believe in something and expect your shame and guilt to evapo-
rate. It is hard to change emotional habits, particularly if they are the
emotional habits that led you to want "more" in the first place. It is hard
even to imagine unconditional love. No humans have truly unconditional
relationships after the complete dependency of infancy, after the expectations of right behavior become part of our relationships with even the
most loving adult. It is hard to feel loved even in an ordinary way by an
invisible being. Yet feeling loved unconditionally is clearly set out as the
true experience of God at a church like the Vineyard. It is the point of discernment and the "let's pretend" play. Who cares if you enjoy chatting to
an invisible force about which shirt to wear in the morning? People who
decide to go to church because they want "more" want what the church tells
them they get if they come to Christ: love, joy, peace, patience, kindness,
goodness, faithfulness, gentleness, and self-control (Galatians 5:22–23).
Those are the deliverables, the bottom line, the rewards that have value
even if all the supernatural stuff turns out to be wrong, and they are
assumed to follow naturally from the promise of God's love. The challenge for the church is to deliver on the promise.

The promise of unconditional love is not an inevitable interpretation
of the Christian God, despite the emphasis on love throughout the New
Testament. For much of the history of Christianity, Christians have feared
God. The great scenes that stretched above the church doors of medieval
Europe showed Christ presiding in judgment. On his one side, the faithful stream to heaven, while on the other, the wicked are cast down to the
demons of hell. The message was clear: Be vigilant and godly, lest you too
slide into the abyss. The medieval historian Rachel Fulton points out that
for many centuries, prayer practices deliberately set out to scare, humili-
ate, and shame the worshipper into the love of God through the fear of

God's damnation. Here, for example, are the early musings of the great eleventh-century philosopher Saint Anselm:

> For I am fearful, knowing the wrath of the strict judge, for I am a sinner, a prisoner deserving punishment . . . the accused stands before a tremendous judge . . . Terrible is the severity of the judge, intolerably strict, for the offense against him is huge and he is exceedingly wrathful.[3]

The theme of a wrathful God echoes down the centuries. Inconstantly, to be sure: by the twelfth century the Christian emphasis shifted into an intense awareness of Christ's suffering humanity and Mary's compassion, a shift enabled in part by Anselm's own rethinking. But the motif of the fear of God's wrath recurs repeatedly across the years. "Sinners in the Hands of an Angry God" is the title of one of the most famous of American sermons, preached by Jonathan Edwards on July 8, 1741. The thoughtful, sober theologian deliberately set out to unnerve his audience. He told them that their God despised them and held them from destruction on his whim: "The God that holds you on the pit of hell, much as one holds a spider, or some loathsome insect, abhors you, and is dreadfully provoked." Edwards told his congregation that they were wicked; that their corrupted hearts were boundless in human fury; and that God should indeed condemn them: "The bow of God's wrath is bent, and the arrow made ready on the string, and justice bends the arrow at your heart and strains the bow, and it is nothing but the mere pleasure of God, and that of an angry God, without any promise or obligation, that keeps the arrow one moment from being drunk with your blood." By the end of the sermon, many in the congregation were wailing, and some had fainted and were slumped upon the floor.[4]

A Portrait of the Artist as a Young Man, published in 1916, feels more recognizable because it is more modern, but Joyce's God draws from the same well of fear. His autobiographical character Stephen Dedalus is seventeen when this portion of the story opens. Curious about sex, he meets with a prostitute; he likes it; he returns, again and again. He begins to eat greedily, gluttonously. He skips his classes. He does not pray. Then, on a retreat with his schoolmates, he hears a series of hellfire sermons, and every word seems spoken directly into his soul.

Consider then what must be the foulness of the air of hell. Imagine some foul and putrid corpse that has lain rotting and decomposing in the grave, a jelly-like mass of liquid corruption. Imagine such a corpse a prey to flames, devoured by the fire of burning brimstone and giving off dense choking fumes of nauseous loathsome decomposition. And then imagine this sickening stench, multiplied a millionfold and a millionfold again from the millions upon millions of fetid carcasses massed together in the reeking darkness, a huge and rotting human fungus. Imagine all this, and you will have some idea of the horror of the stench of hell.[5]

Stephen leaves the chapel with shaking legs, guilty and horrified, to vomit in his room.

The God of the renewalist evangelical church is not this cruel judge. The Vineyard took the basic Christian narrative about the distance between a limited human and a boundless mighty God and shifted the plotline from our inadequacy to God's extraordinary capacity. Gone is the fear of snapping the connection. Gone is the torment of the abyss. The story becomes the delight in drawing closer. Its protagonists fear lifelessness—not death. In this new Christian narrative, the problem is human emotional pain and the human's own self-blaming harshness— a kind of living hell—and the resolution of that pain is God's infinite and personal love that can be had now, today, as long as you truly accept that God is loving; that God is present; and above all, that God loves *you*, just as you are, with all your pounds and pimples.[6]

As a result, the basic task of learning to respond to God is learning to believe that you are truly lovable, just as you are. People spoke of sin at the Vineyard, but what they meant by it was separation. "Goodness, I'd never have stayed if they talked all about sin," Suzanne remarked about her first visit to a Vineyard-style church, as an older woman and a lapsed Episcopalian. Sin is understood not as forbidden behavior but as an inner state of being separated from God. That may be caused by doing something of which God disapproves, but the problem is not that *God* has withdrawn. The problem is that the sinner cannot bear to be close to God. Sin is something you do that interferes with the possibility of experiencing God's joy, something that drives the peace of the Lord from your grasp. And because a behavior that makes you unhappy is understood as a behavior you cannot control, the exemplar of sin is addiction. That idea is not new to the Vineyard. For Augustine, too, addiction was the prototype of sin. But the late twentieth century is more diagnostically oriented than the late Roman world. Here is Augustine: "This was just what I longed for myself, but I was held back, and I was held back not by the fetters put on me by someone else, but by the iron bondage of my own will."[7] At the Vineyard: "We are all addicts!" roared a Vineyard leader at the regional conference I attended at Wheaton College in Illinois. He strode back and forth on the stage, pummeling the air with his fist, insisting that we turn to addiction to fill the emptiness inside, to deal with loneliness, to compensate for our disappointing jobs and marriages.

The message is that while "addiction" solves none of these problems, God does, and would do so immediately—if you could accept that he loves you. One Easter morning at the California Vineyard, an associate pastor began her teaching by observing that most people in the room still felt wretched sometimes, despite the resurrection. "If it *is* true that Jesus died on a cross, and took my shame and my guilt and yours too to death with him, and then he rose back to life, and invites you and me into that new risen life, then how come it still feels so bad in this world at times?" She answered this question not with a philosophical explication but with some practical advice: If you feel lousy, it is because you are not taking advantage of God's offer to make you feel good: "Shame comes when we become aware of our own sin, and also the sin done to us, the wrong things done to us that hurt us. When I feel shame, it feels like I'm a dirty little crow in a room full of fancy flamingos, marked by whatever is dirty and bad and worthless."

That's the human state. You feel like a dirty little crow in a room full of fancy flamingos. You feel like you deserve your filth. "How," she asked, "does the resurrection of Christ reverse that within me, and that within you?" The basic answer: It just happens when you accept that the story is true, and feel loved: "When I see [the shame and guilt] within me and ask Jesus for help, he takes [it] for me and dies it on the cross."

The point is that the real problem with which we all struggle is not God's judgment but our own. *God* believes that we are worthwhile and loves us for ourselves. *We* feel shameful and unworthy, because we magnify our guilt and hold ourselves responsible for our pain. If we really believed in God's love, we wouldn't feel that way.[8] There is no threat of a fiery damnation. The closest I ever heard a Vineyard pastor come to a mention of hell was one Sunday when the speaker said that at the end of time, when they rolled the movie of Christ's life, we could be part of the credits, or we could end up on the cutting-room floor.

It would be too strong to say that in this church heaven has disappeared along with hell. Vineyard pastors do talk about heaven. "If this is good, just think of the joys of heaven!" a pastor exclaimed on a Sunday morning. But the future recedes in these churches. Your pain and suffering are now. Your joy and redemption—if you accept Jesus as your savior—are also now. A sermon is not meant to frighten you out of your misbehavior; it is meant to be like a door opening from a raw, chilly evening into a cozy room. Here is a story given to me when I joined a Vineyard prayer group:

THE SAMURAI AND THE MONK

A big, tough samurai once went to see a little monk. "Monk," he said, in a voice accustomed to instant obedience, "teach me about heaven and hell!"

The monk looked up at this mighty warrior and replied with utter disdain, "Teach you about heaven and hell? I couldn't teach you about anything. You're dirty. You smell. Your blade is rusty. You're a disgrace, an embarrassment to the samurai class. Get out of my sight. I can't stand you."

The samurai was furious. He shook, got all red in the face, was speechless with rage. He pulled out his sword and raised it above him, preparing to slay the monk.

"That's hell," said the monk softly.

The samurai was overwhelmed. The compassion and surrender of this little man who had offered his life to give this teaching to show him hell! He slowly put down his sword, filled with gratitude, and suddenly peaceful.

"And that's heaven," said the monk softly.

Author unknown

In this story, heaven and hell are within us. They are emotions.

Most middle-class Americans continually work to manage their emotions: "I *tried hard* not to feel disappointed . . . I *made* myself have a good time . . . I *tried* to feel grateful." The sociologist Arlie Hochschild drew attention to what she called "emotion work" by pointing out that in late-twentieth-century America, many jobs demand emotion management as a condition of employment.[9] Part of the job description of being a flight attendant is to be kind and warm to passengers, whether or not you got enough sleep the previous night and whether or not you'd really prefer to smash the coffeepot down onto the head of the annoying drunk in seat 27B. But that kind of emotion work is emotional performance. (In fact, Hochschild later called this learned performance "emotional labor.") You *wanted* to hit him on the head with the coffeepot when he yelled at you, but *instead* you restrained yourself and smiled politely. Christians want to do more than politely display certain emotions. They try hard to behave in what they take to be a Christian way, but they also expect that the person who knows God will not simply *perform* those emotions, the way an annoyed flight attendant performs warmth and kindness, but will *feel* them spontaneously and automatically. And they attribute the capacity to feel this warmth and kindness not to good emotional management but to the ability to connect to God and thus to feel his love. They give a special name to this God-nurtured capacity: it is the "heart."

Heart is a near-sacred word for evangelical Christians.[10] In *The Way of the Heart,* the Catholic contemplative Henri Nouwen, whose writing appeals deeply to contemporary evangelicals, presents the heart as a mystic collapse: "that point of our being where there are no divisions or distinctions and where we are totally one."[11] People talk about having "a heart for" something: the poor, leading worship, helping out in a school. They talk about God "putting [something] on my heart," by which they mean that they really want to do something, like play the violin. To say that something happens "in your heart" means that the experience is private, personal, deeply felt, and spontaneous. At the same time, it is a claim that you feel this way because God wants you to feel this way, and that these feelings are really God's. In the Vineyard, people spoke about the heart as George, a graduate student in chemistry, did one afternoon:

Every once in a while there's like times when I'm just, like when it's like wow, something is different in prayer. It doesn't feel like it was just part of the daily routine, I just feel it was something more like there's some sort of connection, I'm more really talking to God.

[How do you feel?] It feels better. I don't feel like I'm thinking of what to say, like everything is just sort of coming from my heart, not from my mind.

Congregants are supposed to develop their heart. Once again, it takes work.

When Sarah talked about the heart, she talked about a physical barrier built out of emotional hurt between one's most private core and the outer world. When you felt hurt, you closed the barrier and withdrew; when God reached in past the barrier with love, the barrier melted, and in turn you felt the pain of others and loved them in turn. "I was praying this weekend for someone who has really closed up a part of her heart," she told me once. "She's just been really hurt. The way I saw it, her heart was doubled over, with a big fold, like she had pressed it shut. And I saw God reach his hand up and his fingers just fit perfectly into that crease, into the dark recesses of her heart." Sarah knew that hidden pain, she said. She had tried to hide from God herself, to not speak out loud in prayer the things she did not want to acknowledge or want God to know. She said that as she began to trust God, she developed a heart that could help her to help others. "Sometimes it hurts physically to feel physical things in your body that are painful to feel. Emotionally it is painful to be able to see things about someone's life, to feel that pain. And if your heart isn't compassionate, you don't even feel it and you don't see it. So it just takes that deepening of your relationship with God to be able to accept more of his love, to let him stretch your heart in these ways. People prayed for me a lot that God would stretch my heart and to be able to take more in."

The "stretching" of Sarah's heart made her feel like she was a different person with other people: "Everything changed. Everything looked different." She felt like she had this private, perfect, almost nonverbalizable relationship with someone who loved her more deeply and more completely than any human. The fact that he didn't have a face to hide behind made him even more intimate, closer, and more personal than a husband. "I feel like there's nobody on earth that knows me, nobody, the way he does," she said.

I remember how startled I was, back in our first conversation, when I asked Sarah whether she felt God was satisfied with her. She told me that God didn't think that way. I had in mind all those medieval damnation images and the angry God in his garden. But Sarah thought of God not in terms of good or bad behavior but as a challenge of recognition. If he was real to you, if you recognized him, you would feel his love. "The effort to be 'good for God'—that's just silly. A rose doesn't wake up in the morning and grunt and try to give off a scent. A star doesn't wake up in the morning and try to shine. The goodness of God is just poured into you. All you do is to reflect it back. It isn't anything you need to create."

Yet Sarah certainly thought that knowing God entailed an enormous amount of work. That's where the concept of developing your heart came in. When you recognize and relate to God, your heart changes, and if it hasn't changed, you do not know him.[12]

If we humans know that it is God with whom we speak, then we must be changed—or we do not know truly know that it is God. (Sarah also believed that the reverse was true: that God changes in response to our recognition and becomes the God we imagine or, as Sarah might say, the God we need.) But while the idea of the heart invites people to imagine recognition in terms of a mystic collapse—God's will becomes my will—what congregants actually do in practice is to think in terms of a mapping back, an attempt to reorganize their interior emotional life by modeling themselves on God or, more precisely, on Christ. That is what spiritual texts like *The Imitation of Christ* teach. *The Imitation of Christ* (published anonymously in the early fifteenth century and still immensely popular today) focuses entirely on emulating the character of Christ: "Whoever wishes to understand fully the words of Christ must try to pattern his whole life on that of Christ."[13] Lytton Strachey reported that one of his eminent Victorians, General Gordon, carried *The Imitation of Christ* onto the battlefield at Khartoum. These days you can buy *The Imitation of Christ* digitally recorded so that you can listen to it as you launder. Its aim and practice is traditionally called "spiritual formation." Dallas Willard, the author of *Renovation of the Heart: Putting on the Character of Christ,* describes spiritual formation as the "process of forming the inner world of the human self in such a way that it becomes like the inner being of Christ himself."[14]

This mapping back from the concept of God/Christ to the self makes the process of coming to know God different from the process of learning the meaning of abstract terms like *time*. If we imagine time by drawing on more familiar experiences of moving through space, and if congregants at the Vineyard imagine God by drawing on more familiar experiences of their mind and everyday social life, then renovating the heart reverses the process. The congregants must learn to take their model of God—given content by the individual but also reinterpreted by the understanding of God within the church—and then use that model to reshape their own emotional worlds. This is an awkward task because one cannot just decide to feel Christ-like love, as if deciding what wallpaper to use in the living room.

As a result, much of what people do and say at the Vineyard resembles psychotherapy. The insight at the core of psychoanalysis and psychotherapy is that we cannot change our emotions deliberately. Psychotherapy is itself a kind of mapping process, what the literary critic Walter Benjamin called "mimesis," or imitation. Clients experience their emotional lives as flawed, and they go to therapists to learn from them a healthier model of self and healthier patterns of response, and then to imitate those models.[15] But the process is notoriously indirect and unpredictable. That is why there are so many different psychotherapies, and why those seeking help move from one therapist to another to find one that works for them.

Emotions are complicated packages of bodily behavior: we have subjective feelings, to be sure, but those feelings depend upon our cognitive appraisal of events (his tone was curt, and so I interpret him as insulting me); our appraisal gives rise to feeling (anger) and to physiological response (my heart races, blood rushes to my face); and we display our emotion for others to read (I clench my fists; I raise my voice). Much of this complexity happens out of our awareness and, seemingly, out of our control. We feel shame (a crow among the flamingos) for an act we did not commit and for emotions we cannot control. Most therapy focuses on figuring out and fixing the cognitive appraisal that generates the bad feeling, but because those models are often not consciously accessible, this can be hard to do. It becomes the therapist's job to make the client feel inherently lovable: to feel like the kind of person who can be loved because the client is not (as the client usually thinks) worthless, inadequate, condemned. When people feel lovable, they are less likely to interpret a curt tone as an insult. The common wisdom is that for the therapy to work—any style of therapy, for any client—clients need to want to change; to be able to decenter sufficiently to see themselves from a different perspective; and to practice new emotional habits. The cliché is that the client must feel strong emotion during therapy for the therapy to do any good, because only when emotions are strong can old, self-punishing emotional habits be recognized and altered.

It is these therapeutic preconditions—strong emotions, decentering, and an intense desire to change and to practice—that the churches that focus on God's unconditional love seek to create in their congregants. The social life of evangelical churches is rich in specific emotional practices—recognizable patterns in the way people act and express feelings, patterns of behavior and response performed again and again, the stuff of which culture is made. The church does not name these emotional practices directly. No one ever lists them off or describes them as so many ways that people learn to behave in church. Nor do people participate in any of these practices in the same way. But if you go to a church like the Vineyard, you know that these are the kinds of things people do and the kinds of emotions they express while doing them, and they probably come to seem not only natural but like the kinds of things you should do in order to know God. These emotional practices create powerful feelings. They decenter the congregant. They lead the congregant to want to change and to practice the change. In short, they create the conditions for real emotional change to occur.

During the time that I spent attending the Vineyard, I identified a half dozen of these emotional practices. They all had the same end. They were all ways of practicing the experience of feeling loved by God. The simplest way of describing them is that just as in therapy, people are pushed to experience powerful, bad, explosive emotions while being told that they are safe and loved. Then they are invited to think about themselves as loved and to practice loving. But these practices are different in a church from ordinary psychotherapy because the "therapist" is more powerful than any human therapist and also more perfect. Because he is also invisible, human members of the group stand in on his behalf, but one does not have to attribute their imperfections to the therapist. And whereas the human therapist coaches the client, takes the client's money, and goes away, God sticks around for all eternity. It is a remarkably effective system, if you can take it seriously.

The first of these practices I came to call "crying in the presence of God." I remember standing in church one Sunday morning, not long after the pastor had finished preaching, when I noticed a large man sobbing in the next section. This was no quiet, embarrassed sniffling. He began with great gulping sobs, and then he began to bawl. The band was playing softly, and the pastor was asking people to come forward for prayer. The big man stumbled up a few yards and then fell to his knees. Members of the prayer team came over and began to pray over him, and as they prayed, his sobs redoubled. Afterward I approached people I knew and asked them what was going on. I think I was expecting some big, dramatic story that everyone would know about. But no one knew any story. More to the point, they were surprised by my surprise. Bawling out loud was just something people did sometimes in church.

They cried a lot. People cried when other people prayed out loud over them. When people went up for prayer at the end of church, someone from the prayer team would stand by them, take a look at their face, and as often as not go over in a businesslike way to tug a tissue out of the box on the amplifier and then walk the congregant over to the side as the band picked up again. People cried at the sermons. They cried in house group. The pastors would sometimes cry as they stood before the congregation. At one conference I attended, four men spoke, one after the other, and every last one of them wept by the time he was done. Crying when people prayed over you was so common that not to cry turned you into a social category. "You know," someone would say, "the kind of person who never cries when you pray for them." If people didn't cry when others prayed for them, it became something they had to explain. "I don't cry," a woman confessed to me. "I mean, it's not that I'm not receiving the Holy Spirit. I'm just a thinker."

And as people cried as others prayed over them, those who were praying aloud were asking God to make them feel safe, loved, and protected—wrapped in his arms, soothed by his embrace, washed by his forgiveness. I came to think of these events as prayer "huddles": one person in the center, usually crying and in distress; the rest of the group crowded around with their hands on the person or (if they could not reach) their hands on the people who were touching the person in the center, as if the physical connection carried a supernatural connection. (Many of them believed it did.) In a prayer huddle, the person being prayed for does not talk, but those around the person do. They see that person's actual emotional experience—sobbing in the center of the huddle—and in many different ways, they say that God loves this person, inadequate and unworthy as that person so clearly feels himself or herself to be.

Praying over someone headed for Africa and visibly anxious about it, the pastor intoned, "God, you know the anxious thoughts she has. Help her to contain them and to feel calm in your presence." The congregants praying for her are loving; she is distraught. Congregants gathered to pray for the young medical student who had been assigned to a medical residency two thousand miles away from her husband, and while her tears redoubled, we prayed that they would reach a decision that would bring them peace. When our house group gathered around one of our members to pray because the young woman had just learned that she had to move out of her apartment and she needed dental surgery and she had no money for either, she became hysterical, while we prayed that God would hold her in his arms so that she would feel his comfort. The people praying usually said some version of this: that the person prayed over would experience, as the pastor put it, "what we were created for, which is to know you and to experience your love."

To me, the pattern evoked a small child crying in her mother's arms. The child doesn't really believe that her mother can change what happened on the soccer field, but the immediacy and the importance of the mother's love can make the moment on the soccer field seem less powerful. When you are hugged by your mother, the memory of that small disaster, whatever it was, loses it ability to cause you pain. It fades from a catastrophe to a blip. That's what the emotional practice of crying as someone else prays is meant to achieve. It is meant to remind you that you are loved completely by a great and mighty God and that the world, imperfect as it is, is good, and all else is like a child's fumble with a muddy ball. Granted, no one ever said that they thought that this was what the crying accomplished. What they said explicitly was that those who cry are feeling the Holy Spirit.

The second emotional practice that I identified I call "seeing from God's perspective." This was a particularly difficult practice for me to grasp because at its center lies a disconnect from the anthropological way of thinking. For me, one of the disorienting things about talking to evangelical Christians is that they say such vague, paradoxical things about God. God is near when he is far away. The years when you saw only one set of footprints, that was when he carried you. Spiritual manuals are full of this language. Here is a sample, from a book used in my prayer group:

> Prayer is not just a means of sustaining us through our linear journey (though it does that too) but is itself the reality of our journey. It is not primarily a calm interlude in our day, a "quiet time," but the very essence of our being.[16]

This is not prose in which the words are like arrows that shoot out and strike something in the world, the way the word *squirrel* picks out a rodent with a furry tail.[17]

I remember visiting a woman who practiced "spiritual direction." I wanted to know what she did during a spiritual direction session that was different from what a therapist would do in a therapy session. I was expecting her to say something about the content of her talk with clients. Instead she smiled broadly, opened her arms, and said, "I love!" I had asked a question that I thought was a simple request for information, and in return, she asserted an emotional feeling.

At first it used to frustrate me to ask someone a question that I thought was clear and direct, and to be given an answer that seemed vague and unspecific. Then I realized that I was thinking like an observer. I was looking at an experience, and I wanted people to put words to it so I could describe it and understand how it differed from other experiences, as if I were a naturalist traveling to another country and trying to characterize the new and different place. But the people I spoke with were not thinking like observers. They wanted to *do* something with their words; they wanted to make a difference to the person who was listening to them, to make them feel confident that God loved them and that the world was good. Many years ago the philosopher John Austin described certain kinds of phrases as "performative": "I christen this ship the *Mary Ann*"; "I promise." These kinds of phrases don't just describe things in the world. They act. When you say the words "I do" in a marriage ceremony, you change the world in a way quite different from when you comment that the sky is a brilliant blue.[18]

One evening I brought my tape recorder to house group. Here is the anthropologist's question:

So what does it mean to say that God is always at work around you?

Here is the response:

> When I hear the words "God is always at work around you," I think
> that okay, God is doing something at this moment to accomplish his
> purposes. The Father is always at work. The Son is looking out for
> his Father.

To the anthropologist—to the person trying to figure out exactly what
the phrase "God is always at work around you" means—this response is
completely useless. It simply repeats the original statement. But to evangelical Christians, it is an invitation to look at your life from God's loving perspective rather than from your own more limited understanding.
When people in church made these vague, broad comments, they were
not trying to describe something. They were trying to change the listener's perspective from that of a scared human looking out at life's challenges to that of a creator God looking down with love.

This is the way the many, many spiritual manuals for sale in the
evangelical world use language. People read these books by themselves,
of course, but they also often read them together in house group. The
group will read a chapter a week and then talk in the group about the
way the chapter affected them. Sometimes the book comes with exercise
plans and questions for discussion, which underscore the point that these
books are tools to teach you how to do rather than a set of observations
that describe.

The most famous and successful of these manuals, as I have mentioned before, is *The Purpose Driven Life,* published in 2002 and written by Rick Warren, which has been used in the house groups of many
evangelical churches across the country and indeed the globe. Evangelical
churches often buy the book in bulk for their congregants.

"It's not about you," begins the first sentence of *The Purpose Driven
Life.* "The purpose of your life is far greater than your own personal ful-
fillment, your peace of mind, or even your happiness. . . . If you want to
know why you were placed on this planet, you must begin with God. You
were born *by* his purpose and *for* his purpose." Rick Warren assumes that
his first task is to persuade the reader that God exists, that God is good,
and that the reader must learn to see himself or herself from God's point
of view. You are not supposed simply to read the book. You are supposed
to practice it. The book has forty chapters, for forty days, which you can

do at the rate of one per day. At its front there is a page that is a contract: "With God's help, I commit the next 40 days of my life to discovering God's purpose for my life." You are asked to sign it, along with your partner. There is a line for Rick Warren's signature too. He has already signed.

For each day there is an exercise, marked by a little box. For day two:

THINKING ABOUT MY PURPOSE

Point to Ponder: I am not an accident.

Verse to Remember: *"I am your Creator. You were in my care even before you were born."* Isaiah 44:2 (CEV)

Question to Consider: I know that God uniquely created me. What areas of my personality, background, and physical appearance am I struggling to accept?

Warren says that you should imagine your life as a test in which you reveal your character in every moment of the day. "God constantly watches your response to people, problems, success, conflict, illness, disappointment, and even the weather! He even watches the simplest actions such as when you open a door for others, when you pick up a piece of trash, or when you're polite toward a clerk or waitress."[19]

Rick Warren never talks about failing the test for good. He never talks about damnation. He never suggests that God will punish you. He identifies those thoughts as the bad thoughts you need to get rid of. In fact, the book reads like a folksy, spiritualized manual for cognitive behavioral therapy, which trains clients to identify and to interrupt specific negative thoughts and to replace them with others. Such therapists often ask their patients to write down the critical, debilitating thoughts that make their lives so difficult and to practice using different ones. That is precisely what Warren invites reader to do. He describes thoughts he thinks readers have but don't want, and offers replacements, which are described as the thoughts readers will have if they really allow themselves to believe that they are watched with great love by God. He insists that this God wants to be there, your best friend, consciously involved in every aspect of your life: God "wants to be included in every activity, every conversation, every problem and even every thought." Warren also reminds readers that this awareness takes practice, but that they can learn to do it: "You must train your mind to remember God." And he insists that if readers practice this awareness of God, they will become the loving, caring, good people God wants them to be, because they will know that they are deeply loved and cared for by the creator of the universe.[20]

The third emotional practice, "practicing love, peace, and joy," was a little more familiar and obvious to me. People set out to rehearse the emotions they would expect to have if God were real. It is thought admirable to create a home that is peaceful, even if—perhaps particularly if—the peace comes at the expense of the normal American life. For example, a young primary school teacher at the Chicago Vineyard felt bombarded by the world. So she and her husband decided not to have a television set in the house. They didn't subscribe to a newspaper. They didn't have a radio. She even turned off the radio in the car so she could feel calm when she drove to her school. She thought that if anything really important happened, someone would tell her.

Sometimes this practice of the right emotions was explicitly associated with acting as-if, despite your doubts. One winter morning in the California Vineyard, the pastor, Frederick, spoke about the time when he first became a Christian. By the time I met him, Frederick was the senior pastor of this Vineyard, a church that he, like Arnold, had built from nothing into a congregation of several hundred.

Frederick, now a tall, bald man of great rectitude, told us that when he was in college, just after he became a Christian, he went to an InterVarsity picnic, and the people seemed so nerdy, he decided he wasn't going to spend time with Christians. Then he started to get into fistfights for no reason. "When I got miserable enough, I turned to God. I didn't quite believe in him yet, but I turned to him because I was desperate, and I said, 'What do you want me to do?' And the words came through my mind: 'Stop drinking, stop chasing women, and go back to that InterVarsity group you thought you were too good to belong to.' I knew immediately that those were not my words." He decided to do what he called an "experiment." He decided to act as if it really were God talking to him and to follow those instructions. And lo and behold, his life changed radically. "The promise of God is that if you follow him, you will be changed. If you practice kindness, you'll get more kind. If you practice love, you become more loving." Behave as if the promise is true. Just try it.

The less obvious consequence of this idea that one should practice love, peace, and joy is that performing the emotion can become more important than its outcome. Feeding the homeless can seem more pressing than calculating when the homeless need food. Supporting the young mission team can feel more urgent than thinking about what the mission effort will do. And asserting a stance on some issue—abortion, pornography, stem cell research—can feel more necessary than analyzing the impact of the stance, a difference of perspective that liberal observers sometimes fail to understand.

Young Christians—usually after they have graduated from college but before they hold a career job—sometimes decide that they should live the mendicant, love-centered life that the Gospels attribute to Christ and his disciples. They quit whatever money-earning job they have, live on handouts from friends, parents, and church members, and express love, peace, and joy in whatever way God leads them. They assume that they are doing his work; he will provide the rent. I watched with alarm as a competent, college-educated woman in her mid-twenties decided that she was going to "depend on God" rather than worry about getting a paying job. She liked to be a loving presence among the homeless people in the park, so she decided that she would give up her apartment, stay in a friend's living room, only spend the money that people at the church gave her, and spend time in the park. To me, it seemed somewhat irresponsible, not to mention of uncertain benefit. When I mentioned this to Arnold, he told me that she was learning what it had been like to be an early Christian: "Go sell what you own . . . and follow me" (Mark 10:21). Arnold told me that he had lived like that for a while in his early twenties. And in fact the more I looked, the more I saw young people apparently dropping out of the workforce to staff the twenty-four-hour "prayer furnace"; to volunteer at a shelter; to go on a mission.

While the determination to practice being Christ-like was sincere, here too there was often an element of play. One morning a woman with a law degree stood before the church to explain that she was committed to serving the poor with Christ's love. She'd been offered a job in Los Angeles, but she felt that God was calling her to stay in Chicago—those were the words she used—so she turned it down. While waiting, she decided that she and her husband should spend no more than ten dollars a week for food, although she was grateful that her roommates spent more. She spoke about how hard it was and how she was learning from this experience more of what people in the developing world suffer. She said that she and her husband were losing weight. But I also thought I caught a twinkle of excitement. She was tapping into her inner hippie.

I call the fourth emotional practice "God the therapist." When congregants talk about their relationship with God, they sound as if they think of God as some benign, complacent therapist. Sometimes this is explicit. "It's just like talking to a therapist," Sarah said, "especially in the beginning, when you're revealing things that are deep in your heart and deep in your soul, the things that have been pushed down and denied." And just as you expect your therapist to take the rage and still maintain the relationship, congregants yell at God with a kind of toddler's rage (as they imagine it), and still their God continues to listen patiently, and he understands. He knows why you are so upset, why you needed to kick. Jane, the young lawyer in Chicago, once told me that she and God had gone off to sulk at each other, but she knew that this wasn't "really" what was going on with God: "With God, like I can throw a temper tantrum in front of God, and God can say, 'It's okay to be upset. We'll resolve it one step at a time.'" She can be childish, insecure, irritable, irrational, outraged. She doesn't have to worry that God's feelings will be hurt.

The psychoanalyst Roy Schafer once described the emotional style to which the good analyst aspired as the "analytic attitude:" perfectly attentive, perfectly interested, empathic, responsive, focused always on the analysand's needs and not his own, interested in understanding the analysand's psychical reality and not his own.[21] Schafer thought of this style as a goal rather than an achievement; so far is it from the everyday mode of human experience that he called the analyst's ability to express it within the analytic session a "second self." But God expresses the analytic attitude perfectly. He is unfettered by the normal human selfishness and petty jealousy that make it so difficult for a human being, however well trained in psychoanalysis, to be perfectly responsive.[22]

Rachael, a petite young Asian woman at the Chicago Vineyard, was very clear that the big disadvantage of her human therapist was that she could lie to him. He didn't really know what she was thinking, so that when she didn't tell him, he didn't know. She liked her human therapist. Like many people in therapy, she talked to him in little daydreams throughout the week—arguing with him about something he had said in the last session, elaborating something she'd said, organizing her thoughts so she would be able to use the next session well. But she didn't always trust him. The fact that he was human meant that there were times when he was tired or distracted, and she noticed this. And of course, he could go away, take a job in a different city, or even just "fire" her, cut her off and refuse to see her anymore: "With your therapist, you play this game you don't really play with God. Like in therapy you have to decide how much to be attached and how much to take risks. Things like that. You don't have to consider that stuff with God."

So she saw God as a better therapist than her human one. He was a more perfect companion, to begin with: "Like you're sitting in the back of a classroom and you have a friend sitting next to you and you're making fun of the professor and what other people are saying. It's very intimate and it's just the two of you and it's kind of like this inside joke." God was more available than her human therapist. She didn't have to save up things to say in that weekly hour. She could talk to him throughout the day. She talked to him about the same kinds of things she talked about in therapy, and when she was upset about something, she talked to God more. "You have all these thoughts, and they all get tangled up. Prayer is almost like housekeeping, like your room's really messy and you're cleaning it up. It's like you gain a perspective."

But God, because he is perfect, has a downside as a therapist, and that was why Rachael still paid good money to a human one. Ultimately, the point of therapy is to see the mistakes we make in ordinary human interaction. Freud thought that the value of psychoanalysis is that people are blind to the habitual, unconscious assumptions that they make about other people and that an analyst who listens carefully and empathically can figure out what those assumptions are and explain them. Analysts give analysands "insight," and insight leads to change. But the insight can occur only when analysands are forced to see those mistakes bluntly. That is why transference is useful. *Transference* is the name for the intense emotional feelings that analysands develop for their analysts, and that each analysand experiences with the unique emotional blueprint through which we each interpret the world none of us can see clearly. When the analyst offers an insight, and the analysand bursts into tears because he is so extraordinarily generous, or becomes angry because he is so stunningly demeaning, she can see in those dramatic responses the implicit assumptions she makes about other people in her life, her "assumptive world." Often it is the analyst's mistakes that provoke the most intense response: he forgets something he's been told before, or misremembers a conversation, and the analysand's emotion explodes.[23]

God makes no such mistakes. Moreover (as congregants recognize), because the most human characteristics of God's personality—the way God loves, the way God criticizes, the tone, as it were, of God's voice— are shaped out of your own private emotional blueprint, God cannot confront you with an interpretation that on some level you do not know. Rachael knew this: "Obviously I believe that God is real. But there are a lot of attributes of God that are true but unreachable by me. So the God I chose to create, I think that has a lot to do with who I am. I think that when you get to know God, you're really getting to know yourself. It's almost like pure transference." Therapists sometimes say that the most important learning in psychotherapy comes when the patient who has deified the therapist learns that the therapist can have feet of clay. God can never be a normal human being whom you, out of your neurosis, have mistaken for a God.

On the other hand, God does offer a collapse into wordless identification that no human therapist provides. Congregants would put time aside to do nothing but talk in their heads (and sometimes out loud) to God. They would talk and talk, and they would daydream in vivid images, and they often felt that they had really learned something about themselves through this time they spent in quiet thinking about their past. But they would also often say that the prayer they enjoyed most was the quiet time when the interaction became nonverbal and they experienced themselves as spending time with God in a happy, soothing, wordless embrace. "I always start off talking," Rachael said, "but then you get into this place where you just feel so connected, and then your thoughts are flowing into God and his response is flowing into you, and then even that gets blurry and you just feel this oneness. And that feels good."

Not everyone can do this. You cannot have these feel-good blurries unless you experience God as fundamentally benevolent. At church, people were sharply aware that many people do not actually experience God as a loving presence. They agreed with Rachael that whatever people were taught by scripture and by sermon, their actual expectations of God's character came straight out of their own emotional history. In particular, most people assumed that someone's experience of God was based upon their experience of their father.

I call the fifth emotional practice "reworking God the Father" because congregants were acutely aware that for many people, this was a problem. Admittedly, for some it was not. (I never heard mothers discussed in this context.) David, a successful middle-level manager at a large engineering firm, said that he had a very good dad. "He wasn't a Christian when I was young, but he was a good father. So naturally when I think of God as a father, I don't have a lot of barriers. I'm not thinking of a God who wants to hurt me and is angry at everything, that kind of thing." But most had to set out deliberately to rework their sense of God as father because their own father did not offer an ideal template.

Robert, the middle-aged realtor, told me that his life with his human parents made it more difficult for him to respond to God. His mother, who was diagnosed with schizophrenia, had psychotic delusions about God, and that made it hard for Robert to take religion seriously when he was young. But when he actually became a Christian in his late thirties, his problem was his father. Robert's dad was a tough, hard man, a diesel truck mechanic who had spent thirteen years in the Marines and, Robert thought, had never gotten over the rigidity and stress of his assignment during the Korean War. He beat his kids freely. Robert said that he hadn't known any better: "He was a really good person in some ways. He did the best job he could. Kids don't come with an owner's manual. He gave us a good Christmas every year. But emotionally he really wasn't there for us. The intimacy wasn't there." Robert believed in God. He'd even had one of those conversion experiences in which he heard God speak to him audibly in the middle of the night. But he was willing to tell me that he didn't trust God. And while many people told me that they expected God to test them in some way, Robert was the only one who told me that he expected that testing to be brutal: "I think that God wants me to experience doing without, and I feel like I just have the sense that something devastating will happen."

The church believed that these representations of God—what a psychoanalyst would call the "inner object" of God, the emotionally drenched ideas about God that act in the psyche the way memories of a father shape the way the adult child responds to the world—could and should change. They recognized that a person's God-representation carried the emotional valence of a life, and they believed that as the life changed, the representation would change. They believed that a healthy, happy life generated a deep-seated belief in a loving God—and they believed that if you could bring yourself to believe genuinely in a loving God, your life would reflect the resilience of someone who believes deeply that he or she is loved. Rachael remarked, "I feel like everyone has a different notion of who God is. All are equally supported by the scriptures. What happens is that you reach a point where you feel like God's not responding or some-thing's not going well in the relationship. Then you realize you think of God as being someone who's angry or unforgiving or whatever. So then you realize that you have to modify it." As a result, evangelicals support an ever more thriving community of Christian therapists who described their primary task as working with someone's inner God-concept.

This would have horrified Freud, who was notoriously dismissive of those with faith: "Religious ideas are illusions, fulfillments of the oldest, strongest and most urgent wishes of mankind."[24] Psychoanalysts who are religious, particularly those who are Christian, might be admired within the tribe for their courage, but they are regarded with astonishment by their peers.[25]

Ana-Maria Rizzuto is one of the few who have dared walk that line between religion and psychoanalysis. She arrived in the United States from Argentina on the eve of the Dirty War. In Córdoba she had taught in a Roman Catholic seminary, and she had become curious about the vicissitudes of faith and about the way a person's understanding of God could shift over the course of their life. In Boston she retrained as a psy-chiatrist and then as a psychoanalyst, back in the era when psychoanal-ysis still dominated psychiatry and when inpatient stays could last for years. She spent a year on an inpatient unit, serving officially as the chief resident but also talking to the patients about God, and she had access to all the rich data that such wards then collected on their patients: records of hours of extensive evaluation, notes on their daily psychoanalytic psy-chotherapy, notebooks of observations by the nursing staff. She asked patients long, probing questions about the way they experienced God and the way they experienced their families. She went out to meet some of their family members. She concluded that God is not simply a projec-tion of some idealized father, as Freud had suggested. ("A personal God is, psychologically, nothing other than an exalted father.")[26] Instead, she argued that a person's internal representation of God is nearly as complex as an internal representation of a parent; that it draws on the important relationships and powerful experiences in the life of the individual; and that, once formed, it has all the psychic potential of a living person, even if it is experienced only in the privacy of the mind.[27] When *The Birth of the Living God* came out in 1979, it upset the psychoanalytic community so thoroughly that only one disciplinary journal reviewed it and did so negatively, and the rumor circulated that the author was a nun.[28]

But Rizzuto was right, and her conclusions are identical to those that guide evangelical Christian therapists, who believe that God functions like a social relationship—a person—in a congregant's emotional life and that any psychodynamic work they do with a Christian is essentially therapeutic work with that person's relationship with and conception of God.

Margaret became a therapist late in life, after she had become a charismatic Christian, joined the Vineyard, and found herself blessed with the gift of healing. She was a gray-haired matron who had worked most of her life as a senior accountant, but she found her vocation in retirement. She told me that the crucial concept at the church was "power." Invoking the Holy Spirit really *worked*. Margaret loved doing physical healing, but she said that God told her very clearly that he wanted her to focus on inner healing, and although terribly disappointed, that was what she did. She was so emphatic that her primary job, as a licensed Christian psychotherapist, was focusing on people's struggles with "closeness to the Lord," that I did not realize at first that this was the way she understood all human suffering—that when people came in complaining of depression and bulimia, she understood their distress as the result of the harsh and judgmental God-concept that they held. "Most people think that God is exactly the same as their earthly father. So if you have an earthly father who was critical and yelling and not loving and not caring, they think that that's who God is. And when you have the concept of a God that you're supposed to trust and love and that you keep hearing in church that God loves you, and you think of God as this yucky father that you had, it doesn't compute."

In some ways, Margaret did conventional therapy (excluding her forays into demonic exorcism). She talked to clients about the encounters that distressed them, and she tried to get them to see those events from another perspective, one less harsh and corrosive. What made it different from conventional therapy was her insistence that this perspective was God's and that God loved them, and that what made their lives difficult was their failure to perceive this love as genuine. In effect, what she tried to do was to get her clients to use her own loving attentiveness as a model for God's. She knew she'd made a difference when she saw their God-concept change: "If someone believes in a punishing God, then they are going to be afraid of God, and they are going to be angry at God, and they are going to be running around doing everything they can think of to please him so he won't zap them. When I see them begin to relax and just praise him—that's a radical shift."

In fact, this slow reworking of the God-concept was the heart of many house groups and prayer groups. In one of the later groups that I joined, we focused our attention on one member each meeting. This person would talk about what was difficult in her life at that moment (it was a women's group), and we would pray for her. No one described herself as doing therapy in the group. Indeed, when people spoke, they were often quick to distinguish the problems they would bring to a therapist from the spiritual problems they spoke about in group. Problems for therapy were problems about your own sadness or a sense of inadequacy: problems about your everyday human experience. Spiritual problems were about "the movement of God" in your life. In practice, this often meant that the group focused on the way people experienced God and the limitations that their own human life had placed on their ability to trust God and to experience God as truly loving.

The result of all this hard emotional work was that when it succeeded, God became more "alive" for people. What congregants meant by this was that they not only identified God's presence reliably, they responded to him emotionally as if he were a real person, unique and specific, with his own particular way of consoling, encouraging, laughing, and grieving. Here is one woman's struggle to explain what she meant by "alive":

I'm not reading the story, it's like the story is coming alive. During the week I'm so busy I don't have that time just to be still before God and let him come and talk to me. All the other voices crowd in, you know. On the weekend—it sounds so stupid, but when you have that freedom to not worry about time and to be open and relaxed—it's like I feel soothed, and God comes, and he's like "You're fine just the way you are, I love you."

"Alive" mixes together interaction, openness, mutual emotional responsiveness, relationship, and love. You are responding to something external, the external is responding to you, and the back-and-forth feels natural, unforced, and real. When people talked about God's aliveness, they sometimes made squeezing motions with their fingers, as if they were pushing against something springy and elastic.

The sixth and final pattern I've named "emotional cascades." I consider it an emotional practice because people talked about the behavior in church settings and because they recognized immediately what I was talking about when I struggled to describe it. "Ah," someone sighed, "you mean those precious moments when you suddenly really know that God loves you." But unlike these other emotional practices, these moments are not deliberately chosen behaviors (like knowing you should cry when people pray for you) but overwhelming experiences that just seem to happen. They are rare, powerful instants of happy emotional collapse that demonstrate to the congregant (and to whoever was listening to the testimony) that they had personally experienced the absolute certainty of God's love.

At some point in my interviews, as I sat with a teacup in my hand and my tape recorder running on the coffee table, some of the people I was interviewing would start to cry. They did this when they began to describe their relationship with God as something deeply precious, private, special. They seemed to cry because the emotions they felt were so tender, as if they were afraid that if they exposed the relationship to the light, it might begin to fade and lose a little of its power, the way the adored fluffy Snoopy of your childhood can seem small and shabby when you find it years later in an attic box. When they cried, they described a specific emotional memory.

I sat with Suzanne, the mature lapsed Episcopalian, in her tidy sitting room as she spoke about how she had come to experience the Bible as alive, rather than as the dull text it had been for her as a young adult. At one point, tears welled up in her eyes. She said that she had been at the kitchen table ("I remember exactly where I was sitting"), waiting for the plumber to finish the job he was doing in the basement. It was a time in her life when she wanted God to be real but when she doubted. That is, she believed in God in a philosophical way, but she did not really experience him as real. She was reading a magazine story about Jesus, and she mused aloud to herself about whether Jesus really existed. Then she heard—she distinctly heard, as if the sound came from outside her ears, the only time it had ever happened—a voice that said, "Yes. Yes." And she began to cry. She has remembered it always.

The associate pastor described a similar moment in a Sunday-morning teaching.

> I was driving home from grocery shopping in the car, and I stopped at a light, and suddenly for no reason that I could come up with, I was weeping, and I felt a massive and awesome sense of the presence of God in the car with me. It just came, and I had absolutely no control over it. I pulled over to the side of the road—I remember thinking that I was so in love with Jesus at that moment that no one else on the planet could come close. After about twenty minutes of real intensity, the feeling subsided somewhat, but the presence of Jesus stayed with me. I drove home not really ever able to fully express what happened without sounding like I'd taken something illegal.

These special moments are not common in the life of the believer, but they are extremely important. They demonstrate that God matters, not just as an abstract principle of the universe, like gravity, but that God is present for you in particular, and that he cares.

These emotional cascades are overwhelming. Like the pastor in the car, people cry, sometimes so uncontrollably that they have to pull over to the side and stop the car. Often the moment happened when someone was alone, although it would be recounted in public. But sometimes the moment happened in church. Sarah told me that she remembered someone who came to church for weeks on end and stood skeptically in the back. One morning that person began to weep and laugh through her hands, saying, "I get it. I get it." Sometimes people had these moments at the beginning of their Christian life, but for others they occurred when they were far along. The moments were for the most part not as dramatic as the mystical experiences described by William James, where the person seems to be having not only a spiritual experience but also a small seizure.[29] But like mystical experiences, these moments were rare—people typically described just a few—and they were associated with confident knowledge. When they happened, people *knew* that God existed and that God loved them.

Where do emotional cascades come from? They happen in therapy too. Sometimes a great bubble of feeling wells up in a client during a session, and the client sobs and sobs. The rhythm seems a little different in therapy—cascades occur more often, although when people in therapy speak of moments of great insight, they are also usually rare and emotion-drenched. Emotional cascades might, in effect, be "catastrophes" in which the deliberate and repeated practice of strong emotion suddenly and unpredictably gives way, like the sudden, dramatic shifts that can arise from small perturbations, the way a landslide can be triggered unpredictably by a rainstorm. In therapy, the cascades are usually negative. The client remembers how desperate and abandoned he felt when his parents fought; somehow those feelings are evoked within the psychotherapeutic session, and the floodgates open. But in these churches, the emotional cascades that are associated with God are positive. When people reported specific, singular, emotionally intense moments when they realized that God loved them, the primary emotion they described was "joy."

At the Vineyard, people mostly use the word *joy* in two ways, as a rush of happiness (in phrases like "tears of joy") and as a long-lasting inner mood (as in "the joy of the Lord"). As a mood, joy was an inner glow. That was what brought Sam, the business major, into the church in the first place. He met a girl with a "joy that could never be stomped on" and followed her into faith. The rush was associated with the sharp, sudden, astonishing awareness of the presence of God. As another man explained it, "There's this rich, unexplainable joy, joy that comes totally unexpected. It just kind of comes, and it's just almost overwhelming." Sometimes people talked about joy as "being filled with the Holy Spirit," a powerful physical sense of God's presence that flowed through the body. "All of a sudden I just felt joy and there's no reason for it." Once I was at a weekend retreat when a young man collapsed in tears across the room. He'd told me that he felt unsettled in his faith, disconnected from God, and I thought he was crying with the loss. But he was crying because the Holy Spirit had come to him, and he felt joy.

C. S. Lewis owes his status among evangelicals as a beloved Christian writer in large part to the way he characterized this joy as specifically Christian. Lewis entitled his spiritual autobiography *Surprised by Joy*. Its point is that joy is an intense longing, and its discovery is that the longing is for Christ. As a schoolboy, Lewis had abandoned his childhood faith for skepticism. He first experienced joy as an intense passing emotion, an overwhelming rush as he looked at a little toy garden that his brother had made. "It is difficult to find words strong enough for the sensation which came over me: Milton's 'enormous bliss' of Eden (giving the full, ancient meaning to 'enormous') comes somewhere near it. It was a sensation, of course, of desire, but desire for what? . . . the central story of my life is about nothing else." He found that as he grew to adulthood, he recaptured glimpses of the moment through the epics and legends of the European past. Something about the myths of Baldur and Loki enchanted him. But he thought of them as magic, childhood, fairy tale, or romance: "Nearly all that I loved I believed to be imaginary; nearly all I believed to be real I thought grim and meaningless."[30]

Certainly the everyday world Lewis knew was grim. England was in her First World War. Young men were shipped out to the squalid horror of the front lines with diminishing hope that the war had a purpose. Lewis was lucky—he went into the trenches, got sick enough to leave, and lived. He returned to an undergraduate degree at Oxford, stayed to teach, and was elected a fellow at Magdalene College, where he could focus on the medieval literature that he loved. Slowly, what had seemed to be a wispy "let's pretend" became more real for him. One day while riding the bus (it is an odd but obdurate fact that in my years as an anthropologist, I have heard several people describe intense spiritual experiences that took place on buses) he had a moment of joy and realized that he believed in God.

Evangelicals love C. S. Lewis, both for his children's books about the enchanting land of Narnia and for his more explicitly theological writing. Christian Book Distributors, the popular website for Christian books, describes Lewis as the most influential Christian writer of the twentieth century and says of *Mere Christianity* and *The Screwtape Letters* that "no thoughtful Christian's library is complete without these two classics." Indeed, his influence has increased substantially in recent years. *Time* magazine called him "the hottest theologian of 2005."[31] I remember a young woman pausing in the middle of an interview and reaching over to fish out Lewis's *Collected Writings* from the shelf to find a better description of what she wanted to say. "I *love* his writing," she sighed, and pressed the book against her chest.

For many evangelicals, Tolkien, too, is a Christian writer. In fact, Tolkien helped lead Lewis to Christianity, although he was Roman Catholic and Lewis remained true to the Ulster Protestantism of his childhood.

Lewis and Tolkien were part of the same writers' group, the Inklings, the Oxford literary equivalent of the Cambridge Apostles. (Its other famous member was Charles Williams.) For decades they met every Thursday and read aloud their drafts: *The Hobbit,* and then *The Lord of the Rings; The Screwtape Letters, Surprised by Joy, Till We Have Faces,* and eventually, near the end of Lewis's life, *The Lion, the Witch and the Wardrobe,* which Tolkien never liked. Still Lewis and Tolkien meant much the same thing by joy, and they saw it at the center of their stories. In an essay Tolkien wrote:

> The consolation of fairy-stories, the joy of the happy ending . . . a sudden and miraculous grace. . . . It does not deny the existence . . . of sorrow and failure: the possibility of these is necessary to the joy of deliverance; it denies (in the face of so much evidence, if you will) universal defeat and in so far is evangelium, giving a fleeting glimpse of Joy, Joy beyond the walls of the world, poignant as grief.[32]

Joy is the happy fictional ending you believe to be true.

You do not need to be evangelical to know the tears at the heart of Christian joy. For some, reading *The Velveteen Rabbit* is enough. *The Velveteen Rabbit* is a beloved children's tale about a little plush rabbit made real by love—a sawdust-stuffed bunny that belonged to a boy who slept with it every night, took it for picnics in the park, and hugged it so tightly and so often that the plush wore off its nose and its button eyes fell off, but none of that mattered to the boy. Then the boy fell ill with scarlet fever, and the old bunny was put out with his clothes to be burned, to rid the house of germs—and then the bunny discovers, through the grace of nursery magic, that he truly is alive. He discovers that he has hind feet that are not filled with sawdust but can kick, and he bounds off to run with the other real rabbits who have come to the edge of the clearing.

Some people always cry when they read *The Velveteen Rabbit.* They cry because they feel that it *should* be true. They *want* it to be true. It is *emotionally* true. But they know that it is *not* true, not in the world they know.

That is joy, and it is an evangelical Christian emotion because the core of this Christianity is the hope in the face of hope's failure. The difference between the joy of *The Velveteen Rabbit* and the joy of Christ is the enormous amount of work that these Christians do to allow the individual to experience the story not as a tale for children, which is never really true, but as a story that really is true, just not in an ordinary way, not yet. They learn to infuse the absent, invisible being with presence by cherry-picking mental events out of their own familiar experience and identifying them as God; they integrate those events into the awareness of a personlike being by using "let's pretend" play; and then as they shape their own interior world through modeling it on their understanding of this invisible person, they learn to react emotionally to that being, as if that being were alive in an ordinary way, right now.

Another way of describing the learning process is that it takes the imagined dialogues we all live with—the inner voice that comments, guides, interprets, and reflects, not always nicely—and works to make some of the dialogues both more real and more good. When you talk to yourself about your upcoming presentation, you may remember the time you flubbed. When you talk to God, you should experience him telling you that you'll do a good job and that whatever happens will be for the good, and you should believe this inner dialogue. To do this, you must not only learn to feel that the inner dialogue is in part external; you must be able to have a helpful, soothing dialogue.

It is a profoundly social process. It is the evangelical church that teaches discernment, encourages the play, and models the six emotional practices. It is no easy matter to become confident that the God you imagine in the privacy of your mind exists externally in the world, talking back. In the struggle to give the invisible being its external presence, the congregation surrounds the individual and helps to hold the being out apart from the self, separate and external. It is the church that confirms that the invisible being is really present, and it is that church that reminds people week after week that the external invisible being loves them, despite all the evidence of the dreary human world. And slowly, the church begins to shape the most private reaches of the way congregants feel and know.

CHAPTER FIVE

Learning from the Experts

Then Jesus said,
"He who has ears to hear,
let him hear."

Mark 4:9

May Your voice be louder
May your voice be clearer
Than all the others
Than all the others in my life

Jeremy Riddle, "Full Attention"

B Y THIS POINT, we have seen that this kind of evangelical Christian-ity solves the problem of presence with specific faith practices. The problem of presence is that an immaterial God cannot be seen, heard, smelled, or felt in an ordinary way, and so worshippers cannot know through their senses that God is real or, if real, where and in what he is—a problem particularly acute for churches that encourage an inti-mate personal relationship with the divine. So churches like the Vine-yard teach congregants to find God in their minds and to discern which thoughts, images, and sensations might be God's word. The congre-gants practice having minds that are not private but open to the experi-ence of an external God. The churches encourage the imaginative play through which congregants practice interacting with an invisible per-son. In many different ways, they coach congregants to practice feeling loved.

These faith practices change people. At least, after people have spent some time in the church, they begin to speak as if they recognize when God talks to them in their minds. They report vivid imaginative encoun-ters with God that feel like more than "mere" imagination. They say that they feel that God loves them, and that this makes them happy.

A skeptic might scoff at this as so much "discourse"—just the kind of thing that people say when they join such a church and want to demonstrate that they are part of the group. Even anthropologists are sometimes tempted to see culture as shaping the content of thought but not its process. But as I listened to people talk about God, and about the way they experienced themselves in prayer, I began to think that these faith practices and the way they taught people to pay attention to their minds and emotions shaped something about the process of mind itself and that these changes helped people to experience God as real.

I came to this conclusion because I began to notice a pattern in the way people talked about prayer. As we have seen, all the faith practices involve prayer. They are, in fact, prayer practices. The central point of the renewalist evangelical church—on Sunday mornings, in the small house groups, in the endless numbers of books people read, and in the lyrics of the music they play—is that one should build a personal relationship with God through prayer. No instruction is made more plainly or more emphatically. Prayer is understood as the only way to create a relationship with God and indeed the only way to reach God at all.[1] There are manuals about prayer, teachings on prayer, and people who meet together weekly to pray. Every service ends with prayer ministry.

But not everybody prayed easily, and not everyone enjoyed prayer. And then I noticed that hearing God seemed to fall along a continuum, with people who were frustrated in prayer at one end and people who loved to pray at the other. People who didn't enjoy prayer did not pray much, did not think that God talked to them much, and did not have wonderful imaginative experiences with God. They sometimes worried that God did not love them very much. On the other hand, those who loved to pray were likely to talk about becoming so absorbed in their prayer that the ordinary world could fade for them, and their sense of time and place and self would alter. They talked about how vivid their internal world became. Indeed, they talked as if the very architecture of that internal world—their mental images and their sensations—became sharper and richer and more powerful, and they spoke as if their sensory perceptions of the materially external world became heightened. They imagined God vividly, and they had rich, deeply emotional, often playful relationships with God. They felt his love intensely, and they mourned his absence deeply. They said that sometimes they saw or heard or felt the presence of something that was not there in a material way. Most of the sensing was interior, akin to what we think of as the imagination. But every so often, they heard or felt God as if he were a body among bodies. Such occasions were rare, and some people had those experiences, while others did not.

Moreover, people repeatedly told me that prayer requires training and discipline; that learning to pray is hard; that some people are naturally good at prayer; and that some people, who are naturally good at it and who practice, become experts. This suggested to me that there might be a real psychological *skill* to responding to prayer, and that these reported changes were not just pious assertions that people learned to say so that they could appear to be devout. It suggested that as people develop the skill, something changes about the way they use their minds. It also suggested that some people develop the skill more readily than others. But what is this skill, and why are there differences in the way people learn? We begin to answer this question here by narrowing in more precisely on the experts.

As Sarah began to pray intensely, something shifted in the way she responded to her world. By then she had learned how to identify thoughts and images as interactions with God. She had learned to pay attention to her mind with the expectation that God would communicate in images and impressions, and she had begun to identify some of the mental events as instances of hearing God. Part of what she was learning was sheer interpretation. Here, for example, she interprets past thoughts as incipient prayers, responses to God's nudging.

> When I first moved [here], up on the twelfth floor, I used to watch out my window. There was this school right there, and there was a really busy intersection. And I used to do what I called "think" about the people that were driving through the intersection. I would just get like ideas, like they have a medical problem that they're gonna be dealing with today, or there's this on their mind, or I'd watch interactions with kids on the playground under my window and just sort of get ideas about it. I think those were prayers being born, you know, without me really knowing what it was.

But Sarah also made comments that suggested that the quality of those mental events had changed. She was quite clear that prayer practice had altered the way her mind worked: "Everything looked different to me." She told me, for example, that her mental images actually got sharper: "Depending on the prayers and depending on what's going on, the images that I see [in prayer] are very real and lucid. Different than just daydreaming. I mean, sometimes it's almost like a PowerPoint presentation." She told me that over time the images got richer and more complicated. They seemed to have sharper borders. They continued to get more complex and more distinct. She felt that as she became more expert, words would just come to her when she shut her eyes to pray for people, and in her mind they began to crystallize into the forms imprinted by a printer on a page. Sometimes, as she listened to people talk, their words would appear to her almost as if they were being transcribed on paper.

When Sarah talked about these changes, she talked about them as capacities she needed for the "technical" side of the prayer process: what someone praying had to do to enable the prayer process to "work," to reach both God and the person she was praying for in a way that would connect them together. Sarah explicitly understood prayer as a technique, a bidirectional link created by an expert that enabled God to act through the Holy Spirit and enabled the person being prayed for to receive God's act. Sarah believed that to forge that link, one's mind needed to be what she called "open": flexible enough to take in many sensory impressions and disciplined enough to recall the ones needed to connect to the unique person for whom one prayed.

Whatever one makes of the ontological claim that the person praying is a link, prayer clearly *is* a technique: a skilled practice that has to be learned. Like many skills, acquiring it seems to have consequences. Sarah understood the changes she experienced as gifts from God that enabled her to do the work for which he had selected her. I thought they were the consequence of repeated focus on objects held in the mind in a particular way.

It reminded me of learning to run. I began to run back in college, and initially, I ran to lose weight (those pesky ten pounds). But as I learned to push one mile to two, and then to three and five, more changed than my weight. My legs grew lean and taut, their muscles more defined. That's the way Sarah talked about how she changed when she began to pray: "It was like just opening it up, opening up your perceptions and tuning them up in a different way so that even just walking down a street and looking at flowers took on new significance."

Sarah's running muscles were mental images. She didn't set out to change the way she paid attention or to change the intensity of her mental images. Instead, she set out to learn to pray, and she prayed for hours at a time, and her prayers centered on the images that happened to appear to her. As she did that, she seemed to give more focused attention to her sensory world.

> As we were praying, those images came back to mind. For example, one of them was tulips. I noticed as I was walking how different the tulips were. They're all the same species, but they were different colors, they were different sizes. Some of them were still such tight buds, you couldn't even tell what color they were. Some had just started opening, so you could see that they were red or white, but it didn't even look like a tulip yet. Some were perfect, some were past prime, all on the same block. Some in the same bed with one another.
>
> While I was praying for this woman, those images came up. So we prayed that it would be God's timing that would open up those flowers, that she wouldn't try to push a bud open before its time, that she would know what color she was going to be in and things like that. Those things might have come to my mind anyway, but I'd really opened myself up for that in the morning for God to really be planting whatever images I was gonna need in the afternoon. I didn't consciously recall them, I didn't consciously think, *What can I use as an example to get across what I think is happening?* They just came.

Sarah explained to me that it is important for her to be "opened up" because she has to be able to let God give her the images and sensations that she will be able to use in the prayer. But notice the way she sees—how much she remembers about those flowers, how carefully she reconstructs the details, how she has learned to pay attention and to recall. She delights in those flowers, some of them open, some just in bud. And in the process, her mental images seem to get richer, more complicated, and even more defined.

Moreover, the very structure of her experiencing seemed to shift, particularly when she was praying. She told me that she had become more focused when praying, less distractable, more fully engaged with what happened in her mind. She said that when she was praying, time seemed to pass at a different pace than it did when she washed the dishes and answered e-mail. At the same time, she began to feel as if as what she experienced in her mind were more out of her control, as if the experiences were happening *to* her, rather than being images and thoughts she summoned at will.

> It's more spiritlike, and it's like being in a different dimension, being on a different plane of existence. I can see what's going on around me, I can hear the things that are going on around me, but I'm removed from it. It's sort of—to put it in a maybe new age kind of term—it's like an out-of-body experience almost sometimes. And that's the Holy Spirit dimension of God.
>
> The word that sometimes I think of is *flow* . . . when you're just so intensely and completely absorbed in something that you're like, what's going on around you, it's like not a part of your exact consciousness.

Sarah had read Mihaly Csikszentmihalyi's *Flow* some years before I met her, probably along with the rest of America, when Dallas Cowboys coach Jimmy Johnson spoke in a feature aired during the Super Bowl about how much the book had helped his team. Then they won. You can't buy better advertising. Csikszentmihalyi describes a state in which you are so fully absorbed in your work or your play that you don't notice the passage of time. Your mouth feels dry, your mind, alert, your senses, sharp.[2] It's easy to feel skeptical when reading *Flow*. It doesn't really sound like science. It reads like wishful thinking, like an invocation of the state you would like to be in if you made it to the Super Bowl. When one mentions the book to academic psychologists, they sometimes get a quizzical, hesitant look in their eyes. But *Flow* captures something real.

Sarah thought that prayer was an experience of flow, at least when it was working well, when it was good: "Sometimes [when I pray,] I'm amazed at how much time has gone by, how long I've been praying. It is like time is spent a bit differently." She also felt that what happened in the flow of prayer was, in some real sense, not just in her mind—and not under her personal control: "Like my mind is just a screen that they're flashed on. So it's more like watching for the images rather than generating images, I think. Somebody else is controlling that clicker."

God, of course, was the one in charge of the clicker. The images were hers, but they were also of and in another world. She talked about this sense of otherness as if she lived both in a spiritual realm and here on earth; what she seemed to experience was that her internal world—her mental images, her thoughts, her imagination—became as real to her as her everyday external world, but was superimposed upon it.

> I'll be worshipping and hearing the music, worshipping through my own heart, and God will highlight somebody to me, and it's literally like a spotlight is turned on, and I'll just pray for that, whatever. Generally that's prayer not with words, like words can't go on at the same time, but it's also not just babbling incoherently out of one part of your mind while you're concentrating with the other. Somehow processes can happen at the same time, and actually I'll see it like my music, almost like a treble clef and a bass clef, where there's harmony between the two things. Where there's words, there's stuff of the world, and then there's like this melody that's going on that kind of flows between both things.

Sarah was acutely aware of participating in both worlds simultaneously. She would speak as if she were aware of them separately and intermingled: "One day, and it was right when I had been praying for this, I realized that I was praying in the spirit at that same time I was carrying on a very worldly conversation with somebody. I was seeing things like for them and praying about it without a lot of conscious thought. At the same time I was talking to them about something extremely ordinary." At times like these she sometimes felt compelled to pray, to go on and on, as if she could not stop.

Sometimes it seemed as if there was a kind of overflow, as if that intense internal experience "leaked" into everyday perceptions of the dull and normal world. Sarah began to have sensory experiences of immaterial things. She had one back in the beginning, back when she was learning to pray, not long after she began to get up before dawn, as her husband slept, to read her Bible for hours. Back then a voice startled her awake. *Read James,* the voice said, and she knew it was God. "I didn't even know then that James was a book in the Bible." She clearly and distinctly experienced this voice as audible, and she knew that no human had spoken. She said that this had happened a few times—not very often—and each time stood out in her memory like a streetlight on a darkened road. When God tells you to get off a bus, you remember it.

These events happened in many different sensory modalities. She didn't just hear. Almost all of her senses leaked, so that what had to be imagined—because it was spiritual, immaterial, and not externally available to be sensed in the ordinary way—she began to sense as if it were material, real in the world like a table. When she became one of the most relied-upon prayer experts in the church (such people are called prayer "warriors" because they fight for God) and she began to pray for people who were struggling with what she described as evil, she sometimes saw the evil. Here she describes praying for a woman:

> You know, like when you can see a cup of coffee, not the steam, but you can just see how things are distorted behind it from heat rising or the heat rising off the pavement or something like that? It was just like distortion, kind of behind her head. . . . It was like a change in the force field, . . . and I could see it behind her and I could feel it behind me. I didn't have a clue what it was.

For a while Sarah was involved in praying for a local school. Some church members worked there, and they had spoken to her about tensions among the staff. She found that as she prayed, she actually smelled the badness she thought was there.

> I would get these intense smells of like baby poop or rotten meat or horrible . . . [You could really smell that? I asked her.] Yeah. Horrible, almost gaggy kind of thing. Somehow I just knew that it was time to pray for the school. And I didn't know if kids were being molested or kids were being mistreated or what was going on there.

She never tasted God or the devil—to my knowledge, I never met anyone who did—and she never told me that she felt God's touch, possibly because I never asked. Back in the beginning of my research, back when I was talking to Sarah, I didn't probe too closely. I just let her tell me what she thought I ought to know.

As time went on, Sarah's unusual experiences happened more often, although they were still rare. Then there was a whole new category of things that she sensed as being external to her mind but not as external in the material world: they were in her mind, but not in her mind. These things did not seem to have happened before she became a member of the Vineyard and began to pray so intensely: "But lately I've been starting to see things that aren't there, and I know they're not there, and yet they're not just in my mind. It's like being able to see in a different realm."

Sarah spoke to me as if what she was learning to do was to take her inner sensational world more seriously, to treat her thoughts and images and sensations as more meaningful, and deliberately to blur the line between what she would attribute to an internal cause and what to an external one. That, after all, is the point: to learn to experience God—an external presence—interacting with you through phenomena you ordinarily interpret as internal and often as simply distracting. She learned to identify her own internal sensations as partaking in a spiritual realm that was external to her even if it was not part of the material world.

What was striking to an observer was that as she lovingly attended to these internal sensations, the sensations seemed to take on a life of their own and become more and more vivid until she occasionally experienced some of them as if they were located in the external material world, so that she saw and heard and smelled and felt sensations not caused by material things.

If this were just Sarah's story, one might wonder about her stability. After all, we worry about people who see and hear things that are not materially present. But it wasn't.

David's report of the way he had changed after he became a serious prayer person was very much like Sarah's, except that he was unsure how to interpret theologically the psychological changes that he clearly recognized were taking place. When I met him, he was a successful middle manager at a large engineering firm, but he first became an evangelical Christian at the end of high school. He'd grown up in the Texas Methodist Church and found it pretty boring. When he turned sixteen and got his own car, his parents told him that he was old enough to make his own decisions about God, and he stopped attending services. A friend of his urged him to come to a Christian youth group at school. He did and liked it, and he decided to give this more charismatic and engaged Christianity a try. "I felt I had to make a decision," he told me. "You know, the engineering background. Let me think this through logically. So I did the whole 'how do we know the Bible is true' stuff. Then I decided, 'Okay, I'm gonna make a decision based on faith. Like the bridge is gonna stand, and I'm gonna walk on it, and if it falls, I'm gonna blame you.'"

For him, the bridge held. David is a wiry, intense man, with a restless energy that kept him pacing back and forth when he spoke to the congregation on Sunday morning. He wasn't comfortable with the politics he found in evangelical churches down in Texas. He wasn't always comfortable navigating the conversational terrain at work, where some people were deeply religious and others just as deeply secular. By the time I met him, however, he was the kind of committed Christian who tithed and served on committees and in general ran things that needed running. He often spoke to great effect on Sunday morning ("he's so amazing," someone gushed after one of his teachings); he and his wife, Madeline, hosted a weekly house group; and David in addition had begun to shepherd a men's accountability group, a small group where men spoke intimately about the ways they felt they weren't responsible enough for their families and how they wanted to become more so. He and Madeline had the kind of neat, well-decorated house that made me think uncomfortably of my life in my own late twenties, when I lived in university housing with piles of books around an unmade bed. When I admitted this to Madeline, she laughed. "We feel that the house should be a place people from the church can spend time in."

In high school, when David decided that he should pray, he prayed for about an hour a day. He was then reading the Gospel of John. He would begin his sessions by reading for a while and taking notes. Then he would actually get into his closet because it was quiet there—"I had a decent-size closet in my parents' house"—and he would pray on his knees. (Many prayer manuals talk about finding a closet to pray in; David was among the few people I knew who took that injunction literally and plunged in among the boots.) In college, for about a year, he increased his efforts. He fasted every Monday. In the evening, after the fast, he'd pick up a Burger King Whopper and fries—"yeah, I know"—and drive out to an abandoned field. "There used to be a huge cattle field north of this school, and I'd drive there, and I had a blanket. I'd just drive up into this huge field and I'd put the blanket out and I'd eat dinner and [then] I would just pray." He described praying with intense, driven, focused yearning. Time vanished in that field. At first, he said, nothing happened. "I remember there for while I was kind of disappointed because I didn't feel any different." He clearly thought, at the time, that praying intensely should make him feel different. Soon it did. "After a few weeks, it was like God was waiting for me." He could really feel God's presence, he said, as if God were there. He also felt profound rest, and a kind of emotional openness and freedom. He cried a lot. He also told me that people seemed to respond to him differently, which he interpreted as a consequence of supernatural contact. "Things started happening around me." He went to the field every week for a year.

These days when David prays, he gets a lot of imagery. The face of someone he hasn't thought of for a long time will come to him, or he will "have someone on my heart for no particular reason." When that happens, he will pray for them. He was praying one night, and much to his surprise, the image of a woman he knew from church popped into his mind, and she was dancing with grace and freedom. "I felt, praying about the image, 'God, what is this?' Because I wasn't thinking about her . . . So I told her about it, and she was struggling then, and she was so encouraged by that image, that God still sees her just dancing for him." *God* sees her, he said. It was an image in David's head—but both he and she took it as a message from God. He told me that those images had gotten clearer over time.

David told me that sometimes he saw something as if it were real in the world before him, although he knew it was not materially present. When he told me this, he hesitated. He knew it was weird. But he went on to explain that things like that had happened after he had begun to pray. He had felt God touch him, and the touch had been so real, he was startled to discover that no one was there. He had felt that sometimes when he was praying out loud, the Holy Spirit would more or less take charge, and he did not remember what he said, but he felt he had to pray. He felt compelled. And when I asked him whether he had ever heard God speak audibly, he said yes. "Not often, but when I would hear it, it's like when I would hear someone else, like that kind of an audible, not like *Moses* but still . . ." Outside your head? I continued. "Yes." How often, I asked, had that happened? "Very rarely. Probably twice. The first time was when I believe God said my name when I was praying. Actually before I was praying. I was just lying in bed, and I was definitely clearly awake, but it was like my name. I told the pastor about it because I was a little concerned like, am I going crazy? But God wasn't telling me what to do. It wasn't *that* kind of voice."

Not that kind of voice: he paused, he hesitated, he doubted. But the voice had also seemed real to him. "The second time I was at a grocery store, and it wasn't so audible, but I felt like God did a hiccup or something. It was about like a person standing next to me. The voice was like, 'He's Mormon,' and so I started talking to the guy, and sure enough, he was a Mormon. It was as silly as that."

These experiences made him anxious. He took them to be experiences of God, and yet he hesitated to treat them as divine revelation, and he was insistent that an individual's unusual experiences—however real they felt—should not become the foundation of anyone's faith, because there was too much risk that the individual could be mistaken. "I think the safest position to be in is that God doesn't speak to people outside the Bible," he told me. "I mean, people say, 'God's telling me to go shoot an abortion doctor.' It's craziness. Maybe it's a spiritual experience; maybe it's a lot of caffeine."[3] David came back to the ambiguity of these experiences repeatedly. He enjoyed them. He thought they brought people closer to God. But he worried that someone who heard voices could be crazy, and he worried that if people came to faith because of their experiences, they might ignore the teaching. "[The apostle] Paul wasn't going out and saying, 'Hey, experience Jesus.' He was saying, 'Study the word.'"

Sam did not have this uneasiness; he also did not have what he thought of as mental imagery. He is an example of someone with a different sensorium—a different personal pattern of using and attending to one's senses—who nevertheless finds that sensorium enriched and sharpened through the practice of prayer. Sam also illustrates another pattern: that those who become experts are more likely to report dramatic spiritual experiences.

Sam is a blunt working-class guy, blond and big and earnest. He was in high school when he decided to become a Christian. At the time, he was the kind of student other students call a party animal. He used a lot of marijuana, and he drank until he passed out. He liked his blackouts: "The thing I loved the most about drinking was the stories I'd hear about myself that I didn't remember in the morning. I'm funny when I'm drunk." Still, he scared himself one night when he woke up in the backseat of a car belonging to people he didn't know. He started to talk to his girlfriend about his worry and his guilt, and she told him that God could change all that for him. "She's like, 'If you want to accept Christ, he can take that stuff away and give you a new heart.'" He'd encountered Christianity already, when he went to Christian youth groups at his middle school, but those Christians had made him angry. It felt to him as though they wanted to force him to believe something. Now, with his worry and his pounding head and a girl he found captivating, he decided to give it a try. She led him in what many Christians call the sinner's prayer—basically, a confession of sin and repentance coupled with the acceptance of Christ as savior—and then she prayed over him. He told me that he bawled.

Why did he cry? Most people do when they are saved. And most of them say that they do not know why, and that they didn't really know what they were doing. They also talk about feeling light and free. It is one of the great paradoxes of Christianity that these moments, which secular outsiders can interpret as a capitulation to peer pressure and the taking on of prescribed rules and beliefs, are experienced, by someone like Sam, as sacred moments of exquisite freedom. "It just felt like every single thing I had piled on top of me was gone. What I'd said— 'Yes, I accept Christ my Lord and Savior'—it didn't mean a ton to me. But I felt that a million pounds on me were gone, just after I said it." Sam started going to church, but it wasn't until he took the Alpha course and went on its retreat that he felt the power of God flood through him.

The Alpha course is possibly the most common vehicle through which new evangelicals learn about the faith they have embraced. In 2011 the Alpha website stated that more than two million people in the United States and more than sixteen million worldwide had taken the ten-week course. Every Vineyard church I visited ran Alpha at least once a year. The course was created in 1991 by an Englishman named of Nicky Gumbel who had been an avowed atheist until he read the New Testament during his first year at Cambridge and fell in love with it.

When you take the course, as I did in 2005, you attend ten weekly evening sessions, each with a home-cooked meal, and a weekend retreat informally dubbed the "Holy Spirit weekend." You watch a half-hour presentation by Gumbel, speaking in a pleasing, intellectual British accent, to a church full of young, attractive middle-class adults. The tapes are funny, intelligent, relaxed. Gumbel assumes that the listener has doubts. He assumes that it is hard to take this supernatural stuff seriously, although he also makes it clear that those events really occurred. After the tape ends, participants break up into small groups to talk. People are encouraged to talk about their doubt. One evening a woman in my own group explained that she wasn't a Christian because she just couldn't believe that Jesus was the only path to God, and a man remarked that if God hadn't wanted humans to do stem cell research, he wouldn't have made scientists so darn smart.

The Holy Spirit weekend is supposed to change your life. It is meant to be a retreat where the group leaders encourage participants to feel the indwelling presence of God, often for the first time. This does not happen to everyone. But it happened to Sam.

It was the first time that I really felt God's power. So on Holy Spirit Day, my girlfriend and I both went. They were talking about the Holy Spirit and stuff, and then the leader was like, "We're gonna start praying for everybody shortly." She said, "Some of you might be feeling the spirit on you now," and I noticed about myself that my breathing was getting like really deep, and like I was starting to shake a little bit. I just felt like my body had so much energy, and it's like I'm gonna just leap out of my seat and just go running like fifty miles or something. She's like, "Some of you may be sweating," and I'm like, "Yeah, I'm sweating." She's like, "Some of you might have oily palms," and I'm like, "Yeah, I got oily palms." And she's like, "Some of you might be shaking and heavy breathing, and some of you might just be like jittery." And I'm like, "Check, check, check, check, I've got all that." I'm like, "She must have put something in my food or something." She's just like, "I feel the presence of the Holy Spirit right here," and she points at me, but I'm like, "I'm not going up there." You know, I feel really uncomfortable, like nervous and stuff. I don't want to go up in front of all these people. There had to be fifty or sixty people there.

So she's like, "There's also the presence of him over here too," and there's this other girl across the way that's shaking and has the same things going on with her. She stands up and they pray over her. And it was just amazing. They keep praying over her, these two helpers, and the leader is explaining that the Holy Spirit administers to your heart and all this stuff. They have their hands on her, and she just collapses backwards and they catch her. She's just laughing on the floor like you can't wipe the smile off her face.

Then they started praying for me, and I had this, it feels like, not really electricity, but like your body is touched by some kind of extreme power. You're just shaking, like you just can't handle all this stuff that's being poured into you. They're saying, "Come on, Holy Spirit, and fill him up to overflowing." I'm just so jittery, and then they're like, "Is there any gift [of the spirit] you want?" We'd talked about the gifts of the Holy Spirit before. I was like, "I'll take whatever, I'm open to healing, I'm open to tongues, anything, like I don't care, this is amazing." When I said that, I felt like there was somebody else in me like yelling, trying to get out, and I was just overwhelmed in it. And as they prayed over me, my tongue starts moving around, and they say, "Just speak." So I start speaking. I didn't know what was going on, I didn't know what the language was. I got the gifts of tongues that day. It was absolutely incredible. It was the most marvelous gift.

I could hear people praying around me, but it felt like I was in a bubble and that everything outside of this bubble just did not exist. Like it was me and God in this one little tiny capsule, and the rest of the world could go by it a billion miles per hour and I wouldn't care. Time stopped, and where I was felt absolutely weightless.

Note the progression: The group leader suggested, and he experienced. He was one of the few who experienced so dramatically. Yet he does not seem to have faked his response. Sam felt the Holy Spirit with his senses and in his body, and it transformed his life because now, for the first time, he was really sure that God was real. "I would always ask my girlfriend, 'Why do you believe? How do you know that God really exists?' I mean, I know that I accepted Christ my Savior, I mean, I kind of know he's there. But like I'm not a hundred percent sure. And she's like, 'You just know, you'll just know, he'll show you.' After that day, I *knew*."

The experience he reports—he felt electricity in his body; he shook; he spoke in tongues; time crawled to a stop—is a classic Holy Spirit experience within evangelical Protestantism. People describe feeling a great surge of power running through their bodies, so commonly called "electricity" that I started using the term as shorthand to ask people whether they'd ever experienced anything like it. During this surge, people often sweat and shake. They weep or laugh. They feel cut off from the ordinary world, as if they were alone in some private place with God, and they feel terrific. The revivalist Charles Finney, the great preacher of the so-called

Second Great Awakening in the early nineteenth century, may have given the adrenaline surge its best-known narrative form:

> Without any expectation of it, without ever having the thought in my mind that there was any such thing for me, without any recollection that I heard the thing mentioned by any person in the world, the Holy Spirit descended upon me in a manner that seemed to go through me, body and soul. I could feel the impression, like a wave of electricity, going through and through me. Indeed it seemed to come in waves and waves of liquid love for I could not express it any other way. It seemed like the very breath of God.[4]

Finney did not speak in tongues because he lived in an era before people spoke in tongues. Sam had never spoken in tongues before, but afterward he did often. He liked to speak in tongues. He said that it enabled him to pray when he couldn't think of anything to say. That was the kind of thing that people said at the Vineyard. They said it was a way to keep the connection, to keep talking with God, even when they could not think of anything in particular to say. As Sam said later, "You run out of things to pray for, and you just need to pray, to let all these emotions run out of your head. So you pray in tongues. I do that quite often."

I met Sam about two years after that experience. He was in college by that point, majoring in business. He came to church most Sundays and went to retreats, but nothing like the first intense experience had happened to him since. He wished it would: "It's like the first day I got this whole cake, and then from now you get to have little servings of it from time to time again, but sometimes it's bigger and sometimes it's smaller." He still feels the Holy Spirit when people pray for him or sometimes when he sings the worship songs on Sunday morning. His hands will go numb. He'll start to shake. "It's really weird." And he'll swoon with the intensity of his feelings sometimes during the worship songs. "Just that all-encompassing love. It's like faith and hope mixed together with bonding with God. It feels like you just want to explode with how much it means to you. I couldn't even begin to describe it."

Like Sarah and David, Sam too said that something about his mind and awareness changed as he became more accomplished in prayer. At the beginning, he didn't know what people meant when they said that

God spoke to them. Then he began to pray seriously, reading through five biblical chapters each day and trying to see the stories and be in them and have them be alive. He prayed that he would be able to do this without being distracted, and soon he could. As he did so, he began to feel that God was interacting with him, nudging him to do this or that. He began to pray for people, and he would experience what he called "impressions," ideas about what he should pray for and how, which he believed had come from God. He called this "listening." "It's funny when I'm discipling other people now. It's weird hearing how they talk. They come in and say, 'Can you talk to God about this for me?' And I'm like, 'Why don't you talk to him about it?' They say, 'Because he doesn't talk to me.' And I'm like, 'He's always talking. You just have to learn to listen.'" He didn't really get mental images, he said, but he was comfortable in identifying "impressions," and he said that they came more easily and more recognizably now than they had done in the beginning: "To be in constant communion with God is to be *talking* to him. 'Lord, this is what I think about this and about this.' And then you stop a second and let your heart minister to you, and then you just *know*, there's this voice that tells you something, and it is so encouraging. Something just pops up in your mind, and you're like, 'That's the answer.' I started listening, and it gets to this point where you just know it's God's voice." He wished he were more visual. "I know this man, this man is incredible because when he prays for you, he knows exactly what's on your mind. And I'm asking him, 'Chuck, how do you do this?' And he says, 'I see words written on people.' I say, 'You see words written on people?' He says, 'On their foreheads or on their chest I see words, I just read them on people.' That's nothing that I've experienced. I wish I could."

Soon after he began praying, Sam began to feel sensorily aware of God, as if God were a person who was physically present. He reported that he experienced God as more present than an imaginary friend, and when I probed him skeptically, he pushed back. God was there. He *felt* him. "It *is* like having an imaginary friend, in a sense, because I talk to him all the time like he's always next to me, but [it's not imaginary because] you *know* that he's there." He said he would walk down the street with God by his side, talking to him and singing to him: "It's kind of weird, but walking down the street randomly, making up songs no one's ever heard of, and just singing to him—it makes me feel so wonderful to know that he's listening and walking right beside me." I asked him whether it really felt as if there were a person walking right beside him. "Definitely. *Definitely.* You know beyond a shadow of a doubt that somebody is there with you."

Sam also came to hear God speak to him audibly, although (like Sarah and David) only a few times. "There have been a couple of occasions that have come through rather clearly," he told me. "It's just outside your head, and you just hear your name being called. It's like Jeremiah, when Jeremiah starts hearing his voice. You're like, 'What's that about?' Sometimes you'll hear him. It's happened very rarely for me, but he'll say your name, 'Do this,' and you'll be, 'Okay. I can't argue with that.'"[5]

Jeremiah is among the most introspective prophets in the Hebrew Bible, and among the most reluctant. He lived in the years before the southern kingdom fell to Babylon, and his miserable portents were rarely welcomed. He was taunted, imprisoned, and at one point thrown into a pit to die. I learned about Jeremiah at the Vineyard, however, not because of his pain but because of a scene in which God explicitly teaches Jeremiah to prophesy by asking him to treat images in his mind's eye as a divine message. God comes to Jeremiah and tells him that he has been appointed a prophet; Jeremiah demurs. He "does not know how to speak." And perhaps he is aware of the risks of the job. God touches him on the lips, and then asks him what he sees. Jeremiah responds that he sees (in his mind's eye) the branch of an almond tree. God is pleased. "You have seen well." Then he asks Jeremiah again what he sees. This time Jeremiah explains that he sees a boiling pot, tipping over from the north. God again is pleased and now delivers the first of the hard prophecies that he wants Jeremiah to share.[6] When we read this section in house group, Elaine, our leader, practically shook her finger at us when she made her main point. *Listen. Watch. Pay attention. God will teach you how to hear him.*

And Sam had heard. "When I was deciding whether or not to stay at the University of Southern Illinois in Carbondale when God was calling me up here, I was like, I don't have much time, I need to figure out if I'm going to school here next year or if I'm moving. Then I heard him *audibly* telling me, 'This is not your place.' God was telling me that the reason I had not found my place there was because my heart was back at home in Chicago. And I'm like, 'Okay. I'm gonna go back to Chicago.'"

Aisha, another prayer expert, will serve as an example of someone who grew up in this kind of experiential spirituality rather than coming to it on her own as a late adolescent or an adult. She is African American and had attended a Pentecostal church before she arrived at college and joined the Vineyard. When I met her, she had just graduated and was on her way to law school. She did not speak about learning to pray in the astonished, excited way that the others did. But she described many of the same kinds of experiences associated with prayer that Sarah, David, and Sam also described.

Aisha loves to pray. She will retreat to her room, shut her eyes, and lapse into a kind of communion. Often she cries. She cries easily, although she restrains herself at work. Prayer is her way of letting her emotions rip. Like the others, she sometimes lost time in prayer.

> This last week I was in a funk. I had sent out tons of résumés and I hadn't heard anything, and so I was like, "I need to pray." It was the middle of the day. I thought it was noon, and so I'm thinking, "I'm going to do this for like an hour." And then like I'm praying, I didn't really fall asleep—I was praying—and then it's five-thirty. I don't know where the time went.

She could lose track of her surroundings: "Sometimes I want to be in a different place, and so in my mind I'd go to that place." She could get into a state where she started to pray so intensely, it was as if the prayer took over, as if it went on whether she willed it or not. "There are times when I'm just going and going and going," she told me, "and I have to pray and pray and pray." At the Vineyard, people talked about this kind of almost involuntary, pressured prayer, when you felt like you had to pray and couldn't stop: some people called it "puking prayer."

Aisha also said she didn't really have mental images. She had sensations or impressions when she prayed for people. But when she talked about her prayer life, she made it sound as vivid as a good daydream.

> I always pray as if Jesus is really next to me or he's laying next to me. I'm just hanging out, and I'm like on his lap or something like that. It's always that kind of prayer. I think I need that because I cry when I pray, and so I kind of need to know he's there. Sometimes it's like floating on a cloud. Sometimes it's on a beach or like in a cabin surrounded by nature. I'm always surrounded by nature and really beautiful things when I do it. Never with people, though. I never— when I pray it's never been with someone. It's just me and God.

Aisha told me that she never saw anything spiritual that was as real and opaque as the table on which my digital recorder sat. But when she got baptized, she watched herself as if she were seated by God's side. And she really saw her body, as if she were watching out of someone else's eyes.

I did see myself. I did. That was the coolest thing. I was baptized in the Atlantic. I was deathly afraid of water because I almost drowned in swimming class, so I was scared. The sun hadn't risen yet. I was I think fourteen, or nearly fourteen. We got there, and you know there are big waves in the Atlantic Ocean. I was scared of what I was gonna do. But I was mostly scared of the water. Those waves were huge and crashing. And then like the sun started to rise, and then my dad prayed, and it just calmed down. Like the waves kind of kissed the shore, no more crashing, and then the sun. As I was praying, I looked up, and it was cloudy and the sun shone through the clouds, and it looked like a hand. There were seagulls, and they kind of like were kissing the ocean again. Everything was very intimate. I remember walking into the water, and I *saw* myself doing it. It's the most mystical thing that's ever happened to me. By far it's the most spiritual experience I've ever had. And I really did feel like I was seeing myself. I felt like a bird at that time. I was so happy. I was really scared, really really scared, but afterward I was so happy.

In "out-of-body" experiences, people experience themselves as seeing their own body from a distance. In the United States, many reports seem to come from the operating room, where the patient awakens during surgery—it is thought that their anesthesia has failed—and experience themselves as in the corner of the ceiling, looking down. Out-of-body phenomena are also associated with intense fear, as it seems to have been in Aisha's case. A young man in a motorcycle accident awakens to find himself hovering above his inert body, watching the activity on the ground as if from afar. And out-of-body phenomena can be induced, at least for some. One can buy instruction manuals for "astral travel" that instruct the eager to stare hard at small geometric shapes and then imagine that the shape grows larger and larger until it is large enough to step through. Does the soul really leave the body? Social science cannot answer that question. But the discrete, identifiable experience has been reported in many cultures. Scientists have found that if people have had one out-of-body experience, they can be trained to experience another, and that while in that state, their brains look predictably different in the scanner.[7]

Even though Aisha grew up in this kind of spirituality, she had begun to pray far more seriously and systematically once she arrived at the Vineyard, and she found that her impressions grew more intense. She said explicitly that the more she took her imagined sensory experience seriously, the more God became real to her. "I feel the more I treat God as if he is sitting where you are, the more real he is to me, and the more I treat him as if he is nonexistent, the more nonexistent he becomes."

What we see in the accounts of these experts is that their mental experience shifts in specific ways when they become experienced in prayer. Stepping back from the theology and the God-language and the impassioned account of Christ's presence, Sarah, David, Sam, and Aisha reported, each in their own way, that as they prayed more intensely, they felt an increase in their capacity to concentrate all attention in the moment of prayer. That attentional focus so engrossed them that they reported that they lost time when they prayed. They would look up and be surprised by how much time had passed. They could get so absorbed in the prayer that they felt that they were in another place. "In my mind I'd go to that place." Aisha said. All felt that as their attention became more concentrated, their willful control over the prayer process declined. They became more like a conduit, or as Sarah said, "almost like a tube the Holy Spirit is feeding through me." All described some period in which they experienced an intense compulsion to pray and a sense that they could not stop, that they must pray, and the prayer would take over and move through them.

All also reported that as they began to pray, over time, internal sensations became stronger. Those who were more visually oriented reported sharper mental images: for Sarah, "sometimes it's almost like a Power-Point presentation," while for David, the images became like dreams. All spontaneously described the vividness of these experiences. Sam and Aisha did not think of themselves as particularly visual; they talked about impressions. But they said that those "impressions"—thoughts, sensations, a sense of presence—had become stronger. All talked about experiencing God with their senses—not in an abstract, distant way, such as discovering God in the quiet beauty of nature or pausing on a hike to draw breath, but actually feeling God's presence, being aware of him through a feeling on their skin. It was as if for each, the inner imagined worlds grew more vivid. All described an emerging category of sensation that felt neither like thought nor like sensory perception but somehow in between. In Sarah's words: "Things that aren't there and I know they're not there, and yet they're not just in my mind."

Finally, all reported moments in which they had compelling sensory perceptions of something not materially present. Sarah reported these experiences in several sensory modes: she heard, she saw, she smelled. David heard, twice, and he felt God's touch as real as a person's. Aisha saw herself as if from outside her body, as if with her eyes. Sam heard God speak on several occasions. They were sometimes perplexed and even frightened by these experiences, and yet they also cherished them, as moments when they felt the divine take solid form. These experiences were rare, spontaneous, and unexpected. It was not clear to me that any of these experts had ever mentioned them to anyone else before.

These experiences are not the stated goals of prayer. Nowhere in Vineyard theology does a text set out the explicit intent of developing sharper mental imagery or losing time or, for that matter, having sensory perceptions of the immaterial. While many texts invite their readers to hear God speak, their authors often caution their readers that auditory hallucination is not really what they have in mind. These features appear to be by-products of using the mind in a particular way, the ancillary consequences of prayer practice rather than goals people deliberately set out to achieve. They teach us that what people do when they learn to pray really changes them. Something about prayer practice has a powerful effect on the mind.

Not everyone was able to pray as the experts prayed. Not all who came to church were able to experience God in the intimate way the Vineyard modeled for them, even when they wanted to. They did not all have personal encounters with God; nor could everyone hear God speak, however they understood that phrase, despite their earnest efforts and despite the books they read, the sermons they heard, the retreats they attended, and the encouraging conversations they had with other people. Not everyone went on dates with God, or danced with God around the living room, or asked God what kind of shampoo would suit them best. Sometimes this was because they didn't want to. Alice, the engineering student, was quite clear about not wanting some of these experiences: "I don't understand the gift of prophecy completely. I probably never will and I don't have it and I don't want it because it would scare me." Moreover, people come to a particular church, after all, for different reasons: their spouse likes the church, or they like the music, or the service is convenient, and they just don't want to pray in the intense and involved way that the church recommends.

But sometimes they do want to but they say they can't. Jacob was one of my favorite people at the Vineyard. He had a dry, acerbic wit. He was direct. He was kind. He and his wife were the hosts of the house group I joined in Chicago, and he seemed to be the only one, at the time, who had a sense of what it meant to take an anthropologist—an active observer, always asking questions—into the group. He was intrigued by my questions and by the way his Christianity would seem to an outsider. He seemed less surprised than the others that I came to the Bible with scholar's questions. He tolerated me, and he trusted me, and I came to see him as someone whose faith in the fundamental goodness of the world was part of his character and interwoven with the choices he made in the world. He was in many ways an exemplary Christian. But he did not hear from God, except on very rare occasions, and never with the kind of vividness he wanted.

Jacob had grown up in a Vineyard church. When he was in high school, the church had a revival. Many people were saved, and many of the saved found that they had dramatic experiences of God's personal presence. That never happened to Jacob. "I remember really desperately wanting to draw closer to God," he recalled, "having one of these inspired Holy Spirit moments that maybe sometimes get more attention than they deserve . . . mountaintop experiences, tangible signs and wonders. I wanted those and I sought those out, but I never really found myself encountering them." It was hard for him, and he was demoralized when nothing happened. "There was a time when I was seeking God during that period of high school where that was very frustrating. Why doesn't God speak to me in ways that I hear when Dad speaks to me or Mom speaks to me?" By the time I met him, he had made his peace with his sense that he was just not someone who experienced God that way. He experiences God as close, but he does not have the chatty relationship with God that others seem to have. He doesn't find himself talking to God routinely throughout the day: "I mean there'll be sporadic prayers, quick prayers. Mostly not deep long prayers." He doesn't have many images when he prays, and whatever images he does have do not seem important to him. "I don't picture anything when I pray," he told me. "I know some people picture things when they pray, or praise an image of God or something. I don't."

Nor is Jacob so unusual. Nearly a quarter of the people I interviewed systematically at the church—six out of twenty-eight—told me, sometimes with discouraged voices, that they just didn't hear God the way other people did. "Please pray that I will hear God speak in a booming voice," one of them pleaded in Bible study. Like most people in the church, Fred, an earnest young economist, wanted concrete encounters with God, and he felt bad that he did not have them. When I sat down with him in an interview, he was glum: "I don't have these superpowerful experiences that make me fall to my knees."

Does it matter? In some ways, not at all. Congregants do not actually lose social standing in the church through their failure to hear God speak easily in prayer, although they are unable to become known as highly accomplished at prayer, which does confer visibility and importance. The everyday discussions around prayer in the social world of the congregation are quite tolerant of those who fail to experience themselves as hearing from God in their minds, even though those same discussions repeatedly hold up an experience of intimacy with God as the most important relationship of one's life and even though the discussions repeatedly represent that intimacy as hearing from God in one's mind. People talked quite comfortably about their sense that people had different "gifts." They admired people who prayed easily and well, but someone like Jacob could be deeply respected if he became involved in the church in other ways, like serving on the finance committee or running a house group.

At the same time, being known as a person who prayed powerfully was distinctly good. The term *prayer warrior*, a soldier who fights on Christ's side in a spiritual war, suggests that this is a goal toward which all should reach. People talked about other people as being powerful in prayer. They often agreed on who was good at prayer. When I asked people at the California Vineyard for examples of prayer warriors, everyone mentioned Sarah. I never encountered a Vineyard pastor who was not described by other people as someone who prayed with passion and power. It was clear that being known as someone through whom the Holy Spirit flowed in prayer was a source of great respect, and that people liked it when the experts prayed for them.

Yet most people did not believe that their prayer life was as good as it could be, and most did not feel that they prayed as much as they should. Falling short was just part of the experience of being at a church in which people talked about prayer all the time. Most people seemed to think of themselves as people who would be able to pray more easily if they just worked a little more at it. In some ways, being not-so-great at hearing God was a bit like being a not-so-great dancer at a dance party. You watch the good dancers with envy. You wish you were a better dancer, but you get out on the dance floor anyway, and even if you decide that you must take dance lessons, mostly you don't. Lessons take time, and they are for your own personal benefit. In the press of a busy life in which most of what you do is for other people, something you do for yourself often comes last.

That happens with prayer too. People were quite aware that being a prayer expert took time. Sarah was willing to spend three hours a day praying. Not everyone could do that, even if they wanted to. Many found it hard to set aside the half hour a day that you were supposed to spend in prayer. They knew that praying daily should be as much part of their routine as brushing their teeth, and they wanted and intended to pray. In practice, prayer seemed to be like doing thirty minutes of daily aerobic exercise and eating good, healthy food. Not everyone does it, even when they know they should and even when they want the body these practices will deliver. And just as people feel bad when they break their diet, people like Jacob often feel bad when they can't seem to have the experiences other people have. They feel bad about not praying enough, and they feel bad about not having those cool experiences those other people have. They can feel like bad Christians and even unloved by God.

That is why it is so important to understand the skill dimension of prayer practice. For Christians, it is important because they want to know whether there are ways to teach this skill more effectively. For non-Christians, it matters because we cannot understand how God becomes real to someone until we understand that a person's experience of God emerges out of the vortex not only of what they are taught intellectually about God but also of what they do practically to experience God—above all, the way they pray, and what they bring to their prayer experience as unique individuals.

CHAPTER SIX

Lord, Teach Us to Pray

Rejoice always; pray without ceasing;
in everything give thanks,
for this is God's will for
you in Jesus Christ.

1 Thessalonians 5:17

Prayer is the irresistible urge of our human
nature to contact and communicate
with the source of love.

Sophy Burnham, *The Path of Prayer*

WHAT DO PEOPLE ACTUALLY DO when they pray? When you ask evangelicals that question, they often talk about praise and worship and petition. Indeed, there is a common evangelical acronym for what you should do in prayer: ACTS. It stands for Adoration, Confession, Thanksgiving, and Supplication. You are supposed to describe explicitly your sense of God's greatness, spell out your failings, thank God for what he has done for you, and then bring to his attention what you think you need. This is what an observer might call the content of prayer.

Nonevangelicals might answer the question by describing behavior. Anthropologists point out that prayer is a *genre*. To call prayer a genre means that someone within that *genre community* who hears or sees another person pray would instantly recognize the behavior as prayer. One might describe the prayer genre within an American family as including a distinct set of body postures (being seated, head bowed, eyes closed); an expectation of quiet voice and quiet behavior while in the posture ("throwing hands aren't praying hands"); a verbal act of request, praise, and thanks to a being called God; and at the end, a verbal marker: "amen."[1]

But the question can also be answered by focusing on technique, on those mental muscles that Sarah learned to exercise and that seemed to change something about the way she experienced her mind. There is what you might call a technology of prayer that centers on attention.[2] That is, if you put to one side the theological purpose and supernatural efficacy of prayer, prayer changes the way the person praying uses his or her mind by changing the way that person pays attention. People learn to attend in specific, structured ways when they pray, and some people—the experts—become skilled at doing so.

For the most part, these techniques are taught obliquely. People learn to pray by watching other people pray, which is a very common sight in the evangelical world. Pastors pray out loud whenever they deliver a teaching. People pray for each other in the weekly house groups. At the end of any Vineyard service, as much as a quarter of the congregation stays behind to pray in little groups, heads bowed and hands on one another's shoulders, speaking out loud their hopes and fears to God. Admittedly there is plenty of explicit teaching about prayer. There are hundreds of manuals about prayer, teachings on prayer, even classes on how to pray effectively. And yet for the most part the explicit instruction emphasizes content: ACTS. Adore, confess, give thanks, and ask. It does not spell out the mental techniques that are inherent to prayer practice because people perform these techniques automatically when they imitate what other people do when they pray and follow the advice their pastors give. But it is important to understand the mental mechanisms of prayer because they are powerful. Those techniques have consequences, not only for the expert but for the ordinary person who prays. In order to make sense of how prayer changes people, we need to understand what its technology demands of the mind.

From an anthropological and psychological perspective, the central act of prayer is paying attention to internal experience—thoughts, images, and the awareness of your body—and treating these sensations as important in themselves rather than as distractions from the real business of your life. In some sense, of course, we do this all the time. When we work through things in our mind, when we reenact a conversation, when we daydream, we are paying attention to our inner experience. But prayer asks the person praying to treat those thoughts not as private, internal musings but as in some sense public and externally real speech. This is true for all prayer, but it is true in spades for the kind of evangelical prayer in which God is immediately present and in which he speaks back. The person praying has to learn to use the imagination to experience God as present, and then to treat what has been imagined as more than "mere" imagination. That twofold shift in attention—toward the internal, as the external—is the heart of the skill in prayer.

Some modern prayer manuals spell out a learning process in numbered steps. These steps provide a hodgepodge of practices that direct a person's attention toward their own thoughts; that shape those thoughts in certain ways; and that then push them to treat those thoughts as if they were external speech and action. The book I picked up in a weekend Vineyard course on how to speak with God, *Dialogue with God,* was the clearest in laying out a progression. The first step is learning what God's voice sounds like when spoken within (reading your Bible so that you recognize the kinds of things God says and when he says them). The second is knowing how to go to a quiet place and still one's own thoughts and emotions. The third is attending carefully in the mind, and to images and thoughts and dreams. The fourth is writing out the dialogue, so that it is clear, external, and remembered: real.[3]

The Beginner's Guide to Hearing God presents a similar sequence. To hear God, find quiet places to listen—"over a period of time, I learned to get up out of bed (highly important—get out of the bed!) in the middle of the night"; read the Bible to direct the way to pay attention—"if we haven't read our Bible, we should not act like we know where were are going"; actually pay attention—"I really didn't know what to do with all this stuff—impressions, mental snapshots, hunches, knowledge, short thoughts and full phrases that were being released into my heart and mind"; and treat that inner life seriously, as if it matters: remember it, follow it, and store up the memories of the experience. And practice, the author says again and again. Focus internally. Bend the mind to imagine God, and imagine him so vividly that he springs to life outside the mind.[4]

The aim is to allow what must be imagined (God has no material form) to be experienced as more than mere imagination. That means changing the way one uses one's imagination. Many evangelicals talk about using the imagination in prayer, but again, they often think of this as a matter of prayer content. Bill Hybels, pastor of the evangelical mega-church Willow Creek in the Chicago suburbs, writes that when he prays, he cultivates his imagination to bring him to God. In *Too Busy Not to*

Pray, he describes the way he learned to imagine certain things so that the imagining would catapult him into a state where his mind and emotion were focused on God.

> When you create a secret place where you can really pray, over time you will look forward to going there. You will begin to appreciate the familiar surrounding, the sights and smells. You will grow to love the aura of the place where you freely converse with God.
>
> I created such a prayer room near the credenza in a corner of my former office. In my prayer place I put an open Bible, a sign that says, "God is able," a crown of thorns to remind me of the suffering savior, and a shepherd's staff that I often hold up while making requests . . .
>
> That office corner became a holy place for me.[5]

His point is that readers should focus their imagination on God and away from thinking about the afternoon shopping. He clearly considers the practice to involve training: "As with anything else you take up— racquetball, computer programming or a new job, you have to get disciplined, stretch yourself and work at it to do it well."[6]

But notice what Hybels trains: the "sights and smells." The real work here is not only to shift attention away from the distracting world but to use the everyday imagination to make God vivid. He does it by drawing attention to sensory detail. He uses the props—the crown of thorns, the shepherd's staff—to help him to see, smell, feel, and taste, in his mind's eye. They help him to hear. Richard Foster gives much the same advice in his book on prayer, *Celebration of Discipline,* which *Christianity Today* calls one of the ten most important religious books of the century. "Seek to live the experience [of scripture]," he writes. "Smell the sea. Hear the lap of the water against the shore. See the crowd. Feel the sun on your head and the hunger in your stomach. Taste the salt in the air. Touch the hem of his garment."[7] The Vineyard pastor Ken Wilson makes this point clearly in *Mystically Wired:* "Words are useless without the imagination . . . So imagine that you are part of the scene the words invite you to imagine. Notice the greenness of the pasture [in the 23rd Psalm]. Feel the texture of the grass as you lie down on it. Stay there for a while in the grass. Notice the smells. Feel the warmth of the sun."[8] Take the imagination away from the world, but use sensory knowledge of the world to make what you imagine more real.

I believe that the central but often implicit technology of evangelical prayer is an intense focus on mental imagery and other inner sensory experience. The focus is structured in specific ways and directed toward specific goals, but the techniques first and foremost heighten and deepen internal sensation: seeing, hearing, and touching above all. Not all evangelicals would recognize this description of prayer practice. That is because they do not realize that what they do in prayer is rooted in older practices that go back to the early church and became explicit through centuries of systematic instruction in what are called the spiritual disciplines. The spiritual disciplines are to everyday prayer what elite gymnastics is to fooling around on the monkey bars. They help us to understand what the disciplined mind can accomplish, and how.

There are two named styles of spiritual discipline within the Christian tradition: *apophatic* and *kataphatic* prayer. As a form, both can be found in other faiths, and they are, arguably, the two dominant forms of spiritual discipline (at least mental spiritual discipline) in any faith.[9] *Apophatic* prayer practice takes its name from the Greek *apophasis,* "denial." It is a cluster of techniques through which attention is shifted away from internal and external sensation. The thinker detaches from thought. Any mental event—words, images, awareness of the body—is treated as meaningless in the search for God, because God is the unknowable, the unimaginable, the not-this. The apophatic rejects the human to find the divine.

By contrast, kataphatic prayer, which takes its name from the Greek *kataphasis,* "to affirm positively," treats thought as more important than an ordinary mental event. It shifts attention from the external to the internal. It asks people to dwell lovingly on what is imagined, and its techniques help to intensify the imaginative act. They engage the senses, they evoke vivid memories, and they generate powerful emotions. Kataphatic prayer uses the human capacity to go beyond itself. It is, as one scholar remarks, the verbose element in theology.[10]

Yin and yang, these two disciplines share the same goal: in Foster's words, "to center the attention of the body, the emotions, the mind and the spirit" upon God, and to diminish attention to the everyday.[11] Evangelicals use both types, but without a doubt, the heart of evangelical prayer is kataphatic. Still, the two have much in common, although each is defined by what the other is not. To understand the one, you must know the other.

Apophatic prayer, the *via negativa*, is often described as the way of the desert fathers who abandoned world and word to reach for God. These men, beginning in the third century, fled the social life of village and city for the solitude of the Egyptian desert. In that stark landscape they sought God through silence, fasting, and hard manual labor. Saint Anthony, whose story was told in 360 by Athanasius of Alexandria, lived for twenty years alone in an abandoned Roman fort, surviving on food left at the door for him by villagers.

It is not entirely clear what these men did when they prayed. They seem to have spoken words of scripture slowly, repetitively, as if the words themselves had a magical power to heal and to shield them from the demonic spirits that tormented them in the desert night. But the story of their quest for God—historian Peter Brown calls it "the myth of the desert"—gripped early Christians. (It was learning of Saint Anthony that drove Augustine to convert.) It also grips modern evangelicals. In the Gospel of Matthew, Christ instructs his followers to "go into your closet to pray," a phrase many evangelicals know. The prayer tradition that was built upon these stories from the desert fathers (it came to be called Hesychasm, or "inner silence") made prayer a closet in the mind, an inward withdrawal from the world and from the senses through which we know the world.[12] Here one seeks to know the unknowable by negating all one knows. Hesychastic texts speak of detachment and renunciation, of breathing exercises and prayer posture, and of the varieties of holy silence.[13]

The classic expression of the apophatic method is a text written in the fourteenth century by an anonymous English author that has come down to us as *The Cloud of Unknowing*.[14] It is the kind of text that you might expect to emerge from a fourteenth-century English monastery. Its short passages are digressive, circular, and obscure. They veer from high theology to practical advice. But the text is also a work of great beauty and charm. "Do not suppose," the author writes, "that because I have spoken of darkness and of a cloud I have in mind the clouds you see in an overcast sky or the darkness of your house when your candle fails. If I had, you could with a little imagination picture the summer skies breaking through the clouds or a clear light brightening the dark winter. But this isn't what I mean at all so forget this sort of nonsense."[15]

To the author of *The Cloud,* the darkness of unknowing cloaks God, and God can be reached only through a willing abandonment of thought and image, the detritus of a selfish, human mind. The author urges those who wish to touch God to fashion a cloud of forgetting, to remove them from the world they know. Above all, the author explains that those who seek God must get rid of the stuff in their minds, even when those thoughts are holy, even when they are thoughts about God. The author hastens to assure his readers that thoughts about God are good and indeed necessary, but not in this task. Thoughts teach you about God's nature, he says, but they do not bring you to God himself: "A man may know completely and ponder thoroughly every created thing and its works, yes, and God's works too, but not God himself. Thought cannot comprehend God. And so, I prefer to abandon all I can know, choosing rather to love him who I cannot know . . . Beat upon that thick cloud of unknowing with the dart of your loving desire, and do not cease come what may." If you cannot manage to clear your mind, he adds, choose a single word, a one-syllable word. Focus on it; use it to beat upon that cloud of unknowing and to subdue your many inevitable distractions. "If your mind begins to intellectualize over the meaning and connotations of this little word, remind yourself that its value lies in its simplicity. Do this and I assure you that these thoughts will vanish. Why? Because you have refused to develop them with arguing." For many years those in the monastery sought God along the *via negativa.* But as the Reformation arose and closed the monasteries, this hard road to contemplation faded from the ordinary Christian landscape.[16]

Thomas Merton was no ordinary Catholic. Born four hundred years after the Reformation, he was not only a poet but also a social activist, and his route to Catholicism had many winding side paths. His autobiography, *The Seven Storey Mountain* (it was called *Elected Silence* in Britain), tells the story of his discovery of the apophatic tradition. God, Merton writes, is found in the desert of surrender. You find God by giving up an expectation of finding an answer to your prayers. His answer will be "his silence itself suddenly, inexplicably revealing itself to him as a word of great power, full of the voice of God."[17] *The Seven Storey Mountain* sold more than sixty thousand copies when it came out in 1948. But Merton did not teach a method per se: "Let prayer pray within you."[18] He taught an attitude and a passion, in vaulting prose that spoke of peace and limpid beauty. Many followed his lead, but others found themselves drawn toward Eastern spiritual practices like Zen that taught a more explicit technique.

In the 1970s three Trappist monks inspired by Merton—Thomas Keating, Basil Pennington, and William Meninger—distilled the practical points of *The Cloud of Unknowing* into a method that could be summarized on a page.[19] They called it "centering prayer" because they thought that the cloud metaphor was too difficult. "Few of us have been in a cloud," Pennington calmly comments.[20] The word *center* came from Merton: "Monastic prayer begins not so much with 'considerations' as with a 'return to the heart,' finding one's deepest center, awakening the profound depths of our being in the presence of God, who is the source of our being and of our life." The three monks thought the phrase represented the movement both of the technique and of its imageless theology: "This place—which we make no attempt at pinpointing physically or imaginatively—is deep within, deep within our spirit. It is the place of encounter with the living Triune God."[21]

The method begins with the technique that *The Cloud*'s author recommended as the last resort for those who could not focus. You choose one word—perhaps *God*, perhaps *Abba*, or *love*, or *peace*, or whatever else appeals to you. Then you use the word, as in *The Cloud*, to block out distraction, like the white noise of the fan that drowns out the street sounds as you work. Thus armed with your word, you sit; you focus on the word; and whenever you find yourself distracted by thoughts and feelings, no matter how good or noble, you gently bring your attention back to the word. The monks suggest that the minimum length of time for such a prayer is twenty minutes each day, and they suggest that you do two such sessions a day.[22]

Centering prayer is hard. Your mind jumps and frets and starts. You settle in to find God, and instead you construct the weekly shopping list and reach in your imagination for a pen. "Monkey mind," the leader of my prayer group called it, borrowing the Buddhist term. Many people find it difficult just to be still for twenty minutes, to sit without scratching their arms or fiddling with their fingers. To be still and to halt thought is harder still. Your thoughts seem to gather force when you set out to try this method, as if they have been waiting, subdued, to ambush you. "Wandering thoughts surge about my soul like boiling water," said Abba

Isaac in the first written description of this mode of prayer.[23] The author of *The Cloud* warns his readers that this will happen at first.

> No sooner has a man turned towards God in love when through human frailty he finds himself distracted by the remembrance of some created thing or some daily care ... Don't be surprised if your thoughts seem holy and valuable for prayer. Probably you will find yourself thinking about the wonderful qualities of Jesus, his sweetness, his love, his gracious mercy. But if you pay attention to these ideas they will have gained what they want of you, and will go on chattering until they divert you even more to the thought of his passion. Then will come ideas about his great kindness, and if you keep listening they will be delighted. Soon you will be thinking about your sinful life and perhaps in this connection you will recall some place where you have lived in the past, until suddenly, before you know it, your mind is completely scattered.[24]

You can find yourself resisting even the thought of trying, like people who buy an expensive treadmill that sits unused in a bedroom corner. Even for those who manage to still their minds, the practice can still be frustrating. "I just didn't see the point of it," one young Christian woman told me after she had tried it every day for a month.

Despite these challenges, evangelical interest in centering prayer and desert spirituality has surged in recent years. Richard Foster writes approvingly of Thomas Merton, and he teaches breathing techniques to calm chaotic thoughts. In *The Purpose Driven Life*, Rick Warren explains the value of "breath prayers," brief phrases like "you are with me" that can be spoken in a breath and repeated as often as possible throughout the day. Books on the spirituality of the desert fathers, like Henri Nouwen's *The Way of the Heart*, sell briskly. Evangelical prayer groups build long periods of silence into spiritual retreats. And the very difficulty of apophatic practice has become a lure, the way hard peaks and desolate cliff faces draw young mountain climbers, as if mastering that tough challenge will change one's life. Sometimes Christians go off to reenact Jesus's testing in the wilderness; a young man I knew from the Vineyard did, before he found his wife and settled down. For three months, he lived in a camp in the Californian desert. He fasted and prayed and passed his days in silence among other ardent Christians—no TV, no e-mail, no phone.

Young Christians come back from these camps gaunt and focused, like young Sioux warriors returning from a vision quest. The venture seems now to be imagined as a young man's rite of manhood. An evangelical publishing house recently brought out a book on Anthony and the desert fathers with the subtitle "extreme faith."[25]

The method works, if by *works* one means that those who become expert practitioners find that the practice changes them. At least, we know that the meditation practiced in Buddhism—until now the only spiritual practice that has been deeply studied as a practice by scientists—has clear physiological consequences. The neuroscientists Andrew Newberg and Eugene D'Aquili sought out expert meditators in the Tibetan Buddhist tradition to enact their spiritual discipline within the brain-mapping device of a single-photon emission computed tomography (SPECT) machine. They found that in the peak state of a meditation of an expert meditator, the brain changes significantly. There is decreased activity in the posterior superior parietal lobe, an area that orients the self in relation to the world. Buddhist meditation is not centering prayer, but the formal similarity to what people do in centering prayer—shifting attention away from the senses and from thought—is sufficient to suggest that they might have the same kind of bodily impact. Even among nonexperts, meditation can decrease your heart rate, lower your blood pressure, alter your brain wave pattern, improve your immune function, and help you to sustain attention. These are, to borrow a famous phrase, the "relaxation response," and at least for those who can respond to the practice, the effects are real.[26]

More to the point, the *via negativa* can lead to spiritual transformation. The great Christian mystics have often described their deepest and most intense form of prayer as the withdrawal of the mind from all thought and sensation. In her *Life*, Teresa of Ávila compared prayer practice to the task of watering a garden "in soil most unfruitful and full of weeds."[27] How do you water such a garden? At first the ground is dry, barren, hard. The gardener must work to draw water from a well by hand and carry it painstakingly to the struggling plants. Teresa called that work "mental prayer": "nothing but friendly intercourse, and frequent solitary intercourse, with Him Who we know loves us"—more or less what ordinary Vineyard prayer is like. Soon, Teresa wrote, prayer becomes easier. The effort of finding time and words lessens. The garden can be watered by a nearby stream, and then there is heavy rain. At this point, she wrote, at the most advanced stages of prayer, the person becomes blind to the world and to its senses. The soul, wrapped in the love of God, refuses to use the intellect at all. This stage, she wrote, brings rapture: "It comes like a strong, swift impulse, before your thought can forewarn you of it or you can do anything to help yourself; you see and feel this cloud, or this powerful eagle, rising and bearing you up with it on its wings."[28]

This style of prayer is also deeply controversial within evangelical circles, partly because in the end it just seems too much like Buddhism. The Trappist fathers carefully (and appropriately) placed centering prayer in the rich lineage of the Christian contemplative tradition that descends from the desert fathers. But the technique is essentially the same as in the many forms of Buddhism and Hinduism that independently discovered the practice of being still in thought. Merton understood himself to be bringing Eastern forms of prayer into the West; he thought the West needed the peace that they could bring. When Merton's *Contemplative Prayer* was reissued in 1996, the Zen teacher Thich Nhat Hanh wrote the introduction.

Theologically conservative Christians are careful to separate themselves from anything that evokes the non-Christian. I once attended a workshop in which the leader explained that all forms of Hinduism were inherently demonic and that a Christian should not practice yoga lest Hindu influence creep into the body and corrupt the soul. This is a widely shared view. Some Christians try to manage such skepticism by creating "Christian yoga" or "doxapractice," a kind of body movement similar to yoga but taught by and to Christians. More conservative Christians frown at it. One website describes Christian yoga as "an unfruitful deed of darkness."[29]

The other reason for evangelical hesitation arises from the very idea that humans should reach for God without language. The opening of the Gospel of John is clear: "In the beginning was the word and the word was with God and the word was God." Jesus is that word, and to critics, without that word we find in our stilled minds no more than an empty vastness.

In 1989 Joseph Ratzinger, not yet Pope Benedict XVI, published a letter in which he explained that apophatic prayer was an erroneous way of praying and had been a mistake for the desert fathers in their isolation. The attempt to immerse oneself in that which can neither be sensed nor conceived is found deep within the religious impulse of many non-

Christian peoples, Ratzinger argued, and the God that one finds by the method is no more real than theirs. To dive into your center is to wallow in your soul. The author of *The Cloud* was right, Ratzinger said: We humans cannot know God. That is why, he continued, we were given Christ, and that is why Christ and the word are crucial, for they enable the twofold movement through which humans can reach God and God can reach back to humans. Ratzinger has a point: If prayer leads to an experience of divinity that escapes words and representation, one might conclude that the words of the Christian scripture are as a kind of elaborate window dressing, no more accurate in their description of the real than a Buddhist *stupa*.[30]

That is why for many evangelicals, prayer rich in the images and stories of Christ, the *via imaginativa,* seems like a more appropriate form of prayer. It is, in any event, what they do when they pray. Few evangelicals name it *kataphatic,* and—as we have seen—they do not all pray in the same way. But the daydreams with God, the imagined conversations, the waiting for thoughts and images to appear in the mind during prayer, the desire to experience the scriptures as if one were there—all these cultivate the mind's capacity to imagine God. The history of Christian kataphatic tradition allows us to see, in the loose accumulation of different imaginative practices, which techniques seem to be selected again and again because they work.

In the beginning, imagination-rich prayer was described as a second-tier kind of prayer, a stepping-stone for dull and blinkered humans. Dionysus the Areopagite—he wrote as if he were the convert who followed Paul from Athens in Acts 17:34, but he was in fact an anonymous fifth-century theologian—coined the term *kataphatic* to identify the type of prayer that would enable Christians to know an unknowable divine through their imagination. Just as a child needs a small chair to clamber up to the bathroom sink, those who see childishly, in Paul's famous phrase, need to imagine God in order to grasp his unimaginableness. Consider, Dionysius wrote, this passage from Psalm 78, when God loses patience with his stiff-necked people and blasts them from the earth: "the Lord awoke, like a strong man, powerful but reeling with wine." God does not drink, and neither does he sleep. Dionysius wrote that when we imagine the immensity of God drunk with wine, we are led into an awareness of the incomprehensible intensity of his presence. That pushes language to its breaking point, the Areopagite argued, and moves us beyond to meet divinity in the brilliant darkness of a hidden silence.[31] To the modern reader, these tracts are a strange but beautiful defense of poetry.

By the era of the medieval monastery, however, these views were neither literary criticism nor metaphysics but explicit technology. For the early desert fathers, sometimes isolated without a written text, perhaps sometimes not even literate, praying to God through scripture involved not reading but recollecting. They had called this *mneme theou,* "the memory of God," and they understood it as a craft one had to learn. Asked what a man should do to please God, Anthony replied: "Wherever you go, always have God before your eyes; whatever you do, have [before you] the testimony of the holy Scriptures." It was a skill Anthony possessed, as Athanasius wrote: "For he had given such heed to what was read that none of the things that were written fell from him to the ground, but he remembered all, and afterwards his memory served him for books."[32] Medieval monastics reconceptualized this mnemonic practice as an intricate skill, fine and delicate and practiced. At the center of this skill stood the making of mental images that could be meant to draw upon a vast personal storehouse of scripture so that thoughts could be entwined within scripture, like a vine carefully trained around a gatepost.

In deeply learned books, the medieval historian Mary Carruthers argues that in medieval monastic culture, contemplative prayer was primarily understood as a process of crafting thought. In this culture, she says, memory was understood not as a mirror of the past, or as a record of what has happened, but as a tool to make real what God desired. In his first letter to the Corinthians, Paul compared himself to a "wise master builder." In medieval monasticism, this phrase would become the dominant representation for understanding what prayer did. Mental images were the building blocks. The thinker, the one who prayed, was the mason who set the stones in place to create a building in which God could dwell. Recall that in the medieval world, one did not snuggle into the corner with one's own beloved Bible. Texts were all important, but printing had not yet made it possible to own them individually. Books were manuscripts, rare and shared. Reading aloud was commonplace. One was explicitly expected to make a mental representation to remember what had been read. Mental images were understood as the means to take in what was perceived through the senses and to shape and store that awareness in the mind. Those mental images determined what one remembered and how one remembered it. And unlike a modern psychology that imagines such mental images as unchosen and epiphenom-enal, flitting through the mind like formless moths, monastic psychology treated images as chosen and substantial, as acting on the person and upon the world with power.[33]

The monastics set out to teach themselves to use their mental images like instruments. Augustine spoke of "painting in the heart." Those who listened to scripture were expected to "paint" in their mind's eye, as the fifth-century monk Arnobius invites his audience to do when contem-plating Psalm 98, vague but glorious: "Make a joyful noise to the Lord, all the earth." Arnobius advises:

> Paint, paint before your eyes the various fabricated things, whenever you chant of these [while reciting the verses of the psalm]. Of what sort? Those which were seen with wonder by the apostles [chiefly John]: paint the temples, paint the baths, paint the forums and the ramparts rising on the high summit.

Many of these medieval instructional texts presented scripture in highly visualizable language, and their readers—or more likely, listeners—moved from scene to scene and picture to picture as they progressed. Those pictures were meant to become part of their memory and thus their means to think and act; thus their character, who they were. This was an Augustinian psychology. In his *Confessions,* Augustine remarks: "Inside me, in the vast cloisters of my memory, are the sky, the earth, and the sea, ready at my summons, together with everything I have ever perceived in them by my senses."[34]

The result of this insistent interest was that medieval monastic society became a visionary culture in which people sought out and celebrated the visual experience of things not present in the material world. From the centuries that stretch between Augustine and the death of the mon-asteries in the Reformation, we have inherited a rich store of texts that describe, analyze, theorize, and critique what the writers call "visions": vivid image-rich narratives that have their roots in the Bible but that reach out sometimes into fantastic and astonishing realms. For reasons we do not understand, the authors of the great majority of these vision recitals were women, although their critics were mostly men. (At this point, the twentieth-century Carruthers comments: *plus ça change.*) Yet both male and female monastics were steeped in this culture that paid exquisite attention to mental imagery. Meditation texts instructed readers how to visualize the life of Christ. We have the prayer records of those who used them and other methods, like those of Julian of Norwich and Teresa of Ávila; we have the theories of those, like Alcher of Clairvaux, who attempted to categorize and analyze the phenomena they reported; and we have the writings of the suspicious, skeptical clerics, who struggled to make sense of what people described and to sort out the godly and the demonic from the merely wishful or the mad.[35] So much of this world has faded from our grasp, but these writings do imply an important psychological hypothesis: that mental imagery practice will lead to visionary experience.

In the little Dominican monastery of San Marco, in the sun-warmed town of Florence, you can see even now an illustration of techniques people used to shape their thoughts into the right building blocks for God. Up on the second floor, in the rooms off the long corridors where the monks would sleep and work and pray, are the delicate *quattrocento* frescoes of Fra Angelico. Each chamber has one scene. An angel bows before Mary, whose folded arms show that she accepts God's plan; the baby lies adored by humans, angels, and a heifer and an ass; Jesus sags upon the cross as images of his betrayal encircle him. The frescoes were not decorations but tools in the making of the monks. Most of them have witnesses standing at the side of the main story—Dominic himself, Thomas Aquinas, Peter Martyr—and the way they held their hands and bodies told the monks how to pray. A Dominican treatise on prayer, *De modo orandi,* spelled out the meaning of those gestures and the specific states of mystical awareness they were thought to create when deliberately assumed in prayer and held in thought. These frescoes were not painted as representations of a story to be observed as if it were external from the mind; they were painted as mental images to be held internally, and so used, they were thought to be as transformative as wine.[36]

Mental imagery was thought to impact not only the mind and soul but the world. As the medieval age gave way to the early modern one, imagery practice emerged as the primary technique not only of prayer but of the Renaissance magic that some scholars believe ushered in the scientific revolution. Scholars created complex symbolic systems—alchemy, astrology, and kabbalah, not yet parceled out from astronomy and physics—that mapped earth and heaven, and they used imagery practice to manipulate the symbols to act upon the world. In 1564 John

Dee, adviser to Elizabeth I, owner of the greatest library in England, introducer of Euclid's *Geometry,* and one of the most learned men of his time, published the *Monas Hieroglyphica.* It is a strange, moving treatise, dense with arcane scholarship. Dee thought he had discovered, through long, careful study, a symbol that could change the world—a sorcerer's stone that would really work. It was a sun and moon interlocked and set atop the cross of the elements, with the sign of Aries at its side. Dee wrote that if this symbol were visualized by a magus in the right state of spiritual purity, with the skill to know and understand the meaning of the form, reality itself would change. The magus would become invisible, and a new and better era would be born. Dee seems to have believed that it could really happen: that a trained man who bent his mind with pure intention upon this image could, with the intensity of his focus, bring a new world into being. "Oh my god, how great are these mysteries!" he wrote.[37]

During this period of intense interest in imagery, the prayer practice that most resembles modern evangelical prayer emerged, so elaborate and systematic that it lays out the structure of evangelical prayer practice like a dissection.

Iñigo López do Loyola, the father of this practice, was born in 1491 in the Basque region of northern Spain. Columbus would soon land on the shores of the New World. The future Henry VIII had just been born. Loyola's noble family had fought in the great battle to drive the Moors from Spain, and Iñigo was sent to the royal court at fourteen as a page, to become a soldier in turn. He did not remain one for long. In 1521 he rode into Pamplona in the service of his duke, to fight the French, and a cannonball shattered his legs. He would fight no more. But war would remain at the heart of the way he imagined God.

It was as he recovered that the Spiritual Exercises were born. Loyola was given *The Life of Christ* to read, and rereading it again and again, he found that he would put the text aside and continue the story in his own mind. He told his biographer, Father Luís Gonçalves da Câmara, that he spent many hours dreaming about chivalric deeds in the service of a noble and beautiful lady, but that those secular daydreams left him restless and unsatisfied. Daydreaming of going to Jerusalem barefoot and hungry but with Jesus at his side left him happy. One night when he was awake, he had a vision of Mary with the holy child. It seems to have been that vision that changed the course of his life. Loyola became a pilgrim and a penitent and made his way to Jerusalem and back. He was theologically unschooled, and it seems that he managed periods of uncertainty and confusion by immersing himself in imaginative daydreams of the Gospels. He took notes on what worked for him: what enabled him to retain his focus on these daydreams and what did not. He turned the notes into a system.

Loyola began to lead other people in his exercises. He was denounced to the Inquisition; he and his exercises were examined and passed. He left for Paris, where he studied theology. He acquired followers to whom he gave the exercises and was denounced and examined and passed again. Eventually—having studied, taught, and given his exercises from Paris to Spain and back—he found himself with his companions in Rome. By 1540 they were granted the status of a religious order. By 1548 the exercises were formally approved by the pope and printed, and in the same year, Loyola, renamed Ignatius (he seems to have chosen the name out of devotion to an early church father, Saint Ignatius of Antioch), established the first Jesuit college in Messina. One of the many remarkable things about the man is that he combined organizational efficiency with his daydreamy intensity. From that year until his death eight years later, he approved two new colleges a year. The education was systematic, and it was free.

What remains to us of *Spiritual Exercises* are notes, not much better than early cookbooks by Apicius or Mrs. Beeton, with their lists of ingredients and vague instructions, intelligible only to those who already know how to cook. Loyola seems to have put his notes into order in 1540 and ignored them thereafter, apart from getting them translated in Latin for the pope's approval in 1548. They remain notes. As a text, *Spiritual Exercises* is no more than a handbook. There is no abstract theory. Perhaps that was because Loyola discovered the method before he had been schooled in theology, but more likely it was because he was a resolutely practical man, more concerned with how to bring people to God than with philosophical argument.

Within the Jesuit fold, the text became a guide to an oral tradition, signposts given to those who underwent the exercises and loved them and took over the role of giving them to others in turn. A modern Jesuit editor of the text remarks:

Ignatius took Pierre Favre through the Spiritual Exercises. Favre directed Jerónimo Doménech, who then directed Diego Miron. Miron became expert at guiding others and directed an Italian youth who joined the company. In his time, that youth directed another youth who joined the company, and so on. The ways of guiding and directing changed, but the very real linkage has continued for more than four and a half centuries, down to the writer of this commentary.[38]

The exercises never died. Every Jesuit does them and has done so since the order was first started. But Loyola never meant them to be exclusive to his order. Over the years the oral tradition became stabilized and structured, and these days many people do the Spiritual Exercises without being Jesuit or even Catholic. Increasingly, that includes evangelical Christians.

The Spiritual Exercises are not without controversy within evangelical Protestantism. The Christianity that Martin Luther created sought a relationship with God that was direct and unmediated. Protestantism took away the selling of indulgences, the full or partial remission of heavenly punishment that a priest could grant in return for cash, because indulgences presumed that another being could intervene between a human and his maker. The same logic led Protestants to jettison the sensory feast that was offered in so many Catholic churches—the sweet incense, the votive candles, the pictures crammed against one another on the walls. In the images that spill out from a Catholic church, the cross hangs heavy with the dying Jesus. His haloed, blue-cloaked mother reaches out her hands. Saints and martyrs and followers jostle each other in side altars, so many that these churches seem impossibly dense and crowded to Protestants, whose churches are spare and often unadorned. To some Protestants, the Ignatian exercises and the monastic practices are a soft slide into the demonic because just as in the churches, images are used to intervene between human and God.[39] But those evangelicals who love the exercises say they bring them closer to God. These days there are books and websites that make the Spiritual Exercises accessible for evangelicals. Evangelicals participate in the exercises as they are given in Catholic retreats, and they lead other evangelicals in turn.[40]

The difference between the Ignatian exercises and ordinary Vineyard prayer is that the Spiritual Exercises spell out what the participant must do in precise, systematic detail, and then demand that the participant do it for hours on end. To follow the exercises as Loyola gave them in the sixteenth century (more or less as they are now done), a participant must commit a full thirty days. One must move into a retreat house for a month and spend each day in silence, except for daily meetings with a "spiritual director." The participant is expected to spend perhaps five hours a day in prayer, following specific, structured assignments. In such retreat houses, there are often no phones, no e-mail, no daily newspapers. The Jesuit retreat house near my home offers the exercises in this month-long version every summer. The housing is modest, and the cost runs to $3,400. Yet every year dozens of people participate.

Such withdrawal, however, is difficult for many. As a result, many retreat houses offer the exercises over a longer period, for nine months or a year. Even Ignatius offered these longer but less intense versions. Noblemen, he explained, cannot leave their houses for a month. These days most people probably do the exercises over this more extended period. (Retreat houses also offer weekend and weeklong retreats, which shrink the traditional curriculum abruptly.) In the nine-month version, one commits to do the exercises for an hour a day; to meet with a group of fellow participants once a week; and to meet with a spiritual director each month.

Whether you undergo the exercises as a full retreat or in the longer format, oral tradition has settled the curriculum into a specific progression through the Christian story. Each day involves an intense imagination of specific passages of scripture organized to unfold across four themes: a contemplation of God's generosity and human sin; the story of Jesus's birth and his ministry; his passion and death on the cross; and finally, his resurrection and transcendence. The participant is asked to be there in the scene: to imagine it as if present in the story. You can choose any perspective. Perhaps you choose to be a disciple; perhaps you elbow others in the crowd, a curious but skeptical observer. The next day you might imagine the scene again from another perspective: to see the story from Mary's eyes, or from Joseph's, or perhaps as blind Bartimaeus heard it. You are asked, in short, to daydream the story richly enough that it becomes vivid in your mind. Here are Loyola's instructions for praying around the nativity:

The salvation story, which this time is how Our Lady, pregnant now for nine months and (as may piously be believed) seated on a donkey, set out from Nazareth. With her went Joseph and a serving maid who was leading an ox. They travel towards Bethlehem to pay the tribute imposed by Caesar on all those lands (see Luke 2:1–14). [Then I] compose myself in the place. Here it will be seeing with the eye of the imagination the road from Nazareth to Bethlehem, considering how long it is and how wide, and whether it is level or goes through valleys and over hills. In the same way, it will be seeing the place or the cave of the nativity, considering whether it is large or small, deep or high, and how it is arranged. [Then] . . . I turn myself into a poor and unworthy little servant, watching them, contemplating them, and serving their needs as if I were actually there.[41]

At this point in the exercise, Loyola asked the participants to talk to Mary and Joseph—perhaps to help them with their bags, perhaps to hold the baby. He did not seem to care whether the participants imagined the cave or the road as long or short, as wide or narrow. He cared that the participants imagined intensely: that they felt that they were there in the scene as if they were present, and that when they saw Mary, and spoke with her, they felt that the conversation was meaningful.

I did the Spiritual Exercises in California across nine months in 2007–8 in a women's group at the Vineyard. There were four of us, the other three all long-standing members of the church. We met as a group once a week for three hours under the direction of an evangelical woman who had done the exercises and been trained to lead them at a Catholic retreat house with an offbeat sense of spiritual inclusiveness. Every day, alone at home, we each spent an hour with an assigned scripture and wrote about that time in a journal. When we met, we took turns describing our time in prayer that week. Then we did another contemplative exercise in that group, although we did the exercise alone, parceling ourselves out into different rooms in the building. Afterward we met again to report on our time. We used the same syllabus, with the same assignments, as the Catholic retreat that had trained our leader. Here is a truncated version of our Nazareth exercise:

I ask for the grace to know Jesus intimately in his humanity, to love him more intensely, and to follow him more deeply.
    It is late afternoon—dusk—the day is waning. Mary has just placed the finishing stitches in a small baby blanket she is knitting

for her soon-expected baby. Take a moment to gaze upon this young girl. Observe her now as she lights the candles in her small home. Note the peace in her movements. As Mary looks down the pathway, she sees Joseph approaching. His pace is hurried, and as he approaches, he looks like he carries news. What might this be?

He greets Mary with a warm embrace and then says, "Mary, the news is out—Emperor Caesar Augustus has sent out an order for all the citizens of the Empire to register themselves for a census. We must go to Bethlehem to register." Observe the expression on Mary's face as she receives this news. She knows the trip is a long one and a dangerous one, approximately ninety-five miles from Nazareth to the town of Bethlehem. Take a moment to be with her as she receives this startling news. How does she feel?—almost ready to deliver, and a long journey to make. What are her thoughts? What do they, Mary and Joseph, say to each other? Imagine their conversation. Watch them as they begin to make preparations for the long journey, in the cold of winter. They must travel light. What food provisions does Mary choose to bring? What clothing for herself, Joseph, and the newborn Jesus? Joseph prepares the donkey for the long, arduous trip. Imagine walking ninety-five miles with a pregnant woman on the back of a small donkey.

Watch as Mary and Joseph make inquiries among their neighbors. Who else is traveling to Bethlehem? Who else is of the family of David? How relieved they are to find others who will be in the caravan of travelers. Imagine the faces of these fellow travelers. Imagine yourself as one of them. How do you feel about the long journey?

Be very present to Mary and Joseph.[42]

The evangelical interpretation of the process was not as it would have been in a Catholic context, though I did not realize that until I participated in an Ignatian weekend at the local Jesuit house and found the differences so striking, they made my head hurt. In the Jesuit house, we seemed to be invited to do these imaginative prayers to learn what Jesus had experienced; to know more from the inside what Jesus had felt and tried to teach. In the evangelical context, the aim was to experience God directly and to learn to be more attentive to the way he showed up (or not) in our lives. Still, the actual process of doing the exercises was identical. The prayer techniques were the same.

What astonished me was how intensely emotional the experience was. Every week when we gathered in our group, the women cried. They talked about their feelings—how moved they were, how frightened, how glad. They seemed rubbed raw by the time they spent in prayer. They wept about how much more intimate their relationship with God had become, how they felt his presence, how he had become more alive. All of them said that they knew Christ better: that before the exercises, their belief had been abstract—despite all that encouragement from the Vineyard to experience God personally. (Admittedly, people decide to do the exercises because they feel that their prayer life is not all it could be. It is also true that a Vineyard congregant's "abstract" belief may be considerably more personal than that of an Episcopalian's.) All of them reported that the exercises made God real for them in new ways.

Julia had been a member of the Vineyard for twenty years before she did the exercises. She was a good, conscientious Christian, and I knew she had been praying daily before our group began. But these exercises made possible something her previous prayer had not. She explained:

> Maybe the best analogy would be that before the exercises, it was like I had a relationship with a pen pal. We would write letters to each other. You get to know a pen pal, and you feel like you know them pretty well. But then, imagine after years of writing letters, you finally met that person, really sat down and talked with them and really heard their voice. And experienced how they moved and could hear the color of their voice.

The color of their voice. She knew God with her senses now. She had decided to do the exercises because she could not see Jesus's face in her mind. Now she could. Krista had also been a Christian for twenty years. She worked in ministry and spent much of her time talking to people about God. Still, she thought the exercises drenched her sense of God with feeling and sensation. "I just felt more known than I have in a long time. More connected and more sure and more known to God, more open to Him, more vulnerable."

I felt this too. I cried in prayer, and I cried in the group. Even now I can remember the weeks we spent en route to Bethlehem and the flight to Egypt. I remember imagining the donkey and the dusty heat and the vivid blue of Mary's robe. I had complicated philosophical thoughts about whether God was real—but I remember gazing into the baby's eyes, and I wept.

This is where the quest to understand prayer technique becomes deeply interesting. Remember that what Ignatian prayer asks of the mind is also what evangelical prayer demands: intense focus on words and mental images, with a playlike, daydream-like interaction with God. Why should these practices be so emotional? The simple explanation is that the Ignatian process identifies significant emotional experience *as* God. Our spiritual director, a warm-eyed woman in her early fifties who had come to the exercises after her mother died and had found that they made her death tolerable, spoke, as Loyola did, of what she called the "movement" of God in our lives, as if God were a tide that ebbed and flowed. She had us notice the times when we felt we had made an unexpected emotional connection with someone; when we were able to say something easily, so that someone felt heard and touched; when we had a sense of peace; when we felt happy. That, she told us, is God.

As my Ignatian group became more sophisticated in this identification of God through their own emotional experience, they used the phrase the "movement of God" to describe the way they noticed and responded to their everyday world. For the most part, they used a language of emotions. They talked about periods when they felt sad or when things were difficult, and they called these periods "dark." Then they used the soft psychological language of the urban American middle class: they were "shut down," "isolated," "slow." They would talk about periods of happiness and activity and call them "light." The difference from secular psychotherapy is that these emotional experiences were understood as connected to an external being, God. The women spoke about "what God is doing in my life now," what God was "leading" them to do. The spiritual director did not think of herself as a psychotherapist. "I'm not trying to cure anything. I'm not trying to solve anyone's problem. What I'm trying to do is to help a person learn to understand their own interior movements and to cooperate with what's happening for them on their interior." But it was clear that when we went around the circle each week in group, reporting on that week's prayer meant giving a rich and subtle account of feeling states. That alone heightened participants' emotional awareness.

This, however, would not explain the emotionality of Vineyard prayer experience because labeling emotion as God was not, in fact, a Vineyard practice. God was the cause of emotion, not the substance of emotion, just as a person causes you to feel emotion but is not that emotion himself or herself. And yet because God is the most important person and most important causal actor in an evangelical life, this language of emotion-as-God came comfortably to these Vineyard women.

The more complex explanation for why the exercises are so emotional is that something about their structure and the way they direct the imagination generates intense feeling. As Loyola laid out the formal structure of these prayer practices, they have three explicit features: interaction, interweaving, and sensory enhancement. These features are also found in Vineyard practice.

First, the practice is not passive. The practitioner interacts with what she or he imagines. For Loyola, the intense focus on mental imagery served to enable an interaction with God. He shared this goal, of course, with modern evangelicals, for whom the point of the daydream is to experience that personal back-and-forth with God. During each Ignatian exercise, the participant is supposed to talk to the main characters of the scene directly (the "colloquy"). Usually, this main character is Christ. Loyola said that this talk should be intimate; that it was "really the kind of talk friends have with one another, or perhaps like the way a servant speaks to his master, asking for some kindness or apologizing for some failure, or telling him about some matter of business and asking for his advice."[43] His notes tell us that he thought that each participant would have a different experience and that each would imagine God in different ways. He thought that was fine—not an obvious conclusion for someone to reach in the midst of an Inquisition.

For a Christian, such an interaction is bound to be emotional, like a match to lighter fluid, because the practitioner has such intense feelings about God. Loyola, however, understood that there would be times when participants would enjoy the prayer process, and feel as if they could talk to God, and times when it would make them very unhappy and they couldn't really believe that God was there to listen. Many of Loyola's notes are about these emotional fluctuations and the way a spiritual director should handle them. He called them "consolation" and "desolation." Consolation occurs when the participant feels good: when one has joy, or loves God, or has any experience that leads one to love God more. Desolation is darkness of soul, confusion of spirit, hopelessness, laziness, unhappiness. Loyola thought that both were inevitable and that they emerged for individuals in particular ways. For all the scattered inconsequentialism of a text written as a set of notes for himself, a modern reader can discern a psychological intelligence as acute and sophisticated as any psychoanalyst's.

Then the Ignatian exercises repeatedly interlace scripted prayers (like the "Our Father") with private, personal reflection. You recite the "Our Father," and then examine your feelings of the moment. You think about the scripture, and then about yourself in relation to the scripture, and then about the scripture in relation to yourself. I wrote this journal entry during the week we spent on the annunciation (Luke 1:26–38):

> I felt that I could participate in Mary's excitement and joy and fear. I began to think more deeply about self-sacrifice and the role of trust, her willingness to trust. That Jesus participated in human pain: it becomes a way of saying, trust me, I have been there with you, I know. [The man] who was so angry the other day—I thought of him, and I began to see him as self-hating. To get him to relax, he'd need to trust. He'd need to believe he was lovable. That is hard for him.

The most insistent form of this tacking back and forth is called the Examen, in which you are supposed to reimagine each moment of the previous day in relation to God and in relation to the specific scripture you were reading, attaching the ordinary events of an ordinary day to a biblical story the way upholstery cloth is tacked onto an armchair.[44]

The interweaving blurs the boundary between what is external and what is within. All language does this, of course; all language is given from without but is used within as inner speech. That is why Wittgenstein asserted that there was no private language and why Vygotsky thought that the child's first use of inner speech was its most profound sign of membership in the human community. But the layering of external given verbal structure and internal personalization takes the process one step further by using past personal memories to create the details of the scriptural story. When you imagine Mary kneeling before Gabriel, you bring to bear all you carry within the vast cloister of your own memory: your museum visits to see medieval and Renaissance paintings, your vacation trips to dry and dusty lands, your recollection of a rustic bench, which becomes a model for the bench you conjure up for Mary, who rises up from it in surprise.[45] Mary then shares your own personal past—and that past, of course, is dense with remembered feeling. To frame that personal daydream with the "Our Father" reminds you that this is not your personal fantasy of Mary—this is Mary, and she is part of you.

Finally, the Ignatian exercises use sensory detail to intensify that process and make the abstract personal and near. Loyola clearly and repeatedly insisted that participants use all their senses to engage the story. The most explicit example of this "application of the senses," as it is called, is in the contemplation of hell, scheduled for an early segment of the practice. This is the version in Loyola's text:

> I imagine that I see with my own eyes the length, breadth and depth of Hell. I beg God for what I want. Here I ask for an intimate sense of the punishment suffered by the damned, so that if my failures ever make me grow forgetful of the love of my eternal Lord, at least my fear of these punishments will keep me from falling into sin.
>
> First heading: to see in imagination those enormous fires and the souls, as it were with bodies of fire.
>
> Second heading: to hear in imagination the shrieks and groans and the blasphemous shouts against Christ our Lord and all the saints.
>
> Third heading: to smell in imagination the fumes of sulphur and the stench of filth and corruptions.
>
> Fourth heading: to taste in imagination all the bitterness of tears and melancholy and a gnawing conscience.
>
> Fifth heading: to feel in imagination the heat of the flames that play on and burn the souls.[46]

Loyola always wanted people to see, hear, feel, touch, and taste the scripture with their mind's senses. He wanted his participants to see the characters of the texts they used, to envision the details of how they stood, held their shoulders, and where they rested their arms. He wanted people to listen to what these characters were saying as if they could catch the words with their ears. He wrote that whenever he contemplated a scene from scripture, "I will smell the fragrance and taste the infinite sweetness and charm of the Divinity." He wrote of using his sense of touch to "embrace and kiss the places where the persons walk or sit."[47]

We do this all the time with moments of the day we savor or wish that we could rerun. We revisit upsetting or exciting conversations, speaking again in our minds the words we spoke, feeling our bodies tensed and sprung. The sensory details—the light on the other person's face, the way our stomach jolted when we entered the room—make the reenactments vivid, and the vividness catches up our emotions as if we were there responding to the event as it took place, and as it takes place in different ways as our fantasies unfold. That's the way Loyola wanted his participants to experience praying about scripture: as if the stories were as vibrant as a remembered conversation we nurse over again and again in our daydreams. His sure-footed intuition told him that to make scripture real enough to respond to meant to use sensory memory, and to make scripture sensory made it emotional.

Certainly the women in my Ignatian group reported that they experienced God as more real for them—less like something they believed in, like gravity, and more like something there in the world, like a rock, or like a real person you could lean on. Krista was willing to say that she had never believed in God as strongly she did after the exercises.

> Honestly, I think I'm closer to Jesus than I've ever been. I've been a Christian since—since I was sixteen, which is wild. The Ignation stuff, for me, had to do with really drilling down into what I really believe. Jesus's ministry, resurrection, and death. I don't know if I fully believed until I did the exercises.

Julia said that what changed was her sense of God's presence.

> That sense of presence was really strong. Sometimes stronger than other times. It wasn't perfectly consistent. But when I could quiet my thoughts, when I could sort of get out of my own mind, out of that chatter, I had experiences that I could never—I couldn't have predicted or didn't know that I would want. It felt as if somebody was there.

She explicitly said that this had happened as a result of being instructed to create and to dwell upon specific mental images. "There's reality that I hadn't experienced before. And it came to me through visual imagery." When she tried to explain why, she said that she had never really allowed herself to use her imagination in prayer. Not, at any rate, at length, not deliberately and intensively. (She was too serious, she thought, for date night.) The Spiritual Exercises demanded that she use her imagination; and then God became part of her. "Before, there was an abstract concept. But I think now my experience of that is that Christ is in me. He is part of me at a cellular level. Now I will imagine Christ in me, sense Christ in me. I don't just have to rely on my own resources. That's pretty big." That was what our spiritual director told me. She loved the Spiritual Exercises because when she did them, God became "bigger."

The surprising lesson from this excursion into the spiritual disciplines is that inner sense cultivation—the deliberate, repeated use of inner visual representation and other inner sensory experience, with interaction, interweaving, and sensory enhancement—has been central to the tradition of Christian prayer. It is central to evangelical prayer. This cannot be an accident.

To be sure, modern evangelical prayer privileges a different interior sense than traditional Catholic prayer: hearing, rather than seeing. Evangelical prayer cultivates the auditory imagination, at least in the way people talk about prayer. Book titles like *Hearing God* and *God Whispers* and *The Power of a Whisper* invite the congregant to reach for God with their ears. The auditory is hardly absent from the earlier tradition; Loyola, after all, presented the conversation, or colloquy, as the most important part of each Spiritual Exercise. Nor is the visual exactly absent in the evangelical setting, as Hybels's visual props and the language of praying in the throne room and at the cross suggest. "If it helps," the pastor said one morning, "imagine that you are kneeling at the cross before Jesus and looking up at him." But the differences are real, and they show up in the way people experience God. Catholics seem to see more often; evangelicals hear.[48]

The main point is that the mental muscles developed in prayer work on the boundary between thought and perception, between what is attributed to the mind—internal, self-generated, private, and hidden from view—and what exists in the world. They focus attention on the words and images on one side of the boundary, and they treat those words and images as if they belonged on the other.

Both history and ethnography suggest that the Christian cultivation of the inner senses has real consequences for those who use it. In the first place, of course, inner sense cultivation shapes the content of the cultivator's mind. The person who is focusing all that attention on the man being baptized by John is not fretting about the laundry (or for that matter, about pornography). But the impact appears to do more than simply exclude unwanted thoughts or control thought. Inner sense cultivation seems to make that which is imagined more real in experience, especially when all the senses are engaged. It appears to make what is imaged feel more substantial, more present. The tradition of Christian prayer also suggests that inner sense cultivation, in the form taught by the church, is deeply emotional. Inner sense cultivation seems to intensify emotional response like a hothouse. Emotions become stronger, more intense.

That observation appears to hold across traditions. Inner sense cultivation is common in spiritual practice and has been found in societies of varying complexity throughout human history.[49] For premodern societies, the best-documented example is shamanism. Shamans are religious experts, found primarily in small, face-to-face societies, who are presumed to mediate between the earthly world and the spiritual one. In shamanic societies, the shamans do their work through the use of imagined sight, sound, and feeling. They "see" and sometimes "hear" the objects of the spirit world in their minds, often when they are in trance-like states, and their interactions with those visions and voices constitute their work. For example, when a member of the Amazonian Bororo falls ill, a shaman may go into a trance to "find" the ill person in the other world and "return" them to their human body on earth. Shamans seem to go through extensive training in their use of mental images, both to ensure that they have the right content and to increase their vividness. Apprentice shamans are asked to look for specific objects, and they are rewarded for talking about those objects as if they were real. Here is one ethnographer's account:

> Close by, the payé [teacher] is sitting. "What do you see? Tell me, what do you see?" he will ask insistently, and the apprentice will then find the words to describe his visions. "There is the bend in the river . . . a black rock . . . I can hear water rushing . . ." "Go on, go on!" the payé will insist, his ear close to the other's mouth. "There are birds, red birds, sitting on the lower branches of the tree . . ." "Are

they sitting on your left or on your right?" the payé will ask. And so they continue, haltingly, at times in deep silence, until the older man knows what kind of images and voices his pupil is perceiving and can now begin to interpret for him.[50]

These shamans interact with what they imagine; they are told to seek images identified by their mentors, but they elaborate on those externally provided structures with personal, private experiences; and they add details for the many senses.

Inner sense cultivation is also found in Tibetan Buddhism. In his *How to Practice,* the Dalai Lama presents imagining words and images as central to daily practice: "With a strong determination to attain Buddhahood in order to serve other beings, imagine a Buddha in front of you, or your spiritual teacher as a representation of Buddha. Repeat three times as if you are repeating after him or her."[51] In the hill station of Dalhousie, Himachal Pradesh, in India, where the remnants of the great Tibetan monasteries gathered in the 1960s, a young scholar set out to document the way the monks summoned the divine. They did so through practiced visualizations in which the mind became the vehicle for the nonmaterial to become manifest and the body was transformed through chant and (as in the monastery of San Marco) gesture. "As [the monk] practices, all the parts grow more and more vivid, until finally he should be able to form a picture of what he is deliberately making vivid and to leave unformed everything else, the picture becoming so vivid that he thinks he could not see it better with his own eyes." The ability to do this, the scholar wrote, is the result of long and "really rather frustrating" practice.[52] The monks interact with what they imagine, and they bring all their senses to the task.

One finds these techniques as well in the secluded world of Jewish mysticism, in the practice of kabbalah. The tension between representation and the unrepresentable is fraught in Judaism, yet visualization appears to have been the primary method of mysticism from antiquity. There was a practice known as the "mystical ascent" in the ancient mystical corpus (the *Hekhalot*) in which the practitioner visualized passage through seven celestial palaces to arrive in the throne room of the divine: "His body is like beryl, His splendor is luminous and glows from within the darkness and the cloud and thick darkness surround Him." Over the centuries these texts are clear about the heart of practice: "Simply put, imagination provides the vehicle through which one can have access to God."[53]

These days, as the scholar Jonathan Garb reports, the kabbalists of modern Jerusalem still use visualization practices. Garb describes kabbalists who breathe in to the head while visualizing one name of God, and breathe into the body while visualizing another. They look at objects and close their eyes to imagine the object filled with divinity. They focus upon a letter in the name of God until the letter dissolves into black beads. They go to the graves of the *tzadik* (holy men) and visualize the *tzadik,* and then they visualize ascending to the light and drawing the light down upon the graves. At gatherings, men come to hear a great rabbi speak and then pause, rocking back and forth, and the men rock also, and images come into their minds to which they give significance. They repeat words slowly and methodically until they lose their normal meaning, and they listen for the way the sounds begin to echo in their minds.[54]

None of this implies that the experience of God is the experience of the imagination. In fact, it should be clear that the spiritual impact of inner sense cultivation is not simply the result of the use of internal sensation. That there are two major forms of spiritual discipline—apophatic and kataphatic—tells us that this is true. In the formalized practices called the spiritual disciplines, only the kataphatic techniques increase the flow of thought. Those techniques heighten the significance of certain kinds of words and images, and they draw the thinker's attention to those words and images and give them force. They are techniques of hyperattention. Thought expands, becomes more than thought, becomes (as Dionysius the Areopagite believed) so strong, it overflows into the real. But apophatic practice is understood, within the same tradition, to be at least as effective for those who can do it, and these are techniques of disattention. They teach the practitioner to treat each and every thought as insignificant: to detach from them, to observe them from afar, to treat them as if they were no more than a passing breeze. Thought is meant to still into motionlessness. Both kinds of techniques are associated, in the historical record, with the intense and realistic apprehension of an immaterial divine being. Both hyperattention and disattention work. It's just that hyperattention is a lot easier to master.

What this study of prayer does teach us is that the primary purpose of prayer technology is to manipulate the way the person praying attends to his or her own mind. That makes sense whether you look at prayer from a spiritual or a secular perspective. The point of religious conviction is that the everyday world is not all there is to reality; to see beyond, one must change the way one pays attention. But the lesson from the close observation of prayer technology is that these fine-grained ways of paying attention demand specific mental skills—and that implies that some individuals may be more confident or comfortable in using those skills. This is an awkwardness for evangelical enthusiasm. When John Wimber founded the Vineyard, he thought that everyone should be "doin' the stuff." Everyone, that is, should be feeling the Holy Spirit and talking to God and receiving images in prayer. But we have already seen that not everyone seems to be able to have these experiences, even when they want to. I thought that if I looked more closely at the way individuals use prayer technology, I could understand why.

CHAPTER SEVEN

The Skill of Prayer

I will pour out my Spirit
upon all flesh
And your sons and your
daughters shall prophesy
And your young men shall
see visions
And your old men shall
dream dreams

Acts 2:17

Suddenly I was looking at a map of the world,
only the map was alive and moving! I sat up
and shook my head and rubbed my eyes. It
was a mental movie. I could see all the conti-
nents and waves were crashing on to their
shores . . . the waves became young people . . .
preaching the gospel . . . Then just as sud-
denly as it had come the scene was gone.
Wow! I thought. What was that?

Loren Cunningham,
Is That Really You, God?

W E HAVE SEEN that prayer trains people to ignore the distracting world and to focus on their inner experience. We have seen
that in the kind of prayer taught in evangelical churches, those praying focus on what they think, feel, and imagine. And we have also seen
that prayer traditions presume that these practices alter spiritual experience. Now I wanted to know whether training in prayer did, in fact, have
consequences.

As I delved deeper into the relationships American evangelicals have with God, the patterns that experienced pray-ers reported—better focus, sharper imagery, unusual experiences—began to sound less like words they repeated because they had learned to talk that way in church (as you learn to shrug expressively when you live in Rome) and more like ways their minds had learned to sense a presence for which there is no ordinary sensory evidence. I couldn't know whether they were in fact better at sensing God—whether their new skills had made them more accurate at perceiving the supernatural—but I thought I could figure out whether the mental changes they reported really did take place, and if so, whether those changes were the psychological outcome of the prayer technology they had mastered.

I had a personal reason for being so intrigued. Many years ago, as a young ethnographer, I had studied people who practiced magic in present-day Britain as my dissertation project. I was curious about how magic could come to seem real to modern people. Most of these people thought of themselves as worshipping an ancient goddess under the full and pendulous moon. For them the earth was alive, and they sought to feel its power pulsing beneath their feet. They described themselves as shamans, druids, witches, and warlocks, responsive to the subtle rhythms of the earth. They lived in London, these magicians, and they held modern jobs and had modern lives, but they imagined themselves into another time. When I set out to understand how they came to believe in magic, I did what anthropologists do: I participated in their world. I joined their groups. I read their books and novels. I practiced their techniques and performed in their rituals. For the most part, I found, the rituals depended on techniques of the imagination. You shut your eyes and saw with your mind's eye the story told by the leader of the group. The techniques were pretty close to Christian kataphatic prayer practice. Some magicians even referred to these techniques as "Ignatian."

In the late afternoons, in my London apartment, I practiced these techniques, following the instructions I was given. Here is an example from one of my early lessons, which I did, in some form, for thirty minutes a day for nine months:

Work through these exercises, practicing one of them for a few minutes each day, either before or after your meditation session.

1. Stand up and examine the room in which you are working. Turn a full circle, scanning the room. Now sit down, close the eyes, and build the room in imagination. Note where the memory or visualizing power fails. At the end of the exercise briefly re-examine the room and check your accuracy. Note the results in your diary.

2. Carefully visualize yourself leaving the room in which you are working, going for a short walk you know well, and returning to your room. Note clarity, breaks in concentration, etc., as before.

3. Go for an imaginary walk; an imaginary companion, human or animal, can accompany you. Always start and finish the walk in the room you use for the exercises. Note the results, etc., as before.

4. Build up in imagination a journey from your physical plane home to your ideal room. Start the journey in real surrounds, then gradually make the transition to the imaginary journey by any means you wish. Make the journey to and from the room until it is entirely familiar.

The idea (I came to think of it as the theology of magic) was that if you could learn to see mental images clearly, those images could become the vehicle by which supernatural power entered the mundane world.

What startled me, as a young ethnographer, was that this training worked. At least, it seemed to shift something in the way I used my senses and my internal sensory awareness. After about a year of this kind of training, spending thirty minutes a day in an inner world structured in part by external instructions, my mental imagery *did* seem to become clearer. I thought that my images had sharper borders, greater solidity, and more endurance. They had more detail. I felt that my senses were more alive, more alert. My concentration states seemed deeper and more sharply different from the everyday. One evening I was reading a book about Arthurian Britain and the early Celtic isles (it was written by a magician), I allowed myself to get deeply involved with the story, reading not the way I read a textbook but the way I read books like *The Secret Garden* as a child, giving way to the story and allowing it to grip my feelings and to fill my mind. I read late into the night. And as I woke the next morning, I saw six druids standing against the window, above the stirring London street below. I *saw* them, and they beckoned to me. I stared for a moment of stunned astonishment, and then I shot up out of bed, and they were gone. Had they been there in the flesh? I thought not. But my memory of the experience is very clear. I do not remember that I imagined them, or that I had wanted to see them, or that I pretended to see them. I remember that I saw them as clearly and distinctly and as external to me as I saw the notebook in which I recorded the moment, my sentences underlined and marked by exclamation points. I remember it so clearly because it was so singular. Nothing like that had ever happened to me before.

But other people in the magical world had experiences like that. They practiced the exercises and read the books and participated in the rituals, and then, out of the blue, they saw something—the Goddess, or a flash of divine light, or a shining vision of another world. They saw these as things in the world, not phantoms in the mind, although because the image vanished almost immediately, they knew that what they had seen was not ordinary. I had wondered for many years if something about the practice associated with magic made these supernatural experiences more common. When I encountered the same spiritual techniques in experiential evangelical Christianity, I was determined to find out.

So I decided to do an experiment. I thought that there was something like a proclivity for a certain way of using one's mind, and I suspected that repeated practice in that use might change one's mental experience and increase the chances of an intense spiritual experience. I wanted to know whether that was really true or whether my own experiences were a fluke.

Anthropologists are like old-fashioned naturalists. They go out of their offices to watch people in their own environments, and they spend so much time observing them—an absurd amount of time—that the people more or less forget that they are there. Sometimes even the anthropologists forget that they went there as anthropologists; graduate students end up living in remote Burmese villages and highland New Guinea, their dissertations forgotten, immersed in the vivid intensity of a social world so different from the one of their birth.[1] Anthropologists invest that time because they are after culture: the shared, often implicit patterns in the way people order and make sense of their lives that reveal themselves most clearly in casual social interaction.

But to tease apart psychological change from cultural description, I had to compare different people within the same culture, and that meant thinking like a psychologist, a very different kind of intellectual.

If anthropologists think of themselves as novelists manqué, as Clifford Geertz once said of himself, psychologists are biologists manqué, and these days not so very manqué. Once I gave a presentation to a roomful of psychologists, beginning with my years of ethnographic research and leading up to my first quantitative finding. They listened patiently until the first scatter plot went up on the screen. Then someone smiled at me and said, "Data!"[2]

I met Howard Nusbaum when he and I joined an interdisciplinary group on religion. Howard is a psychologist—the messy-desk-and-untucked-shirt academic kind, not a clinician. He studies the way people use language and understand speech. When I said that some kinds of prayer practice alter the way people use their minds to experience their senses, he was intrigued, and we began to talk. He suggested that I draw up a description of the kinds of changes people reported. I was still in Chicago, and I went back to my Vineyard congregants to interview them more systematically about their relationship with God, the way they prayed, and their spiritual experiences. I interviewed twenty-eight people whom I had met through my house group and through repeated visits to the church. Ten were male, eighteen female; seventeen white, seven African American, four Asian. Twenty-three were between twenty and thirty years old, and five were over thirty. The oldest was in her early fifties. The distribution was representative of this predominantly young, somewhat diverse congregation. I asked them all the same questions, but I let them talk. And as before, I was struck by the differences among them: that not all of them were able to know God as a person who spoke with them, even when they tried.[3]

I then went through every interview and pulled out quotations in which people reported that something had changed in the way they experienced their minds and their senses as they learned to pray. Howard and I organized those different descriptions into clusters. We had a "focus" cluster: comments about how focused people seemed to become in prayer, how deeply they felt that their concentration on prayer took them away from the everyday here and now, like "in my mind I'd go to that place." There was a "senses" cluster: comments about the ways people had experienced the spiritual world with their senses, like whether they commonly got images in prayer or ever experienced something immaterial. And we had a "personlike" cluster: comments about whether people did, in fact, experience God as a person in the ways that the teachings and books of the church suggested that one should—talking freely to him throughout the day, about everything, laughing with him, even getting angry at him. Then we turned the clusters into lists of questions with yes-no answers, the kind of list psychologists call a scale: a standardized list of statements used to measure some quality by the way the subject responds.[4] I went back through each interview and scored it according to these questions. If I could mark "yes" for the question based on the interview transcript, the person got one point on the scale. The score for the list was the sum of the points.

I had also asked everyone I interviewed to fill out a psychological scale. When I started thinking about doing experimental work on the impact prayer has on the mind, I had people fill out psychological scales, plural. One time I showed up at house group and handed out packets of scales to the startled members, which they graciously completed. In the beginning, that packet included a peculiar but often-used scale about unusual experience (the Launay Slade Hallucination Scale); a scale given to people who move in and out of trancelike states, often (it is thought) as a result of trauma (the Dissociative Experiences Scale); and a funny little experiment where you ask people to close their eyes and imagine that they are hearing the song "White Christmas," and then you ask them how vividly they heard it.[5] It is useful to use scales that other people have designed because then you know how some other "normal" group of people has answered them: usually, undergraduate psychology students, who are to psychological science what white mice are to medical research.

Most people in the house group didn't like the scales or answered them all the same way. Almost everyone who did the "White Christmas" experiment said that they had heard "White Christmas" but knew there was no music playing. That didn't help to pick out the differences between them. The dissociation and hallucination scales made them think I was fishing for psychopathology, and that made them flinch and fret about whether I thought they were crazy.

But they liked one scale. That is, they thought that the questions were interesting and reasonable. The questions didn't make them wonder whether they were being secretly examined for mental illness. Moreover, they each answered the scale in a different way. My father, a clinician, had introduced me to this scale back when we were talking about the patho-logical and nonpathological shifts in the ways people experience and perceive, and I threw it in with the others in the packet because I liked the questions it asked. The questions seemed to tap someone's willingness to be caught up in their imaginative experience, and in nature and music, and I had a hunch that what the questions captured was connected to the experience of God.

This was the Tellegen Absorption Scale. It has thirty-four statements that one marks as true or false, meaning true or false for the person filling out the scale. A subject gets a point for every "true." The scale does not measure religiosity per se; it has only one statement that could be construed as religious. Instead, its statements describe experiences of nature and color and music. They describe textures and smells. There are statements that assert that you, the scale-taker, sometimes experience things as a child; that you can "see" the image of something when no longer looking at it; that you sometimes discover that you have finished a task when your thoughts are elsewhere; that different smells call up different colors; that you often sense the presence of a person before seeing him or her; that you can become oblivious to everything else when listening to music; that you sometimes keep listening to a fascinating voice.[6]

I gave the absorption scale to all the people in the Chicago church I interviewed systematically, and then I compared their answers to the answers they gave to the questions I asked about their spiritual experience (the senses cluster, the focus cluster, and the personlike cluster). It turned out that they were closely related. A person's absorption score was not related to the length of time he or she prayed on a daily basis. That is, the scale did not measure prayer practice per se. But the way a person answered the absorption questions was significantly related to the way he or she experienced prayer. The more absorption statements people marked as true, the more focus cluster experiences they reported (for example, that time seemed to change when they prayed, or that they went to a different place in their mind). The more absorption statements they endorsed, the more they said they experienced God with their senses (for example, that they commonly got images and sensations in prayer, or that they had felt God touch them). Most remarkably, the way someone answered the absorption scale predicted whether he or she was able to experience God as a person. You might think that my questions ("Do you speak to God freely throughout the day?" "Would you describe God as your best friend or as like an imaginary friend, except real?" and so forth) would lead people just to parrot back what the pastor and the books and the conferences say about God so often. But those who had high absorption scores were much more likely to report that they experienced God as if God really was a person—someone they could talk to easily, who talked back, with whom they could laugh, and at whom they could get angry. People with low absorption scores said that they couldn't. When I held the absorption score constant, the time spent in prayer turned out to be significantly related to how personlike God was for someone.[7] It appeared that there really was something like talent, and something like training, and that both mattered to the way someone experienced God.

Now that was interesting. A skeptic might look at these results and conclude that the absorption scale simply reproduces what the Vineyard says about God, so it is not surprising that the two overlap. But that's not true. Again, the scale contains only one statement that could be construed as religious. Instead, the scale seems to pick up something about the way people use their minds. That *does* overlap with what the church asks of its congregants, but it overlaps in an interesting way that reveals something about the kind of prayer used in these evangelical settings. We know now that the kind of prayer taught by the Vineyard—and in all experiential evangelical churches—demands the use of one's imagination. Such prayer asks the person praying to be present in a scene one imagines as if one were there. This scale suggests that if you are the kind of person who sometimes experiences things as a child (as one statement has it), then you are more likely to do what evangelical prayer asks you to do with your mind. Everyone in church believes that those who pray are more likely to experience God, but this work suggests that it is the capacity to use your mind in certain ways that allows you to experience an invisible God as if he were present.

There was another reason I thought the absorption scale really picked up something about this evangelical spirituality. The people who did not experience God in the vivid way the church thought they should also did not think that the absorption scale described them. Jacob, who had wanted and expected a mountaintop experience but didn't have one, marked "true" for only four of the items. Fred, who glumly said he hadn't had these powerful experiences (and who later asked our house group to pray for him so that he would hear God speak "with a booming voice"), marked "true" for only five. He even wrote next to one item, "There are such people?" Alice, who said she'd be afraid of prophecy, marked "true" next to only thirteen. When I eventually gave the scale to Sarah, so often held up as an example of a prayer warrior, she marked "true" for thirty-three of the thirty-four items. When she finished writing on the questionnaire that afternoon in my office, she looked up with a smile and said, "The man who created this scale lived inside my head."

There was another interesting thing the absorption scale predicted. If people answered "true" to at least half the items on the absorption scale, their chances of reporting that they had heard God's voice or felt God's touch or seen the wing of an angel or had a sensory perception of something supernatural (like hearing God say "I will always be with you" from the backseat of a car) was six times as high as for those who said "true" to less than half the statements. It turned out that slightly over a third of the subjects reported sensory experiences of something not materially present. They heard with their ears, or they saw outside their head. Again, practice made a difference. If I in effect removed absorption from the analysis by correcting for it (we call this holding absorption "constant"), the length of time someone prayed every day was significantly related to whether they said they had seen a vision or heard a voice. That was striking.[8]

So what on earth does the scale really measure? When Tellegen and his students first drafted the questionnaire, they were trying to develop a pen-and-paper measure of hypnotic susceptibility, or the likelihood that someone will respond to hypnosis. It was a very good idea to see if one could create a pen-and-paper measure, because the gold standard of the field is quite cumbersome.[9] It takes about an hour. It is also quite odd. A person (the subject) sits with another person (the experimenter), who tells the subject to fall asleep—yet remain completely focused on the experimenter's voice. The experimenter asks the subject to stare at a target until it looks funny, to relax his or her muscles one by one, to feel that that the body is becoming heavy, so heavy, and so very, very drowsy, so that the eyelids close of their own accord, it is so hard to keep then open—until the subject is sitting with eyes shut and, apparently, in a dreamy, disconnected state. Then the experimenter gives the subject a set of instructions: to feel a force pushing his or her hands apart; to feel a magnet pushing them together; to hold out his or her arms and experience them as rigid, and to try to bend them, just try; to put imaginary dictionaries on those outstretched (but no longer rigid) arms, piling them on so that the hands fall down with so much weight. An annoying mosquito is buzzing around the room, the experimenter says, now land-ing on the subject's arms. "You can swat it now if you like," the experimenter tells the subject. I do this standard induction routinely now in my classes when I teach about spirituality and health. In the dark, quiet classroom, most students feel their hands move apart almost of their own accord. Very few swat the mosquito.

Hypnosis is a fascinating and frustrating phenomenon because its effects are real but also really hard to interpret. Some people find that in these inductions, their arms float up as if of their own accord; they smell odors that are not present and hear voices that no one else can hear; and when instructed, they forget entirely what happened until the experimenter allows them to remember. About a third of the normal population are "high hypnotizable": they follow eight or more of the twelve suggestions.[10] The scientists who work in this field debate fiercely what explains this behavior—some say it is an altered state, others that the subject is just very suggestible or maybe faking it—but no one doubts that the behavior takes place. Nor does anyone doubt that hypnosis is important. That some people to a great extent, and most people to some extent, have the capacity to treat their own will and memory as under another person's command is among the most compelling of psychological facts. Moreover, for those who can do it, hypnosis is exceedingly useful (if also dangerous in the hands of naïve therapists, as the mad hunt for alien abductors and sexual Satanists has taught us). Hypnosis can help those who respond to lose weight, quit smoking, use less anesthesia in the operating room, and recover more quickly. The problem is pinning the phenomenon down reliably enough to sort out the people who are just very compliant from those who really do seem to enter a different state where they are instructed to feel less pain—and do. That has been hard to specify, and it makes doctors skittish because it seems so much less predictable than a nice, steady, measurable flow of psychopharmacologic drug.

Tellegen and his students came up with the scale after dreaming up a long list of daily experiences and attitudes that they thought might be related to hypnotic "talent," which they seem to have taken as the capacity to get so caught up in an experience that ordinary life (driving a car, the need to do the dishes) fades in one's awareness. The original list had seventy-one items, like "I know that at one point I have walked in my sleep" and "I can tell a story with elaborations to make it sound better and then have the elaboration seem as real to me as the actual incident, or almost so." (Neither of those made it into the final scale.) In the final paper, Tellegen and his coauthor, Gilbert Atkinson, narrowed down the list after giving it to nearly five hundred students (for reasons not clear, they were all undergraduate women) and concluding that thirty-four of the items reliably clustered together. They called what this scale identified "absorption." In the end, the way people answered the absorption scale correlated only modestly (but still significantly) with how they responded to a standard hypnotic induction. So the two men decided they had found something related to hypnotizability but fundamentally different.[11]

Tellegen and Atkinson concluded that absorption is a character trait, a disposition for having moments of total attention that somehow completely engage all of one's attentional resources—perceptual, imaginative, conceptual, even the way one holds and moves one's body. "This kind of attentional functioning is believed to result in a heightened sense of the reality of the attentional object, imperviousness to distracting events, and an altered sense of reality in general, including an empathically altered sense of self."[12] In other words, when you get absorbed in something, it seems more real to you, and you and your world seem different than before. That is why it is related to hypnotizability. Both rely upon your ability to throw yourself into something and then to involve yourself intensely in the experience.[13] Later, Tellegen decided that the real distinction the scale pulled out was the difference between the instrumental and the experiential. There is the way one is when one is pragmatic and effective, focused on what is realistic, making practical decisions and pursuing important goals. Then there is the way one is when one is open, receptive, and willing to dwell in the experience of the moment, whether in the mind or in the world. That, he thought, was the heart of absorption: the mode of the novel reader and the music listener and the Sunday hiker, caught up in imagination or appreciation.[14]

When psychologists use the scale, they have found that it captures the ability to take pleasure in music and literature and the arts. Absorption, as measured by the scale, is related to reading and the imagination. The more highly you score, the more likely you are to be a reader, and the more likely you are to immerse yourself in rich, imaginative worlds; the more likely you are to be the kind of person who can lose him- or herself in movies and literature, the kind of person for whom the story can feel more real than the everyday. You daydream more. You may dance more. And a propensity for absorption has real this-worldly benefits. The more highly you score, the better you are at imagining someone else's perspective, and so the better you are at empathy, which demands that you understand what someone else experiences in his or her world, and the way another person thinks and feels. You may be more responsive to therapy and other forms of healing that rely on the mind's capacity to heal the body. Some psychologists find that high-absorption women are, in the eyes of observing clinicians, aesthetically focused and interesting; that they use unconventional thought processes; that they are imaginative, socially skilled, expressive, and introspective. High-absorption men are warm, giving, aesthetically oriented, nurturing, likable, and interesting.[15]

The clinical literature tells a darker story. Women who report recovered memories of sexual abuse score more highly on the absorption scale than those who report either continuous memories of abuse or no abuse. So do people who remember being abducted by aliens.[16] This suggests that people who are high absorption may become confused about the difference between fantasy and fact. Absorption is thought by clinicians to be part of dissociation, an auto-hypnotic capacity to narrow one's attention to block out awful in-the-now experience: exploding grenades, a stepfather's groping hands, the moment of impact when one's motorcycle hits the tree. The mind uses its capacity for internal withdrawal to protect the person from incapacitation in the face of overwhelming distress and then somehow gets stuck in the escape. A soldier mentally checks out when a blast kills his buddy; he functions mechanically and survives, and the war goes by, but on his return, he finds that he can't let go of the war. He seems to shift back into it so that at times the old war becomes more real to him than the place he now lives. Clinicians think that internal withdrawal involves absorption. The Dissociative Experiences Scale, probably the most widely used measure of dissociation, bases a third of its items on the absorption scale.[17]

All this suggests that absorption is the capacity to focus in on the mind's object—what we imagine or see around us—and to allow that focus to increase while diminishing our attention to the myriad of everyday distractions that accompany the management of normal life. You let a daydream unfold, or you become wrapped up in the hummingbird hovering at the orange trumpet vine, and your trip to the grocery store slips down in your mind. The absorption scale seems to pick up the enjoyable dimension—imaginative involvement, the delight we take in letting a story or sensation carry us away.[18] But the skill—that mental muscle—must be the capacity to allow what the mind dwells upon to take more attention than what the eyes and ears perceive. It seems to be a continuum. Common sense tells us that people vary in their ability to take seriously what their minds imagine. Just as humans can be more or less focused on an object, the degree of absorption varies between individuals and for any individual at different times. Most of us experience light absorption when we settle into a book and let the story carry us away. Some of us get so absorbed that we startle when someone enters the room, because we did not pay attention to the soft tread of the person's feet as he or she approached.

From that perspective, absorption is the mental capacity common to trance, hypnosis, dissociation, and to most imaginative experiences in which the individual becomes caught up in ideas or images or fascinations. That is not to say that absorption is equivalent to hypnosis or dissociation or trance: manifestly it is not. But absorption seems to be the basic, necessary skill, the shared capacity of mind that allows what we choose to attend to become more salient than the everyday context in which we are embedded. It is the ability to use a book to take your mind off your troubles. That cuts both ways, of course. Some people use novels to keep the world at bay long enough to recover and regain the strength to return. Others use novels—or soap operas, or reality television—to escape and ignore the troubled marriage or the needy child. In both cases, individuals use their mind to change their relation to the reality they perceive.

That is why absorption is central to spirituality. The capacity to treat what the mind imagines as more real than the world one knows is the capacity at the heart of experience of God. The very concept of a god, a more-than-natural being, rests on the premise that the world we know is not all of the world, nor indeed the most important part of it. The psychological capacity for absorption allows us to experience that concept as true. It enables that twofold shift in attention: toward the internal as well as the external. It is the capacity to make what we must imagine more real. Absorption gives us the ability to use our imagination to conceive of a being not in the world who nevertheless is the reason that the world exists. Absorption also gives us the capacity to imagine that being as good, because the world as it is does not naturally lend itself to the inference that its creator is wise and good. The anthropologist Maurice

Bloch argues that religion requires the ability to imagine and to trust.[19] He is right.

That is why those who say "true" to many of the questions on the absorption questionnaire are more likely to report that they focus deeply in prayer, that they know God with their senses, and that they experience God as a person. When a supernatural God is imagined as a person who talks to you, the people who are really going to feel comfortable talking to God will be the people who enjoy their imaginative journeys in the first place. It does not follow that those who are low in absorption are not good Christians. But it may be harder for them to know that this God who must be imagined—particularly when this God is understood as so personal—is real on the basis of their own experience.

Can they change that? Most of the psychologists who work with the scale treat absorption as a personality trait. Tellegen seems to have thought of absorption as a personality feature, not a skill, as most researchers have done, and it is true that people's score on the absorption scale is more or less stable over time.[20]

But the way the church talks about prayer suggests that absorption can be trained. I had begun to think about there being a skill in the first place because people at church so clearly agreed that prayer requires training and discipline; that learning to pray is hard; that some people are naturally good at prayer; and that some people, who are naturally good and who practice, become experts. It seemed to me that prayer was an absorption practice, and prayer training was really training in the skill of absorption.[21]

Now I had a hypothesis for an experiment: that when people believe that God will speak to them through their senses, when they have a propensity for absorption, and when they are trained in absorption by the practice of prayer, these people will report what prayer experts report: internal sensory experiences with sharper mental imagery and more sensory overrides (sensory experience in the absence of sensory stimuli). Note the combination: an interest in interpreting a supernatural presence (the participatory theory of mind, taught by the social world of the church); a willingness to get caught up in one's imagination (an individual difference); and actual practice (they do something again and again, which has consequences).

So I set out to train people, in what became the Spiritual Disciplines Project. I had moved to northern California by this point, which meant that no one from Chicago could participate in the project and all my subjects were new. I began by advertising on craigslist, and then in four local evangelical churches, two of them Vineyards and two of them like the Vineyard, softly charismatic but conventional on Sunday morning.

> Are you interested in spiritual transformation and the Christian spiritual disciplines? We are doing a study on different spiritual practices and what people learn through them. Subjects must be willing to spend 30 or more minutes each day for one month, and to come to Stanford University for two two-three hour sessions to participate in surveys, computer exercises and an interview. Subjects will receive a total of $325 for completing all aspects of the task. We are interested in recruiting people who would welcome the opportunity to be thoughtful and engaged in the process of spiritual inquiry. If interested, please contact . . .

It sounds like a lot of money, but it didn't come out to very much per hour. We told people who called that they would be randomly assigned to one of three spiritual disciplines: centering prayer (an apophatic condition); guided imagination on the Gospels (a kataphatic condition); or an intellectual exploration of the Gospels (the study condition). We included the apophatic condition because we wanted to make it clear that each one, including study, was a spiritual discipline; we thought that this interpretation would be more likely if study were one among three conditions, rather than what you got if you did not get the kataphatic prayer. In *Celebration of Discipline,* the beloved evangelical author Richard Foster says, "The purpose of the Spiritual Disciplines is the total transformation of the person. They aim at replacing old destructive habits of thought with new life-giving habits. Nowhere is this purpose more clearly seen than in the Discipline of study."[22] We put that statement in the packet with the lectures for the study condition.

One hundred and twenty-eight people responded and passed our screening questions.[23] Most of them were white, middle-aged, and female. When they came in to our office, they spent time filling out various standard psychological scales: the absorption scale, of course, but also scales about loneliness and stress and spiritual experience more generally.[24] Then they sat in front of a computer and did a series of exercises to see how they used their mental imagery. In one, they listened to a recorded voice that instructed them to shut their eyes and see before them specific scenes, and then to watch those scenes change (for example, to look at a shop they knew well, and at its window display, and door; to go into the shop and buy something, and to see money changing hands). At various times in the exercise, they were asked to open their eyes and to mark down on a scale from one to five how vivid the scene had been for them. We had them do one other subjective visual task—imagining weird, Escher-like forms that they turned in their minds—and then we gave them some objective tasks. They had to watch a rapidly shifting series of letters and pick out whether there had been a particular letter in the series. We faded images and words slowly in through a gray, grainy haze of dots and asked them when they could see the form and what it was, and then we faded them out again and asked them when they could no longer see the form, and we faded in and out some phrases through the auditory equivalent of grainy haze.[25]

Finally, we interviewed them. My assistant Christina spoke with each person for at least an hour and often longer. She asked them whether and how they heard from God and how they prayed, and she asked them about a wide range of spiritual experiences and whether they'd had them, and if so, how often and when. She asked them whether they'd heard a voice when they were alone, whether it was a religious experience, and how—if that had happened to them—they knew that the voice was God. She asked them about seeing and feeling things that were not materially present, and how, if that had happened, they made the decision that the experience had come from God. Finally, she asked them a series of questions that are associated with psychotic illness, so that we could know, if someone reported unusual experiences, whether they might be diagnosable by a psychiatrist as struggling with psychotic disorder. As a precaution, we also screened out people who were taking antipsychotic medications, and we screened out anyone who reported that they had been psychiatrically hospitalized.[26]

When they were finished, the subjects then picked up one of three identical brown packages from a side table. They knew that the envelopes contained different spiritual disciplines, but they did not know which they had chosen. Inside each package was an iPod (pink; the pink iPods had been on sale), which was loaded with one of our three conditions.

For the kataphatic prayer, we provided four tracks of thirty minutes each in which a biblical passage was read to background music, and then reread while inviting the subject to use all his or her senses to participate in the scene. (I made these. Experimental work encourages the development of many new skills, but I had not expected expertise in Apple's GarageBand to be among them.) Along with the iPods came written instructions, taken from a Vineyard leader's manual on Ignatian prayer, which encouraged subjects to use their imaginations: "The core of this method is the use of the imagination to draw close to God, to enter into the scriptures and to experience them as if they were alive to you. This is a different way of knowing than knowing through our reason. In this method of prayer, we daydream."

There were four tracks loosely modeled on the invitational imaginative practices in evangelical churches and on the Ignatian exercises. They invited the listener to see, hear, touch, and smell in the mind's eye (but not to taste, as no one had ever spoken to me about tasting God). The tracks alternated between external structure (listening to the scripture) and internal personalization (imagining the scenes for oneself). There was a track based on the 23rd Psalm; on the nativity; on the passion; and on the transfiguration. Here is an example of the recorded instruction from the track on the 23rd Psalm: "*The Lord is my shepherd* . . . see the shepherd before you . . . see his face . . . his eyes . . . the light that streams from him . . . he turns to walk, and you follow him . . . Notice his gait . . . see the hill over which he leads you . . . feel the breeze over the grass . . . smell its sweetness . . . listen to the birds as they sing . . . notice what you feel as you follow this shepherd."

On each track there were long pauses that invited the listener to carry out a dialogue with the shepherd, or with Jesus, and more pauses that invited the listener to remember a moment from the past and to imagine Jesus present as a comforter in that moment. I created them according to the principles outlined in the previous chapter: interweaving, sensory enhancement, and interaction. Music played in the background against my voice.[27] They were lovely tapes, if I do say so: people cried, and sometimes they played them again and again.

For the study condition, we gave people thirty-minute lectures from the Teaching Company. We started out having people listen to lectures on the philosophy of religion but soon shifted to lectures by Luke Timothy Johnson on Jesus and the Gospels. (For the record, I bought thirty copies of these lectures, one for each iPod.) I had listened to these lectures myself and loved them; they taught me how to read the Gospels. Johnson is a Catholic who holds an appointment at Emory University's well-respected Candler School of Theology, and he approaches the Gospels with the literary techniques of biblical scholars. He teaches the listener to pay attention to the differences between the Gospels and the way they are constructed as narratives. If anything, the problem with these lectures is that they are too compelling: too absorbing.

For the apophatic prayer condition, we provided thirty minutes of "pink noise" on the iPod, with written instructions on centering prayer taken from a website for the practice. Pink noise is a smoother, sweeter version of white noise. We instructed our subjects to play the iPod in order to dampen down external distraction, and then to focus on a single word, bringing the wandering mind gently but firmly back to the single word. Although we always told subjects that there were three conditions, we only began to randomize centering prayer at the halfway mark, when we had already run half our subjects. As a result, we had only a few people—fifteen—who did centering prayer.

We asked our subjects to play the iPod six out of seven days a week, for four weeks, for half an hour at a time, and to fill out an account of their experience on the "daily discipline sheets" we also gave them. We could tell whether they had played the iPod, since it records whether you listen completely to any of its tracks. Most people in the study did. Nevertheless, we called them periodically to remind them.[28]

Then our subjects came back (well, most of them, anyway).[29] They went through another set of surveys, most of them the same, but some different. They repeated the first round of computer exercises and did some that we added just at the end. They heard auditory instructions about creating shapes in their minds, which they then had to draw. (For example, "Imagine a 'plus.' Add a vertical line on the left side. Rotate the figure ninety degrees to the right. Now remove all lines to the left of the vertical line.") They saw twenty pairs of words (for example, *daffodil* and *yacht*) and then were presented with the first of each pair and asked to remember the second—easier to do if you spontaneously use a mental image to remember them.[30] And then we interviewed them again and asked them what the month had been like, and whether and how they had heard from God; we repeated all those questions we had asked them about unusual experience and spiritual experience. Then we called them up a month later and asked them many of those questions again.

It is astonishingly difficult to run an experiment. First of all, you have to hire someone to help. It took my assistant a full year, working more than full-time, over forty hours a week, to bring 128 subjects through all their survey-answering and computer-task-doing and interviews, and then to follow them up and organize their files. And it took more than six months to enter all that data into an enormous spreadsheet. Subjects needed instructions about how to drive to campus, where to park. They needed to be called and rescheduled when they missed their appointments. Their iPods had to be collected and reset for the next person. Their papers had to be collected and kept and not lost in a sprawling chaos. And even the best assistant does not come with mind-reading skills. As one of my psychology colleagues explained to me, given that most psychology experiments are run by twenty-five-year-old assistants who are not the experimenter, it is a miracle that one gets results at all.

We got results. There were, first of all, real training effects. When people came back for their return session, those who had done the kataphatic practices had scores on the subjective measures of mental imagery vividness that were significantly higher, compared to their initial scores, than those who had listened to the lectures. They said their images had more detail. (The test structure makes it difficult to believe that people remembered the way they answered the first time round.) The kataphatic group did better, on average, on objective measures of mental imagery use. At least their mean scores were slightly better, and a higher percentage of those who were really successful came from the kataphatic group. Subjects in the kataphatic group were more able to solve the shapes puzzle and the paired words puzzle, and they picked up more of the target letters that flashed by so quickly that they were almost a blur. When congregants said that people who became prayer experts would develop sharper imagery, on average, they were right. The phrase *on average* is important. Not everyone who did the kataphatic exercises reported that their imagery grew more vivid. But on average, when you looked across the group, if someone had spent thirty minutes a day, more or less consistently for a month, engaging with Christ in their minds through these kataphatic prayer tracks, whether they liked them or not, their mental imagery *did* become more vivid. And when we faded the shapes and phrases out to grayscale and noise, the kataphatic group reported that they heard them for longer, and saw them for longer, than the study group.[31]

We had not set out to get reliable data about the centering prayer group, but we did look at what the results from those few subjects suggested. Those who did the centering prayer discipline improved more in the vividness of their imagery than those who had done the study discipline, but not as much as those who had done the kataphatic practice, and there was a similar pattern with the wheel of spinning letters. The centering prayer group was as good as the kataphatic group in creating shapes in their minds.[32]

If we had made them practice more intensively, the results might have been even more striking. Another study in northern California looked at already-trained apophatic meditators who agreed to retreat to a Zen monastery for three months of full-time meditation. After meditating for at least five hours a day for twelve weeks, the subjects were able to distinguish visually between two slightly unequal lines that they had seen as identical before. They were literally able to see more because they were able to pay attention more closely.[33]

Most Christians, of course, do not pray in this focused way for five hours each day outside the monastery. (They have day jobs.) They are supposed to pray for thirty minutes, and they do not always do that. That we were able to get results with only thirty minutes of daily practice, more or less, suggests that when Christians pray in the ordinary, regular way that their pastors and prayer manuals recommend, something changes in the way they use and experience their minds' capacities.

And again, proclivity for absorption seems to make a difference. The more items someone endorsed on the absorption scale, the higher their initial score on the two subjective mental imagery items. But being high-absorption did not help one to solve the shapes puzzle and the paired words puzzle. If anything, in fact, being high-absorption interfered. Some of the logical puzzles that demanded mental imagery use were done significantly less well by those who scored highly on the absorption scale.

It is as if this intense inner attention makes the world of the mind more vivid, and the vividness enhances different skills in different ways. The same person can, of course, be good at puzzle solving and imaginative daydreaming, but the skills are not the same; in the same way, getting physically fit increases one's chance at getting better at ball throwing and ballet, although in general the people who are good at ballet are not those who have spent a lot of time on a baseball diamond.

The vividness seems to leak into the world. To my mind, the most intriguing results from the experiment were about sensory overrides, those odd moments when you hear a voice when you are alone, or you see something that isn't there—not in a table-and-chairs kind of way—or when you feel or taste or smell the immaterial.

The first finding about sensory overrides is how remarkably common they are. Our initial questionnaires asked our subjects a simple question: "Have you ever heard an audible voice when you were alone, or a voice that no one else present could hear, like someone calling your name?" Nearly half of them said yes. *Half.* We gave them a series of examples of the ways that people might have thought they had heard a real voice, and heard it with their ears, but been mistaken. There were six questions like these:

"Sometimes when I'm in the house all alone, I hear a voice call my name . . . No, it really isn't scary. It was at first, but not now . . . It's just once . . . Like 'Sally' . . . Kind of quick and like somebody's calling me. I guess I kind of know that it isn't really somebody and it's really me . . . But it does sound like a real voice." Has this happened to you?

"Last summer I was hanging up clothes in the backyard. Suddenly I heard my husband call my name from inside the house. He sounded like something was wrong and was loud and clear. I ran in . . . But he was out in the garage and he hadn't called at all. Obviously I guess I made it up . . . But it sounded like a real voice and it was my husband's." Has this or something similar happened to you?[34]

More than half said yes to one of these questions. Admittedly, not all of them were willing to talk about these experiences in the interview, and no doubt some of them were recalling experiences that were not actually auditory. But that was what they checked off on the page.

The second finding about sensory overrides was that both absorption and training make a difference. In the initial interview, people who were higher in absorption were more likely to say that they had heard a voice when alone, and the more absorption statements they endorsed, the more hearing-voices stories they said had happened to them. Meanwhile, those who had the kataphatic discipline reported more sensory overrides on return than those with the study discipline.[35] The overrides were not, in general, very dramatic, and there weren't many of them, but some were meaningful and moving. One subject, for example, had a powerful experience of God holding her hand. Another woman saw her beloved dead dog. Another had a session in which she closed her eyes to visualize the angel Gabriel and found that the angel's light was so bright that she opened her eyes because she thought someone had turned a lamp on in the room.

Indeed, absorption and training seemed to work together. When our subjects came back, we asked them these four questions:

> Are the sounds you hear in your daydreams usually clear and distinct?
> Are your thoughts sometimes as real as actual events in your life?
> Does it often happen that nearly every thought immediately and automatically suggests an enormous number of ideas?
> Are your thoughts sometimes so strong that you can almost hear them?

The people who were high in absorption said yes to more of these questions than those who were low, but the relationship was stronger and tighter if they did either the kataphatic or the apophatic practice. That is, just as with subjective mental imagery, both a subject's proclivity for absorption and the discipline to which he or she was allotted randomly made a difference in the way that person answered those questions.

Of course, we had not so subtly invited people to remember and to report odd sensory experiences because Christina asked each person, in that first interview, whether he or she had heard a voice when alone, or seen something no one else could see. (We had chosen to ask people these questions in face-to-face interviews, because we felt that we could have a more accurate understanding of their experiences than if they just checked off a box on a form.)[36] But she put those questions to all our subjects, including those who found themselves in the study condition. And indeed, some of the people who listened to the lectures on the Gospels came back and reported that they had walked into their living rooms and thought they'd seen the cat—but then the cat was not there. In general, though, when people in the study condition reported those experiences, they were less meaningful. Taking into account the frequency with which those experiences had happened to them in the past, they had fewer of them. Of the seven subjects who, on return, reported unusual sensory experiences that were religious, five had done the kataphatic training (one had centering prayer), and among subjects who said, in the beginning, that they had never had such experiences, or had them once a year or less often, seven of the eight people who reported unusual sensory experiences on return were in the kataphatic condition; one had centering prayer.[37]

In fact, the kataphatic practice seemed to give people more of what the scriptures promise those who turn to Christ: peace and the presence of God. In the kataphatic group, people were more likely to say in their follow-up interviews that they felt they had slipped into an intensely focused state during the month. They were more likely to say that the month was more intensely emotional but less stressful for them; in fact, for those people who had been praying for less than half an hour a day when they came in, their stress dropped significantly more over the course of the month than those who listened to the lectures. Those who did the kataphatic exercises were also significantly more likely to say that they had had a near-tangible experience of God's presence during the month; that God had become more of a person in their life; that they had had more "loud" thoughts and images that seemed different from everyday thoughts and images, even though they were still thoughts and images in their minds. And they said that God had spoken to them (as some of them put it) at last.[38]

That was what Subject 94 said. Now thirty, she had been raised Catholic, with church an obligation. By the time she got to college, religion no longer mattered to her. But when she was struggling with a devastating relationship breakup and was near suicidal, she stopped by the campus Christian community house. Someone prayed for her and gave her a Bible. Hesitantly, skeptically, she began to read. She was (she reported) instantly cured. After that she was able to hear God. In the ten years since that moment, she had heard God speak audibly about ten times, roughly once a year. When she saw our project ad at a local charismatic church, she called because she felt spiritually restless. She thought her prayer life had grown stale. In fact, she wasn't praying much, about fifteen minutes every other day. She wanted more.

She didn't love the kataphatic discipline, at least at first. But it changed her. In the month when she listened to the tracks—usually late at night, so that she was drifting in and out of awareness as she sat (in her mind) on the grass with the shepherd in the 23rd Psalm track—she had a few funny, odd sensory experiences. Once she heard a robotic voice so vividly that she turned on the lights (in her real room) to see if anyone was there. A couple of times she saw something out of the corner of her eye, turned, and found that there was no one. Then early one morning an angel woke her up. The angel was loud and vivid, and in its presence she felt what she called immaculate peace. "This was what I was hoping for in the first place, to be more in touch and more in tune with the Lord, and to hear his voice. To hear him, you know, speak to me."

Subject 15 came to the project with a similar profile of intense spiritual experience. She had grown up in a fundamentalist Baptist church, but now at sixty-eight, her spirituality was considerably more eclectic, a kind of wayward mixture of Christianity and Buddhism. She rarely went to church, although she meditated every day for fifteen to thirty minutes. She told us that she had had many spiritual experiences. One morning before work, shortly after leaving her abusive husband and struggling with caring for her kids by herself with a job that didn't pay her enough, she heard a symphony, like a long-drawn-out chant, and she was surrounded in a shimmer of light. It made her feel good, and not so alone. She had also seen a friend after he died, sitting on the couch. When she did the Ignatian spiritual exercises, through an evangelical church, she saw Jesus on the television, as if he were a character in the drama. She came to the project because the idea of returning to the Christian spiritual disciplines seemed good to her.

But during the month after she walked out with Luke Timothy Johnson's lectures on the Gospels, none of those things happened. She liked them well enough, especially the lectures on the Gospel of John. But she reported no altered states. She said that her mental images hadn't gotten any sharper and didn't seem different in any way. She didn't think that her sense of God had changed. She had no spiritual experiences, no more images or thoughts from God than usual, and no change in the frequency of God's guidance. She experienced no sensory overrides, or even any images or thoughts that seemed "stronger" than normal, although she had a strange dream about an iPod with writing on it.

Subject 14 was a mild-mannered, soft-spoken Catholic man who didn't read the Bible because he thought that there was a danger in people who are not theologians getting their own ideas about what the scriptures are saying. (No evangelical voiced this worry.) He reported a modest array of sensory spiritual experiences when he arrived for his first session. He remembered once having seen a person who wasn't there when he was making his morning coffee. It had scared him. "I don't talk to God" was one of his first comments. He said he had grown up in a church that didn't encourage such things. "Now today it's encouraged to talk to God. Then it was more 'Our Father' and 'Hail Mary,' and then, you know, the rosary." He said that he had felt God guiding his thoughts about once a decade. When he prayed, he said the rosary.

He went home with the kataphatic discipline. In the beginning, he found it boring, but he soon he found himself enjoying it, and it stayed with him: "Now I find myself still thinking those thoughts and communicating." He seemed proud of what he had learned. "I've acquired a knack for doing it," he said, "which is good, because you believe that you are here for a purpose, but you get lost in the world. I found a way to come out of the world." And he began to talk to God: "What I liked best was my ability to communicate with God and actually to visualize him."

In the month when he listened to the kataphatic tracks, this man didn't have any sensory override experiences. But he did find that when listening, he would become so involved in the track that he would forget about his surroundings. He thought that his mental imagery had gotten sharper and that his ability to imagine had improved. His sense of God had deepened. He said he experienced God more as a person, and he thought his relationship with God was less rigid, even somewhat playful. Sometimes as he listened to the tracks, he felt that God was almost tangibly present. "I'm glad I did this," he concluded. "It's great. It really improved my life."

Not everyone liked the kataphatic discipline. One woman found it so offensive to her way of being with God—so directed, so this-worldly—that she never returned. A few got bored with only four tracks for the month. Most liked some of the tracks more than others. The 23rd Psalm track went over the best, but not with everyone. "The word that immediately comes to mind is *annoying*," one person commented. Some objected to the homemade scratchiness of the voice-over and the fact that they could hear when I had turned on the microphone. A couple were simply polite: "I did enjoy it, to a certain extent." But no one who stayed with the project hated the kataphatic discipline, and most listeners really liked it. "I was close to God before, but I feel very close now. I feel like he's inside me." Or "I wanted to feel the peace and it really works." The woman who said that listened to the tracks more than two hundred times. She said it cured her acne.

This was not the way that subjects responded to centering prayer. Centering prayer is hard, and a month is not a long time to practice the focused concentration the discipline demands. Almost everyone who walked out with the apophatic discipline thought it was difficult. About half of them never got beyond how hard it was. "What I hated most," one subject reported, "was the fact that my mind couldn't stay in one spot." Another said, more simply, "For me it was a constant battle." Those people told Christina how frustrated they were and how they didn't think it did them any good. "I don't think I would say that I gained anything spiritually out of it." Or "I just really felt like it wasn't praying."

Those who did like centering prayer were apt to love it, and it became a treasured part of their routine. "The calming feeling I got from it—it became familiar after a while, and I looked forward to it." On them, it had an impact. Subject 103, a young man who worked in biotech in the valley, spontaneously reproduced the language of darkness that the author of *The Cloud* had used five hundred years before.

> I think that the thing that I liked best was probably being able to get to the point where I'm not thinking about anything. I didn't think I'd ever get to the point where I was able to just focus on nothing.
>
> And it was weird because there was—toward the end, there was times where it was almost—I mean, I could see just black. Almost as if my eyes were open, but they weren't. As if I was opening my eyes and I was just looking into dark. And I could feel myself kind of looking around and all of—but there was nothing.
>
> I really felt like my eyes were open. As if I was looking around and I couldn't see anything. Even though I was just sitting there with my eyes closed. Is this what someone who is blind feels like? It was really strange.
>
> But then I would find myself just kind of just listening. To see if God had anything that He wanted to say. Most of the nights it was just stillness. It was nothing. Then some nights I felt like God was trying to talk to me.

Even for him, it was always tough to do. "While the result was awesome," he said, "it was super hard to achieve. It's really, really hard to sit there."

For those who liked it, the pink noise on the iPod seemed to become textured with meaning. Subject 110 came to the discipline during a hard month. Both of her parents were dying, and she had to take charge of the family business while she cared for them. She was fifty. She had been raised Episcopalian, but she no longer went to church. Still, she prayed every day. She had done centering prayer before, and she found that it became a kind of oasis during her day. She said that it was like plugging herself into a battery. She talked about calm and peace, but the pink noise also seemed to dissolve into meaning. One day she heard trumpet notes and the crying of birds. She saw pulsating light against her eyelids. She heard messages: "Cultivate what you have," which made sense to her, and "Excuse me," which she never understood. We never knew how perceptlike, how sensory, these experiences were; in the interview when Christina asked her if she had heard these sounds with her ears, she said both yes and no. But the moments were drenched with significance for her. She felt that God spoke to her in these sessions. At the end of the month, she felt that God had become more immediate and present, more personlike. She said that her mental images had grown sharper, and that she was quicker with the computer exercises. She kept doing centering prayer even after the month ended. When we talked to her in the one-month callback, she had purchased some pink noise.

There is a lesson here as well for those who are low in absorption and who say that they have a hard time hearing from God. We had twenty-seven subjects who scored in the bottom fifth of the absorption-scale scores. As it happened, eleven of them had been assigned randomly to the kataphatic condition, ten to the study condition, and six to centering prayer. Most of them had not prayed much before, as you would expect. Fourteen of them prayed five minutes a day or less when they joined the study, and another seven prayed no more than fifteen minutes. But after the thirty-minute imaginative immersions in the scriptures, those in the kataphatic condition (compared to those who had been assigned to study or to centering prayer) were more likely to say that their spirituality had changed; that their sense of God had changed; that they felt more playful with God; and that God had become more of a person to them. They were more likely to say that they had felt God's presence. And while those listening to the lectures reported more stress at the end of the month, those in both the centering prayer condition and the kataphatic condition reported substantially less.[39] It may be that this technology of recorded imaginative immersion in scripture helps those with low proclivity to experience God more intimately.

. . .

But why should training the imagination lead to unusual sensory experiences? It makes sense that such training should make what is imagined more vivid: that talking with God should help one to experience God more as a person, that attending to mental images should make them feel sharper and more compelling. But deliberately imagining Jesus transfigured is quite different from hearing Jesus speak—and hearing the voice as coming from the outside. None of these subjects had those experiences willfully. They did not intentionally decide to hear God say, "Excuse me." They did not intentionally decide to have an angel wake them up. They entered the project with a broad, generic desire to hear God speak or perhaps just to get their prayer life moving again; they spent thirty minutes a day imaginatively immersed in the scriptures; and then they had unplanned, idiosyncratic experiences that they saw with their eyes and heard with their ears. Why?

Properly defined, a hallucination is a perception, while in a conscious state, in the absence of an external material stimulus. It should have the quality of real perception: it should be vivid, substantial, and located in objective space.[40] Dreams are not hallucinations: they occur in a sleeping state. Illusions are not hallucinations: they involve an external stimulus (the open door), but the person is mistaken about what it is (a lurking monster). To call a sensation a "perception" implies that the source of the sensation is outside the person who senses it and that the source is really there. When you hallucinate, you don't look at the open door and get momentarily confused about whether the door is a monster. You look at where the door usually is, and you see a monster. You feel the touch as if something touched you. You hear a voice as if someone else spoke. Someone who experiences a hallucination has a clear perceptual awareness that the source of the sensation was not in his or her mind—and note that if God himself has in fact spoken, the human experience of hearing God is technically a hallucination, because God is immaterial. He is not a sensory stimulus.

Still, the word *hallucination* implies that there is nothing at all to perceive. So I call these occasional sensory perceptions of the immaterial *sensory overrides* because they are moments when perception overrides the material stimulus. They are not experienced as mis-remembering. They are experienced as the sensory perception of something external.

The judgment is automatic and basic. That's why it's so startling. I saw those druids—I knew they were there. That's why I started up in bed, because it was so abruptly challenging to my expectations of the everyday world to see six druids standing by the window, and then they vanished. That is what people say about sensory overrides: they saw, they felt, they heard, and in so doing, they knew. It seemed real.

These automatic judgments are the result of what psychologists call "reality monitoring." Freud used the term "reality testing," but he treated reality testing as a much higher-level decision—the ability to distinguish between fantasy and the world as it is, between he-loves-me and he's-just-not-that-into-me. Reality monitoring involves the much more basic decision about whether the source of a momentary experience is internal to the mind or external in the world.

Originally, psychologists used the term to refer to judgments about memories: Did I really have that conversation with my boyfriend back in college, or did I just think I did? Cognitive psychologists have known since Frederic Bartlett wrote *Remembering* in 1932 that what we remember is based, in part, on the way events are interpreted, organized, and understood. Bartlett called this process "construction" and, in doing so, was one of the first to chip away at the fond Enlightenment hope that our minds (at least, our rational minds) are mirrors of nature. The work that gave "reality monitoring" its name asked what it was about memories that led someone to infer that they were records of something that had taken place in the world or in the mind.[41] Elegant experiments suggest that memories differ in predictable ways and that people use those differences in judging what has actually taken place. Memories of an external event typically have more sensory details. You remember a comment; if you can remember when it was said, where it was said, or to whom it was said, you are more likely to infer that there was a real event rather than an imagined daydream. If the scent of autumn and the quality of the slanting light linger in a memory of a walk through a field, you are more likely to infer that you really did walk in the field. By contrast, memories of thoughts were more likely to include the memory of cognitive effort, like composing sentences in one's mind. Paul McCartney was confused about whether he had written "Yesterday" or heard it on the radio, because he woke up one morning with the tune running effortlessly through his mind.[42]

The point is that to some extent, our capacity to distinguish between what we have seen or heard and what we have thought is learned. It draws upon our previous experience. Strikingly, our minds do not passively respond to events, like clay upon which impressions are imprinted (the very word *impressions* arises from this old view of the mind as recorder); rather, they act, create, organize, and construct. From the reality monitoring perspective, our minds are always aware of our awareness, always separating out the cognitive events in the burbling stream of our consciousness, distinguishing those that are externally generated from those that are not, those that are real from those that have been imagined. Such a model portrays us as creatures making constant, incremental decisions about the epistemological status of the events recorded in our minds: we decide that the grinding sound is a garbage truck but that the warm conversation was an incidental daydream. Most of this attention occurs below the level of our awareness, and most of it is basic. We rarely make frank mistakes, especially in the judgments of our senses. But sometimes we do—if by *mistake* one means the sensory perception of something that is not materially present.

Scientists have suggested that this kind of judgment explains hallucination and hallucination-like experiences: those who experience sensory perceptions when there is nothing material to perceive are mistaking events in their minds for events in the world. A fair amount of experimental research supports this idea. A standard kind of experiment around what is called *source monitoring* or *signal detection* tries to baffle the subject about how or whether he or she experienced something. The experimenter reads some words aloud and puts up pictures of other words and asks subjects to remember which words they saw and which they heard. A trickier version (once a psychology colleague of mine remarked that his was the only academic discipline that legally tortures its subjects) involves reading out a series of words (*sour, candy, sugar, bitter, good, taste*) and then reading out a new list into which are added words naturally associated with the first list but not actually on it, like *sweet.* Many people mistakenly conclude that *sweet* was on the first list, because it just makes so much sense that it would be. On these kinds of tasks, people who score highly on questionnaires that ask them whether they've had hallucination-like experiences are also more likely to make mistakes on source monitoring tasks.[43]

From the reality monitoring perspective, hallucination-like experiences occur not because there's something wrong with your mind, but because you interpret something you imagined as being real in the world. The issue is perceptual bias, not perceptual deficit. The psychologist Richard Bentall, who is the primary intellectual architect of this interpretation, suggests that the most common conditions that lead to hallucinations— what we might call the ingredients of a supernatural experience—are an ambiguous stimulus, emotional arousal, and cognitive expectation. Someone who perceives an ambiguous noise is more likely to interpret it; someone who needs an answer is more likely to listen for one; and someone who believes that an answer can be heard is more likely to hear one.

We know that culture makes a difference. There are social worlds in which the dead are known to be present and in which experts have direct, unmediated access to the supernatural, and in those worlds, visions and voices are normative. The slight attempts to compare apples to apples across cultures have found that indeed there are differences in rate as well as content. One study in London found that one in ten whites reported a voice or vision; one in twenty South Asians; and one in four sub-Saharan Africans or African Caribbeans. The slight data we have on hallucinations associated with psychiatric illness outside the West suggests that both the sensory mode and the content shift across cultural boundaries. Culture also affects the ease of reporting. Even in the United States, as many as 80 percent of those who have been bereaved will hear, see, or feel the person they have lost, and often that contact gives them comfort. In a Swedish study, 89 percent of the women and 57 percent of the men reported a sensory experience of their lost spouse—they heard, they saw, they felt—but many, out of embarrassment and fear that despair had driven them mad, had told not a soul until the interviewer asked.[44]

Isolation is another factor. Deprive someone of their capacity to see or hear, and many will see or hear something not materially present. In a study of thirteen hostage victims held in isolation during their ordeal and interviewed six months after release (ex-prisoners of war, victims of rape, kidnapping, and terrorism), five reported odd sensory experiences of flashes of light, geometric patterns, and flashbacks of childhood memories. Here is one case report:

An eighteen-year-old female college student was kidnapped by two men and held for ransom. During her solitary confinement for sixty hours, she was imprisoned in a small garage, blindfolded with a black hood, and her legs and arms were bound with ropes. She was denied food, water and toilet facilities. Her captors periodically threatened to kill her. She experienced dull flashes of light in front of her eyes and saw small animals and insects in the periphery of her visual field. She gradually became unaware of her restraints and felt "numb all over my body . . . it was almost like I didn't have a body." She became hypervigilant and heard "strange sounds" and "whispers." Upon hearing loud voices approach the garage, she thought she was going to die and immediately "saw my whole life run off like a slide show before my eyes . . . mostly childhood scenes and my parents." The voices were those of the police who rescued her.[45]

And of course, throughout time, ghosts and spirits have shunned the sun. They dwell in gloomy places that feel unfamiliar in the dark. The ghoul under the bed becomes real only after the lights go out and shapes grow indistinct and there is no one there to laugh away your fears.

The most parsimonious way to explain these sensory phenomena is that perceptual mistakes are common and corrected by the brain to represent the world—except when, occasionally, they are corrected to represent something else. We know that our minds never directly perceive visual information the way it passes over our eyes. When our eyes perceive, the image is curved by the eyeball, inverted by the lens, and doubled by being perceived by two eyes. There is even a blind spot at the back of the eyeball (where retinal photoreceptors are occluded by the optic nerve). These are things we never notice because of our brain's capacity to compensate. Our brains interpret the data before we see what we see.

Idiosyncratically and opportunistically, our brains also seem to do something else. They organize inflowing data to allow us to see images, hear voices, and interpret other sensory phenomena that reflect what we are biased to infer about the world, rather than what is in the world before us. Most of the biases are mundane: expectations about the sounds people make, the behavior of dogs, the organization of space, and whatever else impinges on our world, and probably most of our perceptual breaks are corrections that go unnoticed in our daily lives. But if our cognitive bias leads us to make corrections that are meaningful to larger life issues, those experiences can stand out for us like beacons in the night.

That is what seems to happen with religious experience. No one really knows why we perceive something when it has no material presence, but the reality monitoring model suggests that people who are constantly aware of God and thinking about scripture and reflecting on angels are more likely than skeptics to repair perceptual breaks by reaching for a representation of an angelic choir. It explains that in times of great emotion, they might interpret ambiguous noise with their thoughts about God and find that they experience God's voice with their ears. They have a perceptual bias.

In itself, this is not news. We know that Buddhists have visions of Buddha and Hindus have visions of Krishna. What makes the reality monitoring model interesting is that it explains why prayer training might lead someone to have these sensory overrides more often. Recall that as we scan our own awareness, there are two factors (among others) that cue us to distinguish between the real and the imagined: the amount of sensory detail and the degree of cognitive effort. We have learned to associate more vivid sensory information with the real. I infer that I must have had this conversation with a certain person in reality, not in my mind, because I remember that there was a clock on the desk and that the light fell into the room just so. We have also learned to associate cognitive effort with the imagined. If a memory floods unbidden into my awareness, I am more likely to assume that its source was external, just as we assume that spontaneous thoughts are more significant and freighted with importance.

This is what kataphatic prayer practice does. It invests scriptural passages with sensory I-was-there detail. Someone who has done the Ignatian exercises remembers the dust motes in the sunlight when Mary heard the news from Gabriel because she saw it that way in her mind. Someone who is down at the lake with God on a date knows exactly what that bench looks like and the scent of water in the breeze. And someone who is praying in this imagination-rich way around the scriptures for thirty minutes each day will be someone to whom scriptural stories come effortlessly, the way the details of Frodo's adventures in Middle-earth come effortlessly into the mind of an eager Tolkien reader. A proclivity for absorption probably makes the practice easier and more effective because absorption allows someone to take seriously what must be imagined and to treat it as important; worth attending to; more real. People train absorption by focusing on sensory detail. They practice seeing, hearing, smelling, and touching in their mind's eye. They give these imagined experiences the sensory vividness associated with the memories of real events. What they are able to imagine becomes more real to them, and God must be imagined, because God is immaterial. Proclivity for and training in absorption allows someone to tug on the line that our minds draw between the internal and the external, the line between me and other.

That, indeed, is the great goal of daily practice in an evangelical church where God speaks back: to teach people to tug on that line when it comes to God. The work of a church like the Vineyard is to blur the distinction between inner and outer, self and other, the same line that our reality monitoring system uses to distinguish the source of experience. Congregants go to great effort to interpret, or reinterpret, some thoughtlike mental events as the experience of an external presence; they work hard to experience the God with whom they have been having imagined conversations as hearing and responding in the world. They practice these strategies again and again. The church teaches congregants a new theory of mind, in which thoughts they might have ascribed to random musing are now to be interpreted as the presence of this external being in the mind. The church encourages congregants to pay attention to spontaneous thoughts and to treat them as God-generated (if they pass the tests of discernment). The church encourages congregants to have powerful, personal daydreams around God that give God and God's associates (Christ, the Holy Spirit, angels, and disciples) a sensory vividness in the mind and an immediateness in memory and understanding. The church-learned emotional practices make God and a life with God full of intense deep feeling, in which feelings become the reason to turn to God and feel the effects of God's presence. All of these practices push on the boundary between the mind and the world.

Does that mean that the perception of God is always no more than the imagination? No, no more than the failure to hear God's voice is the mark of someone who is not devout. If the supernatural is real, it reaches to each according to that person's skills and style. The reason that experiential churches worry about discernment is that they are fully aware that congregants will make mistakes about whether God has spoken. But sensory overrides are indications of the possible when it comes to hearing God: the sign that one has a capacity to take inner experience seriously and thus the capacity to experience the immaterial with one's senses.

None of these observations explains the ultimate cause of the voice someone hears on a Tuesday afternoon. This account of absorption training is fully compatible with both secular and supernaturalist understandings of God. To a believer, this account of absorption speaks to the problem of why, if God is always speaking, not everyone can hear, and it suggests what the church might do to help those who struggle. To a skeptic, it explains why the believer heard a thought in the mind as if it were external. But the emphasis on skill—on the way we train our attention—should change the way both Christians and non-Christians think about what makes them different from one another.

People come to faith not just because they decide that the propositions are true but because they experience God directly. They feel God's presence. They hear God's voice. Their hearts flood with an incandescent joy. Moreover, these feelings and sensations are patterned. Despite the deep idiosyncrasies of personality and life path, when people feel and sense the divine, they do so in ways that can be detailed like a naturalist's observation on the flight of birds. The great accomplishment of *The Varieties of Religious Experience,* William James's enduring classic, was to describe these features. It is a brilliant book, but it missed the role that spiritual training can play in encouraging the experience.

James was determined to give a clear-eyed view of what he called our religious "propensities"—to see them as they are, stripped bare of ontological claims. He was equally insistent that attention to bodily pattern does not diminish divine reality. He hated medical materialism.

Medical materialism finishes up Saint Paul by calling his vision on the road to Damascus a discharging lesion of the occipital cortex, he being an epileptic. It snuffs out Saint Teresa as a hysteric, Saint Francis of Assisi as a hereditary degenerate. George Fox's discontent with the shams of his age, and his pining for spiritual veracity, it treats as a symptom of a disordered colon. Carlyle's organ-tones of misery it accounts for by a gastro-duodenal catarrh. All such mental overtensions, it says, are when you come to the bottom of the matter, mere affairs of diathesis (auto-intoxications most probably), due to the perverted action of various glands which physiology will yet discover.[46]

But James thought that if Saint Paul really was an epileptic, it was the honest thing to say so.[47] For James, the difference between the epileptic seizure and the vision was not the physiology of the experience but the way the person who experienced it gave it meaning.

James was right. There is no single experience that is in itself intrinsically religious. No awareness of something not materially present, no warm suffusion of the chest, nor even any moment of inexpressible bliss is ever inherently religious. There is only experience that, as the historian Ann Taves remarks, is "deemed" religious.[48] One of the best illustrations of this insight lies in a classic anthology of mysticism, collected by F. C. Happold and published in 1963. The book is full of remarkable, compelling literary examples of moments of the apprehension of the divine: in Plato, Plotinus, Teresa of Ávila, Saint John of the Cross, *The Cloud of Unknowing*, the *Bhaghavad Gita*, the *Tao Te Ching*, and others. In the middle of the book, tucked away between the definitions and the *Upanishads,* lie the accounts of ordinary folks. Happold tells his own story:

> It happened in my room in Peterhouse on the evening of 1 February 1913, when I was an undergraduate at Cambridge . . . There was just the room, with its shabby furniture and the fire burning in the grate and the red-shaded lamp on the table. But the room was filled by a Presence, which in a strange way was about me and in me, like light or warmth. I was overwhelmingly possessed by Someone who was not myself, and yet I felt that I was more myself than I had ever been before. I was filled with an intense happiness, and an almost unbearable joy, such as I had never known before and I have never known since. And over all was a deep sense of peace and security and certainty . . . It was very wonderful and quite unforgettable.[49]

Happold's experience changed his life. But he also includes in his anthology this fey reminiscence by a man who had what seems to be much the same psychobiological explosion and yet that led nowhere:

> The thing happened one summer afternoon, on the school cricket field, while I was sitting on the grass, waiting my turn to bat. I was thinking about nothing in particular, merely enjoying the pleasures of midsummer idleness. Suddenly, and without warning, something invisible seemed to be drawn across the sky, transforming the world

around me into a kind of tent of concentrated and enhanced significance. What had been an outside became an inside. The objective was somehow transformed into a completely subjective fact, which was experienced as "mine," but on a level where the world had no meaning; for "I" was no longer the familiar ego. Nothing more can be said about the experience, it brought no accession of knowledge about anything except, very obscurely, the knower and his sense of knowing. After a few minutes there was a "return to normalcy." The event made a deep impression on me at the time; but because it did not fit into any of the thought patterns—religious, philosophical, scientific—with which, as a boy of fifteen, I was familiar, it came to seem more and more anomalous, more and more irrelevant to "real life," and was finally forgotten.[50]

Even an exalted mystical state, without a framework to interpret it as spiritual, simply registers and slowly fades.

James was also right that some experiences are more likely than others to be "deemed religious": that we do, in fact, have propensities. He treated these propensities as if they were the data from which God's nature would be known. He would go on to conclude from these propensities the true character of God, and he found in them a divine that was remarkably Emersonian and Unitarian. All faith, he decided, shares this basic core: that we humans feel an uneasiness that there is something wrong about us, and in various ways, faith saves us from the wrongness by a connection with higher power. That power is real, because it changes us. This was a pragmatist philosophical sentiment that produced the most remarkable sentence in the book—"God is real since he produces real effects"—but which James also seems to have believed. He thought, on balance, that the fact that people experience the supernatural means that the supernatural is real.

The whole drift of my education goes to persuade me that the world of our present consciousness is only one out of many worlds of consciousness that exist, and that those other worlds must contain experiences which have a meaning for our life also; and that although in the main their experiences and those of this world keep discrete, yet the two become continuous at certain points, and higher energies filter in.[51]

There, he thought, our knowledge ends. Around the same period, the early anthropologist Edward Tylor wrote that the minimum definition of religion is a belief in spiritual beings. James barely met this minimum because he treated the shared core of human religious experience as the source of the true knowledge of God.

And that was James's mistake. I do not think we should sift through the experiences people have of God to infer the true nature of God, as if we were discovering a common, universal grammar, the underlying structure of English, Tibetan, and Indonesian Piru. Instead I think we can learn from intense spiritual experience how proclivity and practice shape the most basic ways we encounter our world: the way we perceive and judge what is real. The anthropologist Richard Shweder says that when you take culture seriously, you must accept that we live in plural worlds, worlds made so distinctly in the interaction of peoples with one another that the most basic elements of human lives—to whom we respond emotionally, to what we recoil in moral disgust—will shift, so that it no longer makes sense to think about a shared world seen from different vantage points but of multiple worlds.[52]

It's not just about the brain—god spots, peak moments, and universal insights. Knowing God involves training, and it involves interpretation. Each faith—to some extent, each church—forms its own culture, its own way of seeing the world, and as people acquire the knowledge and the practices through which they come to know that God, the most intimate aspects of the way they experience their everyday world change. Those who learn to take God seriously do not simply interpret the world differently from those who have not done so. They have different evidence for what is true. In some deep and fundamental way, as a result of their practices, they live in different worlds.

CHAPTER EIGHT

But Are They Crazy?

*And, behold, the LORD passed by, and a great
and strong wind rent the mountains, and brake in
pieces the rocks before the LORD; but the LORD
was not in the wind: and after the wind an earthquake; but the LORD was not in the earthquake:
And after the earthquake a fire; but the LORD was
not in the fire: and after the fire, a still small voice.*

1 Kings 19:11–12

*From my perspective, the greatest need in the
church today is for believers to clearly hear the
voice of God for themselves.*

James Goll,
The Beginner's Guide to Hearing God

To MANY PEOPLE, hearing a voice when no one is there is a sign not of God but of mental illness. So does it follow that actively trying to hear God's voice might lead the way to madness?

The short answer is an emphatic no. The longer answer is perhaps yes, for some people, at some times. The relationship between spirituality and mental illness is not straightforward. For the most part, prayer practice is good for people, whatever the reality of God. The methods that these American evangelicals learn make a soothing relationship more real for people, and they may help some who would be vulnerable to madness to keep it at bay. At their most intense, prayer practices can carry risks, but there are clear differences between the unusual experiences described by congregants, and psychosis.

Psychosis is the name we give to judgments and perceptions that seem so impaired as to no longer be within the bounds of normal reason. People whom we call psychotic speak furiously to the empty air or talk incoherently. They may fear that they are being followed by the government, tell you that they have radio transmitters implanted in their teeth, or believe that they have been published in leading scientific journals. And of course, sometimes the people who say these things are right. Many years ago I was spending time, as an anthropologist, in a psychiatric clinic, observing the way young psychiatrists come to identify and interpret mental illness, when a disheveled man was admitted to the unit. He was grimy and unkempt, and he spoke grandly of his great astronomical work. He was intermittently incoherent. No one doubted that he needed to be hospitalized. At first, the resident described his astronomical theories as yet another of his psychotic symptoms. Then, on a whim, the resident went to the library, looked the man up, and found his articles. He really had done great astronomical work.

Psychosis is always a judgment. It is also a symptom of many different illnesses—schizophrenia, bipolar disorder, substance abuse, trauma—just as a sore throat is a symptom of many different diseases. Because of this, it is easy to cast doubt on our judgments altogether and to claim, in the tradition of Thomas Szasz and R. D. Laing, that we call people psychotic because they see the truth more nakedly than we do ourselves and we cannot bear their insight. Sometimes they do and we can't. But many of those who are psychotic struggle in a phantasmagoria of blood and horror. They hear people scream at them and curse and jeer. Those voices are real to them, more real than normal voices are. At the same time, they often don't quite believe them. So the very evidence of their senses feels unreliable, the way you feel when your new glasses are fitted accidentally with the wrong prescription, and wearing them, you see the world pitch sideways and you know it doesn't, and yet you cannot trust yourself to step off the curb. Psychosis is even more terrifying, and those who experience it cannot return the glasses. The voices and images throb in their brains. Psychosis hurts.

I have worked for many years with people who are psychotic, because my work explores the boundaries of the real in many different ways. For months, I went to a decaying but gentrifying neighborhood just north of downtown Chicago and spent afternoons with Shirley, a tough African American woman who had lived for years on the street. Shirley easily met the standard psychiatric criteria for schizophrenia. Laid out in the diagnostic handbook, they are:

Characteristic symptoms: Two (or more) of the following, each present for a significant portion of time during a 1-month period (or less if successfully treated):

> delusions
> hallucinations
> disorganized speech (e.g., frequent derailment or incoherence)
> grossly disorganized or catatonic behavior
> negative symptoms, i.e., affective flattening, alogia, or avolition

Only one [of these symptoms] is required if delusions are bizarre or hallucinations consist of a voice keeping up a running commentary on the person's behavior or thoughts, or two or more voices conversing with each other.

Social/occupational dysfunction: For a significant portion of the time since the onset of the disturbance, one or more major areas of functioning such as work, interpersonal relations, or self-care are markedly below the level achieved prior to the onset (or when the onset is in childhood or adolescence, failure to achieve expected level of interpersonal, academic, or occupational achievement).

Duration: Continuous signs of the disturbance persist for at least six months. [This is an American criterion. In the International Classification of Diseases, the length is one month.] This six-month period must include at least one month of active symptoms (or less if successfully treated) and may include periods of prodromal or residual symptoms. During these prodromal or residual periods, the signs of the disturbance may be manifested by only negative symptoms or two or more symptoms listed above in an attenuated form (e.g., odd beliefs, unusual perceptual experiences).

Meanwhile, mood disorders and substance abuse must be ruled out.[1]

As with most psychiatric diagnoses, there is no single diagnostic test like a blood panel that will give you a definitive answer: yes, you have it; no, you do not. But to meet criteria for schizophrenia, your life must be seriously impaired, "markedly below the level achieved prior to the onset."

Shirley was in her midtwenties when she began to hear regularly the sounds that would bother her on and off throughout the years. She had first heard what she called "signals" when she was nine or ten—information about other people carried to her like radio transmission, so she could hear people talking and even thinking about her from a great distance. But the signals had died down in early adolescence. In her midtwenties, she was awash in vodka, and they started up again. She thought of the signals as a kind of supernatural empathy: she would just know about people through the signals, and it felt like she knew too much, more than they would have wanted. She began to feel what she called "pressure." She would put her hands around her head to show me how she felt the signals pressing in from outside. She worried that it was a kind of covert experiment, governmental agents playing weird mind-control games with a poor black woman, a technological Tuskegee.

By the time I met her, twenty years later, Shirley no longer drank heavily; nor did she use the crack she had used for years after she came out of her first hospitalization. She still heard voices. These days she hears people hissing "bitch" to her as she walks down the street, and she hears their echoing laughter through the radiator pipes in her room. She hears them every day, discussing her in the third person, their voices commenting on her behavior, her clothes, her aspirations. She knows that some of these people wait outside her apartment to taunt and threaten her. Sometimes she doubts that these experiences are rooted in reality, but much of the time they feel real. Nor are they just strange ideas she thinks about. They hurt. She feels their thoughts bearing down upon her, and she winces at the sounds. Sometimes things are a little better and people don't listen at the water pipes. Other times they won't let her alone for days on end.

That psychotic hallucinations hurt—that they pound against your head as if they are what drives you mad rather than being symptoms of the madness—is only one of the differences between ordinary sensory overrides and the harsh hallucinations experienced by people with schizophrenia. Most who carry that diagnosis hear voices. Usually, they hear more than one. They can hear a crowd, and the crowd will taunt and threaten and push them in front of cars. I remember a man who told me that he could count seventeen voices that he heard throughout the day. When I asked him how his medication helped, he gave me a defeated look and then turned away. "When I take my medication," he said, "my head gets clear enough that I can decide what kind of soda I want to drink." I remember another man who heard only one voice, but it was that of his fourth-grade teacher, and it spat at him, repeatedly, "Jerk," again and again throughout the day. Sometimes people don't hear voices. They hear a scuffling behind the ears, as if—as one woman explained to me in the living room of her halfway house—a field of rats were rushing toward her from the back.

The hallucinations associated with psychosis are frequent. They can occur many, many times each day—even continuously, like a curtain of rain—when the person is ill. They are extended. People don't just hear a single phrase, like "Get off the bus," although many psychotic hallucinations are short, like "Jerk." People have long, back-and-forth conversations with their voices, and they hear back-and-forth conversations about them in the third person. ("He's so stupid. Look at him, he's going to get on that bus." "He should be under that bus, not in it.") These hallucinations are unpleasant, even horrific, and they are not associated with practice, at least not in any straightforward way.[2] They are also spontaneous: they happen to you, and you are at their mercy.

That is not the way people in the Vineyard hear God speak. When I sat down with individuals and asked whether they had ever heard God's voice outside their head or heard any voice when they were alone, or had any other unusual experience, they told me about one experience, or maybe a handful. The moments did meet psychiatric criteria for hallucinations: people were clear that the voice had come from outside and that they had heard it with their ears, or that the touch or vision felt as if external. Yet the pattern and quality of the experience was quite different from that in psychosis, and there was no associated pathology.

For the most part, sensory overrides—moments when sensory perception overrides an existing stimulus—are rare. They are brief. And while they are quite startling (it is disconcerting to have God speak out of the backseat and say, "I will always be with you"), they are certainly not distressing. Hannah, who liked to go on date night, reported an experience that was typical of the way people heard voices in the Vineyard: "I was walking up the lake and down the lake and I was like, should I go home now? And [God] was like, 'Sit and listen.'" I asked, "Did you hear that outside or inside your head?" "That's hard to tell," she replied, "but in this instance it really felt like it was outside." I asked, "How many times do you think you've heard his voice outside your head?" "Two or three," she said. She said she felt God too: "I have felt a touch, like a physical touch." "Is it real enough so that if you were thinking about it psychologically, you'd say, it's kind of like a hallucination, you feel it sensorially?" "Yeah." But again it was rare. It didn't happen every day, or even every year. That made it special.

Another sign that distinguishes the congregants' voice-hearing from psychotic voice-hearing is that congregants are acutely aware of what their audience might think of their experience. When evangelicals speak of hearing God, they do not in general have an audible voice in mind. In fact, the many manuals that teach you to hear God speak specifically suggest that most people do not hear God speak audibly, although they often first give examples of audible moments of hearing God's voice. Dallas Willard's *Hearing God,* for instance, lists what are clear auditory experiences of God (Moses, Saint Augustine, Saint Teresa, George Fox) and then remarks, as if with a deprecating cough, that an interior or inner voice is the preferred way of hearing from God.[3] In American culture, hearing voices is associated with madness. Because congregants know that hearing voices is not, in general, a good sign, they hadn't mentioned their experiences to many people before I asked them directly whether they had ever heard an audible voice. Sometimes I was the first person they'd told.

When congregants did confess to hearing a voice, they often hedged their account with language that almost disavowed the experience, or marked it as unusual, not part of their normal experience of self. People who are psychotic do not tend to do this. They seem to lack some capacity to interpret accurately what those around them are thinking. They take fewer pains to ward off the negative conclusions their audience might draw. They don't laugh or say that what they've experienced is "bizarre."[4]

Emily, a young twenty-something at the Chicago Vineyard, was so embarrassed by the idea of hearing voices or seeing things that initially she just brushed off my question. When I asked, "Have you ever seen a vision that wasn't in your head?" she said no. Then she paused. "Well, I mean when I was a kid, I sort of once I saw an angel." She laughed here; she didn't want me to think she was crazy. "That's always been my story, I saw an angel." I asked her when. "I was at home by myself after school because both my parents had to work. I was down in my room, sitting by my desk, and I turned, and I swear I saw this wing flutter down the hall, and I was like, 'What is that?' But it was nothing." She had had a few other such experiences; again, she introduced them cautiously, framing them to show that she knew they were unusual, that I might disapprove.

Another difference is the sense of compulsion in the voice. A naïve observer might think that God's voice would have the quality of absolute compulsion: *you must*, just as Abraham knew he must when God ordered him to sacrifice his firstborn son. Psychotic hallucinations sometimes have this quality. Psychiatrists call them "command" hallucinations. Patients feel pushed into complying by a force beyond their will, even though in fact they often resist for years before they act. They feel that they must jump out the window when ordered, even if they manage not to. God's voice, however, did not have this absolute quality for the congregants I knew. For example, Elaine was trying to describe what to do with her life when God told her what to do: "The Lord spoke to me clearly in April, like May or April. To start a school." "You heard this audibly?" "Yeah." "Were you alone?" "Yeah, I was just praying. I wasn't praying anything really, just thinking about God, and I heard, 'Start a school.' I immediately got up and it was like, 'Okay Lord, where?'" But she never did. She never felt she had to. She became a missionary for a few years, and for a while during that period she thought about starting a school. She thinks she still might. That was the way congregants interpreted God, even when he spoke in an imperative. They assumed he might not mean "right now." They also used those criteria of discernment: test the interpretation, judge it against God's character, and so forth. They assumed that what they heard might be colored by their own psyche.[5]

Not only do the sensory overrides reported by the Vineyard congregants differ in many ways from the experience of psychotic hallucinations; the congregation had little difficulty distinguishing between psychosis and spirituality. When people at the Vineyard behaved as if they were hearing distressing voices, other congregants identified them as different: as ill. One morning a woman stood at the back of the church shrieking like a teakettle at someone no one else could see. The pastor did not call her crazy from the pulpit, but he hesitated and described her as struggling, and then he called the police to take her to the hospital.

What I saw at the Vineyard has been seen by other anthropologists in other charismatic churches. The anthropologists Simon Dein and Roland Littlewood persuaded forty members of a Pentecostal church in London, more than a third of the congregation, to complete a questionnaire on spiritual experience. Then they interviewed the twenty-five out of the forty who said that they had heard God speak audibly. Sometimes it was hard for the anthropologists to decide if the voice had, indeed, been heard as if from a source external to the head, but it was clear to the congregants that the voice had not been their own internal thoughts. In fifteen of the cases, the anthropologists were confident that the voice had been audible and experienced as external. For most of those congregants, those experiences were rare. Often they had happened only once. For example:

> There was one time in a church in London and I think they were preaching about forgiveness. I went to the front and there was this peace and joy inside of me, and I broke down and cried in [the] front of the church. God said aloud to me, "You need to serve, just to be a servant." I then joined the church and started serving the ministry and have just gone from strength to strength.

And another:

> Only once ever, that was when I was at university and I was praying about an issue that was quite personal to me. I heard a voice in the room outside of myself giving me an answer to the issue. I opened my eyes and looked around the room but there was no one there in the room or in the vicinity. I concluded that God was talking to me.[6]

The experiences were rare, brief, and startling but not distressing. Whether internal or external, the voices focused on immediate issues. They offered practical direction, not grand metaphysical theology. Many people had the experiences during emotional turmoil, but not all. Just as in the Vineyard, the congregants said that you had to learn how to hear God speak, and they said that God did not compel. One man who had had a psychotic break distinguished between God's voice and the experience of psychosis: "God says something and doesn't force you, so you can do what you like with it." But with the psychotic voices, "you can't refuse to do something when you heard them. They are very pushy."[7]

Still, a skeptic might object that actually hearing a voice is a sign of potential psychiatric vulnerability. This is a deep question. The person who is able to hear an audible voice, even if only once, might indeed be different in some way from someone who strains to hear God and fails. It may be that such a person under unbearable stress would become psychotic rather than depressed, as glass shatters differently from earthenware. But a sensory override is not, by itself, a sign of psychiatric distress, although it is true that a naïve psychiatrist might mistakenly misdiagnose it so.[8]

This is not airy assertion on my part. I began my Spiritual Discipline Project acutely aware that nonbelievers might raise their eyebrows at the unusual sensory experiences people had reported to me at the Vineyard. So in the Spiritual Disciplines Project, we wanted to explore as carefully as we could in that setting what relationship unusual sensory experiences had to mental illness. We asked people to fill out a short questionnaire often used as a broad-gauged screening scale for mental illness. There was no significant relationship between absorption and that scale; nor was there a significant relationship between the scale and the way people answered the question of whether they had ever heard a voice when alone.[9] At the end of our long interview, we asked our subjects a series of questions about experiences associated with psychosis. For example: Have you ever thought that you were being followed or spied on? Have you ever thought that your thoughts are being broadcast so loudly that other people know what you are thinking?[10] Only 14 of 124 said yes to any one of the nine questions in a way that made us wonder whether they might be reporting a psychotic experience (although they were not actually diagnosable with psychiatric illness). Even then, we had often coded a "yes" because we could not be clear that they were not reporting a psychotic experience. That is, we coded cautiously.

Now, those subjects who did say that (for example) when they walked though the cafeteria, they felt other people drawing thoughts from their minds, did mostly report that they had odd sensory experiences. That is, ten of the fourteen subjects who were marked "yes" on one of the psychosis questions also said yes to the question about hearing a voice when alone. That lends support to the claim made by some psychiatric epidemiologists that there is a "psychotic continuum": that psychotic symptoms are distributed widely in the population.[11]

And yet there were fifty people who reported hearing a voice who said no to all those psychosis questions. Five out of every six people who reported having heard a voice when alone reported none of the other symptoms associated with psychosis—even when we coded cautiously and carefully. Moreover, their reports of sensory override experiences were quite similar to those of the Vineyard congregants. They had important spiritual experiences in which God spoke audibly or they saw an angel, or in which they had some other sensory awareness of the supernatural, and those events were rare, brief, and not distressing.[12]

In fact, this pattern appears to be widespread in the normal population. Sensory overrides are much more common than most middle-class Americans think. The first study that established this fact is one of the largest and most thorough that has ever been conducted, and it has been ignored for years because its authors were focused on something no modern psychiatrist believes. This is a shame, because it is a remarkable document, a scrupulously careful and massive report, four hundred pages in tiny nineteenth-century typeface, packed full with data.

In 1889 the newly founded Society for Psychical Research set out to demonstrate that people survived after death by asking a large number of people whether they had ever seen anyone or heard from someone who was not materially present. It was a time of confidence. England ruled a third of the globe. The First World War had not yet shaken the nation's faith in the power of human reason. Russell and Whitehead believed that they could set down the rules that underpinned all mathematics (and thus all knowledge) and guarantee its truth. It was a time before Gödel and Heisenberg, before the bomb, when knowledge seemed like a bottle opener that could uncap the world. And in the face of the challenge posed to Christianity by Darwin and the fossil record, this new society set out to use science to prove that the soul was immortal and that the immaterial was real.[13]

The researchers asked a huge number of people a specific question now sometimes referred to as "the Sidgwick question" after the bearded, brilliant man who led the research team: Henry Sidgwick, the Cambridge Knightbridge Professor of Philosophy.

> Have you ever, when believing yourself to be completely awake, had a vivid impression of seeing or being touched by a living being or inanimate object, or of hearing a voice; which impression, so far as you could discover, was not due to any external physical cause?

The society printed this question on a sheet of paper (Schedule A) with room for twenty-five answers. They handed these sheets out to more than four hundred people they called "collectors," half of them members of the society and their friends. Most of the collectors were educated (medical men, lawyers, university dons, civil servants, and the like), and so their subjects (their acquaintances) were also more educated than not, although there was some diversity. ("A good many collectors have asked the servants of their own or of their friends' households.")[14]

They had a second sheet (Schedule B) on which were listed other questions to ask if the person said yes.

1. Please state what you saw or heard or felt, and give the place, date, and hour of the experience as nearly as you can.
2. How were you occupied at the time, and were you out of health or in grief or anxiety? What was your age?
3. Was the impression that of someone whom you were in the habit of seeing, and do you know what he or she was doing at the time?
4. Were there other persons present with you at the time, and if so did they in any way share the experience?
5. Please state whether you have had such an experience more than once, and if so, give particulars of the different occasions.
6. Any notes taken at the time, or other information about the experience will be gratefully received.[15]

The collectors then collected as many answers as they could, but they were expected to find at least twenty-five people each, an expectation that the society hoped would rule out those eager to find only people who had vivid experiences to report. There seems to have been no other formal means to structure the sampling. Collection went on for three years. It stopped when the number of answers piled up to 17,000. Nearly 16,000 of those were English. The rest came from the United States, Russia, and, improbably, Brazil. William James was responsible for the American sample. You can still find his letter to the editor of *The New York Times*, published in 1890, where he calls for people to help.

Two thousand two hundred and seventy-two people said yes to the Sidgwick question. Sifting through them, the committee threw out responses that, when they read further on Schedule B, seemed not to be hallucinations after all—dreams, or reports of hearing mysterious footsteps, or anything that might have been an accidental overhearing. They threw out reports of visions seen with closed eyes, mysterious lights seen out of doors, anything experienced during fever, anything seen out of the corner of the eye, and the vague shapeless forms one sees occasionally between sleep and awareness. They also threw out reports of vague sounds without human speech—no laughing, sighing, groaning, whistling, or ghostly shrieks. By the time they were finished, 26 percent of the answers where details had been provided on Schedule B were gone. So then they threw out 26 percent of all the "yes" answers on Schedule A where the collector hadn't provided details on Schedule B. That left 1,684—nearly 10 percent of everyone they asked: 8 percent of the men, and 12 percent of the women. Only a quarter of these subjects reported having had more than one hallucination. Most of the hallucinations— 84 percent of them—had a visual element: people reported seeing something, although they often reported hearing or feeling something as well. Many were associated with intense emotion.

The collectors thought that these rates were underestimates. They found that people often forgot or hesitated to mention what they sometimes called "trivial" experiences. They noticed that people were far more likely to report experiences in the year just preceding than in earlier years. In fact, when they looked at the experiences reported in the previous year, half had occurred in the previous month: "As the years recede into the distance the proportion of hallucinations that occurred in them to those which are forgotten, or at least ignored, is very large."[16] Even so, it is clear that these experiences were far from everyday events for most people.

They were also generally brief and generally not distressing, even when the dead seemed to walk again. For example:

On 30th October, 1857, while Curate of Gain's Colne, Essex, I was sitting in my room, in lodgings, in a lonely half occupied farmhouse, about 7 p.m., when I heard the voice of a parishioner, whom I knew well, calling me from the outside, under my window, 'Mr. Maskell, I want you; come.' I went out, but I saw no one., and thought no more of it, til about 9 p.m. I was sent for by the man's wife, distant nearly a mile, and then learned that the man, J.B. had been found dead in the roadway from Chapple Station to the village—a long distance from my abode, perhaps a mile or more. [I was] reading, and in good health.

I was writing in my sitting room at our house in Derbyshire one afternoon in summer. My table faced the open door. I looked up and saw my father coming in with papers in his hands, big blue official looking papers, and a look in his face I had seen a thousand times, a sort of amused look, as if someone had been very funny, in the unconscious way people *are* funny, and he was coming to share the amusement with me. For an instant I forgot that he was no longer on the earth, and I looked up expecting him to speak, and half rose to push across to him the chair he liked to use—when there was just nothing. There is nothing for evermore.[17]

They are strange, these recollections, like half-remembered ghost stories from Henry James. But they are not ghost stories: they are memories, hundreds upon hundreds of them in the thick volume, of moments that stood out in the minds of those who told them like vivid dreams.

The basic story told by the Census of Hallucinations has held up over the following century. If you simply ask people whether they have ever heard a voice when they were alone, or seen something that could not be seen by someone else, and you do not put the question in a religious form or prompt people with examples, roughly 10 to 15 percent of Americans and British will say yes, and for the most part they will report sensory overrides that are rare, brief, and startling but not distressing. In 1948 the American branch of the Society for Psychical Research published a repeat of the census, curious about whether such experiences might take place less often in the bustling commercialism of the mid-twentieth century. They carried it out by mail, using the resources and presumably the sample-collecting skills of one of the new survey firms. They used almost the same language that the original census had used. And they got more or less the same ballpark figure that the original census had reached. Roughly 14 percent of the 1,519 replies reported some kind of visual, auditory, or tactile hallucination. Over half included a visual element. Less than a third were only auditory. Most people reported just one. Nearly twice as many women as men reported hallucinations, and among those who reported having more than one, there were almost three times as many women as men.[18]

Well and good; but this was still the Society for Psychical Research, whose stock has fallen since its founding, when its membership was a roll call of the intellectual elite.[19] In the late 1980s, the National Institute for Mental Health—no haven for wide-eyed optimists—carried out what came to be called the Epidemiologic Catchment Area Study. The sample was tightly regulated, the field surveyors were rigorously trained, and the data were electronically entered and analyzed, not tabulated on piles of fraying index cards. They went to five cities—New Haven, Baltimore, Durham, St. Louis, and Los Angeles—and interviewed more than 18,500 people across the socioeconomic spectrum. Unlike the previous two studies, this one focused clearly on psychiatric illness. Subjects were asked a series of questions based on the standard psychiatric diagnostic manual, questions about depression and anxiety and thoughts of suicide and pain. The hallucination questions were embedded in a series of questions about psychosis: for example, "Have you ever believed that you were being secretly tested or experimented on?" You would imagine that people would be skittish about saying yes.

And yet the numbers came out more or less the same.[20] The interviews asked about visual, auditory, and somatic experiences in questions like: "Have you ever had the experience of seeing things or a person that others who were present could not see—that is, had a vision when you were completely awake?" Thirteen percent of the subjects said yes: 10 percent of the men and 15 percent of the women. The great majority of the experiences were nondistressing, although the ratio of distressing to nondistressing was greater for auditory experiences than for visual ones. At a one-year follow-up, nearly 5 percent of the subjects (somewhat fewer subjects were reinterviewed) reported a hallucination that year alone. As in the previous studies, women reported more hallucinations than men. While the Sidgwick work had suggested that women were more imaginative, the authors of this study just thought that women remembered or reported these events more accurately; in the one-year follow-up, the rates for men and women were close. The one real difference from the Sidgwick study appears to be that the late-twentieth-century subjects reported somewhat fewer visual hallucinations than those one hundred years earlier.

When you prompt people with examples, the number who say yes explodes. In the early 1980s, two psychologists created a list of fourteen anecdotes, typically moments when someone experiences him or herself to have heard a voice and then—this is probably the crucial feature—decides that he or she has made a mistake. Here are the six questions that the psychologists thought captured voice hallucinations experienced when someone was fully awake—not in that twilight period between sleep and awareness, when as many as 40 percent of all people have perceptual illusions.[21] (Two of these questions will be familiar because we used this scale in the Spiritual Disciplines Project.)

"Sometimes when I'm in the house all alone, I hear a voice call my name . . . No, it really isn't scary. It was at first, but not now . . . It's just once . . . Like 'Sally' . . . Kind of quick and like somebody's calling me. I guess I kind of know that it isn't really somebody and it's really me . . . But it does sound like a real voice." Has this happened to you?

"Last summer I was hanging up clothes in the backyard. Suddenly I heard my husband call my name from inside the house. He sounded like something was wrong and was loud and clear. I ran in . . . But he was out in the garage and he hadn't called at all. Obviously I guess I made it up . . . But it sounded like a real voice and it was my husband's." Has this or something similar happened to you?

"I hear my thoughts aloud." Has this happened to you?

"When I am driving in my car . . . particularly when I'm tired or worried . . . I hear my own voice from the backseat. It's behind me over my right shoulder. I know it's really coming from my head, but it sounds like it's little short statements . . . usually soothing . . . like 'It'll be all right' or 'Now, just calm down.'" Has anything like this happened to you?

"I drive a lot at night. My job has a lot of travel to it. Sometimes late at night, when I'm tired, I hear sounds in the backseat like people talking . . . but I can't tell what they say . . . just a word here and there. When this first started happening . . . when I first started driving at night so much . . . four or five years ago . . . it scared the hell out of me. But now I'm used to it. I think I do it because I'm tired and by myself." Anything similar happen to you?

"Almost every morning while I do my housework, I have a pleasant conversation with my dead grandmother. I talk to her and quite regularly actually hear her voice actually out loud." Anything similar happen to you?[22]

Possibly, given the fear and mistrust that surrounds these experiences in American settings, it is easier to remember that that you had such an experience if the jog to your memory is that you were mistaken in your interpretation. Still, the leap in the rates is remarkable. The two psychologists reported that they gave the questionnaire to 375 undergraduates in a psychology class, emphasizing that "hearing voices" meant hearing a voice fully aloud "as if someone had spoken." Over 70 percent said yes to at least one of the six awake hallucination questions. I have given the scale to an undergraduate class five times. Before I hand it out, I explain that unusual sensory experiences are far more common than most people think and that I am curious about how many of them have experienced something like that. Each time, over 50 percent of the class says yes to one. The scale does not ask for a frequency, but looking at the sheets the undergraduates hand in, it is clear that what they report are far from daily experiences. (Few say yes to the dead grandmother question.) And in all of the classes, the more statements someone endorsed on the absorption scale, the more examples they endorsed on this one.[23]

It seems, then, that there is good empirical evidence for two different patterns of hallucination-like phenomena in the population. One is the result of a psychotic process associated with schizophrenia and other psychiatric disorders. In this pattern, hallucinations are frequent, extended, and distressing. They are primarily auditory, and they are often accompanied by strange, fixed beliefs (delusions) not shared by other people (for example, that malevolent government agents are running an electrical experiment in your brain). There is scientific controversy about the cause of these hallucinations: they may well be the result of repairing perceptual breaks, but driven by destructive, repetitive internal thoughts and a habituated expectation of hearing the caustic thoughts aloud. The hallucinations may even be one's own subvocalized speech. Some researchers argue that those who struggle with distressing voices cannot bear to hear their own self-loathing thoughts as their own, and so they allow themselves to identify those thoughts as external in order to protect themselves. Not everyone agrees. But this negative, self-destructive pattern of hearing distressing voices appears to be universal and recognized as illness in all corners of the world. Actually, one of the more curious features of the combination of distressing voices, delusions, and cognitive dysfunction that we identify as schizophrenia is that it may be quite recent. Psychosis goes all the way back (the Greeks certainly knew madness; think of the Bacchae). But schizophrenia may have emerged with industrialization.[24]

Then there is the ordinary, nonpathological pattern in which sensory overrides are rare, brief, and not distressing. This is the pattern described by my evangelical subjects, by other Christian subjects interviewed by other anthropologists, by the Sidgwick study and its follow-up, and by other research that points out that sensory overrides are not uncommon in the normal population. This pattern seems to be associated with absorption. In my Vineyard research, in the Spiritual Disciplines Study, and in each of my five classes in which students kindly filled out those questionnaires, I have found a significant relationship between absorption and sensory overrides. Other researchers have also noticed a relationship between absorption and reported hallucination-like phenomena.[25] Prayer training seems to make these kinds of sensory overrides more likely.

This pattern probably results from the constant perceptual breaks, as our senses reach out to grasp the world, and our top-down cognitive repairs to those breaks. I glance to the left, where I know there is a table, and my mind organizes what my senses take in according to my expectations of what should be there. If the table has been moved, it may take me a confused moment to see the space properly. Those who trust their imaginations more, or who practice attending to their minds, may occasionally repair or reorganize the incoming sensory data in a way that draws from what they know, rather than from what they actually see or hear. Particularly if the stimulus is ambiguous or the emotional need is great, they may see or hear something that springs from some other source than the materially real. And if they expect God to speak back directly, they experience God speaking back in an audible voice more often than those who do not. We know this is true. Nonbelievers do not often report that God speaks audibly to them, but many of my Vineyard subjects had experiences when he did. Does this mean that the voice of God is a perceptual mistake? Not necessarily. But it does mean that someone's capacity to experience the supernatural with their senses has something to do with their willingness to see more than is materially present before them.

Certainly there is a long Christian tradition of people who have heard or seen the supernatural. For the most part, these accounts also conform to the pattern of rare, brief, and not distressing, despite the powerful filtering of those who have told and retold the story. Augustine, for example, sketches his *Confessions* as a long prelude and afterlude to a shining moment of conversion. The book is one of our finest descriptions of the paradox of human intention, an accounting of his slow, sometimes painful effort to turn the unwieldy barge of his behavior out of the currents of accustomed habit. Augustine wants, badly, to be a Christian, but he believes that to be a true Christian, he must renounce sex, and he just cannot bring himself to do it, the way so many who desperately want to be thin still reach for the refrigerator door: "I fought with myself and was torn apart by myself." At the height of the crisis, knowing what he should do yet unable to commit himself to do it, he throws himself at the foot of a fig tree and weeps with abandon. "Suddenly a voice reaches my ears from a nearby house. It is the voice of a boy or girl (I don't know which) and in a kind of singsong the words are constantly repeated: 'Take it and read it. Take it and read it.' At once my face changed . . . I could not remember that I had heard anything like it before."[26] Augustine tells us that he decides that it is a divine commandment to read the Bible. He picks up the book and opens it at random, and his eyes fall on a passage about abjuring wantonness. His hesitation dissolves, and he converts fully and forever.

Augustine gives us good reasons to believe that this was an auditory hallucination. He does not think the child's voice was the accidental overhearing of a human voice: "I could not remember that I had ever heard anything like it before." He tells us that he heard the voice with his ears ("a voice reached my ears") and he gives it a source location ("from a nearby house"). This is the kind of evidence that a psychiatrist uses to judge whether a person has indeed had an auditory experience. And note these other features of the experience: it is a singular event, the only time in the *Confessions* that Augustine reports such a moment; and what is powerful for him is not the intrinsic quality of command in the voice but that he interprets it as divine. Augustine experiences an unusual event that he can make sense of within his religious framework, that is supported by other people (his friends and mother were overjoyed), and that makes him intensely happy.

Sensory overrides show up in particular ways in the annals of the church. They become the moments that found religions and create prophets when they occur at times of great emotion in the lives of gifted people: "As [Saul] neared Damascus on his journey, suddenly a light from heaven flashed around him. He fell to the ground and heard a voice say to him, 'Saul, Saul, why do you persecute me?'"[27] George Fox, founder of the Quakers, was in despair one evening, deeply disappointed in friends who seemed Christian only in name, desperately tempted by their pleasures: "When all my hopes in them and in all men were gone, so that I had nothing outwardly to help me, nor could I tell what to do, then, oh, then, I heard a voice which said: 'There is one, even Christ Jesus, that can speak to thy condition'; and when I heard it, my heart did leap for joy."[28] These events enter into the historical record as turning points in the trajectories of individual lives.

Sometimes the vision or voice becomes famous for itself, as proof of the presence of the divine on earth. In 1858, near a tiny French town called Lourdes, a young peasant girl claimed to see a beautiful young girl in the woods, clad in spotless white. When she told her mother, her mother beat her for the lie. But Bernadette went back to the place where she had seen the beautiful young girl, and the girl reappeared and thanked her for the holy water she had brought. Soon other people came to see, despite the mother's doubts and despite the authorities who soon forbade the visits. By the tenth time Bernadette saw the apparition, eight hundred people came to watch—but they watched Bernadette, her face immobile and translucent, not the apparition.[29] Soon the visions ceased and Bernadette went away, but the shrine that was built at Lourdes would become one of the greatest in Christendom, famed for its healing. When Lourdes became an annual pilgrimage site for Spaniards at the beginning of the twentieth century, pilgrims began to see Christ moving, sweating, bleeding, even writhing in agony in the little towns along the route. In the 1920s, when war made the passage to Lourdes impossible, more than a quarter-million people came to see the Christ of Limpias. One in ten of them saw the image move.[30]

Medjugorje is perhaps the most famous modern Lourdes, although there have been many.[31] In June 1981, six children between the ages of ten and twenty began to report near-daily sightings of the Madonna in this Croatian town. Several million people have since visited the shrine, to see the place of the sightings and sometimes to have sightings themselves. And just as more people see a vision at a place where it has previously been seen, they may be more likely to see visions together as a community. In 1988, in a charismatic Catholic church in Lubbock, Texas, congregants who had been to Medjugorje began to hear "inner locutions" as Mary delivered messages to specific people and to the world. One of these locutions suggested that the Virgin would perform a miracle on a particular day, the Feast of the Assumption. Those who gathered in the late-afternoon sun at the side of the church saw the sun dance (a phenomenon associated with Mary), and many saw visions of Mary and Jesus among the clouds.[32]

And yet while intense desire and expectation play their role, what is most striking about Lourdes and Medjugorje and Fatima and the many other places where the divine is perceived to break in to the everyday is that for all the intensity and yearning, sensory overrides do not take place that often. They are obdurate even in the face of overwhelming longing, even when the divine—at least in believers' minds—is truly present. That surely is the most impressive teaching of the postcrucifixion story. Christ is risen; some disciples see. But they do not see for long. They do not see clearly. And they do not all see. That is what gives the story its ring of psychological truth. Christ is not perceived the way people with psychosis see or hear hallucinations. He is seen rarely, briefly, and without distress, despite the great wish of his followers to see him once again among them.

The story of the Books of Acts is now, remarkably, repeating itself within a different faith. In 1994 Rabbi Menachem Schneerson, rebbe of the Lubavitcher Hasidim, deeply observant Orthodox Jews, died without leaving a successor. During his lifetime, many Hasids thought that he was the messiah. With his death, the messianic fervor grew. Many decided that he had never died, even though his body had gone. They have developed new ways to communicate with him. They place their questions randomly into one of the many volumes of his correspondence, then open the book at that place to read what he would have said—a sobering reminder that so many human problems are the same over the years: work, love, and children above all. In other ways, the rebbe's followers act as if he is still present. When the Sabbath begins in his house in Brooklyn, followers crowd into the room, singing and laughing, waiting for the rebbe to arrive. They have the chair on which he sat, and the ark which held the Torah scroll he used. At one point, the singing crowd parts to let the rebbe reach his seat.

They see him just as the disciples saw Christ. To date, more than eighty sightings of the rebbe have been posted on a website, and a cellphone video of a blur said to be his manifestation as he walks to his seat is used by the zealous as a screensaver. When a photograph of a child at his altar after his death was developed, it showed the rebbe at his side. Here is one of the website-reported sightings. The birth of a son is being celebrated, and the women are bustling about. One remembers:

> Suddenly I lifted my eyes and at a distance of about nine to ten feet I saw the Rebbe! I was completely shocked, and I wasn't able to move. I saw the Rebbe for about half a minute. When I calmed down from the excitement, I got up and went to the place where I saw the Rebbe, but now I already didn't see anything.
>
> I decided to tell myself: stop imagining things, you were hallucinating. I sat down again in my place and didn't say anything to anyone.
>
> After about five minutes, my daughter-in-law's mother came to me with her hands trembling all over and she said to me: "Chavi! You won't believe it!" I asked her: "What happened?" She replied: "I just saw the Rebbe!" I asked: "Where did you see him?" She answered: "I came from the sink to the refrigerator and from the refrigerator I walked back to the sink, and both times I saw the Rebbe!" "Where exactly did you see the Rebbe?" I asked. She pointed to exactly the spot where I had seen Rebbe!
>
> I told her: "Leah, yes, I believe you, I saw the Rebbe in the same place five minutes ago!"[33]

Again, what rings with truth is how rare and precious these sightings are. The absent must be made present. The rebbe's followers burn with the desire to see him here on earth, yet so few have done so.

Are these reports true sensory overrides? It is sometimes hard to tell. People use sensory language metaphorically as well. This is the challenge that confronts the historian. When the Book of Isaiah presents the moment when the prophet learns that he has been chosen by God as his mouthpiece, the words of the text say that Isaiah "saw":

> In the year that King Uzziah died, I saw the Lord seated on a throne, high and exalted, and the train of his robe filled the temple. Above him were seraphim, each with six wings: With two wings they cov-

ered their faces, with two they covered their feet, and with two they were flying. And they were calling to one another: "Holy, holy, holy is the LORD Almighty; the whole earth is full of his glory." (6:1–3)

What does it mean to say "I saw"? asks the medieval historian Barbara Newman.[34] The Bible does not tell us. Neither Isaiah nor Ezekiel—nor John in the Book of Revelation; nor, for that matter, Mary and the disciples, when Christ rises from the tomb—distinguishes between seeing "in the mind's eye" or seeing something solid as an oak. They do not tell us whether their images had clear borders or were translucent like a ghost.

But the people I spoke with at the Vineyard were often extremely clear. They said that they really heard or really saw. It mattered to them because seeing or hearing gave a concrete realness to the supernatural, sometimes at a crucial moment of doubt. The evidence of the senses feels irrefutable. Particularly in a skeptical society, in which God is treated as a lifestyle choice and doubt looms as a constant possibility, when someone who hesitates has sensory testimony to the supernatural divine—as did Suzanne, sitting at her kitchen table and wondering whether Jesus really existed—the moment can be transformative. That makes these moments a source of solace and resilience. Such moments lead those who experience them into health and happiness—not toward madness.

There is another, less common pattern to the way people experience sensory overrides in life and in the historical record. Some people have sensory overrides as often as people who can be diagnosed with schizophrenia, but without the intense distress psychosis carries in its wake, or any of its other symptoms—delusions, cognitive difficulties, emotional flatness. The obvious historical example is Joan of Arc, who was thirteen when she began to hear voices. She said at her trial that there were three voices—Saint Catherine, Saint Margaret, and the archangel Gabriel himself—and that she heard and sometimes saw them every day, sometimes several times. They told her what to do, and she obeyed them. They told her to cut her hair, to adopt men's clothing, to remain a virgin (and so spurn the marriage her parents offered her), and eventually to go to the king's court and insist that he give her an army, which rather surprisingly he did. The voices led her into battle and directed her strategies, and they stayed with her when she was imprisoned, though sometimes her guards were so noisy that she could not hear them. Although when first threatened with death, she denied her voices, some days later she affirmed them and so assured her death.[35]

There are other accounts of long and vivid hearings in our spiritual traditions. Moses took down the commandments. Muhammad received the entire Koran. The psychological state these men experienced at the time is long lost to us, if indeed the men even existed as men. The historian Ann Taves uses the experience of contemporary figures who hear long dictations to argue that the two men who received the Hebrew commandments and the Koran were probably in a trancelike state of intense absorption while receiving the material.[36] Certainly they are described as being in a nonnormal frame of mind. Moses, off with God for forty days and forty nights, returns from a final encounter with a radiant face; Muhammad, in a desert cave, felt that his soul was being ripped away. Taves points out that JZ Knight, who channels a 35,000-year-old spiritual warrior named Ramtha, shifts in and out of altered states, much as the turn-of-the-last-century mediums delivered volumes of wisdom from sages dwelling beyond ordinary human life while they, the mediums, were deep in trance.

Joan's voices seem different from these accounts because there is no clear evidence that her voices visited her in special ways or at special times. But she does not seem to have had schizophrenia, even though she heard voices often throughout the day, and even though her voices seem to have had extended conversations with her. Her life was far from dysfunctional, even if it did end in an untimely death.

The distinction is worth making because in hearing voices joyfully and often, Joan is not unique. There appear to be a small number of people who hear voices often but are not ill. (There are also people who see visions often but are not ill, but no movement has crystallized around them, and as a result, we know less about them.) In the late 1990s, a Dutch psychiatrist, Marius Romme, and one of his patients spoke on national television about the experience of hearing voices and asked people who heard voices to contact them. Seven hundred of them did, and 450 of them had heard audible voices. Many of those voice-hearers did, in fact, meet criteria for psychotic illness. They didn't like their voices and felt that they couldn't cope with them, and they wanted someone to help them make the voices go away. But not all of them. One hundred fifty of the people who wrote in didn't seem particularly troubled by their voices, and yet they seemed to hear them often, even daily.

Typically, the first voice came in childhood, and it had been startling, frightening, and unforgettable: "One Sunday morning at ten o'clock, it suddenly was as if I received a totally unexpected blow on my head." At first, most voice-hearers wanted to escape. They would ignore the voices, or sometimes argue with them, a strategy that often backfired. "Until then," a voice-hearer reminisced, "the voices had always been polite and friendly, but it changed in the opposite way: they said all kinds of strange things, and they made the things that were important to me look ridiculous. It was a full-blown civil war." Those who did best over the long term said that they had decided to respond only to the nice voices (they seem to have heard both nice and nasty ones) and then to interact with them: to listen to them, to understand them, and to incorporate them as part of their lives. Romme decided that the problem for his psychiatric patients was not their voices but the way they and their clinicians were interpreting them. Voice-hearers, Romme explained to a fellow scientist, "are like homosexuals in the 1950s—in need of liberation, not cure."[37]

I met someone like this at church. Jane is a competent, no-nonsense woman who took me in hand to introduce me around the Vineyard in California. She was very well respected at the church. People often called her a prayer warrior, although she laughed the label off. It sounded like hubris to her. But people liked to have her pray for them, and she had been one of the early picks for the prayer team.

Jane was in her midtwenties when I met her. She showed no signs of incipient psychosis. She was not a loner, as one might expect of a person who would go on to develop schizophrenia. She had none of the flamboyant emotional style that clinicians often associate with bipolar disorder. She was measured, and calm, if anything more controlled than the average young adult. Nor were there any signs that her life might slide into disrepair. She had graduated from an excellent university, and she had a good job. When I met her, she was coming up for an early promotion. She had a boyfriend, although they were fading as a couple by the time I met her, and she had a warm, wide circle of friends.

Nevertheless, she heard audible voices, often. We were well into our first interview by the time I figured this out. She told me that when she prayed for people, "I hear a voice almost like someone is kneeling over, standing over me, and sort of whispering in my ear." It soon became clear that this was not a metaphor. "I remember praying for a job and I interviewed, and I didn't know yet whether I was going to take it or not. It was just really random—like, I was cleaning my room—and I hear a voice say, 'That's not the one.' And then I said, 'What?' And sort of looked around, and I'm like, okay, maybe that's someone outside. [Then] I clearly heard God say, 'That's not the one.'"

A second time? I asked. "Oh, yeah. There was no doubt in my mind that was God." But in fact there had been doubt, the way there was doubt for Augustine. Jane gives us two reasons that we should believe she really did hear an audible voice. She turned her head to see who spoke, and then—not seeing anyone—she attributed the voice to a source outside the room. Only when the voice spoke again did she know it was God.

Then she told me about the first time she had had an experience like that. It had scared her.

> I was eleven, or maybe even eight or nine. I remember it was really hot. I remember being in the bedroom. I was watching TV and just hearing things. I was like "Okay, well, maybe I should shut off the TV." I shut off the TV and still heard a little voice, and I thought, "Maybe it's outside. Maybe that's what it was." And then I closed all the windows and went to lay on my mom's bed and then just hearing little bits and pieces. I'm like, "This is very weird." I thought I was absolutely losing my mind.

Again, Jane gave us excellent reasons to believe that she had had an auditory experience. She turned off the television. She shut the window. She worried because she knew that this was unusual.

The voices stopped after that for a while, more or less. At the end of high school—when, as it happened, Jane had reaffirmed her Christian commitment and joined a Pentecostal church—they showed up again. She was driving to a friend's house out in the suburbs, spooked and tense because she had just gotten her license and the streets were so dark and silent outside the city. "I just sort of felt a presence. I stopped the car, looked around, like 'What's going on?' I'm like, 'What is that presence?' Then I just sort of felt a voice saying 'God is here and God is everywhere and God will always be with you.' I'm like, 'OH.'"

Even though she said "felt," she insisted that it was a voice. "You heard that outside your head?" "Oh yeah," she said. "What did the voice sound like?" I asked. "I mean, it sounded like a very sort of monotone male voice. I mean—I don't know, and I think the tricky thing is whether you hear a voice outside yourself or sort of feel it as an impression. I mean, that one sounded a lot more like a voice outside of myself. It was just very, very odd." She said she had stopped the car and then gone on her way. She never told her friend what had happened. But she was sure it was good. "I mean, I knew it was God, I knew it was something good as opposed to I'm losing my mind."

Since that time, particularly after she joined the prayer team and became a leader in the church, Jane has heard God's voice often. She has heard God tell her what to do in prayer. "Recently when I was praying for someone, I heard a voice—it was outside of myself—say, 'Put your hand on her head and pray.'" She has heard God tell her what to do when she was out shopping.

I was downtown on Mission Avenue. I was tired and hungry and late, and I decided to head home. But I really felt like God was saying to me, "You need to walk like a block north and a block over." I was kind of irritated. Why do I need to? I mean, there's no store there, I'm really tired, like I really want to go, but I felt that tugging on my heart so I just went.

"And you heard this voice out—"
"Oh yeah," she interrupted me. "It was outside my head." She motioned.
"Was it behind you?"

Like right here, so sort of around the ear. I was sort of annoyed and frustrated and I didn't really know why, but I thought like, "This is so random, you know, this might mean something." I went over and there was an accident there, right as I turned the corner. There was an ambulance, and I think this woman collapsed. So I prayed for her. I don't know what happened to this woman, I don't know what was going on, but I really very much felt like I was supposed to pray for her and to trust and believe that God definitely was there and would help.

Jane was clear that these voices were external and audible. "How often do you hear something outside of your head?" I asked. "Oh, like all the time," she responded. "Every day?" "Yeah, every day." "Many times a day?" "Yep, many times a day."

What sense do we make of this? I am inclined to think of people like Jane as being different in kind from those who experience the ordinary pattern of sensory overrides. I suspect that the psychological mechanism that enables her voice-hearing shares more with the psychotic pathway than with an absorption pathway. This does not mean that she could be diagnosed with schizophrenia, or even that she is ill at all, but rather that the skills which set her apart are more related to the brain mechanisms associated with schizophrenia than to the sporadic sensory overrides of someone like Augustine.

We tend to think of schizophrenia as a thing, an illness with a series of symptoms like facets that are seen by the world. From that perspective, hearing voices is a symptom of schizophrenia the way sluggishness and dry skin are symptoms of hypothyroidism. But schizophrenia may be less of an organic entity and more of a collection of vulnerabilities, the way being overweight and smoking can be involved in cardiac disease but do not themselves add up to a single organic disease. That, at any rate, is the view of the psychologist Gordon Claridge.[38] I met him one afternoon at Oxford, where we strolled through the tumbled garden behind his house. He argued that schizophrenia is the outcome of a collection of traits shaped through the individual life course: cognitive disorganization, anhedonia, impulsivity, and unusual experiences. Neither cognitive disorganization nor a taste for unhappiness is healthy, and impulsivity is a trait with risks, but he thought that the capacity for unusual experiences is a trait of both the mad and the gifted, genius to madness near allied. From his perspective, a person like Jane has some of the genetic loading that is associated with schizophrenia, but not enough other vulnerabilities and bad life experiences to develop the disorder. This is a radically different way of looking at schizophrenia from the American biomedical approach. But it is gaining traction, not least because increasingly we recognize that there are people like Jane. From this perspective, Jane is able to use a psychological capacity for unusual experiences in a positive, productive way—but had she been beaten up as a child, or had a hard life, she might have acquired the other vulnerabilities that together would produce a package of behavior that looked more like schizophrenia. Without that negative life history, her capacity for unusual experience becomes a gift. Hearing God's voice made Jane feel good. It made her feel useful. And it had never occurred to her that she was unusual, although she did think that she was blessed.

. . .

But there are features of Christian prayer practice and Christian belief that may render someone more vulnerable to psychological distress. This is the other side of techniques that help what must be imagined to be experienced as real. When what is imagined is horrible, the daydream can become more of a nightmare.

Evangelicals who accept that the Bible is true in all it affirms ought to believe that demons are real. Jesus battles with demons throughout the Gospels—it is his major form of healing. Not all evangelicals do believe in demons, but churches that emphasize the holy spirit tend to take demons seriously, and in fact, some observers argue that there is more interest in demonic possession now than there has been for many years. (A 2005 Gallup poll found that 42 percent of Americans believe in demonic possession.)[39] Many evangelical books explain how to recognize and deal with demonic spirits. The most influential is probably Charles Kraft's *Defeating Dark Angels,* which has sold thousands of copies.[40] Kraft is an anthropologist, now retired, at Fuller Theological Seminary. In *Defeating Dark Angels,* he argues that Africans are more spiritually effective because they have the wherewithal to deal with the demons Americans refuse to acknowledge. He writes that he loves to fight demons, even though he says that he doesn't fully understand what they are, and he encourages others to leap in: "Go for it, even without understanding it all! It's worth it."[41]

These days, the phrase *spiritual warfare* is commonplace in American evangelical churches. The idea is that humans are mired in a world shot through with dark forces. Jesus has come to battle them, but he is not fully present, and as a result, the war has not yet been won. Congregants are encouraged to understand themselves as fighting by his side in battles raging between the darkness and the light. This view is central to the Vineyard. John Wimber took demons so seriously, back when his church was part of Smith's Calvary Chapel, that he was prepared to change the affiliation of his church rather than to abandon his exorcisms. You might say, then, that the Vineyard was founded on the belief in demons. One leader defended this position at a Vineyard conference: "If we're not casting out demons as a church, we're leaving people in bondage, we're leaving people in darkness, we're leaving people who are drinking themselves to death, addicted to pornography, thinking about suicide, along with all the medical and all the therapeutic needs that they have, and this is complex and needs inner healing." It's a little like *Star Wars* and a little like Freud.

Indeed, demons are central to much Christian therapy. One woman told me that psychological suffering was usually caused by an evil presence that not only incited abuse from other humans but moved into the victim's body during the pain, much the way rats move into a house with a cracked and broken foundation and take up residence in the walls. She worked with her clients the way therapists worked with recovered memory clients back in the day, encouraging clients to imagine something while in trance and then encouraging them to treat what they had imagined as real. When this woman works with someone, she asks them to relax with their eyes shut; she prays over them; she asks them to describe a safe place in their inner world that belongs to Jesus and where Jesus will take them when the healing has occurred; and then she asks them to describe the experience of abuse. Every detail must be told: any untold detail can fester and ruin the healing like a splinter left in a wound, and so sometimes these sessions must be repeated time and again. When her clients tell their story, she asks them to describe what they see most carefully. She knows, she told me, that demons do all in their power to interfere. She tells them to look for anything dark or weird or frightening. In particular, she asks them to look for a cloaked, black-robed figure that hovers at the edge of inner sight. If the client reports one, she casts it out in the name of Jesus. Sometimes it fights and speaks in strange, gibbering sounds before it leaves.

In the congregations I knew well, most congregants did not talk as if evil spirits were relevant to their lives. Most would say that demons existed, but it seemed more like abstract knowledge. They spoke as if they ought to take the idea of these spirits more seriously, but didn't. Even congregants who did take demons seriously often thought that attributing misbehavior to demonic activity was something of a cop-out. Jane, for example, was quite clear that demons existed, but she went on to explain that people often talked about demons to avoid facing up to their own bad behavior. "I have a co-worker at work, and she's being manipulative and conniving and not particularly truthful. Do I think she's being influenced by demonic forces? No. I think she is committing a sin."

But the pastors took demons seriously. There were sermons and classes on how to recognize demons and what to do about them. (After one of the sermons, I turned, incredulous, to a woman I knew from my house group and asked her what she thought. "Oh, it was really interesting!" she said. "I wish we'd have more sermons like that. I don't know very much about demons.") Still, they often dealt with demons in private. In Chicago, a pastor told me that early on in the life of the church, he'd had a funny feeling that there was a demonic "issue" with one of his congregants. He had taken in a temporary roommate who had been a member of a gang, and the man came to church to ask for prayer. The pastor waited until the room was nearly empty, and they prayed. And then the man fell over, and five demons (the pastor counted) came out of him with strange guttural cries. The pastor told me this to explain how you can recognize demons: by the distorted voices they use. But the story also illustrated his caution. He didn't wanted to spook newcomers by exorcizing a demon in their midst.

It seemed to me that the people who found themselves drawn to dealing with demons were the prayer warriors: those high-absorption, high-practice people who loved to pray and prayed intensely and seriously. As they developed their prayer expertise, they sometimes found themselves taken with the idea of spiritual warfare. Sometimes, when that happened, the demons became palpably real for them—too real.

Grace was sixteen when a friend gave her Loren Cunningham's *Is That Really You, God?* The book is subtitled *Hearing the Voice of God.* It's a popular book in this world, breezily cheerful and eager to teach its readers how to do what John Wimber used to call "the stuff." "This is a book about the outright supernatural," the preface opens. Cunningham is the founder of a large evangelical ministry for young people usually abbreviated as YWAM, Youth With a Mission. *Is That Really You, God?* is the story of how he came to found that ministry. Throughout the book moments of sensory experiences float between the perceived and the imagined. Cunningham describes God's voice as an inner voice, "at times quite audible."[42] This is the kind of dialogue he reports:

> Could it be that God wanted me to give up food for a while and pray? I opened a door to the idea. "God, do you want me to go on a fast?" Immediately the answer rushed into my brain. *Yes, and I want you to withdraw from people for seven days. Starting when you arrive.* I was dumbfounded. With house-to-house evangelism in Auckland we had so much to do! "Am I hearing you right, God?" I asked again.

Withdrawing from people meant I'd shirk my duties. Jimmy and Jannie would have to do the work of preparing for our outreach, the very thing we'd come thousands of miles to do. "Is that really you?" The only answer I got was another quiet voice saying, *The Dawsons are going to ask you to stay with them. Say yes.*[43]

What Grace loved about the book was the intimacy: that God was right there, talking about little specific things, and that you could learn to experience him that way yourself. You didn't have to be Moses. "When I read the book, I was like, maybe this is something I might want to learn." She went to one of the summer youth programs.

There Grace discovered demons. The camp taught her that we live in a time of great spiritual warfare, and that God seeks warriors to fight under his standard and will equip them for the fight. Grace loved the stories the leader told, about God speaking so specifically and in such puzzling but wonderful ways: "It was really cool. It was like so cool." The leader told a story about getting his hair cut, and God had spoken to him, telling him to share the word *bicycle* with his hairdresser. It sounded like a dumb thing to do ("he was like, *bicycle*, Lord?"), but it worked. "The man was like, 'Bicycle.' It linked back to a childhood memory, and then he opened up and shared his whole life story, and because of that, the guy came to know God. Crazy stories. Crazy stories like that." Then the leaders taught the students how to hear God in their own everyday lives.

At first, Grace thought she wouldn't be able to hear God speak: "I was like, I am so rational. I don't hear God." But once she prayed, "God, I really want to hear you," and all of a sudden she felt that she should read Isaiah 55. She told me that she had never read it before. Right there in the middle of the chapter, God announces that he will make a covenant with the reader just as he made a covenant with David. Grace was thrilled. It seemed to her that this was evidence that God really was speaking directly to her, in a personal, specific way meant for her alone. "It all came in the same week, and it came together. It was so cool."

Grace went to other, similar conferences and retreats. She attended another camp. She liked going to these events because she found that she could hear God so much more easily when she was surrounded by people who believe that you could. "You go there to do these things," she told me, "you're around people who are doing these things, it's a very charged atmosphere, a spiritual atmosphere, there's a special grace over it, the atmosphere is very conducive." She began to pray more intensively. She read her Bible aware that God might use it to speak to her. This made reading the text much more exciting, as if it were living, breathing, responding, like a person. "Before I would read stuff and sometimes be like, 'Okay, I know that, blah blah, this is boring,' close my Bible. But when I would read my Bible then, during those times, it was very direct. Everything I read would just speak directly to me. At those times, it sort of feels alive."

She came back to college after that summer with a sense of purpose about prayer. "I returned with that kind of mind-set, like, I have to pray for this place." Increasingly that meant, to her, that she should pray against the powers of darkness. She met another student who shared these views. They began praying early in the morning, for the campus and for their dormitory. They thought their dormitory was depressing, and they prayed against its gloom and the gloom of people within it. She began to feel that her prayers really made a difference in the lives of the people she prayed for. Not that she hadn't thought that they mattered before, but somehow this was different. She quoted Isaiah 62:6–7 to me: "I have posted watchmen on your walls, O Jerusalem; they will never be silent day or night. You who call on the Lord, give yourselves no rest, and give him no rest till he establishes Jerusalem and makes her the praise of the earth." Now she felt responsible for the fight.

In this new life of intense, focused prayer, hours and hours of prayer, Grace found herself more alert than usual, as if her senses were somehow heightened. She was quick to notice the atmosphere of a place, as if she could sniff out evil. She would walk into a restaurant and immediately sense some evil, and she would know she had to pray in order to get rid of something spiritually bad. It was as if the world were drenched with a darkness that not everyone could see, that she had never seen before. She was much more conscious of God's presence, and much more conscious of evil. Once she woke up thinking that someone was trying to rape her: "I woke up and it felt like I was struggling against this figure. Then I saw it. It was kind of dark, and as soon as I shouted *Jesus,* it kind of flew out of my room."[44] She paused to give me some advice. "You always need to shout *Jesus.*"

Grace began to feel like a conduit, as if the Holy Spirit would flow through her to do God's will. She said that she had become open in the way Paul, in his letter to the Romans, says that you are supposed to be open, to allow the spirit to move through you to act on behalf of God. She would feel the Holy Spirit, physically, tingling in her fingers. She felt like she was offering herself as a sacrifice, and the structure that she thought of as who she was had broken down and she was flooded by new intensity. She found that she became much more emotional, much more in touch with what she felt and what the feelings meant to her, that they mattered to her in a way they'd never done before. She began to get deeply emotionally involved with her prayers.

She found herself weeping when she prayed. She wept with sadness or even happiness, weeping sometimes as if the emotion were bigger than she was, as if it were out of control. At one point she found herself alone in the city at her parents' house, studying for exams. She knew that YWAM had a plan to pray for all the pain in all the cities, but at that point she had not felt drawn to the project. Then she found herself out on the streets of the city praying, and sobbing with the intensity of her prayers. She began to sob in the services and to sob in her own prayer time. She said that sometimes she cried without understanding why exactly, feeling God's love so intensely that she wept with the grief of being human. But this intense need to pray also began to frighten her: "I found suddenly like I was praying like crazy. I was like, whoa. This is kind of strange."

Yet she kept on praying. Now when she wept, she wept about all the sad things that happened on the earth. She began to feel that her prayers were needed to keep the darkness at bay, and she felt both empowered and overwhelmingly sad as she began to see how much pain and sadness there was in the world. When I asked her what she felt as she wept, she said, "I was grieving. It wasn't only about this place, it was also about different nations, and it was like such a mess because God is not there as he should be; God is not worshipped as he should be worshipped; these people just don't know him. And I cried like you might cry if someone died."

The more intense the experience became, the more Grace began to wonder, off and on, if she was going crazy. She was not really worried about this, but she noticed that as she was beginning to pray more and more intensely, she felt increasingly different from her friends. They did not sense the strange atmosphere in the restaurants. They did not feel this intense burden and this compulsion to pray, pray, pray. She noticed that she would get so involved in praying that she had trouble doing her classwork. She thought that she talked to God in an almost obsessive way, "just kind of walking round all day, thinking of him, bringing every small thing to him—should I go out with this person now, should I do this other thing—being so much more intense." She knew she was supposed to pray always; but she also knew that what she was doing was unusual, on the edge. "After a while you become so removed from your friends," she told me, "because other people aren't attending the same way you are. They don't see things the same way you do." She called it being in a "zone." "You step out and you're like, maybe I'm making everything up and working myself up. I just seemed so out there, you know."

Eventually she stopped. It was too exhausting. The pastor attributed her exhaustion to spiritual attack; people said that the more intensely you prayed against the demons, the more eagerly they launched themselves against you. But Grace thought it was just exhausting to pray so much, whatever the demons did. And she pointed out to me someone else in the congregation who was known as a prayer warrior and had gotten drawn into spiritual warfare, and she said that this person was also beginning to worry that she was crazy. (That young woman refused to talk to me about her experience when I asked; she found it too upsetting.) "It is so crazy," Grace said. "It's like we're addicted. It's so crazy. Why do we do it?" Some weeks later I drove her back from an event, and we began to talk about that period in her life again. "It's so strange," she said. "You get into that zone, and you know that the students around you think about things completely differently, and you really do wonder whether you are crazy."

Sarah, too, struggled with demons. Things had begun to go badly for her some months after I met her. It was not difficult to understand the strain. She felt that so many people depended on her. She prayed hard for hours every day—for the church, for the pastors, for people she knew who needed God's help. Then the spring I joined the church, her son was shipped to Iraq as part of a military unit. Sometimes he was in Baghdad, sometimes Fallujah. Within months, her husband developed terminal blood cancer. It was a slow, unpredictable cancer. She was told that he might be dead within the year—or live for a decade. The uncertainty and the anguish became nearly unbearable.

By July Sarah was beginning to feel worn down. She described this as being "toughened out." "Like when you are learning to play the guitar and there's a sense of practicing to get the skills and the practice, but you also develop calluses on your fingers," she said. "That's what I feel like I'm doing." She made it very clear that she felt peace in the face of these very difficult events. "Everything that has happened, there has just been this supernatural sense of peace. My son being in Baghdad, my husband's diagnosis, I'm not escaping from it. I'm in it. I'm not denying my husband's cancer. I'm not pretending that my son is really in Texas. There's just peace in it."

Around this time, the church leadership went to a conference out of town. Sarah knew that she was too stressed to drive, but she was looking forward to the trip. "I knew I was burned out," she said. "I knew I was frazzled, I knew I needed a rest, I knew I needed to be restored and I would be there." She'd already begun to think of her troubles in the context of spiritual warfare. She told me that she'd seen an imp—some kind of evil presence—run across her bed. "When I told the pastor about it, I called it an imp. That's what it looked like to me. I saw it in my house running across the pillows in our bed. I felt like I wasn't supposed to see it and yet I was supposed to see it. And it was frightening. I was not wild about seeing something I knew wasn't there. But you gotta know what you are fighting."

Sarah clearly recognized that not everyone in church believed in these materializations of evil or even in spiritual warfare: "You're really putting yourself out there on the lunatic fringe when you even tell somebody you saw something running across the pillow." And yet she felt that her ability to see the imp was a natural progression from all that she had learned so far. She didn't like the fact that she'd seen it, but she also thought that it was cowardly not to go forward in prayer and in knowledge. "I mean, I've been asking God to give me eyes to see what it is that he wants me to see," she said. Still, her language worried me. I thought she might be more vulnerable than she let on to others. And she seemed angry and irritable—understandably but also noticeably. "Sometimes you feel almost schizophrenic," she said. "'Give me more, Lord, give me more'— and then, 'Go away, I don't want to see this, I don't want to be seeing creepy little gremlins in my bedroom.'"

At the conference, someone with expertise exorcized her. Sarah found the exorcism terribly confusing. "When we got to the point where he [the conference expert] was calling off the demons and laying the demons at the foot of the cross and calling on God to—I can't even remember what his words were because I stopped being able to hear him—but it was stuff like break their teeth, dismember them, throw them out." To her own horror, she resisted. "I heard my own voice defending them. Just in my head. I was like talking to God and begging for mercy. At the same time I knew it was a lie, I knew that it wasn't right, I knew it was stupid to do that, but it was like defending your own children or something like a crazed mother bear." She didn't like the experience at all.

Yet Sarah decided that she couldn't move forward spiritually unless she accepted that she was indeed struggling with demons and worked to be delivered from them. "I wasn't growing anymore because there was this inner feeling that something needed to be done, and there was demonic deliverance that needed to be done. I fought it for a long time, and I just wasn't going to fight it anymore."

She decided, then, to understand her own internal hesitation as part of the spiritual attack, as the kind of thing that demons would do. The expert at the conference told her that the demons were feeling scared, and that was why they were making it so difficult to come out. She remembered that in previous weeks, she had heard her own inner voices condemning her, calling her stupid. She said she'd even gone into episodes of near-suicidal despair.

After the conference, Sarah read Kraft's *Defeating Dark Angels.* She decided that God was calling her into spiritual warfare: "Now God's in it, now it's his time, now he is equipping me for it, and he's there. I got that through that book. It was very truthful." She and the pastor agreed that not only did Sarah need more exorcism but that they needed to understand how to deliver it and make it available for other people at the church as well. "A lot of the people coming to church," Sarah explained, "are really in need of that kind of deliverance and that kind of inner healing, and those needs just aren't being met with the ten to fifteen minutes of prayer ministry per person you can get on Sunday morning."

Over the summer, Sarah, the pastor, and another woman began to meet weekly for a couple of hours. They would have Sarah talk about the parts of her life about which she felt shame or anger. That made sense; those were the parts, they thought, where she thought she needed healing. She talked about this as "shining God's light" on her wounds. But these were also deeply personal, deeply embarrassing areas of her life: "It was just like ripping open your guts and your heart and your soul." They worked chronologically, going back to early memories and moving forward. "It was just like talking to a therapist," she said. "I'd talk in general about what was going on in a particular season of my life, and then we'd wait a little more, and God would start revealing specific people or circumstances, literally things I had forgotten, or pushed down so much. Abuse by a teacher, an attempted rape, things that were just horrible, things with my family, my husband."

The pastor was in his thirties, the other woman not quite out of her twenties. They were wise for their age, and careful, thoughtful individuals. The woman would pray for the process. The pastor would name the demons and expel them, and pray for peace and healing. They were praying in the way that the church had taught them, the way so many publications teach, and they were following the clear direction from leaders at the conference. But Sarah was twenty years older, used to being the mother, the caretaker, and the source of support—not the one who needed supporting. And many of the issues that bothered her were not issues that either of the two people praying for her knew much about, and she felt they were so young, so good, so clean, that it was difficult for her. She had the kind of terrible embarrassments that come with twenty more years of life.

For Sarah, things only got worse. She had a bad car accident, although she emerged unharmed. She fell down the stairs and was convinced that a demon had pushed her. She stopped sleeping. The voices of inner condemnation got worse. She began to quarrel with people at church. The pastor, uneasy, consulted with another pastor and also with a Christian therapist. Both said that it sounded like the issue was demonic, but to proceed with caution. They continued with the prayer sessions, then, but nothing changed. Sarah still felt awful. She left prayer ministry. And then the prayer sessions stalled out. They had been praying around forgiveness, and Sarah felt that she could not forgive. The Christian therapist suggested that it would help if she listed each and every issue that bothered her in her relationship with the young man now serving as her therapist-confessor. She presented the pastor with a four-page typed memo. "That was completely disastrous."

In October there was another conference. During the evening prayer sessions, someone had a "prophetic word" for the pastor that he should be doing more work with spiritual deliverance—the code word for the process of diagnosing demonic possession and then delivering the host person of the demon's presence. They decided that they should pray again for Sarah. The man who joined them was more direct and authoritative than anyone who had ever prayed for Sarah before, naming and commanding and shouting at the demons that inhabited her. Afterward she still felt awful, and now she felt hopeless. She knew that none of the prayers had worked and that she still had demons. The pastor remembers that she cried out in anger: "I'm stuck with these demons. What do I do now?" She left the church. Within weeks, she was hospitalized for major depression.

Over the next six months, Sarah went in and out of the hospital. She had two suicide attempts, one of them serious. She was diagnosed with bipolar disorder. She tried a series of antidepressants, none of which seemed to work. Eventually she agreed to electroshock therapy, and slowly, over the course of many months, the bleakness lifted.

Had the demonic exorcisms made things worse? Sarah's family thought so. In fact, they laid the illness at the door of her faith. "They blame the depression on being born again. Here I'd hoped to be a good testimony and a good witness to them, and it's sort of worked the other way. When I told them that I was thinking of going back, they were horrified that I would go back to the place I was ruined." Her new Christian therapist was appalled at the prayer she had been receiving at the church. The therapist wasn't charismatic and didn't believe that Christians could be demonized or, for that matter, that people could really speak in tongues.

But Sarah still prayed in tongues. In fact, she was pleased to know that she could, that it hadn't been taken away from her: "Now, when I'm in a completely different situation and I don't need to display anything to anyone, sometimes my prayers will just change into tongues without doing anything or thinking anything or anyone else hearing."

Despite her family and her new therapist, for Sarah the idea of demonic presence remained very much alive. She told me, long after she left the church, that demons had tried to kill or maim her: "I was walking downstairs to the basement, and I literally felt something take hold of my shoulder, turn me, and I walked off the side of the stairs. There was no reason for that to happen." She said that when she looked at the ceiling, she could see creatures waiting for her, trying to destroy her. "I look up trying to pray, and there's this whole nest of horrible creatures just waiting for me as I'm walking that path to God." She could see them and hear them and smell them, not quite so clearly as if they were flat-out hallucinations, but clearly enough to be aware of them and to be bothered. "They're—they're like they have no hair, they're like E.T., those waxy faces. Sometimes I see their teeth, which are very pointed, and their mouths are big and open, and their teeth are dripping, they're drooling and stuff comes out. But it's their cackle that's just unbearable."

She told me that the pastor had given a sermon about demonic possession one Sunday before I arrived in the church, and she had dug it out and read it. She wrote out the symptoms of demonic possession the pastor had given, and the symptoms she thought were associated with bipolar disorder—and they were, she thought, the same. Her list contained these symptoms:

a. Bizarre or violently irrational behavior, esp. in opposition to the gospel (Mark 1:24, 5:2–5, 9:28, Acts 16:16–18, Rev 2:10)
b. Malicious slander and falsehood in speech (Jn 8:44, 1 Jn 4:1–3)
c. Increasing bondage to destructive behavior (Mark 5:5, 9:20)
d. Stubborn advocacy of false doctrine (1 Jn 4:1–6)
e. Sudden unexplained onslaughts of emotion such as fear, hatred, depression, anxiety, violence, anger, etc. (the Enemy's flaming darts in Eph 6:16; contrast to the fruits of the spirit in Gal 5:22)
f. Deep uneasiness or discernment of spiritual evil (1 Co 12:10)

And she wrote this in her journal: "Every 'symptom' applies/applied to me. Every one. But they're also the symptoms of depression and anxiety disorder. So which is it? Does it matter? The treatments are so different. Lord, please help me."

"You know," she said after showing me the journal,

when I was first starting to go to my psychiatrist—to tell a psychiatrist that you're hearing voices or you're seeing things that aren't there—psychiatrists interpret that outside of the spiritual realm. So I knew I couldn't describe those experiences to them. Then you wonder, "Well, should they know it? Would it make a difference to the way I'm treated or the medication they give me?" It's confusing . . . And the stuff about demonization just seemed to really articulate what I'm experiencing, and I went and looked up all those scriptures, and it seemed like that was what was going on with me. But by this time, I wasn't going to church anymore, I was disconnected from everybody, and I had no way to get help. Where do you look up "exorcist" in the phone book?

. . .

To the extent that prayer techniques can help make more real a loving God, they can also make more real a leering demon. Of course, it is hard to draw the causal arrow. Grace eventually just stopped the behavior that made her feel odd. Had the circumstances of Sarah's life not been so difficult, perhaps she too could have turned away. There is also the possibility that the bare circumstances she confronted—son and husband both at such terrible risk—were such that without any talk of demons, she would have become dangerously, suicidally depressed. One might also infer that Grace and Sarah were drawn to demons because the negative images spoke to them, rather than being imposed on them through the church. But it was hard for me to avoid the conclusion that ruminating on demons is dangerous, even when the goal is to rid the world of them, even when they may not actually exist, because when people are drawn into working with demons, they become more psychiatrically vulnerable—not because the demons are necessarily real, but because through the intense practice of prayer the demons become real to the those who pray, and haunt them.

What we carry in our minds really can become our world if we encourage it and allow it to be present. That is the promise of faith and also its curse. God-concepts and spirit-concepts are not neutral. They have great power for those for whom they are real, and when they are real for those who embrace them, they can be a problem, especially when they are negative. That is the risk for the high-absorption practitioners who learn to make them real: that the evil spirits become more real for them, as well as the good spirits. It is not a necessary risk. Not all the prayer warriors I met went down the path of spiritual warfare. Many got deeply caught in prayer without worrying about demons and their evil presence. But for those who did, it could be costly. Those who did were the only Christians I spoke with who seriously worried out loud to me about being crazy.

CHAPTER NINE

Darkness

My God, my God,
why have you forsaken me?

Psalm 22:1

God is real, no matter how you feel.

Rick Warren,
The Purpose Driven Life

A LMOST ANY discussion between a believer and a nonbeliever eventually comes down to the nonbeliever's strongest argument: How can anyone believe in a God who is all-powerful and benevolent in a world that is filled with suffering?

It is an old problem. God has always disappointed. The Hebrew Bible sings with the anguish of a disappointed people, bound by covenant to a God who fails them repeatedly for reasons they do not understand: *I cry out to you, God, but you do not answer.* The Book of Job is the sharpest example, a meditation on a blameless man whose life shatters for what seems like God's whim. Scholars date its composition to shortly after Jerusalem fell in 560 B.C.E. to the Babylonians, who destroyed the great temple and took God's chosen people into slavery. But many biblical texts are full of helpless pain. *I saw all the deeds that are done under the sun; and see, all is vanity and a chasing after wind.*[1]

Yet not until the eve of the Enlightenment, with its love of explicit reason, did the various intellectual solutions to the problem of unjust suffering get a name: *theodicy,* a term coined by Gottfried Leibniz in 1710 to describe the philosophical solutions to the problem of why a perfectly good, almighty, and all-knowing God permits evil. There are three general solutions. Evil is the lack of God's goodness, and humans create it when they do not choose God (Augustine); the world will be good in the end (Iraneus); and despite appearances, we live already in the best of worlds (Leibniz's explanation, and the one with which Voltaire made hay in *Candide*).[2] None is entirely persuasive, and the inability to reconcile God's goodness, omnipotence, and omniscience with human suffering is the compelling logical puzzle that has led many out of faith.

Churches like the Vineyard handle the problem of suffering with a fourth solution: they ignore it. Then they turn the pain into a learning opportunity. When it hurts, you are supposed to draw closer to God. In fact, the church even seems to push its congregants to experience prayers that fail. This is not, of course, anything pastors actually say or believe. They say very clearly that God always answers prayer. But prayer failure is an inevitable consequence of the way these churches encourage people to pray. Congregants pray for admission to specific colleges, for the healing of specific illness—even, it is true, for specific red convertible cars. They pray far more specifically than most mainstream Christians. Many of these prayers fail unambiguously in ways that prayers for world peace do not. (You can always see a little improvement in the health of nations if you look for it.) Clutching a rejection letter or looking into the mirror at a botched haircut, it is hard to say that your prayer was answered. The logical problem then becomes glaringly obvious. When God is very close and very powerful and always very loving, there is no easy explanation when he does not deliver. Vineyard congregants do not have the theological resources available, say, to those beleaguered congregants for whom Jonathan Edwards laid out so bleak a vision. Their God is never angry. He loves, unconditionally. As a result, cognitive dissonance is sharper at a church like the Vineyard than at any of its mainstream counterparts.[3] Why would people pray like this?

The answer is that in-your-face failures force people to get something different out of prayer. When prayer fails, people at the Vineyard simply shift the focus and say that this is when you need God. Indeed, the more powerful the apparent assault on faith—how could God have let this happen?—the more intensely congregants insist on God's role as friend to help them through tough times. His friendship becomes its own reward. That is what makes churches like the Vineyard work. People stay with this God not because the theology makes sense but because the practice delivers emotionally. Under these conditions, it is often when prayer requests fail that prayer practice becomes most satisfying.

. . .

At the Vineyard, people explicitly and repeatedly explained that asking for specific, concrete outcomes was important. "God doesn't just want to know that you want to pass the MCAT," a medical student announced to us in house group. "God wants a number, and he wants to be reminded of it often." That woman did well on her MCATs, and she passed her boards. "It's all him," she said to me. "I'm not very smart. I couldn't have done it on my own." Early on in our house group, the second or third time we met as a group, our leader, Elaine, gave us this verse:

So I say to you, ask, and it will be given to you; seek, and you will find; knock, and it will be opened to you. For everyone who asks receives, and he who seeks finds, and to him who knocks it will be opened. If a son asks for bread from any father among you, will he give him a stone? Or if he asks for a fish, will he give him a serpent instead of a fish? Or if he asks for an egg, will he offer him a scorpion? If you then, being evil, know how to give good gifts to your children, how much more will your heavenly father give the Holy Spirit to those who ask Him! (Luke 11:11–13)

Elaine was a serious, confident Christian. Our problem as Christians, she told us, is that we don't ask. You just have to ask. And ask for specifics! "Don't tell God you want a car. Let him know that you want a red car. He won't give if you don't ask, but he will give if you ask." (This is sometimes described as "name it and claim it.") The medical student told us that a friend of hers had been about to take the medical licensing exam and was refusing to do more than pray not to fail. She had badgered her friend to come up with a score, but her friend thought it was presumptuous to give God a number. Then the medical student laughed as she explained that when the scores came back, her friend got a score that passed by one point, but no more. Yep, another member of the group nodded sagely. "Sometimes I think, you know, we pray so hard to get God's, attention and then what do we ask for when we get it? You've got to get specific."

But inevitably, God didn't always come through. When that medical student entered the residency match, she really wanted to work as an obstetrician, and she really wanted to live in Indianapolis, where her brother was—and she didn't get to Indianapolis. She didn't even get into an obstetrics residency. She ended up in family practice in St. Louis. She was so upset and mad that she left Chicago for the spring. "I'm struggling with God," she said to us. "I don't know what to say. I'm struggling. Actually, I'm screaming."

But that prayer gets results—specifically, directly, demonstrably—is a constantly reiterated theme of Sunday-morning gathering, of house group discussion, of all those training sessions. Indeed, congregants often describe being hungry for proof and then fed by confirmation. At first, Sarah said, she really needed to know that her prayer was having a concrete impact: "Very often, in the beginning—when I kind of had training wheels—I would get immediate feedback, that [what I'd prayed] was right on, or I'd find out in another way that something I'd prayed had actually happened." She no longer needed that confirmation every day, she said, but she did need it sometimes. "I don't get it as much anymore," she told me, "but when I get it, it's bigger, and it's enough to carry me." Prayer is real for these congregants; it is a pragmatic, actual connection to God's power, and knowing that it gets results was central to Sarah's faith experience: "To me that's part of faith, to know that what you're doing is making a difference, that you are hearing God correctly, and that it is having an effect."

Of course, there are ways to judge prayer as effective even when the red car does not come through, the same ways people find evidence for the accuracy of horoscopes and lucky charms.[4]

a. God answered your prayer but gave you what you needed, not what you wanted. You wanted Yale. He knew you'd be happier at Colorado State.
b. God heard your prayer, but for reasons we cannot understand, he chose to refuse. A popular bumper sticker announces: "God answers every prayer, but sometimes the answer is no."
c. God's time frame is different from yours. You need to be patient. (People say this particularly when praying for love.)

And yet at the Vineyard I was startled by just how much congregants risked by praying so very specifically—a red car, not a blue one—and, as a result, just how often they were forced to confront prayer's apparent failure. In mainstream churches, one has the sense that to pray so specifically is not only unseemly but unwise: that to do so is to tempt fate.[5] (A version of this that one does hear at the Vineyard is the assertion that you must not test God. *Bruce and Stan's Pocket Guide to Talking with God* has a sidebar box in which they say that God is not a lab rat.) That people take such risks even when the outcome upsets them and makes them mad suggests that prayer failure is doing something useful in this spirituality.

Indeed. At the Vineyard, when everyday prayer seems to fail—prayer in which someone's life does not hang in the balance—people explain that the failure is part of God's plan to build a better relationship with the person praying. God gives evidence of his existence to those who need it, they say, but he wants his more mature followers to turn to him for the sake of a relationship and not for his stuff. In this developmental trajectory, God always answers your prayers specifically only if you are new to belief. He gives you concrete signs of his supernatural reality because you need to know that he is really there. Then, people say, he leads you into a relationship in which you do not need these trinkets, as if answering prayer directly were like getting a gift bag at a wedding: nice, but not the point. Madeline put it this way:

> When I first became a believer I saw all these sort of miraculous answers to my prayers. It seemed like I would just pray and then things would happen . . . like, amazing things. And then as I grow and grow and grow in my faith, and as the years go by, I see these things less and less.
>
> When we're young in our faith, we're babies. We're weak. We're immature. We need those kinds of miraculous, amazing, fireworks kind of displays because our faith is so small, and our understanding of God is so small. We need that. More mature Christians don't rely on those things. They know God.

You can argue that this is more or less the story that the writers of the Gospels tell. Christ begins as a miracle worker, bringing people to his side as he heals and casts out demons. He amazes them, and they pursue him, and the more miracles he performs, the larger the crowd he draws.[6] But Christ wants people to believe in him and to love him without the bells and whistles. The last and latest Gospel ends with Doubting Thomas, who refuses to believe that Christ has risen until he puts his finger into the marks of the nails and his hands into the wound on his side.

Jesus appears; Thomas has his proof. Then Jesus says, "Have you believed because you have seen me? Blessed are those who have not yet seen and yet have come to believe."[7] In other words, God starts out as Santa Claus and ends up as best beloved.

People called this "spiritual maturity." They contrasted the giggly euphoria of being a new Christian with the sober demands of being there for the long haul. They spoke of the first stage as "falling in love" with Jesus. Everybody agreed that this was a fabulous period in your life. God always seemed to be there and to indulge every whim, to care for you in ways you hadn't expected, to create—as one woman put it—"a relationship with the man of my dreams." You developed spiritual maturity when you loved God even when he didn't act like a sugar daddy. People used the word "walk" to frame their experience of God as a journey, speaking casually about where they were on their "walk with God." The journey begins with falling in love and develops as the love ripens and becomes mundane, love in the context of diapers and mortgage payments. When small prayers weren't answered, or when in hindsight it was clear that God's choice had been a good one (you really liked Colorado State), people would say that God knew better than you what you needed. But when bigger prayers went wrong—and especially, it seemed, when the unanswered prayers concerned money—people often said that God gave them the hard times because he wanted them to depend upon him alone.

I spent a morning with Trish, the medical student, talking about Elaine and her ambitions. Elaine had organized the house group that I attended, and I could see those ambitions. She wanted intense, powerful, intimate experiences with God, and she wanted to be known for having those experiences. "She's so hungry," Trish said. She wanted so badly for God to fill some hole in her life, Trish explained; she wanted so badly to have these intense visions or some kind of amazing relationship with God, and she was going to fail. Trish said this matter-of-factly. She thought that Elaine's prayers weren't going to be as effective as she wanted and that her relationship with God wouldn't do for her everything that she wanted. "The failure will be good for her," Trish said, nodding wisely. "It will be a maturing experience. It will make her relationship with God a better one."

Elaine lived on a budget considerably smaller than most students in the area. She came to Chicago specifically because she was looking to work in a church like the Vineyard, but her only actual employment was working ten to twenty hours a week in the church office. (Her evangelizing efforts kept her considerably busier than that implies.) She took this to be a form of dependency on God, and she was proud of and excited by her commitment. Her parents had wanted her to be a lawyer, or maybe an engineer, but she had decided to serve God. This made it all the more painful when God seemed to turn away.

When Elaine's roommate moved out of their studio apartment in the summer of 2004, and Elaine decided, on the basis of her prayers and those of her friends, that God wanted her to stay put, she did. She explained to me that while she could not afford the rent on her own, she had faith that God would solve the problem. She thought that he wanted her to get a new job.

As the months went by, Elaine kept the apartment and did not take a roommate, but she also failed to land any job that would help her pay the higher rent, despite her own continued prayer and the prayers of other people. In fact, she even lost her small income from the church, which decided that they no longer needed the work she had been doing for them. Into November, she still didn't have any job, and she was still in the apartment, because she believed that that was where God wanted her to be. Her parents—who may have been covering the rent—were quite worried about her, not only financially but because they distrusted her willingness to believe that God was speaking directly to her (they were conservative Christians of the noncharismatic kind), let alone telling her to stay in an apartment she could not afford. I was her prayer partner in house group, and week after week we prayed for specific upcoming job interviews, in response to specific applications that she had made. Week after week those interviews failed. To me, she looked unhappy and scared.

When we read the parable of the prodigal son in house group that autumn, most of us announced, with some self-mockery, that we identified with the older son, the one who worked hard and dutifully for his father and never had a party thrown in his honor. Elaine—still in her studio, still without a job—led the discussion. She opened by pointing out that the problem with the older son was that he just didn't ask for things. If he'd asked, his father would have given him a party. She quoted the scripture that we'd studied just some months earlier: "If you ask for an egg will he give you a scorpion?" "You just have to ask him," she said. Then Nancy, a middle-aged, single African American woman who had been silent up to this point, abruptly announced that this passage told her that her relationship with God just wasn't what it should be. She worked hard, she ate properly, she exercised, she did all the things she was "supposed" to do, and yet all those things just took her away from God. You don't read your Bible in the gym, she said bitterly. The younger son was broken, she said, because there was no other way God could get him to listen. "He was a prideful dog," she said. Murmurs of assent went around the room.

Soon Elaine began to talk about her sense that God wanted her to be dependent on him. She explained that worry and poverty were giving her so much more intimacy with Jesus because she realized that he really wanted her to depend just on him. A few months later she stood up in church on Sunday morning and explained how much God had taught her in the months of unemployment, and how close they had become. "In the midst of not knowing whether the rent would be paid," she said, "God has really taught me to laugh. My soul has become more deep."

The concept of spiritual maturity allows people to reinterpret a disappointment as, in effect, a promotion. We do this all the time in secular contexts. *He didn't reject you because he didn't like you but because he was intimidated; they didn't follow up on your application because they thought you were too good for them and you'd never stay.* It is a constructive move, whether it is true or not, and it helps many of us handle the phone call that never came and the letter that went to someone else. In the Vineyard setting, the promotion takes one out of if-then logic and into relational intimacy. God wants your love, not your gratitude, this interpretation insists; he wants you to pay attention to him, because he loves you. Again and again what counts is recognizing God—not whether ideas about God are coherent, not whether prayer is actually effective, not whether faith delivers on what humans think it promises. In this spirituality, it is all about the relationship.

Elaine did eventually get a job, but not one she liked. Despite the unsatisfactory job, she now talked as if her relationship with God had never been stronger. In the months since she had begun to figure out what God was saying about the apartment, she became more and more interested in things supernatural and, at the same time, almost wantonly uninterested in probabilistic logic. We went together to a Vineyard-sponsored conference called "The Art of Hearing God" shortly after she got her job. The leader explained to us that scientists had discovered that if you slow down the sounds a cricket makes, you will find that the cricket is actually singing the "Hallelujah" chorus to Handel's *Messiah*. Elaine thought that this was really neat and repeated it to our house group without a trace of irony. She went to another conference where she felt the Holy Spirit sweep down the auditorium and knock her over. She spoke of praying for things that popped into her mind all the time. She said she'd been learning to hear God's voice more clearly: "He loves to talk to his children. I mean, wouldn't a father love to talk to his child? They love to get phone calls from a child—'Hi Daddy, I just wanted to say hi.'" She became extremely interested in prophecy and was beginning to feel that she was prophetic. She wanted God to trust her and speak to her more; she told me that God knew she wouldn't add words or change things around when she reported to people what he said to her. She said that she'd begun to hear from him in such a way that suddenly something would switch—"like something switched in my head, just switched"—and another voice would speak, for ten to thirty seconds before it stopped. And indeed, during our conversations it seemed like she would get lost in her own thoughts and look at me quizzically, as if she were listening to something else.

A few months later Elaine decided to become a missionary. She had had a vivid dream about being on an African safari, with some majestic lions, and when she'd gone to a conference on prophecy, one of the speakers told her that it meant that God was calling her into ministry. I asked her how a dream about a safari could be interpreted as a call into ministry and she responded: "Sometimes the Lord just gives you enough information because other stuff would confuse you." Then she prayed that the Lord would show her a path. The next day she went to the Sunday service, and she met a woman called Ann who gave a testimony on missionary work in the Philippines.

> I ended up putting my stuff in a certain chair, and then I went off and someone else took the chair, and then my friend said, "Why don't you sit over there?" and I ended up sitting right next to Ann. I felt a deep connection to her. I wanted to hang out with her after the service, but I knew I had a prayer meeting with the pastor. After church he came running up to me. He'd just forgotten about our meeting! Did I want to go out to lunch with her. And at lunch she said that she'd been praying and she felt like the next step in the ministry was to start a school for the street children. And she gave

me this pamphlet she'd written, and I realized that I'd dreamt about that very booklet, with that cover.

Elaine still didn't know exactly what she would do. Her plan was to go get some basic medical training at this woman's mission school and then head to Africa. She didn't have a particular destination, although she was praying for one. She needed, she thought, $10,000 a year, and she made up a letter asking people to donate. (When I expressed surprise about this to another member of the church, he told me that it was pretty cheap. Sending a family to Africa, he said, could cost $80,000 a year.) She didn't raise as much as she needed, but she decided that this was part of God's plan and resolved to go anyway, as long as she had enough for a one-way ticket. "Even since then," she told me, "I've been like a walking prophet, leaving things behind. I never used to leave things behind." She lost her cell phone and then her planner. She described this as being like a prophet walking naked in the wilderness.

And everywhere Elaine looked, it seemed as if her choice to be a missionary had been confirmed: "I talked to a friend last week about what I'm going to be doing, and she was just really excited. She said that in April she had a vision of me in a kitchen with this woman with glasses and a skirt. She's a mother, she's a wife, and I'm just sitting at her feet. Obviously, that was Ann." She said that she really tried to follow the Lord in everything now, although she still found herself failing. "His plans, not mine," she said, discouraged. To get to her job, she needed to take either two buses or a bus and a train. She told me that one day she had taken the first bus and gotten off to see her second bus, she thought, in the distance. She ran to catch it, found that it was the wrong bus, and ran all the way back and just barely caught her train. She interpreted this as imposing her plans on the Lord: He had intended her to take a bus and then a train that day. She had not been patient with his plans for her, and she felt ashamed.

All this provoked mixed reactions from the congregation. By the end of the spring, Elaine had developed a reputation for being prophetic. The pastor had been impressed by some of her prophecies; one day she reported to him that she had had a dream that the church would receive a large donation, and out of the blue, someone gave the church its largest donation the very next day. People also commented on her close relationship with God. "Jeez," Jacob said in house group, "sometimes I think God's whispering in her ear all the time." But they were also sometimes openly scornful of her willingness to think that God was speaking to her so frequently. Another Vineyard congregation, known for its interest in prophecy, had an after-hours session on prophecy at Elaine's church, and people came for prayer and for prophecy. One of the visiting leaders picked Elaine out of the crowd (he'd seen her before; she came to many of his events) and said that he felt that God was telling him that she was his daughter and that he loved her. At this, another church member abruptly walked out of the service. That woman told me later that she thought the comment was outrageous. "Scripture says that everyone is God's son or daughter," she said. "What did that guy think he was doing?" And yet Elaine had stood there listening, hands clasped, an expression of bliss on her face.

One might say, from the viewpoint of a secular observer, that cognitive dissonance threw Elaine into the arms of God. She certainly believed in God before he failed her so spectacularly. That is, she would tell anyone who asked that she believed in God; she went to church regularly; she prayed every day. But God's failure to deliver when it counted—she really needed that job—forced her into a choice between abandoning belief or experiencing God in a way that helped her to deal with distress even when the ostensible reason to believe in a God ("He won't give if you don't ask, but he will give if you ask") fell flat. And quite possibly, the contradiction pushed her faster and farther than she would have traveled if one of those good jobs had come through. It was not inevitable that she would have made the choice she did. Not all people do. In a secular society, it is always possible for an individual to abandon belief. But the practices of faith within this kind of evangelical church make it possible for someone in trouble to learn to experience God as an internal source of comfort, whether or not the idea of God makes coherent logical sense. That is what Elaine did. Faced with the failure of her passionate prayer, she decided to plunge into the faith practices associated with hearing God speak back— and she began to experience God more intimately and personally than she had done before.

That is why I thought of these faith practices as tools: they are like the hammer and nails you can use to build a table, except that in this case you build in your mind. The tools are the pattern recognitions that identify God's presence, the daydream play of conversation and dialogue, the feeling-suffused prayer huddles in which people repeatedly insist on God's love, the intense prayer that helps what one imagines to seem more real. Someone can choose to use those tools in pursuit of an experience of God.

The word *choose* might seem odd to some readers. Many scholars these days—as I have earlier pointed out—argue that there is something evolutionarily hardwired about a belief in God. They argue that because our minds evolved to help us survive the assault of predators, human or otherwise, we are quick to infer the presence of agents, even when we cannot see them, or to see human faces in clouds and machines. They are undoubtedly correct. But the problem of faith is not finding the idea of God plausible but sustaining that belief in the face of disconfirmation. Elaine's problem was not that she could not believe in God; her problem was that she did believe, and she had acted on her belief, and her belief—as she had understood it ("he will give if you ask")—crashed into real-world fact. She had prayed repeatedly, insistently, and determinedly for God to give her a job, and every one of the prayers, before each of those interviews, had failed. Yet Elaine wasn't ready to give up on God, so instead she learned how to experience God so that his being real to her became the point of her prayer—not the job she had prayed for. That is the way prayer disconfirmation can paradoxically strengthen spiritual commitment.

From the congregant's perspective, the take-home lesson of Elaine's renewed experience of God after his failure to deliver a job is that she had not worked as hard as she could have done to master the use of those tools until she ran into difficulty. Elaine hadn't really tried to experience God personally in the way that she did until after her prayers had failed. These faith practices are hard. They take time. Most people do not work hard to master the skill of prayer until they purposefully structure their lives in some way to allow themselves to pray and feel an intense need to carry through. It was only after Elaine started having trouble paying the bills that she started going to the conferences that gave her such a direct experience of the Holy Spirit, and took courses that insisted that she pray at length and pay attention to her dreams. It was only then that she began to pay such attention to the signs that confirmed the way God spoke to her in her mind.

. . .

The community is crucial, snarky as its members can be. It is tempting to look at this modern evangelical experience of God and see it as profoundly individualistic: me and my relationship with God. And that view certainly captures something real.[8] But it takes a great deal of work for the community to teach people to develop these apparently private and personal relationships with God. The community can help someone to stick it out and keep them at it, just as community can help to keep someone sober and to get them to the gym. It may take a kick in the rear to get people to the gym in the first place—thus, the value of prayer failure—but it is the friends they work out with who keep them there. Elaine did not persuade all the members of her community that her interpretations of God were always accurate, but they were there when she was told that she was God's daughter. They came to the house group she ran. They greeted her in church. They welcomed her at the conferences. They bought her a ticket to Africa. For Elaine to walk away from God would have been to walk away from all those people.

The community is also crucial because those powerful personal moments when God does speak (Elaine's safari dream), and those precious moments when someone finally knows, deeply and truly, that they are loved by God, are not enough to sustain a faith commitment by themselves. The great sociologist Emile Durkheim recognized this. He thought that when the nomadic aboriginals he took to be representative of earliest human society gathered for their rituals, they had moments when the divine became real and reality as they knew it changed. Those moments made their divinity come alive to them. But he thought that they needed to experience these moments again and again, because the memory of any particular moment would weaken and the reality of the divine would fade. Faith, he argued, was like a battery that needs to be constantly recharged by ritual.[9] At the Vineyard, the community stood in for God when God seemed distant and particularly when he seemed unreal.

"When I first graduated from college," Krista explained one Sunday morning, looking out at the two hundred church members in shorts and sundresses seated on folding chairs in the gym, "I looked for a job.

I looked and I looked and I ended up getting a job at 7/11. I had a degree from the University of California, Santa Cruz, and the only job I could find was at 7/11, the morning shift, six a.m. to one p.m., four to five days a week. And you know something? They used Slurpee mix to clean out the coffeepots. I know this. I did it.

The worst thing about my job, though, was the shopping habits of people who come in at six in the morning. Lots of hung-over people. Lots of grumpy people. Lots of inappropriate interaction. I can't tell you how many times I had to deal with someone trying to get money out of the ATM machine with a library card. They were so out of it. People would come in, and they'd buy beer and cigarettes and cat food. That was pretty common. And I'll be honest with you, I was about as judgmental as you can get. I was like, "You have *got* to be kidding me. Why am I here"—and I'll use an expression I don't use anymore—"*with these people?*"

One morning this woman came in, and she looked like she'd been up all night. She looked like it had been rough. She threw her stuff on the counter. Two six-packs of Miller Lite, some cat food, and a food product of some sort—doughnuts, I think. And she looked at me and said, "Hey, can you get me a carton of cigarettes?" And I'm thinking, "Excellent. *This* is what I want to be doing with my life." So I turned around, rolled my eyes, and started thinking my judgmental thoughts. In that moment, I literally *heard* the voice of God say to me, "Do not judge this woman. I have created her in my image, and I love her." And—poor woman. I almost fell over. I'm trying to give her change, and I'm like, "Whoa, the voice of God spoke to me."

I have been changed ever since.[10]

But years later, for months Krista came numb and angry to church services. A friend of hers in the church died unexpectedly in his middle thirties, leaving a devastated wife and two toddlers. The death was quite unexpected and completely unjust from a God-is-good standpoint. Her friend was a lovely man, an upstanding church member, a decent and honest human being. Krista was with him soon after he became suddenly ill, and she was at the hospital hours later when he died. She was in my Ignatian group. When she came to the group the week after the death, she was angry and confused and horribly distressed. She did not pray in the following weeks, maybe even for months. Every Sunday night we took a break in the middle of our group to go off and pray, and week after week, when we came back, she reported that she had sat there in silence and that God did not come.

This is the problem of "empty" prayer. At the Vineyard, people use the phrase "God showed up" to mean that they felt the presence of God in that setting. Often, they use the phrase to describe a group activity— for example, when women from the church held worship services with inmates at the local jail, as if they were a group of early disciples reporting that Jesus had been physically present in their midst. The implicit model is found in those passages of the Gospel where Jesus begins to appear to the disciples after his death, as if he is among them in an ordinary way once more. Here is such a passage from the Gospel of John: "When it was evening on that day, the first day of the week, and the doors of the house where the disciples had met were locked for fear of the Jews, Jesus came and stood among them and said, 'peace be with you.'"[11] God shows up as if he's a person at the service.

But if God can show up, he can also go away. This is the special challenge of any spiritual tradition that seeks to experience God's presence, for anyone who learns to experience God more intimately will find periods of time when God will seem to become more distant. The book *Enjoying God* meets this problem head on:

> There will be times when the Lord will lift the sense of His presence from our lives in order to communicate various truths to our hearts. He may use such times to humble us by making us aware of our need for Him. He may also use such occasions to alert us to some specific problem in our hearts. He may even remove the sense of his presence from us just to awaken in us a deeper hunger for Him.[12]

The language of God's absence speaks of someone who yearns to experience God but cannot, as if someone sat down to pray but found that God had strolled off to spend time with someone else. In fact, congregants really did describe it like a romantic date gone wrong. You sat down to pray and "nothing happened." Prayer became "empty," "cold," "mechanical," "dry," "dead."

The contrast of wet/alive and dry/dead runs throughout this way of talking about prayer. Wet/alive evokes the experience of connection to a speaking, interacting God; dry/dead evokes a God who does not speak and does not answer. Another evangelical prayer manual explains:

> One of the great benefits of God's silence is that it makes you appreciate the times when He speaks. God's silence teaches that when the faucet of God's revelation is running, when you can feel his sweet presence and comprehend His sweet words, get all you can get . . . You never know. He may be pouring out on you because a wilderness period is around the next corner. God reserves the right to be silent. He reserves the right to delay answers, leave certain issues unaddressed, and become seemingly quiet.[13]

Here the author describes these dry, desolate periods as the "wilderness." Another term is the "desert"—not the desert of mystical inspiration but an empty stretch of unconnected absence.

At the church, people often spoke about dryness. People would come in to house group and complain about how hard prayer had been—great on Tuesday, perhaps, but "dry as bones" the other days. Most people had days where they prayed easily and times when they sat down to pray and the prayer was dry. One evening I asked the house group what they meant when they described something as "dry." They said things like "discouraging, feeling directionless, unable to connect"; "like in the wilderness, you're not connected, you're dried out"; "not connecting with his work, not in sync with him"; "he's just silent, like he doesn't speak." One man gave a more active image, not of absence but of intervention, destruction with the goal of pruning growth: "When God brought the Israelites into the desert, he allowed those Israelites who did not know God or resisted God to die. I think there have been times in my life when there has been that sense of pruning, when God takes me to a place where he can work out those relational issues." He called this "doing business with God."

The metaphor of water as the experience of God comes from a passage in the Gospel of John, though its source is far older.[14] Jesus, tired from a long walk back to Galilee from Judea, stops at a well in Samaria and asks for a drink from a woman who has come to draw water. She is startled; Jews, the Gospel writer tells us, do not share food or water with Samaritans. Jesus tells her that if she asks, he will give her living water to drink: "Everyone who drinks this water will be thirsty again, but those who drink of the water that I give them will never be thirsty. The water that I give will become in them a spring of water gushing up to eternal life."[15] When, in the fourteenth century, Teresa of Ávila took this metaphor and developed it into an image of an internal garden watered with the joy of prayer, she described dryness as an opportunity to experience the life of Christ by suffering in some small way as he did. Late in my fieldwork I met an evangelical man who, tired and frustrated by his workplace, embarked on a process of spiritual renewal through working through the Spiritual Exercises with a Catholic director. Renewed and invigorated in his prayer life, he found to his horror that the conflict around him at work had only intensified. His spiritual director smiled at him when he complained. "Congratulations. You asked for more intimacy with God. He has rewarded you by allowing you to share in the life of his son."

In my experience, congregants at the Vineyard did not reach to explain dryness in prayer as a process of identifying with Christ's suffering. This may have been the result of their Protestantism, that mode of Christianity having a distinctly more triumphalist bent. What they said was that in times of dryness and desolation, you needed community, because when an individual's private experience of God fell short, that individual needed their community to pull them through. That was the way the pastor ended his teaching as he spoke about the death of Krista's friend that Sunday morning after he had died. You need to see God in each other, he said, when you cannot see him for yourself: "The majority of us, we need others to help us. If you're gonna lose weight, you need Weight Watchers. If you want to get into good physical condition, you need a trainer or a group of people to play with. If you don't do it together, it won't get done. And if that's true on a physical level, it's even more true on a spiritual level."

Many months later I asked a member of my prayer group why people kept believing in God when things went terribly wrong. "Community," she said. "You learn to see Jesus in each other when you cannot see him for yourself."

"What does it mean to follow God when you are dry, very dry?" a young woman asked one morning as she gave the Sunday teaching one winter morning. She spoke on Psalm 42:

As the deer pants for streams of water,
so my soul pants for you, O God.
My soul thirsts for God, for the living God.
When can I go and meet with God?
   My tears have been my food day and night,
while men say to me all day long,
"Where is your God?"

Sometimes, she said, it feels like God destroys hope. You're so dry that the only wet thing in your life is your tears, and they are running out. Perhaps your prayer for healing hasn't worked; perhaps things are not happy in your marriage; sometimes, she said, it's something like wondering why, fifty years after segregation, kids still go to all-black schools. The psalmist is asking one question, the when question—"When will God come through?" Those around you are asking the where question—"Where is your God anyway?"

It had been a hard time for her, she said; she felt like a deer dying of thirst. How, in the face of the intense thirst and emptiness, did you retain your hope in God? she asked. She did not invite us to remember Jesus's suffering. She did not suggest that we seek for ways that we had sinned. She told us that we needed each other and to stay in fellowship—to keep coming to church and to house group and to men's ministry and women's ministry—and to cling to God anyway. Then she asked everyone who felt parched to come forward so that other people could stand around them and lay hands on them in love and pray for them.

The concept of dryness naturalizes the failure to feel God's intimacy, just as the concept of spiritual maturity naturalizes prayer failure. These concepts allow people to hang on to a belief that the world is good by giving them a way to acknowledge the excellent evidence to the contrary. The concepts give them a kind of space to be in doubt or distrust and yet to think of themselves as good Christians, and it encourages them to turn to other Christians for support when things get hard. What neither concept does is to explain why God allows things to go terribly, unbearably, wrong.

They are the body blows of life: loved ones die before they grow old; good marriages end in divorce; dreams shatter on the rocks of circumstance. Unlike ordinary prayer failure, which is explained by God's desire to have one depend on him, the failure of really important prayer is left deliberately unexplained in Vineyard spirituality.

That, of course, was what happened with Job: "Let God weigh me in honest scales, and he will know that I am blameless." Job curses his birth as he sits in misery, covered with boils, his home and herds destroyed, his children and servants dead, the result of a bet God made with Satan and lost. God never explains to Job why he has suffered. He ignores Job's question about justice. Instead, God thunders on about his power: "Where were you when I laid the earth's foundation? Tell me, if you understand." They can seem almost mocking, the bold claims God makes for his authority. "Have you comprehended the vast expanses of the earth? Tell me if you know all this!" The theological point of the Book of Job is clear: God's presence is enough. We do not need an explanation. We do not need wise judgment. We do not need stuff. All we need is to know that God is. Note that what Job gets from God is not simple knowledge of God's existence but his own sensory perception of God. Nowhere in the book does Job doubt God. What humbles and satisfies Job is not new belief but felt experience: "My ears had heard of you but now mine eyes have seen you."[16]

People at the church did report moments in extremis when they perceived God with eye or ear, and when they were in despair, those moments did for them something of what Job's moment did for him. They somehow satisfied the person in pain, even though they explained nothing of where the pain had come from. At least, that was the way people told the story.

Julia, for example, had become a Christian in her twenties and remained one for decades, but there had been a moment in her thirties when she was ready to leave the church. She had grown up in a safe, middle-class world, and someone close to her had been brutally murdered—a violent, horrible death. She no longer trusted God, and she wasn't sure that she believed God existed. "It was the only time I'd been really angry at God," she told me. "I felt like I'd been dealt a dirty deal. I felt I'd been duped. I was furious beyond belief at God, and in this melodramatic way, I raised my fist to curse him." At that moment, she saw a figure in the corner of the room.

About four feet high. Absolutely external. Absolutely visible. This white, glowing messenger. And words were emanating from this messenger, whoever it was. Just full of authority. I felt the voice said, "I am good." My experience was that God wasn't good, that he allowed death and destruction. It wasn't a sweet cajoling voice. It was simply a statement of fact. Right after that, I was on my knees on a hardwood floor. And that was it.

Julia was embarrassed about this experience. She called it "bizarre." But she told me that after it, she had never doubted again.

Lainie was in seminary by the time I met her, but she too had nearly left the church when she was much younger and her marriage was a mess. One evening her husband went out on a date while they were still living in one house. She lay in the next room, listening to him blow-drying his hair in the bathroom, and she told God that she wanted God to pin her to the bed, because otherwise she would kill the man. She seems to have really considered killing him. And then she found that she could not move, that she was physically immobilized. When her husband left, the storm erupted. She took all his clothes out of the bedroom and threw them into the other room. She took everything he owned from the closet, the dressers, and even the walls and threw it out of the bedroom. She was breathing hard, worried that she would explode with the rage and the passion.

> I said, "God, you have to get ahold of me." And I dropped—this was bizarre. I dropped to my knees, and there was a Bible that was open and it was Psalm 73. It was so bizarre. I remember dragging it over, and I just opened it up. It says in there, "Even though I behaved like a beast before you, you took ahold of my hand and you led me." And I was sitting there and I'm reading this and I stuck up my right hand and I felt something grab my hand and it shot through my body and I went, "Thank you," and all of a sudden I just calmed down.

Like Julia, she marked the moment as "bizarre." She felt it as physical: "I definitely felt something touch my hand, and then there was a tingling that went all the way down the arm and right into my chest." And it made her feel that God was real. She hadn't paid attention to God, or even gone to church, for years. "So I said, 'Okay, who are you, God?' Not in a challenging way. More, 'If you are really real, how does that work with who I am?' And that began the journey."

. . .

Stanley was ten when his parents divorced, and he was devastated. He began to be obsessively interested in whether he would go to heaven when he died. He would read his Bible, pray to be saved, and go to sleep. One night, he was.

> I woke up in the middle of the night at some point, and there was this overwhelming [sense] of peace and calm. There were these words that just kept coming to my mind. Not of my own doing. I woke up hearing them in my mind, over and over again: "I will never leave you, I will always be with you." Just sort of over and over again. I have never felt that way before and then rarely felt that way afterward.

He did not hear the voice with his ears, but he knew that the voice was God and that God was real and God was good.

For these individuals, the moment was definitive, a moment that, as Thomas Merton put it, turned notional assent into real assent.[17] Lainie finally knew beyond a whisper of a doubt that God was real and would protect her. Julia knew once and for all that God was good. Stanley finally believed that God loved him. After that moment, each would have experiences when they thought they had heard again from God but were not quite as sure. "In subsequent events," Stanley said, "I have been more left with the sense that I can choose to believe this is from God or I can think, 'This is just from me,' and the reality is that it could be either, and I know that. But about that one, there was never any question. Everything else, there is a question. Not that." The moments explained nothing, but they made God seem real when the world they thought God had created was senseless.

Whether or not the congregant has one of these intense experiences, these congregants repeatedly reject the idea of needing an explanation from God when things go badly wrong. When I explain this to a secular audience, or even sometimes to a Christian one, people tend to bridle. They don't see how it can be true. But I observed this rejection time and again.

"God doesn't want to be analyzed," Aisha explained to me one Sunday morning. "He wants your love." She was reading an evangelical book about God's apparent failure to deliver on his promises. Philip Yancey organizes *Disappointment with God* around three questions: Is God unfair? Is he silent? Is he hidden? Like most spiritual texts, Yancey's gives many answers, winding around the questions like a circuitous track up the side of a tall hill. What is most striking about the book is what it does not do. Yancey does not explain why bad things happen to good people. In fact, he explicitly rejects the best-known mass-market explanation found in *When Bad Things Happen to Good People.* Harold Kushner wrote that book because he was horrified when, as a young rabbi, a couple lost their only child to a brain aneurysm and attributed the death to God's wrath because they had not fasted on Yom Kippur. Kushner concluded that God is good but not all-powerful. That is not Yancey's God. Yancey settles for a God who is logically incoherent but emotionally available, and the point Yancey makes is that the awesome, mighty creator of the universe is desperate that we should like him and hurt when we turn away, regardless of the devastation going on in our lives. "Our choices matter, not just to us and our own destiny but, amazingly, to God himself." Yancey goes on to speculate about why we do not understand God's intentions, but this is clearly not important to the way he imagines God.

> One bold message in the Book of Job is that you can say anything to God. Throw at him your grief, your anger, your doubt, your bitterness, your betrayal, your disappointment—he can absorb them all . . . You can't really deny your feelings or make them disappear, so you may as well express them. God can deal with every human response save one . . . an attempt to ignore him or treat him as though he does not exist. That response never once occurred to Job.[18]

Get mad at God or sad at God, but do not turn your back on God.

It can be tempting to ascribe this refusal to give a logical account of human suffering, this philosophical recalcitrance, to a kind of theological cluelessness, but it would be more accurate to treat it as an indication of what this imagining of God does for his followers.[19] This is not the God conceived of by Thomas Aquinas, who laid out the features of the Christian deity with a theological argument as precise as a Gothic filigree. This God is a great furry lion who walks by your side and keeps you from falling off the cliff, as Aslan did with Shasta in *The Horse and His Boy.* In times of personal struggle you are meant to reach for God the way you reached for a beloved stuffed bear or a puppy during childhood. You are supposed to imagine that you stand cuddled by God as you look out together at the wreck that is your life. That was what the pastor said in church when Krista's friend died. He simply refused to give an explanation, and he told the church to experience God as present.

> This is a difficult philosophical issue for Christians. We believe in a God who's both good and all powerful, and when you see hard things, to put it bluntly, either God is good and not powerful or powerful and not good, or he's not there. Atheists don't have this problem. Buddhists don't have this problem. Deists don't have this problem. We who believe in a loving personal God who created the earth and can intervene at any time—we have this problem.

His answer? That's the way it is: "Creation is beautiful, but it is not safe." He called our everyday reality "broken." "God is doing something about it. There's a fix in progress. It will be okay." What should you do? Get to know God. "Learn to hang out with him *now*."

There is some hard evidence that the experience of a relationship with a loving God is good for people and may even be at the heart of what gives religion health-boosting properties. We have known for some time that weekly church attendance keeps people healthy; on average, it adds two or three years to one's life. Religious observance boosts the immune system and decreases blood pressure. But the biological mechanisms have never been clear. The effect could be the result of the social support of a committed community or the healthy behaviors of people more hesitant to drink, take drugs, or have casual sex.[20]

Increasingly, however, there is evidence that the quality of someone's relationship with God has consequences. In a study of the relationship between prayer and mental illness, when God was experienced as remote or not loving, there was a direct relationship between prayer and psychopathology; but that when God was experienced as close and intimate, the more someone prayed, the less ill they were. In another study of caregivers, prayer was associated with fewer health problems and better quality of life. In a study of people with devastating medical conditions—cancer, spinal cord injury, traumatic brain injury, and the like—belief in a loving higher power and a positive worldview were associated with better health. In a private Christian college in southern California, the quality of someone's attachment to God significantly decreased perceived stress and did so more effectively than the quality of that person's relationships with other people. A secure attachment to God (compared to an insecure attachment) protects college women against eating disorders and college men against excessive drinking and drugs.[21]

And in general, consciously reflecting on the importance of God seems to make people more relaxed. In one recent study, psychologists gave a hard task to a group of subjects, some of whom were religious and some of whom were not. Those who were religious and encouraged to think about their religion (by writing a paragraph about what religion meant to them) were less distressed physiologically when they made errors than either the atheists or the religious subjects who wrote about their favorite season. That is, whereas the "control" subjects felt agitated when they made a mistake (inevitably, given that the task was deliberately frustrating), those who had been thinking about God were less bothered, and the calmness showed up in their brain scans.[22] Indeed, a relationship with God makes people happy. White Protestant evangelicals—for whom a personal relationship with Jesus is the route to salvation, whether or not they are charismatic—are more likely to report that they are very happy than white mainstream Protestants. In fact (as John Micklethwait and Adrian Wooldridge report in an eye-opening book entitled *God Is Back*), going to church weekly, as compared to not going at all, has the same effect on reported happiness as moving from the bottom quartile of the income distribution to the top quartile.[23] That's a jump.

The Spiritual Disciplines Project also supported the claim that the direct experience of God's love is beneficial. When people came to the project, we gave them a series of statements about experiencing God and asked them to tell us how much those statements described them:

> I feel God's presence.
> I experience a connection to all of life.
> During worship, or at other times when connecting with God, I
>   feel joy which lifts me out of my daily concerns.
> I find strength in my religion or spirituality.
> I find comfort in my religion or spirituality.
> I feel deep inner peace or harmony.
> I ask for God's help in the midst of daily activities.

I feel guided by God in the midst of daily activities.
I feel God's love for me, directly.
I feel God's love for me, through others.
I am spiritually touched by the beauty of creation.
I feel thankful for my blessings.
I feel a selfless caring for others.
I accept others even when they do things I think are wrong.[24]

This is the Daily Spiritual Experiences Scale, developed by Lynn Underwood to capture people's spiritual experience rather than their religious beliefs or practices.[25] Underwood and others have shown that the more highly people score on this scale, the less anxiety, depression, and stress they report. In the Spiritual Disciplines Project, that pattern also held. We found that the more of these spiritual statements people affirmed, the less lonely and stressed they described themselves as being, and this was statistically significant. In addition, the more spiritual statements people affirmed, the more they experienced well-being, and the more they were satisfied with the life they lived (both of these were measured by standard scales), and again this was statistically significant. Strikingly, if you looked at people's responses to just one statement— "I feel God's love for me, directly"—all these relationships became stronger and more significant.[26]

The quality of someone's attachment to God—whether you trust God; whether you fear him; whether you expect him to hurt or abandon you—seems to have its roots in early parental relationships, but it is not simply the reflection of those relationships.[27] What the church does is to work tirelessly to transform that attachment through the faith practices it teaches and models. The effort to push people to experience God in relationship through prayer—at times, it seems, through deliberate invitation to experience the failure of prayer to deliver stuff—is the central goal of the many different faith practices that congregants practice again and again.

But the soothing process does not happen automatically, and it does not always work. I met Peter and Amanda, a couple in their early twenties, at the Chicago church. Peter had always been a Christian, although the church he'd been raised in was more conventionally conservative than the Vineyard. He had little doubt that God was real. When he was eighteen, he was rattled because he'd been given a college roommate who wasn't a

Christian, as Peter understood the term; the man was a Mormon—and Peter really didn't see much difference between their lives. "I felt that if what I believed was really true, then there should be something different between my life and the life I saw lived by this guy. And there wasn't." He went off, a little skeptical, to a Christian camp that summer. On the penultimate day, he happened to get up very early. He went out to the tennis court, lay down on his back, and said to the sky, "Okay, God, I want you to show yourself to me. I want to get something real." He got it. "I just closed my eyes, and I remember this sort of feeling of awe that I had never felt before just creeping into my head. The only words that went through my mind were, 'God, you are big. God, you are big.' It was as if somehow I had been able to see something I had never seen before spiritually. Some small part of the greatness of God was revealed in some supernatural way."

It seems to have been a classic mystical experience, the kind of that William James wrote about: short-lived, with a sense of being suspended in space and time, your worldview fundamentally askew, your head spinning with a conviction of knowing something more real and more true than any other knowledge. "I had always been a thoroughly rational person from a very young age, incredibly rational," Peter told me. "So I didn't quite know what do to with this experience, but I realized that if God had shown himself to me, then I needed to pursue that." He began to read the Bible seriously, as he had never done before. He spent a lot of time learning to pray. When I asked him what he had learned, he said, "The balance between standing in front of the Grand Canyon and seeing the vastness, and then speaking to the vastness as an intimate friend." That first year was a honeymoon, he said. (Meanwhile, he was getting his doctorate in mathematics.) It felt like things were becoming clear to him all the time about God and about what the Bible said. He often felt that God was speaking to him, placing thoughts in his mind, or talking to him through scripture. He had times when he felt that his prayers didn't seem as good or as "connected," but that didn't really bother him. Not until the baby died.

Amanda hadn't grown up in a family that went to church. She described her first year in college as a wild, depressing party. Six months later she was sitting in church because she was dating someone who took her to meet his parents and that weekend his parents took them both to church. "At the end, the pastor starts talking about becoming a Christian," she told me. "I don't even remember what he said, but it resonated. I remember thinking, 'That's what I need.' So I became a Christian. But I didn't tell anyone." She was too embarrassed to tell even the boyfriend who had taken her to church. Still, after a few months—and having dispensed with the boyfriend—she started to go to church on her own, and she started to read the Bible. Then she went to Bible study, where they used the inductive method, and the text came alive for her. She said that it moved from black and white to Kodachrome. She began to feel that in some way it spoke directly to her. She learned to pray. She didn't really know how to think about God as a person, though. A friend tried to help her by explaining that because God was like a good father, you could imagine him based on that, but Amanda didn't feel like she had had the experience of a good father. She started looking around for different human models for a good dad. One day she was driving home in her car, and she heard the words "I love you" in the car. She heard them as an audible voice, coming from outside her head. She knew that the words came from God. It scared her to hear a voice spoken out loud, but it also made her feel good and secure. The voice told her twice that it loved her.

Peter and Amanda met at a church mixer in graduate school. They soon married and had their first child unexpectedly early. Their second child was planned. The pregnancy was fine until they walked into a routine checkup a month before delivery and discovered that the baby was dead. I talked to them two years later, after they had a new second child whom they loved, and still they felt the loss intensely.

They held God responsible for the death, but they were clear that they found attempts to explain God's actions downright stupid. Most of their friends and most of the people in the church were in their twenties, and at that age most were embarrassed by death. Sometimes, with the aim of being comforting, these people would say that the death must have happened for a good reason, or that Amanda would soon get pregnant again, as if the new child would simply make the memory of the dead child go away. Peter and Amanda felt hurt by these well-intentioned but awkward efforts. "That is not," Amanda said, "how Jesus would have responded." She and Peter felt better when someone saw the pain but offered no explanation. "At the funeral," Peter said, "someone said, 'This sucks, and I am so sorry that it happened to you.'" It was the only thing, he said, that helped at all. "It's the only thing you can say."

At the same time, they refused to let God off the hook. They repeatedly said that God was ultimately responsible for the death. When I asked them whether they thought demons might be involved (an easy out for God), they shrugged: "God still could have prevented it." Peter said that he took comfort in knowing that people had wrestled with this problem for centuries. He pointed out that when God confronted Job, he did not explain and he did not excuse. "No religion grasps God as a loving being and a thinking being in quite so challenging a way as Christianity," Peter said. Neither of them suggested that they had sinned in some way and that the death was God's judgment on the sin. Neither of them said that they welcomed the death because it helped them draw closer to Jesus and experience his trials more deeply. Neither of them, despite my many questions, offered any theological account of why the death had occurred. They simply said again and again that when disaster struck, you had to be comforted by knowing that God exists. Peter quoted from memory a passage in the Gospel of John where many followers abandon Jesus because of his teachings. Jesus says sadly to his twelve disciples, "You do not want to leave too, do you?" and their leader responds, "Lord, to whom shall we go?"[28]

Now when they read the Bible, they saw pain and mystery. Amanda said that she had come to realize that when Job's wife told him to curse God and die, the wife wasn't thinking about logic. She was hurt. Amanda said that when she'd read Job earlier, back before the baby's death, she'd focused on the part of the story where Job gets his stuff back. Now she realized that that wasn't the point of the story. The point, she said, was that the pain of the loss never really goes away. It helped her to know that.

But Peter and Amanda did not experience God after the baby died with the joy they had before. For all the church's emphasis on God's thereness, God's presence as friend, they still felt a terrible rupture. They felt numb immediately after the child's death, and when I sat down with them two years after the funeral, they still felt numb. Yet they came to church regularly. They believed in God, and they believed that their relationship with God would, in time, recover.

For Krista, it did. A few months after her friend's death, she began to talk about praying and about her sense that Jesus loved her. She never explained why her friend had died, and she never ever suggested that some good would ultimately come of his death. But she said that God had come back.

. . .

The way this evangelical Christianity handles the classic logical puzzle of how a powerful and loving God permits suffering makes it very clear that for these Christians, religion is not about explaining reality but about transforming it: making it possible to trust that the world is good, despite ample evidence to the contrary, and to hope, despite loneliness and despair. Anthropologists have come to realize that this is true of all faiths. It was the "armchair" anthropologists like Sir James George Frazer, so called because they theorized on the basis of travelers' tales and missionary reports read in upholstered comfort, who presumed that religion emerged primarily as an explanation of reality, the science of prescientific people. Once anthropologists began to do fieldwork and to live among the people they sought to understand, they recognized that while religion did make sense of the world for its people, it was far more a way to manage fear and disappointment. The British ethnographer Godfrey Lienhardt captured this insight in a moment in his fieldwork among a nomadic cattle-owning people in southern Sudan. He was with a Dinka man hurrying back to his family in the late afternoon when the man stopped to tie a knot in the grass to prevent the sun from going down. Lienhardt realized that the man didn't think that the knot would hold the sun up, as if it were a string to tie a ball. Tying the knot was a way of making his hope more real for him.

Yet while faith is generally more about managing pain than explaining it, the straightforward rejection of God-as-explanation in experiential evangelical Christianity is really rather striking. I think it results from a social world where, in some quite fundamental way, modern believers don't need religion to explain anything at all. They have plenty of scientific accounts for why the world is as it is and why some bodies rather than others fall ill. What they want from faith is to feel better than they did without faith. They want a sense of purpose; they want to know that what they do is not meaningless; they want trust and love and resilience when things go badly. In short, they want help when their dreams fall short. This can be confusing to nonreligious observers, because the evangelical talk around God is all about God's power and God's ability to deliver. But when you look at what people actually do in the religion, you see that they want a God who helps them to cope when the going gets tough.

This is no accident. The social upheaval of the 1960s ushered in not only a spiritual revolution but a psychotherapeutic one. Americans became intensely interested in their emotional experience and in the ways in which their emotional habits could be understood and transformed. They began to think of happiness as a kind of birthright, not only as something they had the right to pursue but as a state they should expect to achieve. (I still remember the Sunday morning my mother, raised in the shadows of the Depression, lowered a book review on the dilemmas of working women's lives and said, "Why do they assume they should be happy?") Psychotherapy exploded as a profession.

That shift had an enormous impact on American spirituality. The evangelical Christianity that emerged out of the 1960s is fundamentally psychotherapeutic. God is about relationship, not explanation, and the goal of the relationship is to convince congregants that their lives have a purpose and that they are loved. For that relationship to work, the congregant must be able to tolerate moments when it seems to fail. It is a psychotherapeutic cliché that failure in the therapeutic relationship helps the psychotherapy to succeed, because when the client learns to tolerate the therapist's inadequacy and still experience the therapist as helpful, the client is able to act as if the helpful therapist is present despite his or her mistakes. The client is said to have "internalized" the supportive therapist despite the external therapist's momentary lapse. The philosopher and psychoanalyst Jonathan Lear argues that this capacity is in fact the engine of therapeutic action.[29] The one thing we know unambiguously about psychotherapy, he points out, is that therapist and patient get each other wrong all the time. If the patient cannot learn to trust the process despite the misunderstandings, the therapy is doomed.

In some sense, what psychotherapy does is to practice the failure and the misunderstanding. The patient comes in because he feels badly about his divorce. But what the patient and therapist talk about so often is not the divorce; rather, it's the patient's experience of feeling wronged in some silly interaction with the therapist. That moment becomes an opportunity to capture the patient's spontaneous feeling of shame and failure—and to change it, by understanding it differently. If the therapy works, the patient's sense of failure abates during times when things don't work out the way he hoped. His trust in the future grows more supple.

Psychoanalysts have a name for the mental construct that creates this trustful resiliency: a *self-object*. This term was coined by the Chicago analyst Heinz Kohut, who created an uproar in the profession back in the 1970s when he suggested that therapeutic work was more about helping the patient to have better relationships than about giving the patient knowledge. Freud had thought that psychoanalysis cured people by explaining what was wrong with the way they interpreted the world, but even Freud had published a late, bleak essay ("Analysis Terminable and Interminable") in which he observed that some people did not change no matter what you told them and that the whole business of cure had become a mystery for him. Kohut argued straightforwardly (at least as straightforwardly as jargoned prose can argue) that what makes intensive long-term psychotherapy effective is that patients learn to experience the empathic therapist as an internal "object" that is loving, caring, and concerned with what is best for them. This object does not exist anywhere in space. Instead, a patient who is helped by therapy is able to act and think and feel as if always aware of that therapist's loving concern, as if the patient has become the person created within that responsive, attentive relationship. When the patient is able to maintain the behavior shaped by the awareness even after the therapy has ended, analysts say that the patient has "internalized" this awareness as a self-object. People who are healthy enough not to need therapy already have helpful, soothing self-objects. Their reactions to everyday life are shaped by a complex set of internal memories of someone who loved them. Holding these memories close, they are able to respond to other people with empathy rather than fear or anger. The ideal self-object is a sort of cross between a coach and a teddy bear, always available, never intrusive, someone whose emotional presence keeps hope alive and self-doubt at bay.

I am not the first anthropologist to observe that spiritual practices can build self-objects for those who practice them. In a moving account of the emotional trajectory of young postulants at a Mexican convent (postulants are nuns before their vows), Rebecca Lester argues that the successful nun learns to create and continually re-create a sense of self as seen by God and in the presence of God, and to carry God internally as a self-object who loves, cares, and attends always.[30] It is a Catholic story: God is more judgmental, sin is more important, the corporate church more emphasized, than in the evangelical setting. Nonetheless, much of what these postulants do is familiar. They come to the convent restless and unsettled. The community around them teaches them to pay attention to the presence of God in their lives, to think of him always, and to evaluate themselves in response to God. And if it works for the postulant, God will become a constant presence in her life, in her but not her, an external presence within her interior subjectivity, and God's presence will make her feel good and loved and with purpose.

Failure drives the process. These young postulants make God present by seeking out the ways in which they feel "broken"—ways they are unhappy, ineffective, inattentive, or, as they put it, distant from God. Only when they learn to experience God when they feel broken do they experience God as fully alive.

When things began going so badly for Sarah, she felt that God wasn't there: "It was like the lights were on, but nobody was home. I'd go to pray, and I knew he was there, but he wasn't coming to the door." She never stopped believing in God, but she was angry, frustrated, and depressed: "It was him hanging on to me, not me hanging on to him." She still believed, but in an abstract sort of way. She couldn't feel anything. The worst of it lasted two months. And then, slowly, God came back. By that she meant that she felt a response, a sense of give-and-take when she prayed. She heard God tell her, audibly, that she would be a "face of mental illness," which she took to mean that her experience would allow people who were afraid to feel more confident. The voice seemed very different from the self-condemning voices inside her head that she associated with her illness. She began to read spiritual books and to pray over the daily biblical texts verses she had arranged to receive online. Praying over them made her feel more peaceful. She began to notice nice things that happen during the day: someone smiling back or looking pleased to see her. She said that her relationship with God was quite different now, and in some ways better than it had been when she became this kind of Christian. Back then, she said, it was like the high of dating someone you loved who loved you: "You're together, you're holding hands, everything is just sweet and really nice. And then you get married—and your baby dies. It's when you go through those kinds of situations when your love really deepens." In other words, she loved and felt loved now even though the dream had shattered. Before she was hospitalized, she had tried to read Job and couldn't. It was too upsetting and, really, distasteful. Job was so angry. She couldn't get through it. About a month after she came out of the hospital, she turned to it again, and now she loved it. She recognized the anger and the frustration, and she adored that God hung in there and showed himself to Job. "I just love to read the ending," she said.

Sarah had learned to value hope more than outcome. Early in our conversations she had quoted Hebrews to me: "Faith is the substance of things hoped for and the evidence of things unseen."[31] She said that God becomes more real to her in the absence of any evidence at all, because then God is her hope, and her hope feels alive and resilient—whatever happens in her world. "It's contradictory, but it's exactly right," she told me. "I feel really close when it seems as if he's far away. I think that's the only way you can trust."

For American evangelicals, that is what this idea of God is trying to achieve. They want to know that what is truly real—what the anthropologist Clifford Geertz called the "really real"—is good, despite the pain and ugliness they see around them. They want to hold on to hope, despite their doubt. They care about transforming their own suffering, not about explaining why suffering persists. Their faith is practical, not philosophical. Odd as it may seem to a skeptical observer, it can help to have small, specific prayers go wrong.

CHAPTER TEN

Bridging the Gap

Lord, I believe; help mine unbelief

Mark 9:29

"Tell me one last thing," said Harry. "Is this real? Or has this been happening inside my head?"

Dumbledore beamed at him, and his voice sounded loud and strong in Harry's ears even though the bright mist was descending again, obscuring his figure.

"Of course it is happening inside your head, Harry, but why on earth should that mean that it is not real?"

—J. K. Rowling,
Harry Potter and the Deathly Hallows

THIS BOOK BEGAN with the nonbeliever's puzzle: How can sensible, educated people believe in an invisible being who has a real effect on their lives? The puzzle sits in the middle of many relationships. Maybe your running partner is a woman your age who shares your taste and humor, but every so often she says something that just stops you in your tracks. Or the guy in the next cubicle tells you that God wanted his neighbor to survive a terrible car accident to give him time to accept Jesus, and you react with stunned perplexity. At those moments, the nonbeliever can feel—and however kindly, convey—that the believer is simply out of touch with reality. And yet the believer and the nonbeliever may share so much. They may have similar educations, careers, and hobbies. They may vote the same way, or share a lawn mower or child care. They live in the same world and yet in very different worlds. How are Christians able to hold on to their faith despite the frank skepticism that they encounter again and again?

The answer is that they understand their God in a way that adapts to the skepticism. The God described in these pages, the vividly human, deeply supernatural God imagined by millions of evangelical Americans, takes shape out of an exquisite awareness of doubt. In fact, in the course of doing this work, I came to believe that the very features that seem so irrational to skeptical observers—God's right-here immediacy, the insistence that the worshipper should pray specifically and that God will answer every prayer, no matter how trivial—actually help Christians to manage their own doubts and the doubts of others. This God is not, as some people have argued, a rejection of modernity—a refusal to embrace the modern or a denial of modern ways of thinking. This near-magical God is an expression of what it is to be modern.

What do I mean by that? This modern God is "hyperreal": realer than real, so real that it is impossible not to understand that you may be fooling yourself, so real that you are left suspended between what is real and what is your imagination. In literature, this style of representation is called "magical realism," where the supernatural appears unpredictably and blends almost seamlessly into the natural world, as if the magical were real and the prosaically material were imaginary, and both perspectives are real and true together. You find magical realism in the novels of Jorge Luis Borges, Gabriel Gárcia Márquez, Salman Rushdie, Isabel Allende, and Alice Hoffman, where the characters unquestioningly accept the magic and the reader is left to interpret whether the magic took place for them in historical time or only in a symbolic dream.[1] In this modern experiential evangelical faith, this way of understanding God insists on a reality so vivid that it demands a willing suspension of disbelief while generating direct personal experiences that make that God real and integral to one's experiences of self. As a result—because most of our basic judgments about reality do not have this supremely self-conscious quality—the process of believing splits off belief commitment to God as something special and different from other kinds of beliefs. And ultimately what Christians learn to do to experience God as real despite their doubts tells us something about the experience of the mind in our complex modern world. It tells us that evangelicals reach out to use these ancient prayer practices to experience God, but that they do so with a very modern epistemology.

What is it about this moment in time that supports the enormous growth in belief in a personal God? After all, in the mid-twentieth century, most social scientists thought spiritual faith would simply disappear. This was widely known as the secularization hypothesis: that modernity gradually leads to a widespread collapse of the plausibility of traditional religions.[2] The cause was largely attributed to what the philosopher Karl Popper called the "open" society, a society with science and religious pluralism. In an open society, the remarkable success of science and medicine made it possible to explain reality without recourse to the supernatural, while knowledge of the astounding variety of ways to understand the supernatural could make any particular religion seem more like culture— like speaking French, say—than like an account of what is real and true. In scientifically oriented and culturally diverse societies, these scholars argued, religious allegiance became voluntary. There were alternate religiosities, alternate ways of doing things, alternate ways of making sense of life. Spirituality was thought to have become a consumer good that adherents would sample and discard as if they were buying cosmetics in a department store aisle.

And so these midcentury scholars assumed that faith would soon diminish or disappear. They identified liberal Protestantism—perhaps Unitarianism—as the natural outcome of faith in a scientific society. They anticipated a church retracting its claims to supernatural miracles and pulling back its commitments to God's creation, in the face of geology and evolutionary theory. They predicted that in an open society, Jesus would become understood as a wise but human teacher whose life story had been embellished by myths and metaphors.

We now know that those scholars were wrong. There are pockets of liberal Christianity left in America and in Europe, but Christianity around the world has exploded in its seemingly least liberal and most magical form—in charismatic Christianities that take biblical miracles at face value and treat the Holy Spirit as if it had a voltage. This book has been about that kind of God in America. This kind of vividly present God is at the center of the many forms of Pentecostalism, and Pentecostalism is among the fastest-growing religions in the world. From Melanesia to Africa to Latin America, this kind of supercharged God is the vehicle through which Christianity spreads most easily, and it has been stunningly successful.[3]

But for part of the nineteenth century and most of the twentieth in America, it looked as if the secularization thesis was accurate, and as if the liberal Christian God would become the kind of God most Christians would follow. The second half of the nineteenth century threw up great challenges to the belief that the biblical scriptures were a reliable record of human history. As the world shrank, as Europeans colonized other countries and became familiar with people who had different skins and bodies and customs, as Americans began to catalog and describe their own native peoples, and as the question of slavery ripped apart the United States and the problem of the rights and status of Africans became a practical moral problem, it became an intellectual's cottage industry to arrange humans beings on hierarchical ladders by brain weights, tool development, marriage systems, and so forth, and to call those ladders "evolution." Most Christians did not see these claims as a challenge to their faith because God's purpose could still be discerned. God could be understood as immanent in the evolutionary process, with his intelligence and purpose expressed within it.

Darwin's version of evolution was disturbing to Christians because with natural selection he provided a mechanism that could explain evolutionary change independent of some overarching divine purpose pulling the puppet strings behind a curtain. Moreover, Darwin's evolution seemed horribly cruel, an account of life to which justice and mercy were simply irrelevant. Natural selection is the result of purely random variation, small and apparently meaningless differences between siblings and cousins, and the engine of change is death. Only those who survive carry on their traits. Perhaps Darwin would have seemed less of a threat to Christians had engineers not created railways that made it possible to travel from one end of the country to the other in days rather than weeks, had factories not darkened the skies as they turned out mass-produced goods, had the telephone not been invented. There was something crudely and obviously effective about what people called science that made biblical accounts of supernaturalism seem increasingly awkward.[4]

Nor was it just that there were new technologies and new explanations of how we came to be. The existence of other civilizations, always known but never so intimately and with such awareness, made it clear that there were other ways of relating to God and that some of them were rich and profound. On the most mundane level, Americans now had Catholics on the streets and in their cities, a novel experience for a country whose religious orientation had been almost entirely Protestant. By the end of the nineteenth century, millions of immigrants had arrived in the new country from Europe, many of them Catholic. By 1906 Catholics were about one in six of the population but one in three of the churchgoers.[5]

Meanwhile, by the end of the nineteenth century, scholars had begun to translate the spiritual texts of Asia. The *Vedas* and *Upanishads* and other texts were published first in German and then in English translations, great volumes of intricate poetry and theology that seemed very different from the texts of the ancient Mediterranean world. A newly founded discipline of anthropology argued that religion itself was part of the evolutionary development of human society, from magical animism, to polytheism, to monotheism, and eventually to the rejection of faith for science. The closing metaphor from James George Frazer's *The Golden Bough*, an awesome magpie's trove of myth and custom from around the world, captures the general argument:

> Could we thus survey the web of thought from the beginning, we should probably perceive it to be at first a chequer of black and white, hardly tinged as yet by the red thread of religion. But carry your eye further along the fabric and you will remark that, while the black and white chequer still runs through it, there rests on the middle portion of the web, where religion has entered most deeply into its texture, a dark crimson stain, which shades off insensibly into a lighter tint as the white thread of science is woven more and more into the tissue.[6]

Those who were willing to accept the scholarship but sought to reject the interpretation sometimes did so by explaining that while the narratives of faith were shaped by the local culture of those who wrote them, the underlying spiritual impulse was nevertheless fundamentally Christian.[7]

And yet it could be difficult to believe that the Christian sacred texts were transparently true while other sacred texts were written by scribes whose understanding was obscured and distorted by the time and place in which they wrote. The awareness of other religions, some so eminently sophisticated, raised the uncomfortable question of what in Christianity might be merely cultural, artifacts of the limited understanding of scribes enmeshed in local social worlds. By the end of the nineteenth century, German scholars had suggested that the Torah or Pentateuch— Genesis, Exodus, Numbers, Leviticus, and Deuteronomy, the foundation of the Hebrew Bible that both Christians and Jews took to have been given directly by God to Moses—had been created out of four different accounts that had existed independently until some editor sat down to stitch them cleverly together.[8] This became known as historical criticism. Scholars pointed out that there are two different versions of the creation story and the flood, each associated with a God (Elohim in one, Yahweh in the other) whose tone and temper differ markedly. (In the creation stories, a distant Elohim placidly surveys the creation of the earth and all its creatures; a hot-tempered Yahweh throws his blundering humans out of the paradise he made for them.) The scholars argued that these had once been one story, but when Judah separated from Israel, the traditions had developed differently. There seemed to be another textual source of legal and priestly matters, and yet another source in Deuteronomy, different from all the rest. Scholars discovered that ancient Babylonia, too, had had a story of a flood. Perhaps the Jewish exiles had simply picked up the story. Perhaps it was a myth. Perhaps, in the end, the armchair anthropologists were right, and the Bible was a collection of animistic magic and local folklore knitted together to give authority to the memory of a wise and thoughtful teacher, so regrettably killed before his time.

The belief that the Bible was true to the letter was a direct response to these currents.[9] Prior to the late nineteenth century, Christians did not insist that every word of this complicated, sprawling text was literally true and historically accurate. Centuries of interpretation had emphasized that the book was a text of mystery and symbol. It was not until the last decades of the nineteenth century that there emerged a "scientific" approach to the Bible that explicitly set out to derail this critical approach. "Religion has to fight for its life against the large class of scientific men," wrote one of the founders of the new approach, Charles Hodge, author of *Systematic Theology*. His son Archibald Hodge, together with Benjamin Warfield, set out the tenets of the approach in 1881: "The scriptures not only contain but are the Word of God, and hence all their elements and all their affirmations are absolutely errorless and binding on the faith and obedience of men."[10] They argued that this approach was rational; that it was scientific. It was as modern as historical criticism but came to entirely different conclusions.

As the nineteenth century turned into the twentieth, most Christian institutions across the United States, regardless of their denominational affiliation, began to liberalize. They did so in a deliberate attempt to save faith from the onslaught of scientific and scholarly developments that seemed to challenge the worthiness of the sacred biblical text. They de-emphasized the supernatural elements in the scripture—the virgin birth, the miracles performed by Christ, his bodily resurrection, and his prom-ised second coming—and instead drew attention to Christ's humanity and his teaching about love and compassion. They argued that the scrip-tural texts, however divinely inspired, were written by human scribes and contained the scientific errors and misjudgments of their day. Some even embraced the concept that Christianity was merely one of many human efforts to comprehend that which the mind cannot encompass. They were eager to persuade their followers that a modern world, with its science, its technology, and its humanistic knowledge of many different societies and different ways of living, was neither intellectually nor cul-turally incompatible with Christianity. A turn-of-the-century modern-ist Sunday school curriculum for a Methodist church in Chicago used a teacher's manual that stressed that "the teacher has no right and probably has not sufficient wisdom to impose his own opinion upon his pupils." Teachers were told to "discover in the laboratory of the world's thought and experience, together with your class, who Jesus Christ was."[11]

This appalled a broad array of antagonists who would come to be called fundamentalists because they fervently believed in the fundamen-tals: the accuracy and authority of scripture (including the miracles) and the need for personal salvation through Jesus Christ. Their name was taken from a series of pamphlets entitled *The Fundamentals*, first pub-lished in 1910 and mailed to more than three hundred thousand pastors, missionaries, and others.[12] The pamphlets were meant to be a decisive attack on the modernist scourge of historical criticism. They laid out what the authors took to be the fundamentals of Christian faith, which included the literal truth of the Bible and thus of the supernatural ele-ments written off by modernists as fable or hyperbole: the virgin birth, Jesus's miracles, his bodily resurrection, his second coming.[13] From this perspective, the whole point of Christianity—Christ's power to redeem us from damnation—was lost with the modernist interpretation of the text. These authors insisted that liberal Christianity was not a new inter-pretation of the faith but a new religion entirely, and thus was entirely false and un-Christian.

And yet these conservative critics for the most part denied that the supernatural events described in the Bible would be possible in their own day. In the language often used to describe this theological position, revelation was now "closed." The theological justification for this was that the needs of the founding church were different from those of the evangelizing church. At the Princeton Theological Seminary, Benjamin Warfield explained it thus:

> [Miracles were] the characterizing peculiarity of specifically the Apostolic church, and it belonged therefore exclusively to the Apostolic age ... these gifts ... were part of the credentials of the apostles as the authoritative agents of God in founding the church. Their function thus confined them distinctively to the Apostolic Church, and they necessarily passed away with it.[14]

As the battle over Christianity's essential nature took shape, the two sides were clear: a rationalist modernism in which biblical supernatural elements were no more than folkloric remnants, and a fundamentalism that held that the supernatural events had indeed taken place—in the past.

It is true that there was a third major strand of American Christianity as the nineteenth century turned into the twentieth. That strand drew on old Protestant taproots, on John Wesley's Methodism and on the English holiness tradition that ran alongside the nineteenth-century evangelical revivals. This was Pentecostalism, which emerged out of Topeka, Kansas, when a white minister called Charles Parham studiously read the second chapter of Acts with his followers.

> When the day of Pentecost had come, they were all together in one place. And suddenly from heaven there came a sound like the rush of a violent wind, and it filled the entire house where they were sitting. Divided tongues, as of fire, appeared among them, and a tongue rested on each of them. All of them were filled with the Holy Spirit and began to speak in other languages, as the Spirit gave them ability.[15]

As we saw, they discovered or invented the art of speaking in tongues, which was not much reported outside of the biblical text until Parham and his followers proclaimed that baptism in the Holy Spirit was always accompanied by speaking in a language that the speaker did not understand.[16] But while Pentecostalism grew steadily if not meteorically through the course of the twentieth century, for many decades it seemed a small ripple in the larger Christian stream, a weird and embarrassing eddy in a swift and powerful modernizing current. Most of those who clustered under the banner of "fundamentalism" saw Pentecostalism as self-indulgent emotionalism or (less generously) as a religion of illiterates, hillbillies, and rednecks.[17] The fundamentalists understood their primary struggle to be with those who rejected traditional Christianity because it was irrational. They set out to prove that fundamentalism was perfectly rational and to win back the modernists through reasoned argument.

Over the span of barely more than a generation, from the 1890s to the 1930s, they failed. All major denominational seminaries became more liberal, and none (except in the South) hired Bible-believing scholars. The huge battles in the North American Baptist convention and the (northern) Presbyterian church fell to the modernists. Entire denominations, like Congregationalism, became liberal.[18] Public opinion abandoned the antimodernists. The Scopes trial became a public humiliation of the attempt to claim biblical inerrancy with intellectual integrity. As *The New York Times* drily remarked, "Mr. [William Jennings] Bryan's complete lack of interest in many of the things closely connected with such religious questions as he has been supporting for many years was strikingly shown again and again by Mr. [Clarence] Darrow."[19] Prohibition, an enactment of conservative Christian policy, had been a colossal failure. Fundamentalist Protestants had almost no presence in politics, in mainstream media, or in major universities.

So the antimodernists retreated. They saw themselves as cultural outsiders, and they began to insist on being apart. By the 1930s, being separate from the mainstream denominations and even from mainstream society became an article of faith.[20] The fundamentalists became cautious, defensive, closed. Some who had failed to win over their denominations split dramatically from them, like the Southern Baptists. Others built new nondenominational churches. The moral strictures of the antimodernist impulse led most of its followers to opt out of most of mainstream culture. They didn't drink, they didn't dance, they watched no movies. They saw the church as a pocket of refuge in a doomed and corrupted world. They became inclined to view scholarship as the source of apostasy. Many turned to a view of human history—"dispensationalism"—that held that human society was inherently corrupt and divided into stages that would end, inevitably, in a depraved chaos from which only the second coming of Christ would rescue us. It was not a perspective that oriented believers toward participation in the world. Some denominations seriously debated the question of whether it was morally defensible even to vote.[21] Modernist observers, looking across at this walled-off culture, were likely to conclude that the claim that the Bible was a record of historical truth was the product of rural culture, unschooled and naïve. "By 1947," the eminent historian George Marsden notes, "fundamentalism seemed a cultural and intellectual wasteland."[22]

That was when a group of men set out to create a theologically conservative Christianity, committed to what they understood to be the biblical fundamentals but accepted and respected within mainstream American society. The astonishing thing is not that they succeeded so admirably. The astonishing thing is that as they did so, they embraced an experiential supernaturalism as vividly present as that of the Pentecostalists from whom they worked so hard to distance themselves, and as alien to liberal Christianity as Mongolian shamanism.

The men who founded Fuller Theological Seminary in 1947 on a beautiful estate in southern California represented this new kind of conservative Christian. These Christians had been raised in fundamentalist homes but were now, in the aftermath of the war, becoming more affluent. They were no longer comfortable living on the outskirts of American culture. Charles Fuller was a radio evangelist, the son of a prosperous California orange grower, wartime host of *The Old Fashioned Revival Hour.* The man who would be the first president, Harold Ockenga, had served as the pastor of Boston's Park Street Church, one of the rare remaining fundamentalist strongholds with an intellectual bent. These Christians sought to engage with the world, to transform what they took to be its secular culture, and they wanted to do so in terms that elite intellectuals and mainstream denominations would respect. Ockenga's convocation address announced that the school's task was to save civilization itself, to rethink and restate "the fundamental thesis and principles of a western culture."[23] They called themselves "the new evangelicals."

In the world of today, when evangelical Christianity has become so politically powerful that secular observers fear it like a monster, it is difficult to imagine how strange and unsettling these sentiments would have seemed to the conservative Christians of 1947. Today it is hard to imagine evangelicals who view political action, or for that matter even running a soup kitchen, to be spiritually unsound. But if you view the world as inherently corrupt, any social action apart from saving an individual soul is of necessity spiritually bankrupt, perhaps even trafficking with Satan. Militant antimodernists often quoted 2 Corinthians 6:17, "Come out from among them, and be ye separate."[24] To be faithful was, in the eyes of most conservative Christians of the day, to "come out" and be separate. One of the thirty-nine students registered in the first class at Fuller actually left the school after Ockenga's convocation speech because of his attack on separatism. "The statement of Dr. Ockenga that he repudiated come-out-ism *nauseated* me."[25] Yet the new evangelicals persisted.[26]

They were more eager to reach out than worried about the doctrinal purity of those for whom they reached, more concerned about bringing people in than about protecting the threshold over which those people would cross. That not only vitiated the commitment to separatism; it weakened the commitment to the belief in biblical literalism, which most conservatives treated as the dike against the rising waters of modernism, the levee that would keep out the storm. It was difficult to insist upon the literal truth of each word in the Bible—its "inerrancy"—while also engaging with the scholarly world outside of fundamentalist circles. Faculty still signed every year a statement of faith that included the sentence that the original scriptures are "free from error in the whole and in part."[27] But cracks were appearing.[28] In 1962, in a meeting so tense it became known as Black Sunday, the newly appointed dean of the school—he also happened to be Charles Fuller's son Dan, recently returned from studying with the theologian Karl Barth in Europe—announced that he could accept only what would become known as "limited inerrancy," the view that the Bible is inerrant only in "revelational" material, not in incidental historical details. He carried the day. Nevertheless, the wounds were so raw that all the transcripts carefully taken by the school stenographers were removed by Charles Fuller and have disappeared. After 1965 in conservative Christian circles, the words *inerrant* and *infallible*, previously used as synonyms, no longer referred to the same thing. Progressive evangelicals—still the "new" evangelicals—began to say that the Bible was true in all it "affirmed." It was literally true in all matters of faith and practice, but it could be mistaken in details that are irrelevant to salvation, like the age of the earth.

It was in this era that the mainstreaming impulse of conservative Christianity encountered the hippie Christians who had embraced the Holy Spirit with such enthusiasm. The streams merged. The rebels became conservative, the evangelicals more experiential, and the resulting spirituality became not only mainstream but drew enough converts to transform the cultural and political landscape.

By 1975, Fuller was one of the largest and most powerful conservative Christian seminaries in America. Many of the leaders who dominated American evangelical Christianity had shaped or been shaped by the institution. Billy Graham has been associated with Fuller since the beginning and was a trustee from the late 1950s, a visible symbol of fundamentalist theology without fundamentalist separatism, a man who was comfortable in Washington and comfortable (after some coaching) with middle-class sophistication. The faculty and alumni list is like a roll call of American evangelical Christianity: Rick Warren, pastor of Saddleback Church and author of one of the best-selling books in American publishing history; Richard Foster, author of the much-acclaimed, much-beloved *Celebration of Discipline;* George Eldon Ladd, a leading evangelical theologian; C. Peter Wagner, who founded Global Harvest Ministries and coined the term *third wave;* Dallas Willard, another leading evangelical theologian; and John Wimber, who founded the Vineyard or, at least, led it to its current form.

And as Fuller and evangelical Christianity became mainstream, both became experiential. By 1982, over 40 percent of all Fuller students were willing to describe themselves as "charismatic," a term they seemed to use loosely to assert that they were interested in feeling the presence of God tangibly and realistically. About the same number said that they had spoken in tongues.[29] They are not alone. In 2005, *Newsweek* found that nearly 40 percent of Americans said that "the main reason" they practice religion was "to forge a personal relationship with God."[30] There are still theologically conservative Christians who do not believe that God will speak back; they still hold, as they put it, that revelation is "closed." But probably half of the conservative Christians in America are experientially oriented.[31] Membership in charismatic congregations has exploded since the 1960s. Over the same time span, mainstream denominations have seen their membership plummet relative to the population size. The Presbyterian Church is down 50 percent. The congregations of the

United Church of Christ fell by 60 percent; the United Methodist Church by over 50 percent; the Episcopal Church is down 58 percent.[32]

This history tells us that the liberal Christian God has failed. The mainstream churches are often empty now, their pews unfilled, their hymns unsung, while the churches of the supernatural God blaze with life. For most Americans—and for many people around the world— understanding God in a desupernaturalized way just doesn't keep them in their seats on Sunday morning. But the lesson about the way conservative Christianity has changed is just as striking. For perhaps half or more of those that call themselves born-again, their God has become *more* supernaturally present than he was in the days when the fundamentalists first set themselves apart. The miracles are no longer true only in the past. They are true now, and any congregant can encounter them.

What makes this conception of God so successful in a late modern world? Why does it bring people to church and keep them there? Part of the answer is the intense attention this intimate and personally real God demands. In these experiential evangelical churches, the way Jesus and God are imagined insists that a congregant pay constant attention to his or her mind and world, seeking God's presence, listening for something God might say. This personlike God can comfort, like a friend, and respond directly, like a friend. He can be a real social relationship for those who make the effort to experience him in this way. But because that social relationship lacks so many features of actual human sociality—no visible body, no responsive face, no spoken voice—such a theology demands constant vigilance from those who follow it. They must scrutinize their spontaneous thoughts and their mental images, their perceptions and their feelings, looking for moments that might be God. They are asked to create elaborate dialogues in their imaginations, and to get emotionally involved in those daydreams (or God-dreams). They work to build up a model of God by interpreting it out of their own familiar experience in a way shaped by the social world of the church and the sacred text, and then they work to reorient their own interior emotional responsiveness by matching it to this representation. Faiths that imagine God differently make fewer demands on attentional habits. But it may be, perhaps, that such a God is easier to take for granted. Paradoxically, this high-maintenance, effortful God may appeal to so many modern people precisely because the work demanded makes the God feel more salient. More real.

At the same time, the practice of this attention may produce actual perceptual evidence of God's presence. That is the psychological consequence of the type of prayer this kind of Christianity encourages. As congregants learn to pray and to practice prayer, they sometimes experience God with their senses. They may feel the touch of his hand or the sound of his voice; they may catch a glimpse of a vision he wants them to see. Such experiences cannot be willed, and the more sensory they are, the more rare they become. Those rare moments can be quite powerful, even transformative. When someone hears God—directly hears, with his ears—say that "I will always be with you," it can make God real in a way that feels definitive. The more common but less powerful sensory moments when you sense God's presence, feel his response, have a thought pop into your mind that you know comes from him—these experiences make God come alive in a way no sermon can match.[33]

They also make God of the mind. This way of paying attention shifts the reality of God into a form grasped by the mind and experienced in the mind, and that too has consequences. God becomes more real—you heard him speak—but also more private. He is known through an interaction no one else can share. When the mind is the place one meets God, one gets an acute sense of the deeply human filter through which God is known. The more intimately someone comes to feel connected to God in this style of spirituality, the more sharply he or she feels that God speaks uniquely to each. Those who seek God in this way come to deeply respect the way God is different with each person: and with this respect grows an understanding that all people reach for God through the thick density of their own thoughts and feelings. And since minds are private from each other, no Christian can have full knowledge of any other Christian's relationship with God.

At a church like the Vineyard, the language of the congregants is full of the awareness of one's limits in knowing other minds. Here, for example, is the way one woman describes her response when someone else reports what God has said to him or her:

I'm kind of postmodern in some ways. You know, if that's what someone else is experiencing, I can't discount that experience. I might see different ways in which they might be thinking from a falsehood rather than a truth, but it's fundamentally up to them to decide what they experience or didn't experience or feel or didn't feel.

This woman is not saying that it does not matter what the other person believes; she is not saying that there is no fact of the matter. She really believes that there is a truth condition: God did or did not speak, and the person to whom he spoke did or did not interpret God accurately. But she is sharply aware that because God speaks to each in his or her own mind, as an observer she will never really know whether God spoke to someone else and, if so, whether that other person interpreted God accurately. And she is acutely conscious of the complex filter of her own mind. The more confident she grows in hearing God speak in her own life, the more she is aware that her conversation with God is also just a conversation she is having with herself. "Prayer is often an introspective conversation," she told me. "You know, I am asking my conscience, which is really the Holy Spirit, 'What do you think about this idea?'" She must work to remember this: it is a conversation with herself, but it is also a conversation with God.

And so the need to suspend disbelief becomes inherent to the experience of this God. When God is known through the mind, God is always both immediately present and profoundly cloaked. The insistence on the inevitability of this uncertainty, this cloud of humanness through which humans reach for God, is a constant theme in church sermons. One Sunday morning, we sang a series of worship songs in which God was intimate and close and unquestionably real, and then the pastor stood up to deliver a teaching on the kingdom of God. In this church that encourages people to have coffee with God, he said that God's kingdom does not come with a bang. "Those early Christians, they wanted Christ to say, now, now we are going to overthrow Rome and take over the city." But Christ did not do that, he said. Instead, he said, Christ told a story about a mustard seed, to show that faith grows from small and insignificant beginnings. "It's an ugly seed," the pastor said. "Seeds are ugly." And then he told a story about the early stage of his own Christian journey.

I became a Christian right before my nineteenth birthday. My mom gave me a Bible with tears in her eyes. But every time I opened that book, I fell asleep. Every time. And I began to ask, does Christianity work? I was going to this church called the Vineyard. They were really focused on prayer and how you should pray out loud. So I went home and shut the door and knelt down—that was the image I had of someone praying—and I started talking. Praying. I go on for a little while, not long, and I thought, "I have lost my marbles. I'm talking to myself." I fell backwards and started laughing hysterically. I'm insane. I am actually talking to the ceiling and thinking that that will do something.

When God is imagined in this way, the skepticism of an outer social world is also an inevitable part of the inner dawning awareness of the divine.

These stories of doubt and the fear of being foolish are an integral part of what it means to be an evangelical Christian. They are reiterated repeatedly in prayer manuals and spiritual narratives. John Wimber's anxiety is the title of the documentary about his life. "I'm a fool for Christ," he said again and again in his teachings. "Whose fool are you?"[34]

Almost every Christian I have described in this book tells other people straightforwardly and unambiguously that they are Christians and that they believe in God. And yet every one of them, when talking among themselves or at the end of an interview with me, uses expressions that acknowledge an acute consciousness that their belief has a complicated relationship to the everyday world in which they live.

One evening as women gathered for prayer group, all of them long-standing and firmly committed members of the church, Susan regaled us with a description of her afternoon. She told us that she had seen her five-year-old daughter outside in the pool without her floaties, those air-filled pillows that beginner swimmers wear on their arms, and ran to yank her out. "She said to me, 'Mom, if I had gone down to the bottom of the pool, God would have whispered into your heart and told you I was down there.'" Gales of laughter from the women. "I wanted to say," Susan went on, "'Honey, I *know* this God. You wear your damn floaties.'" More riotous laughter. A woman who had recently dumped her boyfriend for bad behavior gasped that we all need floaties. A different woman, finding this vaguely sacrilegious and deliberately ignoring the up-yours irony in the daughter's retort, said piously that we should all believe in God like that little girl. But another woman responded, "Yeah, I dunno, I think those floaties aren't a bad idea." Nor was that kind of laughing ambivalence so uncommon. After a bad week, the woman who had convened the group—a deeply devout woman—opened the evening with this: "I don't believe it but I'm sticking with it. That's my definition of faith."

The need to damp down disbelief is sharpest when people talk about the direct experience of God. They use phrases like "it sounds lunatic"; "it seems bizarre"; "it sounds like total goofiness." They are explicitly and confidently committed to the fact (as they understand it) that they experience the supernatural directly, and they say this as members of a church that earnestly encourages them to know God in this way. And yet talking about that experience, they mark it as disbelievable by describing how it must appear to others: "I figured out very quickly that you didn't talk like this [to non-Christians.]" "At the time it never struck me how weird I may have been looking." "I know it's true, but it sounds just off the wall."[35]

This anxiety about how what one experiences or believes might appear to others is a constant theme of Sunday-morning sermons. Speakers talk about becoming Christians but not wanting at first to spend time with other Christians because they seemed so nerdy. They talk about feeling like an idiot when kneeling down to pray. Amanda (as we saw) was so embarrassed about believing in God when she became a Christian, she didn't tell anyone for months. In the Spiritual Disciplines Project, when people were talking for the first time to someone they did not know—even though the interviewer was obviously interested, knowledgeable, and sympathetic—they presumed their interviewer's disbelief in the supernatural. "I hope that doesn't sound really mysterious or stupid," one woman began, "but it's—sometimes I think God *does* warn you of something." Speakers fear their audience's response. They fear that they will be seen as crazy. And they worry that what they take to be God is no more than their own wandering mind.

And so there is another paradox: the most direct evidence for God—the evidence of one's senses—is also the clearest evidence for folly or madness. That in-your-face contradiction punches home the need to suspend disbelief, to create an epistemological space that is safe and resilient.

John Wimber was so clear that reason was the biggest stumbling block for contemporary Christians that he used the term "power evangelism" to title his major theological statement. "Power encounters" was an old term, used by missionaries to describe a visible, practical demonstration that Jesus was more powerful than the local spirits, a supernatural shoot-out for pagan souls. Writing of his twenty years in the South Pacific in

1971, one evangelist said, "They did not doubt the power of the God about whom the missionaries spoke . . . but the superiority of that salvation had to be proved by practical demonstration. Somewhere there had to be an actual encounter between Christ and the old god."[36] Wimber expanded that concept more broadly into the encounter of a Western Christian with the Holy Spirit, and for him the real enemy was not a pagan faith but reason, which leads people to doubt God's supernatural power. One of his followers told this story:

> Melinda [was] a young person who manifested all the signs of demon possession. When John Wimber first encountered Melinda—he had been called late one night by a scared friend of hers—the demon said through Melinda, "You can't do anything with her. She's mine." Eventually the demon left Melinda, but not until first putting up a fight. An event like this is a remote village in Africa would result in many members of the tribe converting to Christianity. In the United States it only raises questions about the relationship between mental illness and demonic delusions.[37]

In *Power Evangelism,* Wimber spelled out his understanding of the impoverished framework that is so basic to Westerners that they cannot even see the assumptions as assumptions but rather as fundamental truths about the world. Westerners, he said, assume that we live in a material universe closed off from divine intervention, in which we find truth only through empirical study and rational thought. We feel confident in our ability to control our environment, and we feel little need for any help from anything outside ourselves. We assume that only that which has been tested and proven is true. And finally, we accept reason as the only and highest authority in life.[38] This secular, self-reliant, materialist, and rational culture is, Wimber argued, the greatest impediment to a Christian's authentic personal encounter with Christ. Now, he argued, we live in a world in which most intellectuals have abandoned the hope that we have a purpose for being, and we live in a moral crisis and a miasma of existential doubt.[39]

Yet we have always lived with skepticism. When women reported their visions in fifteenth-century Europe, observers were often exceedingly skeptical, and their explanatory options were identical to those available today: the vision could be the product of divine or demonic inspiration, but it might also be the result of psychiatric illness or an overeager imagination. Nor is the supernatural ever treated, in medieval Europe or in modern Melanesia, as the same order of being as trees or tables.[40] By its nature, the supernatural is nonnatural, and the commitment to its presence is inherently complex. In medieval Europe, as the scholar Steven Justice explains, belief was "routinely taken to be a thing mobile and multiple: shifting, partial and unregularizable in its cognitive components; reliant on hypothesis and metaphor, sustained by imaginative habits and improvisations."[41] The anthropologist E. E. Evans-Pritchard described the knowledge of God among a preliterate Nilotic people, the Nuer, this way: "If we seek for elucidation beyond these terms, a statement of what Spirit is thought to be like in itself, we seek of course in vain. Nuer do not claim to know. They say that they are merely *doar,* simple people, and how can simple people know about such matters? What happens in the world is determined by Spirit and Spirit can be influenced by prayer and sacrifice. This they know, but no more."[42] God is always other.

On the other hand, Wimber is right: There is something different about modernity. Presumed atheism—atheism as a social identity—is a postindustrial Western phenomenon, an odd blip in the long history of our species. As the psychologist Justin Barrett puts it:

> The markers of societies in which atheism seems to be able to spread and develop a noticeable following seem to have emerged late in history. Before the industrial revolution, atheism almost did not exist. People might have rejected organized religions, but they did not cease to believe in God or gods of some sort, including ghosts and spirits. The industrial revolution opened the door, but few walked through until after World War II. The distinctive characteristics of societies in which atheism seems to have a foothold include urbanization, industrial or postindustrial economies, enough wealth to support systems of higher education and leisure time, and prominent development of science and technology.[43]

The clerics who doubted that the late medieval visionaries had truly seen Jesus did not doubt that Jesus existed. The early modern skeptics who challenged the idea of the presence of any particular spirit usually did not doubt that spirits were real. In 1628, for example, an ill woman in France was visited by a ghost who came all in white to clean her house and to care for her and her newborn baby. She came every day for forty days. The author of the long contemporary pamphlet reporting on the events described how many people came to examine the ghost, to determine whether it was godly. He reported the strange sightings that indicated that something supernatural was afoot (the cradle moved without assistance; things put purposefully out of place were tidied up), but most of all, he described the way people tested the spirit to see if it was good. They made the spirit touch crosses and rosaries; they made the ill woman (the only one who could actually see the spirit) examine its feet and smell it; they taunted the spirit and asked it trick questions. They wondered whether the ill woman was making the whole thing up. But neither the pamphleteer nor the people he reported upon dismissed the idea of ghosts as nonsense.[44]

Christians in late-twentieth-century and early-twenty-first-century America, in Europe, and perhaps even in Africa and elsewhere, live in a world in which it is entirely possible to take for granted that talk of the supernatural is bunk. That is what is modern. It is why the philosopher Charles Taylor has characterized our "secular age" as one in which the spiritual is present but different: "We tend to think of our differences from our remote for[e]bears in terms of different *beliefs,* whereas there is something much more puzzling involved here. It is clear that for our forbears, and many people in the world today who live in a similar religious world, the presence of spirits, and of different forms of possession, is no more a matter of (optional, voluntarily embraced) belief than is for me the presence of this computer and its keyboard at the tips of my fingers."[45] Faith has become more self-conscious; doubt of the idea of the supernatural itself hovers as a plausible reality. And what it is to believe has changed.

In a remarkable book called *Believing,* the great historian Wilfred Cantwell Smith argued that the state of mind we moderns take to be central to religious conviction—belief—is simply irrelevant to the way most human beings over the course of human history have engaged with the divine. We assume that belief is central because we assume that the person who is religious—we call that person a believer—must assent to a proposition, that divinity is real. But before our doubt-riddled age, force-fed with information like so many passive and unhappy geese, the great word was *faith.* Faith was about the way you related to reality, not an assertion of what that reality was. Cantwell Smith observed that in the

King James Bible, the magnificent 1611 English translation of the sacred text, the word *faith* occurred 233 times and the word *belief* but once. To be fair, in English there is no verb form of the word *faith*, and in the King James translation, *believe* was used to describe what the faithful did. But in 1611, *to believe* meant to hold dear, to treasure, to trust. Its sense has changed since then. In 1611 *believe* took a person, and not a claim or a statement, as its object—"I believe him" rather than "I believe that." In those days, it would have rung oddly to say of a man that you believed what he said, but you did not trust him. As Cantwell Smith wrote:

> Indeed, one might perhaps sum up one aspect of the history of these matters over the past few centuries in the following way. The affirmation "I believe in God" used to mean: "Given the reality of God as a fact of the universe, I hereby pledge to Him my heart and soul. I committedly opt to live in loyalty to Him. I offer my life to be judged by Him, trusting His mercy." Today the statement might be taken by some as meaning: "Given the uncertainty as to whether there is a God or not, as a fact of modern life, I announce that my opinion is 'yes.'"[46]

Belief is no longer about a moral state but an epistemological conviction.

It is my belief that the God of the late twentieth and early twenty-first century has become imagined as magically real because that way of imagining God helps those who wish to hang on to God manage the doubts that surround them. This God is so real, so accessible, and so present, and so seamlessly blends the supernatural with the everyday, that the paradox places the need for the suspension of disbelief at the center of the Christian experience. The supernatural is presented as the natural, and yet the believer knows that it is not.

It is, in effect, a third kind of epistemological commitment: not materially real like tables and chairs; not fictional, like Snow White and the Seven Dwarfs; but a different conceptual space defined by the insistence that you must suspend disbelief and so by the awareness that disbelief is probable. We saw that ambiguity in the serious play of "let's pretend" prayer. We saw that in play, there is a "play frame" and a "reality frame," and when we play, we act within the play frame. But when evangelicals pray to God in a back-and-forth dialogue—when they go on date night and sit on a park bench with God's arm around their shoulders, when they ask God which shirt they should wear that morning or which medical school he thinks they should attend—the play frame is also and self-consciously a reality frame. They know that they are "pretending" to talk to God. Much in the way they talk about their interaction indicates that they know that this is not "really" God. Yet congregants also insist that the daydream-like prayer is a way of encountering God. It is play but not play, the place where the distinction between belief and make-believe breaks down.

Johan Huizinga, medieval historian and author of *Homo Ludens,* believed that all sacred ritual partakes of this quality of play/not play. But modern evangelical practice takes the ambiguity and accentuates it. The Christian plays at relating to God and understands the play as serious, and the truth of the experience becomes a third form of truth, more real than real, which is what Coleridge intended to invoke when he coined the phrase "the willing suspension of disbelief" in the first place.

The result of the emphasis on paradox is that the practices through which one knows God become more important than the abstract question of belief, and belief becomes in turn an assertion that one has chosen to see an ambiguous world in a certain way.[47] In *Love Wins,* the evangelical pastor Rob Bell frames this as a choice about which story you accept: "What the Gospel does is to confront our version of our story with God's version of our story." What do you choose to believe? he asks. "These are ultimately issues that ask what kind of universe we believe we're living in . . . Are we the ultimate arbiters of what can, and cannot exist? Or is the universe open, wondrous, unexpected, and far beyond anything we can comprehend?"[48]

Insoo Kim, a Vineyard pastor, placed this on his Web page:

I spend most of my time imagining . . . imagining the "what ifs" and "why nots." The excruciatingly delightful tension between what is imagined and what is real is where I live. I choose to live in the tension. Not ignore it. Not hide from it. Not dismiss it. I choose to embrace it fully, with all of its glorious mystery and pain. Because the alternative is not a life worth living.

If there is a God . . . What an incredibly mind-blowing thought— a thought that every human being should wrestle with at least once every few hours. If a person would seriously take a moment's pause and really grapple with this idea, I imagine life will look and feel [and actually be] quite different. What if?

Life is a journey. Often, quite often, we walk along the same path where most people tread. Mindlessly, aimlessly, we live simply to survive, to endure, to get by. But for those who dare to walk along a different path, a narrower path, where the blind see by faith, where the hungry are satisfied by love, there is a hope that awaits. What if there is a narrow path that leads to life, to God. What if?

So I wake up every morning trying to bridge the gap between these two worlds—the world of what is imagined and the world of what is real. Most of the time I fail miserably. But once in a while, not very often, these two worlds collide beyond my wildest dreams. And it makes me imagine, again, "what if . . ."

Insoo Kim believes in his God. But he cannot escape his doubt. It is part of his social world. It is part of the way he comes to know God. In the face of his doubt, his embrace of the uncertainty allows him to make sense of his faith as a way of choosing to live within the world, a way of being more than a proposition. The playfulness and paradox of this new religiosity does for Christians what postmodernism, with its doubt-filled, self-aware, playful intellectual style, did for intellectuals. It allows them to waver between the metaphorical and the literal, between what they fear to be true and what they yearn to be true, in what George Eliot called the doubt and hope and effort which is the breath of life.[49]

There are other factors that play a role in the emergence of this type of modern God. A postindustrial, highly literate, information-saturated society has created the conditions in which people take the explicitly fictional seriously. For one thing, the explicitly fictional is, relatively speaking, a recent phenomenon. It was not until industrialization created the conditions for leisure time, when family size fell and when childhood became venerated as a special time of life, that pretend play became highly valued by the majority.[50] In agrarian societies, children are not particularly encouraged to play, and when they do, they tend to imitate adult activity: farming, cooking, child care. In urban, middle-class families from America to Taiwan, adults actively encourage pretend play. They often believe that play is important for the child's cognitive development.

And they promote fantasy play—play that does not reenact the everyday world but alters it. They tell stories about dragons and princesses and talking dogs. They participate in pretend play directly, making a stuffed animal talk or waging war with space aliens. Parents even initiate pretend play for a younger child. They turn the bedtime story into a ritual, and adults often encourage children to participate in the storytelling, explaining what else the character on the page is doing or thinking at different points of the story. By early childhood, these children are highly active in pretend play and capable of elaborating complex, imaginative, fictional scenarios with others.[51]

What is true of the play of children is true, broadly speaking, of the play of adults. Of course, societies across time and space create stories in myth, drama, and ritual. Everywhere there are narratives both solemn, in sacred texts, and comical and commonplace, like folklore. But narratives that are explicitly fictional—explicitly not true—that adults take up and cultivate as private realities may be a more modern phenomenon. Novels read by many are a relatively recent cultural creation, emerging in Europe around the turn of the nineteenth century. (Admittedly there were what could be called novels even in antiquity, but these had a limited readership.)[52] With widespread literacy, by the early twentieth century these explicitly fictional stories became available to all and widely consumed. The leisure time that modernization created made novel reading possible. And then there are movies and television, which we know to be make-believe and yet can surround us with great vividness. The very juxtaposition of these explicitly fictional worlds and our repeated practice in shifting between them must affect the modern sentiment that we can choose what to believe, and that what we imagine can be more important than the world we perceive to be real.

Meanwhile, the radical technological innovations of our time have fundamentally altered the conditions of our perception and the very way we experience with our bodies.[53] Television, the virtual reality of the Internet, and the all-encompassing world of music we can create around us are techniques that enhance the experience of absorption, the experience of being caught up in fantasy and distracted from an outer world. We play music to create a shell in which we work or to soothe ourselves from a daily grind. We put on headphones on buses and subways specifically to create a different subjective reality from the frazzled one that sways around us. We park our children in front of videos so that they will be absorbed into their own little universes, and we can cook or clean around them undisturbed. Television, with its gripping images and mood-setting music, now provides that experience every night, and for hours each day.

And then there is what one might call the attenuation of the American relationship. A great deal of sociological data suggests that the American experience of relationship is thinner and weaker than in the middle of our last century. Robert Putnam's massive analysis of the decline of civic engagement in the United States argues powerfully that American citizens have become increasingly disconnected from friends, family, and neighbors through both formal and informal structures. Union membership has declined since the 1950s. PTA membership has plummeted. Fewer people vote in presidential elections (except in the South). And with data collected since 1975, one can see that people have friends to dinner less often (and they go out with them no more often). Time diary studies suggest that informal socializing has declined markedly. Between 1976 and 1997, family vacations (with children between eight and seventeen) nosedived as a family practice, as did "just sitting and talking" together as a family. Even the "family dinner" is noticeably in decline. Putnam uses this data to argue that social capital is on the wane in late-twentieth- and early-twenty-first-century America. It also suggests, however, that Americans citizens might feel more lonely. They are certainly more isolated. More Americans live alone now than ever before: 25 percent of them do, compared to 8 percent in 1940 and none in our so-called ancestral environment, when we roamed as hunter-gatherer bands on the open savannah and no one slept alone.[54]

These social changes have facilitated the modern faith practices that build an intensely intimate relationship with God. Our strange new absorbing media probably make us more comfortable with intense absorption experiences. As we switch our DVD players on and off, we practice living in multiple realities. And it seems quite likely that the closely held sense of a personal relationship with God, always there, always listening, always responsive, and always with you, diminishes whatever isolation there is in modern social life. The route to this God is complex and subtle, at once childlike and sophisticated, drawing on skills and practices found throughout human history but doing so in a form specific to this time and space. It is a process through which the loneliest of conscious creatures can come to experience themselves as in a world awash with love.

. . .

And there is another factor that shapes the way the individual experiences God. That is the real presence of the divine. I have said that I do not presume to know ultimate reality. But it is also true that through the process of this journey, in my own way I have come to know God. I do not know what to make of this knowing. I would not call myself a Christian, but I find myself defending Christianity. I do not think of myself as believing in a God who sits out there, as real as a doorpost, but I have experienced what I believe the Gospels mean by joy. I watched people cry in services, and eventually I would cry in services too, and it seemed to me that I cried the way I sometimes wink back tears at children's books, at the promise of simple joy in a messy world. I began to pray regularly, under the tutelage of a spiritual director, and I began to understand parts of the church teaching not just as so many intellectual doctrinal commitments but as having an emotional logic of their own. I remember the morning it dawned on me that the concept of redemption from sin is important, for example, because we cannot really trust that we are loved until we know that we are loved even with our faults. It was (as my spiritual director put it) like believing—really, deeply, believing; believing "in my heart"—that I did not need to lose those ten pounds I always thought I needed to lose before I would be truly lovable. This is, perhaps, not exactly what Paul had in mind, but he would have agreed that unconditional love is hard to understand and that, once grasped, it changes whatever else you thought you understood. It changed me. I came to call my own experience of joy and love, with respect to C. S. Lewis, my furry lion problem.

In the end, this is the story of the uncertainty of our senses, and the complexity of our minds and world. There is so little we know, so much we take on trust. In a way more fundamental than we dare to appreciate, we each must make our own judgments about what is truly real, and there are no guarantees, for what is, is always cloaked in mystery. On the edge of night, when you can hear the surf crash against the distant shore, and see a white horse upon a silver hill, you reach to touch it, and it is gone.

ACKNOWLEDGMENTS

This work has been many years in the making. It is a great happiness to thank those who have been with me on the journey. My first thanks go to those from the Vineyard who accepted me, supported me, tolerated me, and pushed me to see differently: above all Rand Tucker, whose human wisdom is deep; Insoo Kim; Liz Milner; Mark Petterson; Alex Van Riesen; Ken Wilson; Jane Piller Wilson; Caleb Maskell. Thank you to Adeline Coleman. Rand, Liz, Jane, and Ken read parts of the manuscript and helped me to see more clearly. The women in my prayer group were a source of great comfort, maybe more than they knew. More generally, the wider Vineyard community—many of whom I am not naming to protect their privacy—took me in and taught me how to see something of the world they lived in, and did so with grace and without fear. Thank you.

Sharon Broll gave me enormously helpful feedback on the manuscript. Carol Janeway was as always an inspiring editor, and Jill Kneerim, a wonderful agent. Richard Saller and my father, George Luhrmann, read each chapter in its early stages and helped me go forward. Joel Robbins, with whom I have been talking about religion now for over ten years, read the entire manuscript at the end. He has been a true intellectual friend.

The experimental work arose out of my involvement with the Chicago Templeton Network. This group, headed by John Cacioppo, pushed me to support my ethnographic observations with quantitative evidence. I would not have done such a demanding project had they not encouraged me. Howard Nusbaum and Ronald Thisted, whom I got to know in this network, have been remarkable intellectual collaborators. They helped me to design the Spiritual Disciplines Project and have been involved throughout. Christina Drymon was my first research assistant. She did the actual running of the project: calling people, arranging for them to come in—interviewing them, organizing their transcripts, computer exercises, and surveys, and then entering the data. I am enormously grateful to her. Then I brought in Rachel Morgain, who listened to all four hundred hours of our interviews, coded them, entered more data, and worked with great focus on analyzing it. I have learned a very great deal from her. The John Templeton Foundation and the National Science Foundation, along with the University of Chicago and Stanford University, financially supported the project. It gives me great pleasure to express my thanks here.

Books are born from conversations. My students and colleagues from the University of California at San Diego, the University of Chicago, and Stanford nurtured this project, argued with me about it, and ultimately enabled it to emerge in its current form. The project ultimately arose out of time spent observing church worlds with Richard Madsen. Geoffrey Lloyd and Michael Cole first engaged me in thinking about theories of mind, and Roy D'Andrade first encouraged me to march across disciplinary boundaries. Rebecca Lester has been an intellectual partner since she arrived at UCSD twenty years ago. Suzanne Gaskins showed me how to think differently about play and about minds. John Lucy, Richard Taub, Susan Goldin-Meadow, Rick Shweder, Martha McClintock, Jean and John Comaroff, Bert Cohler, and Kathy Morrison framed my discussions about what counts as data at the University of Chicago; my conversations with Jennifer Cole, also at Chicago, have been at the heart of my intellectual career, whether talking about Pentecostalism or the making of books. At Stanford, Lera Boroditsky and Laura Stokes have been co-conspirators in thinking about the supernatural and human cognition. I have talked with Hazel Markus about everything under the sun in recent years, and she has taught me how to analyze psychological data, as have Ewart Thomas and Gordon Bower. Julia Cassaniti and Jocelyn Marrow, my postdoctoral fellows during the final stages of the project, have shaped my approach. Glynn Harrison taught me a very great deal about hearing voices, psychotic and otherwise, as has Kim Hopper. Ann Taves and I have talked long into the afternoon about religious experience. Bill Dyrness, Michelle Karnes, and Richard Kieckhefer have taught me about religious experience across the centuries. My friends in the world of the anthropology of Christianity—in addition to Joel, Jon Bialecki, James Bielo, Webb Keane, Thomas Csordas, Danilyn Rutherford, and others—have helped me to think about Christianity in its many forms. I have given papers on aspects of this material at Cambridge, Chicago, Oxford, Stanford, the London School of Economics, Northwestern, Bergen, UCSD, Fuller Theological Seminary, the Society of Vineyard Scholars, and in Jerusalem. I am enormously grateful for the audiences who listened and responded and engaged.

When you write about something as intimate as God, it is those closest to you who mold your thoughts. I have been thinking about God ever since my grandfather, a minister, walked across the park with me when I was six and tried to explain who he thought God was. My mother, his daughter, continued the conversation, and my father and sisters helped me to know what I know of grace.

This book, and my understanding of love, would be very different without Richard.

NOTES

PREFACE

1. The main reported finding of this representative survey of some 35,000 adults was that Americans have a nondogmatic approach to religion. Even 57 percent of evangelical Protestants were willing to say that many religions can lead to eternal life, and 53 percent of evangelicals agree that "there is more than one true way to interpret the teachings of my religion." The findings about supernatural reality are however equally impressive. Pew Research Center 2008.

2. The authors are Daniel Dennett, Pascal Boyer, and Stewart Guthrie. Remarkably, although this is the conclusion Dennett 2006 draws, not all who contribute to the literature are atheists. Justin Barrett is an eminent evolutionary psychologist (*Why Would Anyone Believe in God?*) and a committed Christian. He argues that God has allowed evolution to shape us for belief. It would be fair to say, however, that most of these scholars are not religious.

3. Indeed, Barrett has demonstrated that people remember God's actions as if God were a person, despite the theologically correct view that God is omnipresent. Tell people that God has prevented a man from drowning in California and saved a child from suffocation in Pennsylvania, and they will talk about God turning his attention from one to the other, as if he were a single person rather than an omniscient and omnipresent force. See Barrett and Keil 1996.

4. Religious readers will recognize that many Christians go through at least one period of significant doubt in their lives and struggle with mild doubt often. It will be nonreligious readers who find the idea of doubt surprising. Many Christian books target doubt: Yancey's *Disappointment with God*, Young's *The Shack*. Frank Schaeffer's *Patience with God* is directly focused on "faith for people who don't like religion." The sociologist Christian Smith (1998:165) reports figures from the General Social Survey 1988–91. Asked "to what extent is your religious faith affected by doubts?" with a scale from one

to seven, only 27 percent of respondents checked one, "faith completely free of doubts"

5. Genesis 32:24–29.

6. Mark 8:17, 9:32, 9:24.

7. 1 Corinthians 13:9–12; King James version.

8. Paul is of course a major figure in Christianity; arguably, without Paul, there would be no Christianity. That there is a sea of scholarship on Paul goes without saying. It is a little more surprising to see, bobbing across that sea, work on Paul by two mandarins of critical theory: Giorgio Agamben, *The Time That Remains,* and Alain Badiou, *Saint Paul.* In that rarified world, they argue, the deconstructionists have deconstructed the idea of what it means to be a person (the "subject") into an ineffective, indecisive wimp. A deconstructed subject is, after all, quite incapable of political action. Whatever one makes of Paul, he was clearly a man of decisive action and as a result—as Bialecki 2009 points out—he seems to have become for these theorists an icon of the possibility of politics. It is an odd kind of salvation, but one imagines that Paul would have been pleased.

9. I owe this observation to Don Randel. One of the more compelling confrontations with this question is Søren Kierkegaard's *Fear and Trembling,* a subtle, haunting book that argues that any decision to believe is equivalent to the choice Abraham made to sacrifice his own son, a choice Kierkegaard describes as fundamentally irrational in the face of utter uncertainty.

10. What one might call an avalanche of medical data has demonstrated that, for reasons still poorly understood, those who attend church and believe in God are healthier and happier and live longer than those who do not. Some of this work is reviewed in Koenig and Cohen 2002; Miller and Thoresen 2003; Powell, Shahabi, and Thoresen 2003; and Seeman, Dubin, and Seeman 2003. John Cacioppo's work on loneliness has demonstrated that in many, many ways— immune response, stress hormone, blood pressure—people do better when socially connected. He and his colleague Nick Epley have demonstrated that those who are more lonely seek out God (Epley et al. 2008), and their work suggests that those who create a relationship with God become less lonely (Cacioppo and Patrick 2008). The MRI work demonstrating that God functions for people as a social connection was reported in Schjoedt et al. 2009. In my own work reported in Chapter Nine, affirming "I feel God's love for me, directly" is significantly negatively correlated with a standard scale for loneliness, the UCLA Loneliness scale. Some work has found that the loneliness reduction associated with a belief in God is effective for women but not men (Kirkpatrick, Shillito, and Kellas 1999). It also appears to be the case that the way God is imagined affects whether belief reduces loneliness: in a West German study, belief in a wrathful God was positively associated with loneliness, while belief in a helpful God was negatively associated with loneliness

(Schwab and Peterson 1990). In 1982, Ray Paloutzian and Craig Ellison demonstrated that Christians whose faith emphasizes a relationship with Jesus were less lonely than Christians whose faith emphasizes moral and ethical teachings. Increasingly, we have evidence that the relationship may have different health consequences than religious practices. A study of mildly symptomatic HIV-positive men found that religious belief (placing one's trust in God, finding comfort in religion) was associated with lower depression, and religious practice (service attendance, prayer, spiritual discussions) with improved immune function (Woods et al. 1999). These matters are further discussed in Chapter Nine.

11. The phrase *problem of presence* is the title of a fascinating 2007 book by Matthew Engelke, about the Friday Masowe Church in Zimbabwe. These "Friday apostolics" refuse to read the Bible because they think of it as a thing, and they want a relationship with God that is "live and direct," not obstructed by the stuff of this world.

12. Miller 1997.

13. This study found that 23 percent of all Americans call themselves charismatic, Pentecostal, or speak in tongues at least several times a year (as people often do in the Vineyard, but rarely in church). Pew Research Center 2006.

CHAPTER ONE. THE INVITATION

1. Conversion narratives are remarkably interesting because they are both records of deep personal transformation and publicly scripted stories that catch up the emotional attention of those who deliver them. Stromberg 1993 is an example of the former, part of an ongoing project to understand the way that the self (perhaps) is transformed through symbol and narrative. Stromberg argues that conversion narratives enable the new congregant to reorganize emotional distress. Harding 1987 is a compelling example of the social power of these narratives. Harding left an interview with a conservative Christian pastor and found herself in a near-miss car accident. Despite being a non-Christian—indeed, despite having little sympathy with some aspects of the fundamentalist world she sought to understand—she immediately asked herself: What is God trying to tell me? For a synoptic account of conversion, see Rambo 1993. Other discussions of conversion narrative and transformation include Csordas 1994, Robbins 2004b, and Luhrmann 2004.

2. The Vineyard is in fact on the intellectual end of the spectrum. Arnold went to seminary because he liked the idea of reading the Bible in Greek. Not all evangelical pastors do. Often evangelical churches are scornful of intellectual learning, as if it offends their sense of just-plain-folks authenticity. In the meth-and-redemption church I attended, the pastor made that quite clear one Sunday morning: "The people of this government, they've been

to Harvard and Yale, they just passed a law saying that pornography can be shown on television at any time, because it's protected by the freedom of speech. But that's not what free speech is about!" he shouted. "We all know that free speech is about having the freedom to criticize the government, not to allow rubbish on television." This outright contempt for learning drives many evangelical scholars nuts. In his remarkable history of Jesus, the historian Stephen Nichols writes, "Contemporary Christian music represents for many evangelicals the sum of their theological training and discipleship" (2008:16). A famous evangelical historian, Mark Noll, summarizes his view of this anti-intellectual approach to the Bible in a title: *The Scandal of the Evangelical Mind* (1994).

3. Smith 1998:106.

4. Gallup polls have asked "Would you consider yourself as 'born again' or 'evangelical'?" every other month or so for years. Those who say yes have wavered between 39 percent and 47 percent since 1996. In the aggregate, Gallup concludes that in 2006, 43 percent of all American adults would describe themselves that way. That figure includes Catholics, 19 percent of whom said yes. According to these polls, 28 percent of all Americans are white evangelical Protestants. A large study by Baylor found that 34 percent of all Americans are evangelical Protestants. For the Gallup poll, the yes that people gave may have been in part a simple commitment to an experiential spirituality: Gallup reports that the percentage of Americans who say that they would like to experience spiritual growth rose from 6 in 10 in the early 1990s to 8 in 10 by 2001, and it also reports that if you ask specifically about what are assumed to be the defining features of evangelical Christianity—the literal truth of the Bible; salvation through Christ; and sharing belief with nonbelievers—only 22 percent of those questioned agree that they believe in or have done all three. The data on pro-choice evangelicals is reported in Gallup and Lindsay 1999:40; the figure on biblical literalism is reported in Pew Research Center 2008. I explore the relationship between fundamentalism and evangelicalism in Chapter Ten.

5. This is the definition that Christian Smith eventually determines to be what most people mean when they call themselves evangelical: "an activist faith that tries to influence the surrounding world" (1998:242).

6. This is not true of all evangelicals, as the final chapter recounts. Some evangelicals are "cessationist": for them, miracles ceased at the end of the biblical age. Even so, they may seek to experience God in some way. The Brethren, for example, accept the three main principles of evangelical commitment and are classically cessationist. But in the born-again experience, they often expect a special psychological experience of God. See Brett Grainger's *In the World But Not of It.*

7. The word *charismatic* has a rich scholarly and theological history; see Robbins

2004b. Charismatic spirituality is often described as having had three "waves" in America: Pentecostalism, emerging at the turn of the twentieth century; the Catholic Charismatic Revival in the 1960s; and the neo-Pentecostal turn, of which the Vineyard is a part, emerging in the 1970s and 1980s, although there are charismatic expressions that fall outside these periods. Marsden 1987 and Marsden 1991 provide an excellent history; Smith 2000 and Smith 1998 present impressive survey-driven work that in some ways complicates the understanding of evangelicalism one might infer from that history.

8. At the time of writing, *The Purpose Driven Life* has sold more than twenty-five million copies. It must be said that Warren explicitly rejects an experience-driven approach to God. He does not think that Christians should be spiritual junkies. But he does insist that God wants to be the reader's best friend, and he does set out to teach readers how to experience God in that way.

9. The classic essay is McLoughlin 1978. But see also Lambert 1999.

10. See McLoughlin 1978 and Fogel 2000, among others.

11. Ostling 1993; Wuthnow 1996.

12. Roof 1993.

13. Gallup and Lindsay 1999:68.

14. As we saw in the preface, a 2006 Pew study concluded that 23 percent of a representative sample of Americans could be called "renewalist": they either attended a Pentecostal church, described themselves as Pentecostal or charismatic, or spoke in tongues at least several times a year. Twenty-six percent of them reported that they had received a "direct revelation from God." Eighteen percent reported that they spoke in tongues at least several times a year. Fogel 2000 concluded that as many as one in three Americans practices an experiential spirituality. Burgess 2005 reported that 23 percent of all Protestant churches are charismatic; that 46 percent of all adults who attend Protestant churches are charismatic; and that 51 percent of all those who call themselves born-again are charismatic. These judgments, however, are typically made about Christians who accept the more dramatic forms of charismatic experience. The percentage that accepts a less dramatic experiential spirituality is far larger. Remember the more than twenty-five million copies sold of *The Purpose Driven Life*. It is not alone. *Celebration of Discipline* is a practical introduction to experiential spirituality; more than a million copies are in print. *Experiencing God* is a how-to manual, a step-by-step guide "to *experience* God, not merely to know about Him." More than four million copies are in print. These are just some of the many, many manuals available.

15. Miller 1997 may have coined this term.

16. The Jesus Freaks were not, of course, the only source of theologically conservative Christians in the country. But the Christian hippies played an important role in enabling an experiential spirituality and making it public, and both the hippies and the existing conservative Christians shared the sense of

being hurt by the age's social tumult. This was the period when, for example, existing conservative Christians began to focus more heavily on the family. That story is well told in Harrington-Watt 1991; Tipton 1982; and Shires 2007.

17. Eskridge 2005:81.

18. The documentary film is *Frisbee: The Life and Death of a Hippie Preacher*, written by David di Sabatino and produced by Jester Media in co-production with KQED. It is a terrific film. Otherwise unreferenced quotations about this period are taken from the film.

19. *San Francisco Oracle* 1 (5):2.

20. Eskridge 2005: 75–76.

21. Di Sabatino 1999:5.

22. Eskridge 2005:10, 180.

23. In the late 1960s less than ten million dollars of the modern music market were earned through Christian music. In 2007, sales of contemporary Christian music topped three-quarters of a billion dollars. Vitale 2002.

24. Prothero 2003:127.

25. Reading the Bible literally is in fact a late-nineteenth-century phenomenon that emerged as a response to the challenges of evolutionary theory and the new Higher Criticism, which gave a historical (and not theological) account of the source of scripture. However, this style of reading—which assumes that: "the scriptures not only contain but are the Word of God, and hence all their elements and all their affirmations are absolutely errorless and binding on the faith and obedience of men" (Hodge and Warfield 1881)—was specific to the staunch conservative Christians who came to be known as fundamentalists until the 1960s. Karen Armstrong, who quotes this statement (2007:199), has a nice discussion of this shift in *The Bible*.

26. Marsden 2006 provides a helpful account of this history.

27. John 14:12, Acts 1:8, Acts 2:2.

28. Newberg et al. 2006.

29. Acts 2:3; 2:8, 11.

30. Anderson 1979:54.

31. Pentecostal histories may trace tongue-speaking through many centuries, but non-Pentecostal historians tend to identify only small pockets of Christians as speaking in tongues prior to the twentieth century, and those primarily in the nineteenth: some early Mormons, some British Christians called "Irvingites," and perhaps some early followers of George Fox a century earlier. Since the second century, the established church had interpreted tongues as evidence of demonic possession, as in the comments of the twentieth-century century Catholic theologian Ronald Knox: "to speak with tongues you never learned was, and is, a recognized symptom of alleged diabolical possession." Quoted in Samarin 1972:13.

32. Wacker 2001:232.

33. Eskridge 2005:97.

34. Kittler 1972:12.
35. Lindsey and Carlson, 1970:156.
36. The comment can be found in a history of Calvary Chapel, written by Chuck Smith and posted on various Calvary websites, for example: http://www .calvarygp.com/the-History-of-Calvary-Chapel.
37. Prothero 2003:138, 139.
38. Miller 1997:34.
39. Smith 1992:1.
40. He seems to have been more of a manager and producer for them, but his biographer reports that he also played sax.
41. In *Empowered Evangelicals,* (Nathan and Wilson 1995), Ken Wilson emphasizes how unusual this focus was within the Christian church, and how powerfully it drew Wimber's early (and current) followers. Wilson also points out that this emphasis on Jesus's supernaturalism is quite different from the Pentecostal emphasis on tongues, which draws its inspiration from Paul's first letter to the Corinthians. Wimber instead turned to a theology that insisted on the real presence of the supernatural Jesus in the everyday world. This was the "kingdom theology" developed by George Eldon Ladd, a theologian at Fuller Theological Seminary. Wimber popularized Ladd's theology in a course he taught at Fuller in the early 1980s. The course became famous, oversubscribed, and controversial because Wimber taught theology as a practical lesson: that anyone could learn to use the supernatural power that broke through into the world. It is said that the theology faculty voted not to give students credit for taking the class.
42. Jackson 1999:69.
43. Jackson 1999:70. Carol Wimber gives a different date for the first healing, but this is the account Wimber presents: March 1978.
44. Jackson 1999:71.
45. Carol Wimber in Springer and Wimber 1988:12. Jackson reports that Lonnie may not have actually said "Come, Holy Spirit" (1999:73). The event became so momentous that it has its own chapter in the only written history of the Vineyard, Jackson 1999.
46. Wimber 1985:44. It is in fact a fairly common Catholic and Pentecostal prayer, an observation that reinforces the sense of Wimber as theologically naïve, as Jon Bialecki pointed out to me.
47. C. Wimber 1999:151.
48. C. Wimber 1999:136.
49. C. Wimber 1999:148.
50. E.g., Smith 1992:3.
51. "This whole doctrine and practice was developed entirely upon experiences, with no solid scriptural foundation . . . That demons can and do possess the bodies of *unbelievers* is an accepted fact of scripture, and that they can be exorcised through the authority of the name of Jesus is also evident. But to

believe that a child of God can be freed from the problems of the flesh (such as lust, anger, and envy) by exorcism is charismania." Smith 1992:120–21.

52. C. Wimber 1999:156.

53. It, too, has struggled with routinization. In the middle 1990s, a Vineyard church at the end of an airport runway in Toronto—one of nearly four hundred Vineyard churches in the world at that point—began to report a sudden renewal, an infusion of the Holy Spirit. There were reports of people getting "drunk" in the spirit and experiencing uncontrollable fits of laughter. Soon it was holding services six times a week, with an average of eight hundred worshippers a night and hundreds of people being slain in the spirit and being healed miraculously of physical illness. Demons emerged, howled, and jerked their humans back and forth before they were expelled. Curious Christians began coming from many countries, but the most eager participants came from Britain; they took the revival back into mainstream Anglican churches, and the media perked up its ears. By the end of 1994, some sympathizers estimated that between two and four thousand British congregations embraced what came to be called the "Toronto Blessing" (Hilborn 2001).

The bridge too far (from the Vineyard's perspective) was possession by animals. About five months into the revival, the church pianist in Toronto darted into the sanctuary nursery, shook violently, and then became an ox (apparently). An angry ox, too. She charged on all fours, flared her nostrils, and prophesied in the first, second, and third person that the Lord was chasing this enemy back with great strength (Jackson 1999:312). In England, newspaper reports described worshippers as "barking, crowing like cockerels, mooing like cows, pawing the ground like bulls, and, more commonly, roaring like lions" (Hilborn 2001:184). (Mind you, these actions were understood within the church as "scriptural," supported by, for example, Ezekiel 1 and Revelation 4.) The excitement passed back across the sea to California. On October 26, 1995, *The Orange County Register* carried an article—a sectional front-page article—on the local Vineyard about a young woman "who seemed to be imitating a chicken, waddling with head jerking back and forth as if searching for grain." Then Wimber was quoted as saying that he didn't care if someone "quacked like a duck for three days" if they quacked all the way to Christ (Jackson 1999:326–27). That backfired. In a church primarily white and mainstream, cringe counts. In 1995 the Vineyard withdrew its endorsement from the Toronto Airport Vineyard.

54. You can see it most clearly in the beloved hymns. "What a Friend We Have in Jesus" (1855) sings of the relief of taking every trouble to Jesus in prayer. But he is not a close friend—more someone to relieve the burden you bear alone.

55. Prothero 2003:72.

56. In Exodus, God speaks to Moses face-to-face "as a man speakest unto his friend" (Exodus 33:11), and elsewhere Abraham is described as God's friend.

"O our God, did you not drive out the inhabitants of this land before your people Israel and give it forever to the descendants of your friend Abraham?" (2 Chronicles 20:7). But no one else in the Hebrew Bible is described as a friend of God—just these two, who talked with God one to one and founded the nation of his chosen people. In the Gospel of John, Jesus explicitly calls his followers friends, but here friendship is really about being chosen to carry out God's will: "You are my friends if you do what I command you." That is clear enough. Jesus then explains, "I do not call you servants any longer, because the servant does not know what the master is doing; but I have called you friends, because I have made known to you everything that I heard from my Father." And then he underlines the asymmetry of the friendship: "You did not choose me, but I chose you" (John 15:14–16). Sometimes those who go to great trouble to find him are called "friend," like the men who brought a paralyzed man to be cured by him, but the crowd was so great that they had to clamber up onto the roof to make a hole to let him down (Luke 5:19–20). When Judas betrays him in the garden of Gethsemane, Jesus calls him friend—and makes it clear that Judas is acting under his command and not the other way around (Matthew 26:50). It is true that Jesus does behave, in the Gospel of John, as if he has real human friends. He seems to love Mary and Martha. He cries when he sees how upset they are when their brother has died. But for the most part, friendship implies responsibility, and it is not a friendship of pals.

Luke Timothy Johnson makes a case that at least in the Letter of James, friendship with Jesus is understood as a particularly intense intimacy that becomes a kind of spiritual identity, a statement about one's ultimate values (2004:213–16). In the New Testament, James 2:23 returns to the theme of friendship with God in order to make an argument about the seriousness of faith around the question of whether faith alone can save. James argues that faith without good works is no faith at all: and he turns to Abraham's willingness to sacrifice his son, which is an act made possible by faith. "Faith apart from works is barren" (James 2:20), the writer says—and he says that Abraham believed, and was called the friend of God. The next sentence reads: "You see that a person is justified by works and not by faith alone" (James 2:24). Friendship in this text entails responsibilities that are not easy: "Adulterers! Do you not know that friendship with the world is enmity with God?" (James 4:4). See also Andrews 1997, which makes it quite clear that "discipline is the activity most closely associated with the divine parent"—not cozy cuddling (1997:iv).

57. Hatch 1989 focuses on the spiritually democratic impulse of the early republic, but he identifies as distinctively American the democracy of the teaching that no training or education is required to know God.

58. Mark 11:12, 3:5, 1:34, 1:44, 3:21, 6:3, 4:40, 14:34, 15:33.

59. Mark 6:56, 5:29, 7:34. I learned to see these features of the text after listening to Luke Timothy Johnson's remarkable lectures on the Gospels, available from the Teaching Company.
60. Peter's recognition of Jesus as the Messiah is not the same thing.
61. Mark 5:20, 5:42, 6:2, 4:41, 9:32, 7:14–23, 8:16.

CHAPTER TWO. IS THAT YOU, GOD?

1. Lewis 1980 [1952]:144.
2. See, for comparison, diSessa and Sherin 1998.
3. Bickel and Jantz 1996:68.
4. Goll 2004:39.
5. Virkler and Virkler 1986:29.
6. Boroditsky and Ramscar 2002.
7. Poloma and Gallup 1991:26, 3. Similar figures were reported by Gallup and Lindsay 1999:46.
8. Bickel and Jantz 1996:5–6.
9. Bickel and Jantz 1996:39.
10. Bickel and Jantz 1996:40.
11. The phrase *breaking through* is common in the Vineyard and carries a theological meaning associated with "kingdom theology." Derek Morphew's *Breakthrough* describes this well.
12. The classic statement is Goody 1997.
13. Virkler and Virkler 1986:57; Hybels 1998 [1988]:58.
14. Warren 2002:10.
15. Many anthropologists have written well on dreams, including Charles Stewart, Kilton Stewart, Jeannette Mageo, Waud Kracke, and others. Tedlock 1987 is a good place to start.
16. One of the most famous examples is chess. Expert players literally see and remember more on the board than naïve players. See Luhrmann 2000.
17. 1 Corinthians 12:10.
18. Some psychologists have begun to study the way nonevangelical Americans interpret spontaneous thought and dreams; indeed, they treat thoughts and dreams that they experience as appearing unexpectedly as having more real-world significance. See, for example, Morewedge and Norton 2009.
19. Virkler and Virkler 1986:8.
20. Miles 1995.
21. Goody 1995 collects some quite interesting observations on this theme.

CHAPTER THREE. LET'S PRETEND

1. The calculations of the number of muscular movements and the expressions they form was made by Paul Ekman, whose work has focused on the micro-expressions that communicate emotion.

2. Lewis 1980 [1952]:187–88, 188, 193.

3. 1 Corinthians 11:1.

4. "Believing is not something you can decide as a matter of policy. At least, it is not something I can do as an act of will. I can decide to go to church and I can decide to recite the Nicene Creed and I can decide to swear on a stack of bibles that I believe every word inside them. But none of that can make me actually believe if I don't." Dawkins 2006:104.

5. Blackaby and King 2004:95.

6. Blackaby and King 2004:97.

7. Taylor 1999:10.

8. Taylor 1999:10.

9. The 1934 study found that 13 percent of the 111 three-to-sixteen-year-old children studied had or remembered having one. A later study (Singer and Singer 1990) that included stuffed animals and dolls (if they were treated as humanlike) found a rate of 65 percent. Rates rise if you ask children directly and shrink if you rely on parents or the retrospective memories of adults. A careful recent study, by Marjorie Taylor and Stephanie Carlson, of 152 three- and four-year-olds interviewed parents and children separately and included stuffed animals and dolls. Twenty-eight percent of their children seemed to have an imaginary companion. When they interviewed 100 of the children three years later, many of those who hadn't originally reported companions had developed them, bringing the rate to 63 percent. Reported in Taylor 1999.

10. Girls are somewhat more likely to have them than boys, although it is not because girls are more imaginative. Boys are more likely to impersonate someone or something—to become Superman or a dinosaur—and if you look at persistent impersonation roles, the imbalance evens out.

11. Taylor 1999:5.

12. Such children may be more able to focus. They are slightly more likely to be first-born or only children. They watch less television, although whether this is cause or consequence is not known. "The view that is emerging from recent research is that most of them, in fact the children who create pretend friends, are very social people who particularly enjoy interacting with others. When there is no one around to play with, these children make someone up." Taylor 1999:5.

13. Taylor 1999:78.

14. Taylor 1999:65.

15. See, for example, Harvey 2006.

16. Curtis and Eldredge 1997:13, 14, 14–16.

17. Curtis and Eldredge 1997:143, 180. It can seem quite shocking to those new

to this way of thinking that evangelical Christians might compare the Gospels to a fairy tale, but *The Sacred Romance* is not the only book to do so. Frederick Buechner's *Telling the Truth: The Gospel as Tragedy, Comedy and Fairy Tale* (1997) is another example. Even its title conveys the complex dance around the real and the fantastic. Another example is William McNamara's *Wild and Robust* (2006), which invites it readers on the great adventure of faith.

18. Curtis and Eldredge 1997:82.

19. Blackaby and King 2004:7–8.

20. Best 2005:64.

21. Best 2005:18, 30, 51, 9.

22. Winnicott 1971:6. Winnicott's papers are remarkably terse. It is as if he were trying not to say more than he must, to convey an idea that compelled him to write, or maybe he was just not a writer. Nonetheless the papers are richly suggestive and well worth reading. Another clinician of play is Virginia Axline, author of the luminous book *Dibs,* whose protagonist played his way from cramped fear to freedom by allowing the toys in the therapist's office to become imbued with the real emotional responses he felt toward the human parents in his life.

23. Sadeh, Hen-Gal, and Tikotsky 2007.

24. Curtis and Eldredge 1997:203.

25. www.preceptaustin.org.

26. In some ways, this is an old manner of reading the Bible. For most of the history of the scriptures, when people came to the text, they read it symbolically. Pelikan 2005 tells this story well, as does Armstrong 2007. The idea that the biblical text is literally true is a modern notion, a response to the equally modern idea that the text can be deciphered through the scholarly apparatus. What seems to be contemporary and more particular to this century about the inductive Bible approach to reading the scripture is that this practice can be undertaken by someone who believes that the Bible is literally true while at the same time believing that the Bible is personal and unique for each individual. When the leader of one of my groups was explaining how to read the Bible to me, she said that just as there is a Gospel of Mark and a Gospel of Matthew, there is a "Gospel of Tanya," and my job was to understand that Gospel. This is not unlike the "Sheilaism," the religion of a subject named Sheila in Bellah et al. 1996. These evangelicals are far more constricted in their understanding of the Bible than Sheila is, but the individualistic, personal ethos is similarly clear.

27. One of the very few studies of the house groups in which these readings take place is Bielo 2009.

28. Here I would remind the reader of the Pew statistic that only 59 percent of evangelicals believe that the Bible is true word for word.

29. The example is provided by Paul Harris, one of the leading developmental psychologists to have studied play. His work has demonstrated—in the face of the presumptions by both Freud and Piaget that imaginative play was a failure of realistic, rational thought—that children distinguish between imagination and reality from the time they can talk. Harris 2000.

30. Huizinga 1949:13.

31. Huizinga 1949:25.

CHAPTER FOUR. DEVELOPING YOUR HEART

1. Warren 2002:123.

2. Luther came to this vision out of his own failed attempt to feel that he so sufficiently despised himself that he could not usurp God's judgment by assuming he was saved. The doctrine of salvation by faith emerged as a solution to the problem of his own hubris. See Wicks 1983.

3. Fulton 2002:175.

4. Miller 1949 is one of the best portraits of Edwards, written by the great historian of Puritanism. Marsden 2003 is another fine account. A recent evangelical text translates Edwards on discernment for practical uses by a contemporary audience; Gerald McDermott, *Seeing God.* The quotations in the text are taken from this famous sermon.

5. Joyce 1916:137–38.

6. That God loves truly unconditionally may be a novel feature of late twentieth-century Christianity. Modern evangelicals base their interpretation on John 3:16—a banner that you can see, as Johnson 2004 points out, at baseball games: "For God so loved the world that he gave his only Son, so that everyone who believes in him may not perish but may have eternal life." That God loves unconditionally is a plausible interpretation of that sentence fragment, but it is not the only plausible interpretation. The phrase "God is love" appears only twice in the New Testament, in a letter in the Johannine tradition, 1 John 4:8 ("Whoever does not love does not know God, because God is love") and I John 4:16. ("And so we know and rely on the love God has for us. God is love. Whoever lives in love lives in God, and God in him"). That is the God of *Godspell* and the Jesus People, but it is not obviously the God who threw the moneychangers out of the temple or the God who led the pilgrims to their new land, nor their descendants into war.

7. Augustine 2001 [1963]:158 (book 8, chapter 5).

8. Rob Bell makes this a point in *Love Wins,* a book that became controversial because he spelled it out so clearly that it took some evangelicals aback. But he simply stated what I heard again and again in this community: that God is love; that heaven is the emotional experience of God's love; and that hell is the grasping, self-critical condemnation we too often emotionally experience

instead. As Bell puts it theologically, "At the heart of this perspective is the belief that, given enough time, everybody will turn to God and find themselves in the joy and peace of God's presence" (2011:107).

9. Hochschild 1979:561.

10. Many evangelicals associate the term *heart* with desert spirituality, but in fact the modern meaning of the term probably owes more to Pietism and the search to encounter the divine through the emotions, particularly the love of God. See Campbell 2000 and Bebbington 2000.

11. Nouwen 1981:76.

12. When Hegel built the concept of recognition into the cornerstone of his *Phenomenology*, he meant that who we are depends, in the deepest sense, on our awareness of the way others see us. This is what Sarah meant by "recognition."

13. à Kempis 1947, book 1.

14. Willard 2002:22.

15. I owe this observation to the anthropologist Yehuda Goodman (2009), who observes that clients seek to re-create an ideal self.

16. Silf 1998:4.

17. Arguably, no words are. That is the burden of a line of philosophical inquiry that began with Wittgenstein and that Richard Rorty expressed so eloquently. I still hold to the observation that there is a broad difference between the referential style of spiritual language and, say, a naturalist's account of squirrels and their acorns.

18. Austin 1962.

19. Warren 2002:17, 26, 43.

20. Warren 2002:85, 87, 89.

21. Schafer 1993.

22. Luhrmann 2000 is about the experience of therapy and biomedicine in the context of psychiatry.

23. Increasingly, psychoanalysts have begun to focus on uncertainty and mistake as the source of psychoanalytic understanding. See the work of Steve Cooper and others as described in Luhrmann 1998.

24. Freud 1961 [1927].

25. That said, there have always been a few religious psychoanalysts, including Christian ones. One of the best known was a Jesuit: W. W. Meissner, author of the first psychoanalytic study of Loyola, subtitled: *The Psychology of a Saint* (2002).

26. Freud 1910:123.

27. Or as she put it in the language of her profession: "The image of God is . . . an object-related representational process marked by the emotional configuration of the individual prevailing at the moment he forms the representation—at any developmental stage" (Rizzuto 2007:44).

28. The review comments: "Hers is a brief for religion . . . object relations theory is thus used as a crypto-Jungian basis for psychoanalytic theology" (Stein

1981:126). Outside Rizzuto's work, the psychoanalytic thinking about religion is surprisingly limited. Meissner's biography of Ignatius Loyola uses a classical model to understand the source of Loyola's anxieties. More scholars have developed their thinking out of object relations theory, in which the human being is understood to be driven by a desire for attachment. Winnicott, as we have seen, understands the young child as creating "intermediate" objects between the self and the other, objects that are both self and other: for Winnicott, this is the arena of God, who partakes in both self and other. Self-psychology, which developed out of object relations, is another such fruitful domain. Kohut argued that in therapy the analyst offers a "good object," in the person of the therapist, that can be internalized by the patient and create a reparative relationship. That is the kind of relationship evangelicals are seeking with God.

29. In *The Varieties of Religious Experience,* James described four features of a classic mystical experience: the person feels intensely that they are suspended in space and time (often with an overwhelming sense of light and love); the experience is ineffable; it is noetic (it conveys a sense of knowing something deeply and beyond words); and it is transient, often lasting no more than a minute. The moments I describe here can include such phenomena (the pastor, for example, might have been describing a mystical experience), but they are often more low key.

30. Lewis 1955:16, 17, 170.

31. Biema 2005.

32. Barry 1991:70. For Barry, a Jesuit priest who quotes Tolkien's passage, joy is more than mere happiness. He calls it the "desire of the everlasting hills."

CHAPTER FIVE. LEARNING FROM THE EXPERTS

1. Here is a sampling of the insistence. In the Bible: "Devote yourself to prayer, being watchful and thankful" (Colossians 4:2). In prayer manuals: "God wants you praying because it is part of the process he uses to be involved with your life" (Bickel and Jantz 1996:17); "We can never draw close to God and get to know Him well, or develop the kind of intimate relationship we want, unless we spend time alone with Him" (Omartian 2004:10); and "[Prayer] is communion and intercourse with God. It is enjoyment of God. It is access to God" (Bounds 2007:13).

2. More precisely, Csikszentmihalyi wrote that flow has the following features:

   1. Clear goals.
   2. Concentrating and focusing, a high degree of concentration on a limited field of attention.
   3. A loss of the feeling of self-consciousness, the merging of action and awareness.

4. A distorted sense of time, so that your subjective experience of time is altered.
5. Direct feedback in the course of the activity, so that you immediately adjust your behavior.
6. A balance between ability level and challenge (the activity is neither too easy nor too difficult).
7. A sense of personal control over the situation or activity.
8. The activity is intrinsically rewarding.

The basic point is that in flow, as he conceived it, people become absorbed in their activity, and focus of awareness is narrowed down to the activity itself. See Csikszentmihalyi 1991.

3. Caffeine may in fact play a role, although this study that suggests that it does is purely correlational. People who take in the caffeine equivalent of three cups of coffee are more than three times more likely to report unusual sensory experiences, at least as measured in a group of two hundred U.K. undergraduates. See Jones and Fernyhough 2009.

4. Finney 1876:20.

5. Sam was invoking Jeremiah as a reluctant prophet, but his "what's that about" makes me wonder whether he was also thinking about Samuel, who is the best biblical example of someone who hears God audibly call his name and is frankly confused by the experience until he figures out that it is God. When the story opens (I Samuel 3:1–9), Samuel is a young boy in the service of Eli, a priest of the temple. Late one night, each is lying in his own room when Samuel hears a voice calling, "Samuel, Samuel!" He runs to Eli, who tells him that he did not call and that he should go back to bed. By the time it happens a third time, Eli realizes that it is God who is calling Samuel. He tells Samuel to go back to his room and, if he hears the voice again, to address it as "Lord." The striking phenomenological detail is that Samuel looked for the source of the voice. When someone gives you that detail—they heard a voice and then looked to see who was speaking—it is good evidence that they heard the voice with their ears.

6. Jeremiah 1:1–14.

7. See for example Blanke et al. 2002 and Ridder et al. 2007.

CHAPTER SIX. LORD, TEACH US TO PRAY

1. This is the account of prayer genre given in a lovely essay about the structure of prayer as children see it: Capps and Ochs 2002. See also Keane 1997; Baquedano-Lopez 1999, 2008; and Shoaps 2002.

2. The idea of calling a social behavior a "technology" comes from the work of Michel Foucault, who transformed anthropology by observing that routine institutions—prisons, psychiatric hospitals—emerged out of new expecta-

tions about how to be human, and that those expectations and practices transform ("discipline") what it is to be human as powerfully as the automobile transforms and directs the way we move through space.

3. Virkler and Virkler 1986:6–7.

4. Goll 2004:56, 62, 17.

5. Hybels 1998 [1988]:51.

6. Hybels 1998 [1988]:65.

7. Foster 1998 [1978]:29–30.

8. Wilson 2009:106.

9. See Luhrmann 1989.

10. Turner 1995:20.

11. Foster 1998 [1978]:28.

12. Matthew 6:5–6 (King James translation): "And when thou prayest, thou shalt not be as the hypocrites are: for they love to pray standing in the synagogues and in the corners of the streets, that they may be seen of men. Verily I say unto you, They have their reward. But thou, when thou prayest, enter into thy closet, and when thou hast shut thy door, pray to thy Father which is in secret; and thy Father which seeth in secret shall reward thee openly." The term *hesychia* and *hesychazu* appear as early as the fourth century in the writings of Saint John Chrysostom and the Cappadocians.

13. The story of the desert fathers is told in many places, but among them are Waddell 1936; Brown 1988; and Burton-Christie 1993, a study of the use of scripture in prayer. The development of the apophatic tradition is described in Turner 1995. One of the compelling aspects of Turner's work is that he focuses his analysis not on the mystical experience, which modern readers often associate with meditation-like practice, but on the epistemological structure of the search for God. He treats the apophatic tradition as an answer to the question Augustine poses early in the *Confessions:* How can we be said to be searching for something if we do not know what we are searching for?

14. Pennington 1980 provides a rich history and theology of centering prayer, in clear, inviting prose.

15. Johnston 1973:52–53.

16. Johnston 1973:54–55, 56. The diminution of the role of centering prayer is often attributed to the suppression of the monasteries. The tradition remained more alive in the Eastern church. See Pennington 1980:34.

17. These specific words actually come from Merton 1969:90. They do represent the point of his autobiography, and they are among his most achingly beautiful lines.

18. Pennington 1980:57.

19. The Cistercians of Strict Observation, called Trappists, are a contemplative Roman Catholic order.

20. On the other hand, Pennington does think that being in a cloud really cap-

tures something about the experience of this kind of prayer. He once found himself in a thick cloud on a trip to Barcelona, walking up to the Abbey of Montserrat, perched on a granite mass above the city. He could see virtually nothing, and he was both drawn into the inwardness that the cool isolation invited and afraid that if he did so, somehow the reality beyond the cloud would vanish and he would be lost.

21. Pennington 1980:63, 62.

22. The teaching site associated with Thomas Keating and with centering prayer, which provides more information about how to use and respond to the practice, is http://www.contemplativeoutreach.org.

23. Pennington 1980:27.

24. Johnston 1973:52, 55.

25. *Antony and the Desert Fathers: Extreme Faith in the Early Church;* another example is *Pray Give Go Do: Extreme Faith in an Awesome God.*

26. Newberg, D'Aquili, and Rause 2001; Benson 1975; Newberg and Waldman 2009. Recent scientific reviews describing these effects include Walton, Schneider, and Nidich 2004; Arthur, Patterson, and Stone 2006; Cahn and Polich 2006; Walton et al. 2002; Luskin 2004; and Smith 2005. See also Luhrmann 1989. One of the leading researchers in the field is Richard Davidson: see, for example, Lutz et al. 2009 and Davidson et al. 2003. Austin 1999 is a remarkably wide-ranging book on these matters; shorter but more accessible is Albright and Ashbrook 2001. As "mindfulness," this practice is increasingly pursued as a treatment for depression and schizophrenia.

27. Teresa 1960:75. I love this description of Teresa: "Who that cares much to know the history of man, and how that mysterious mixture behaves under the varying experiments of time, has not dwelt, at least briefly, on the life of Saint Theresa, has not smiled with some gentleness at the thought of the little girl walking forth one morning hand-in-hand with her still smaller brother, to go and seek martyrdom in the country of the Moors? Out they toddled from rural Avila, wide-eyed and helpless-looking as two fawns, but with human hearts, already beating to a national idea; until domestic reality met them in the shape of uncles, and turned them back from their great resolve. That child-pilgrimage was a fit beginning. Theresa's passionate, ideal nature demanded an epic life; what were many-volumed romances of chivalry and the social conquests of a brilliant girl to her? Her flame quickly burned up that light fuel; and, fed from within, soared after some illimitable satisfaction, some object which would never justify weariness, which would reconcile self-despair with the rapturous consciousness of life beyond self." So begins George Eliot's *Middlemarch.*

28. Teresa 1960:54–55, 111, 148.

29. Christian Research Services, http://www.christianresearchservice.com/Christian Yoga.html.

30. Ratzinger 1989. David Brooks once argued in a *New York Times* column

(May 13, 2008) that the risk Christians face from modernity is not so much atheism but the demise of the centrality of the Bible, because once one realizes that powerful spiritual experience can be generated by more than one faith, the texts of that faith seem like culture, not like immortal truths. The future pope seemed to agree with this observation.

31. The Dionysian text that deals most with the kataphatic is *On the Divine Names,* but this phrase comes from the *Mystical Theology.*

32. Burton-Christie 1993:109, Athanasius, *Life of St. Anthony* (Schaff and Wace, 1892:196).

33. 1 Corinthians 3:10; Carruthers 1998; Carruthers and Ziolkowski 2002.

34. Except for the things he has forgotten, Augustine adds. See Carruthers 1998:134, 135, 29, and Karnes 2011.

35. This visionary culture is discussed thoughtfully in Newman 2005.

36. Hood 1986; see also Didi-Huberman 1995.

37. See Luhrmann 1986. The story of early modern magic is best told by the historians who brought it to light, Francis Yates and D. P. Walker, though many others have since joined their fold. Yates 1972 describes a kind of apogee to the vision of magico-spiritual transformation. Fanger 1998 provides a fascinating selection of more recently translated and edited medieval sources.

38. Loyola 1992a:31. *The Spiritual Exercises of Ignatius Loyola* can be found in many translations, by Joseph Tetlow, by George Ganss, and by Thomas Corbishley, all Jesuits. Modern companions to the Ignatian exercises include Barry 1991 and Silf 1998.

39. Dyrness 2004 offers a thoughtful exploration of the way Protestant and Catholic theology and practice encourage different uses of the visual imagination.

40. For example, the website Evangelicals on the Ignatian Road (http://evangelicals ontheignatianroad.blogspot.com); Evangelicals on the Ignatian Way (http://lci.typepad.com/evangelicalsignatianway); and Wakefield 2006.

41. Loyola 1992a, sections 111–114.

42. This exercise was written by Sister Lorita Moffat, RSM staffperson at the Mercy Center near San Francisco, where many people are led through the exercises in their longer, nine-month form.

43. Loyola 1963, section 54.

44. This is one of Lacan's more striking metaphors. The *points de caption* was a phrase he used to account for the way that signifiers and what they signified had a relationship that did not allow slippage beyond a certain point in those who were not psychotic, despite the volatility of human emotion. This anchoring is what Ignatius thought one should achieve with the Examen.

45. Linguistic anthropologists argue that this layering strategy guarantees the authenticity of the person praying, for God is heard to speak through that individual as recognizably both God and individual. Shoaps 2002; Silverstein and Urban 1996.

46. Loyola 1992b, sections 65–70.

47. Loyola 1992b, sections 124 and 125.
48. There is little quantitative evidence for this claim, but Catholicism certainly stands out for its tradition of examining and validating visions.
49. One of the best articles is Noll 1985.
50. Reichel-Dolmatoff 1975: 79, quoted in Noll 1985: 448. In this case, the shaman is taking hallucinogens, but the principle of training the attention remains the same. Crocker 1985 describes the shamanic system of the Bororo.
51. Dalai Lama, 2002: 111.
52. The quotations come from Beyer 1978:70, 71. This remarkable book describes the stages of skill development, details of visualizations, and specific chants and gestures, and places them within their social context (to some extent). It is a rare combination of ethnographic fieldwork and the scholarship required to read the ancient texts.
53. The quotations are taken from Wolfson 1994:90, 280. He engages the debate about how and whether God can be visualized at some length.
54. Garb 2009 and Garb 2011 are perhaps the greatest scholarly studies of contemporary kabbalah and its relation to traditional kabbalah. You see in some of these practices another characteristic found in many other kataphatic forms (but not in Ignatian prayer): paradox. Sensory invitations to do what is not doable can powerfully shift attention away from the everyday.

CHAPTER SEVEN. THE SKILL OF PRAYER

1. Not surprisingly, the enterprise has generated some terrifically interesting memoirs, like Malinowski's *A Diary in the Strict Sense of the Term*, in which the founder of British social anthropology voiced some very inappropriate feelings about the people among whom he was living; and Hortense Powdermaker's *Stranger and Friend*, which talks, among other things, about what it was like to do fieldwork in Hollywood. And there are great novels written by long-suffering spouses, like Elenore Smith Bowen's *Return to Laughter*, and more recent works written by people who are not anthropologists at all but who have been able to grasp the strange intensity of the method, like Norman Rush's *Mating* and Mischa Berlinski's splendid *Fieldwork*.
2. This event took place within the University of Chicago Templeton network, which became the setting for the experimental portion of this work. The group pushed me to do the work and gave feedback throughout the process. Both Howard Nusbaum and Ronald Thisted were members of the network.
3. All these conversations were recorded and transcribed. I listened to them all again and corrected the transcripts and coded them. Note that although the sample was representative, it was not a "representative sample." It was a convenience sample, whose members seemed to me to represent the variety of people within the church.

4. Note that these are stated here as questions we asked of the transcript. I asked more open-ended questions in the interviews, although each interview covered every topic. These were the questions for the "focused absorption" section:

Did he/she describe a sense of being absorbed or experiencing "flow" when praying?

Did he/she report that he/she experienced surroundings to change subjectively? ("in my mind I'd go to that place")

Did he/she report that time seemed to change when he/she prayed?

Did he/she describe experience while praying as being a conduit for God? ("I feel like almost like a tube the Holy Spirit is feeding through me")

Did he/she say anything about "switching" while praying?

Did he/she describe learning to gain increased focus in prayer?

Did he/she specifically say that God flowed through them?

These were the questions for the "sensory intensity" section:

Did he/she specifically say that he/she described God with the senses?

Did he/she say that he/she commonly got images in prayer?

Did he/she say that he/she commonly got sensations/thoughts in prayer?

Did he/she specifically say something about the vividness of those experiences? (e.g., "it's almost like a PowerPoint presentation")

Did he/she describe unusually intense visions or voices—experienced "with the ears" or "outside the head" or "in front of one with one's eyes"—that he/she experienced in their minds but felt were almost external?

Did he/she report smells from something not materially present?

Did he/she report having a physical sensation of being touched by God? (e.g., saying yes when asked, "Did you feel it on your skin?")

Did he/she report auditory or visual experience of something not materially present between sleep and awareness? (hypnagogic or hypnapompic sensory phenomena)

Did he/she report auditory or visual experience of something not materially present while fully awake?

Did he/she spontaneously remark that he/she "loves the Holy Spirit side of God" or similar formulation?

These were the questions about the "God-as-person" section:

Did he/she say that he/she prayed to God about things that might seem trivial to other people, like getting a haircut?

Did he/she say that he/she spoke freely to God throughout the day?

Did he/she say that he/she would describe God as his/her best friend or like an imaginary friend (except real)?

Did he/she say that he/she ever gets angry with God for personal experiences (for example, not getting into the college of one's choice)?

Did he/she say that he/she had a playful, teasing side to the relationship with God?

Did prayer seem to be experienced as genuinely dialogic?

5. Launay Slade Hallucination Scale: Launay and Slade 1981. The original DES Scale was presented in Bernstein and Putnam 1986; it has since been revised. The Barber White Christmas experiment was presented in Barber and Calverey 1964.

6. The scale is under copyright protection, although about half the items have been previously published. It is available through the University of Minnesota Press and is usually available online. The items listed are abbreviated and published with the permission of the University of Minnesota Press.

7. All the reported relationships were statistically significant and are discussed in more detail in Luhrmann, Nusbaum, and Thisted 2010. Ron Thisted was the other person who helped me; he is a statistician and chair of the Department of Health Studies at the University of Chicago. Ewart Thomas, a psychologist at Stanford, was also immensely helpful at a crucial point.

8. Luhrmann, Nusbaum, and Thisted 2010.

9. This is the Stanford C, developed at Stanford by Ernst Hilgard and others. Herbert Spiegel developed a much faster test that asks the subject to roll their eyes back in their head: the more white showing, the more hypnotizable the subject will be. It is not quite clear this should follow, but the eye-roll does seem to pick up hypnotizability. It is not however perfectly aligned with the Stanford C. See Spiegel and Spiegel 2004 [1978] and Gritzalis, Oster, and Frischholz 2009.

10. Roughly 5 to 7 percent of subjects pass 11 or more of the 12 items of the Stanford C; 17 to 34 percent pass 8 to 10. See Bowers 1993; Bowers 1998; Weitzenhoffer and Hilgard 1959; Weitzenhoffer and Hilgard 1962. The major debate in the hypnosis world is between the neodissociation (or "state") model, which assumes that someone enters into a different kind of awareness, and the sociocognitive trait debate. Interested readers should consult the work of John Kihlstrom, David Spiegel, Steven Lynn, Irving Kirsch, and others. One useful if dated collection is Lynn and Rhue 1991.

11. The correlation coefficients tend to be in the 0.17–0.23 range. See Nadon et al. 1991; and Whalen and Nash 1996. Others have agreed with the conclusion that absorption and hypnosis are related but not identical. John Kihlstrom and his colleagues (among the leaders in the field) conducted a comprehensive empirical analysis of daydreaming, absorption, and hypnotizability and

concluded that "whatever it is that absorption and hypnosis share, relatively little of that variance is also shared with daydreaming activity. A good case can be made, however, for a strong tie between absorption and daydreaming activity of all sorts. Both require intense involvement in imaginative activity and the virtual exclusion of extraneous stimulus. Hypnosis, however, requires the individual to interact with the hypnotist." Hoyt et al. 1989:339.

12. Tellegen and Atkinson 1974:268.

13. Spiegel and Spiegel 1978:118. They argue that hypnosis can be understood as one-third suggestion, one-third dissociation, and one-third absorption.

14. Tellegen 1981.

15. Only a handful of scientists have worked with the scale, but their results are quite consistent. This research on imagery ability can be found in Hilgard 1981; on fantasy proneness, Lynn and Rhue 1986; on daydreaming, Crawford 1982; on experiential involvement, Wild, Kuiken, and Schopflocher 1995; on alteration in attention, Pekala, Wenger, and Levine 1985; on imaginative involvement and its relationship with openness to experience, Glisky and Kihlstrom 1993 and Glitsky et al. 1991; on empathy, Wickramasekera and Szlyk 2003; the psychologists' observations appear in Kremen and Block 2002; on dance, see Bachner-Melman et al. 2005. Absorption may also be associated with responsiveness to complementary medicine: Menzies, Gill, and Bourguignon 2008.

16. McNally et al. 2000; Clancy 2006. The relationship between absorption and dissociation is discussed in Spiegel and Spiegel 2004 [1978]. Most work on dissociation does focus on pathology, but many researchers recognize that there is "normal" dissociation.

17. Waller, Putnam, and Carlson 1996 report the three factors of the Dissociative Experiences Scale and go on to argue that those who experience pathological dissociation respond in predictably different ways to this scale than do those who experience nonpathological dissociation. See also Cardeña, Lynn, and Krippner 2000.

18. Hoyt et al. 1989 looked at the relationship among daydreaming, absorption, and hypnotizability and found that the strongest correlation was between absorption and "positive-constructive" daydreaming.

19. Bloch 2008.

20. Test-retest reliability is quite high; Tellegen reported a thirty-day test-retest of 0.91 and Kihlstrom of 0.85 (Roche and McConkey 1990). In the Spiritual Disciplines Project described below, the test-retest reliability was 0.864 across the one-month interval.

21. Absorption seems more like what some psychologists call self-hypnosis than hypnosis. *Self-hypnosis* is the name given to the practice of intentionally allowing yourself to become absorbed in your imagination. Research does suggest that this capacity can be trained: that people are able to become more rapidly and deeply engaged with practice and, indeed, that their imag-

ery becomes more powerful and seemingly sharper. To some extent, their hypnotizability also increases. The most extensive research was done at the University of Chicago, where Erika Fromm and Stephen Katz (1990) had volunteers spend an hour a day in a room at the university library in self-directed imaginative daydreaming. At the end of the month, they reported more imagery, more vivid imagery, and deeper focus and involvement. It is said that the library's refusal to give out keys dates from this period, after one of the subjects forgot to lock up and left the library open overnight.

22. Foster 1998 [1978]:62.

23. The screening was primarily designed to pull out people who might meet criteria for a psychotic disorder or who would be uncomfortable with a spiritual discipline focused on Jesus. We did not use in every analysis all of those whom we invited to participate. A few were spiritual directors whom we chose not to randomly assign and whom we did not use in the analysis of the training. We also had a subject who received the discipline of study, then took up a new kataphatic discipline almost immediately; in effect, this person did not do the experiment. The data from this subject was not used in evaluating the training effects. However, the data from all subjects was used in assessing the relationship between measures taken only at the beginning of the month—for example, the relationship between absorption and vivid mental imagery.

24. These were the Tellegen Absorption Scale (Tellegen and Atkinson 1974); the Daily Spiritual Experiences Scale (Underwood and Teresi 2002); the Spiritual Well Being Scale (Paloutzian and Ellison 1982; see Bufford, Paloutzian, and Ellison 1991); the Hearing Voices Scale (Posey and Losch 1983); the Empathy Scale (Davis 1980, Davis 1983); the UCLA Loneliness Scale (Russell, Peplau, and Ferguson 1978); the Satisfaction with Life Scale (Diener et al. 1985); the Perceived Stress Scale (Cohen, Kamarck, and Mermelstein 1983); and the Berkeley Emotional Expressivity Scale (Gross and John 1997); and on their return, the Dissociative Experiences Scale (Bernstein and Putnam 1986, but with updated response structure); the O-Life (Claridge 1997); and the Kessler Ten-Item Scale (Kessler et al. 2002).

25. These were the Vividness of Visual Imagery Questionnaire (Marks 1973; see discussion in McKelvie 1995); the Dean and Morris Shapes Test (Dean and Morris 2003); the Shapiro Attentional Blink (Shapiro, Raymond, and Arnell 1994; we paid attention only to the first part of the test); and the fade-in fade-out that we constructed ourselves, loosely based on Perky 1910.

26. This was to prevent misinterpretation—not because we believe that someone who has been psychiatrically hospitalized is always ill or that their spiritual experiences are inherently pathological.

27. None of the subjects had ever met me before and so did not have a prior association with my voice, and they did not meet me during the experiment.

28. According to their iPod play counts, they did listen. The mean was 26, the

median 24 times. Only fifteen of them listened fewer than 10 times, by the play count, and the play count tends to underestimate: to get counted; the listener has to allow the track to run to the very end, which not everyone does.

29. Three subjects dropped out.

30. The first of these was published by Finke 1989; the second is an experiment based on Bower 1970b. See also Bower 1970a.

31. The details are reported in Luhrmann, Nusbaum, and Thisted, forthcoming; and in Morgain and Luhrmann, forthcoming.

32. Subjects made comments that suggested as much. For example, subject 108, who had the kataphatic condition, remarked, "I think I was like doing an exercise that we did on the computer, and yeah, I felt like the images came faster, or I don't know, like I was able to manipulate them better." Subject 124, also in the kataphatic condition, said, "Yes, I feel like I got better at doing [mental images] in the month . . . I actually even noticed it just doing the exercises. I felt like they were a lot easier to just like create and manipulate in my head maybe than before." When subject 110, who had centering prayer, was asked whether her mental images were sharper or different in any way, she said, "Well, when I was taking the testing, they definitely were. And I was quicker." Subjects who had the study condition were much less likely to say yes when asked whether their mental imagery had gotten sharper or changed in some way. (Note: When quantitatively analyzing those in the apophatic condition, we compared them only to subjects in the second half of the group.)

33. MacLean et al. 2010.

34. This is what we called the Hearing Voices Scale, published in 1983 by Posey and Losch.

35. The pattern seems not to hold for apophatic subjects, although with so few of them—fifteen—it is hard to feel confident one way or the other.

36. In the one study (Horwood et al. 2010), more subjects asserted that they had a hallucination than were judged to have had one by the interviewers after questioning. We were motivated by a similar caution, and we explored people's initial answers in similar ways, asking them whether they had heard the voice with their ears, whether they had turned to see who had spoken, and so forth.

37. The study group did report more fleeting visual experiences than the kataphatic group. This may have been because those experiences were related to stress, and the kataphatic reported less stress over the month; or it may have been that the fleeting visual hallucinations were the way in which the study group responded to the suggestion that these experiences were common, while the kataphatic group responded to the suggestion with more fleshed-out and meaningful experiences.

38. Details in Morgain and Luhrmann, forthcoming.

39. The numbers of subjects are small, so the relationships are not always statistically significant, but the raw data suggests this pattern. Judging from the mean for responses to direct questions (measured "no=0," "maybe=1," or "yes=2"), no centering prayer or study subjects reported feeling the presence of God; the mean for the kataphatic was 0.6; did your spirituality change post-interview: centering 0.83; study 0.78; kataphatic 1.4; did your sense of God change: centering 0.50, study 0.60, kataphatic 1.0; did you feel more playful with God: centering 0.33, study 0.10, kataphatic 0.40; did you experience God more as a person: centering 0.00, study 0.00, kataphatic 1.80; the change in stress, measured by before-and-after use of the Perceived Stress Scale (a positive number indicates more stress): centering -3.33, study, 3.00, kataphatic -0.5000.

40. One of the clearest explanations is published in an unlikely place. It is the standard view but expressed remarkably cleanly: Chiu 1989.

41. Johnson and Raye 1981. See also Johnson, Hashtroudi, and Lindsay 1993; Mitchell and Johnson 2009.

42. This is reported in Bentall 2003: 365; he quotes from Barry Miles, *Paul McCartney: Many Years from Now.*

43. Slade and Bentall 1988; Bentall 1990 presented the first version of this reinterpretation of the reality monitoring model. Most of the work since is summarized and discussed in Bentall 2003 and Aleman and Laroi 2008.

44. See Grimby 1993; Bourguignon 1976; Al-Issa 1977 and 1995; Johns et al. 2002; see also Suhail and Cochrane 2002; Bauer et al. 2010; Kent and Wahass 1996; Okulate and Jones 2003. Luhrmann 2011 discusses this point more broadly.

45. Siegel 1984, 267. I deliberately did not include in my reanalysis of his data the two cases of UFO abductions he reports.

46. James 1935 [1902]:29.

47. James 1935 [1902]:37. Moreover, he did not think that the science would explode faith—he thought it would make faith more sure. "Religious melancholy, whatever pecularities it may have qua religious, is at any rate melancholy. Religious happiness is happiness. Religious trance is trance. And the moment we renounce the absurd notion that a thing is exploded as soon as it is classed with others, or its origin shown . . . who does not see that we are likely to ascertain the distinctive significance of religious melancholy and happiness, or of religious trances, far better by comparing them as conscientiously as we can to other varieties of melancholy, happiness and trance."

48. Taves 2009b has a most useful discussion of religious experience. She builds on the well-known Proudfoot 1985. Although each emphasizes an opposing point, together they make a powerful argument for the interaction of biological, psychological, and cultural factors in spiritual phenomena.

49. Happold 1990 [1963]:133–34.

50. Happold 1990 [1963]:130.

51. James 1935 [1902]:401.
52. Shweder 1991 and Shweder 2003 make this argument eloquently.

CHAPTER EIGHT. BUT ARE THEY CRAZY?

1. This is a paraphrase of the diagnostic criteria given for schizophrenia in the *DSM-IV.*
2. It is true that one of the theories about schizophrenia is that the heard voices are in fact self-generated self-critical voices that are in effect practiced self-reproaches, much like the harsh self-criticism of obsessive compulsive disorder (e.g., Laroi, Van der Linden, and Marczewski 2004). However, this is quite a different notion of "practice" than the practice of prayer. I discuss psychosis and the homeless in Luhrmann 2010, from which some of these paragraphs are drawn.
3. Willard 1999:20–23, 89.
4. People with schizophrenia may have a diminished "theory of mind," meaning that they are less able to infer what someone else is thinking. See Brune 2005.
5. Jon Krakauer's *Under the Banner of Heaven* describes a Mormon man who heard God tell him to kill his sister-in-law. His unquestioning acceptance of the command should have tipped off his brother that he was psychotic.
6. Dein and Littlewood 2007:219-20.
7. Dein and Littlewood 2007:224.
8. Admittedly, people who have sensory overrides could be diagnosed with "Psychosis, no other symptoms," a wastebasket diagnosis for people who do not fit in other categories, but that is a foolish mistake in the diagnostic nosology.
9. This is the Kessler Ten (Kessler et al. 2002). In our subject pool, 129 people filled out the Kessler and Tellegen absorption scales: the correlation was negative (-0.014) and startlingly nonsignificant (p=0.879). The same number answered the question "Have you ever heard an audible voice when you were alone, or a voice that no one else present could hear, like someone calling your name?" The correlation between their answer and the Kessler scale was r(129)=0.045, with a nonsignificant p=0.624.
10. The psychosis questions were taken from the PLIKS, a questionnaire that assesses psychoticlike symptoms in a manner similar to the SCID, the Structured Clinical Interview for DSM Disorders (Harrison et al. 2004; reported in Horwood et al. 2008).
11. The argument is that there is no radical break between those who can be diagnosed with psychosis and the general population (Johns and van Os 2001; see also Luhrmann 2011). This work supports that conclusion: at the same time, these psychiatrists might assume that the phenomena associated

with absorption are an example of the psychotic continuum. I believe that these absorption-related phenomena are an expression of a different psychological process.

12. Davis, Griffin, and Vice 2001 compared evangelical and psychotic experiences of hearing voices and noted that the evangelical experience was far more positive.

13. One of the best accounts of this era is Turner 1974.

14. Sidgwick et al. 1894:33–35.

15. Sidgwick et al. 1894:404.

16. Sidgwick et al. 1894:63.

17. Sidgwick et al. 1894:74, 258

18. West 1948.

19. In addition to Turner 1974, Owen 1990 contains a vivid account of the period.

20. Tien 1991. These numbers are more striking because the NIH threw out sleep-related hallucinations. Many of the experiences reported in the Sidgwick study occurred immediately after awakening or while the subject was in bed: 38 percent of the visual hallucinations, 34 percent of the auditory hallucinations, and 44 percent of the tactile ones. If you do not count those, the Sidgwick rate falls from 10 percent to 7 percent overall. On the other hand, the NIMH rates include distressing hallucinations associated with psychotic illness, which the Sidgwick group threw out. Adjusting for these differences, the rates are not statistically different.

21. It is quite common to have hallucination-like experiences between sleep and awareness. These are called *hypnagogic* if they take place before falling asleep and *hypnapompic* if they occur before waking up. (My experience of seeing the druids was a hypnapompic experience.) The sleep researcher Maurice Ohayon and his team asked nearly five thousand people in the United Kingdom a range of questions about sleep behavior, in the midst of which he tucked in questions about unusual experiences between sleep and awareness. They asked, "Have you ever experienced:

The realistic feeling that someone or something is present in the room?
A vivid experience of being caught in a fire?
A vivid experience that you are about to be attacked?
A vivid experience that you are flying through the air?
The feeling that you will soon fall or are falling into an abyss?
The feeling that shadows or objects are moving and distorting?
Do you experience other types of vivid perceptions?

Thirty-seven percent of his subjects said that they experienced at least one of these phenomena *twice a week for a year* (Ohayon et al. 1996).

22. These are questions 7, 8, 10, 12, 13, and 14 of the series.

23. One was a class on prayer; another a required social science class; the third

and fourth a class on culture and mental illness; the fifth a class on hauntings, visions, and prophecy. The required class, in autumn 2006, was an introduction to issues about the impact of culture on mind; it had fifty-six undergraduates, with a smattering of graduate students. Fifty-four percent of the students said yes to at least one of the six items; 87 percent said yes to at least one item on the entire scale, which included experiences between sleep and awareness. The class on prayer in 2006 had thirty-one students. Seventy-seven percent said yes to one of the six awake-hallucination questions and 96 percent to some item on the scale. There were twenty-eight students in the class on culture and mental illness, in spring 2009; 60 percent said yes to one of the six awake-hallucination questions, and 96 percent said yes to something on the scale. There were thirty-four students in the same class taught in 2010: 94 percent said yes to one of the questions, and 88 percent yes to one of the six. There were thirty-two students in the hauntings, vision, and prophecy class in 2010: 94 percent said yes to one of the questions, and 82 percent yes to one of the six. It is quite possible that not all of these reported experiences were really hallucinations, but all in all, this work suggests that at baseline, at least 10 to 15 percent of the population, and perhaps many more than that, have had a sensory perception of something that is not materially present.

24. Gottesman 1991 develops the claim that schizophrenia is a recent illness in human history; certainly Midelfort 2000, in its effort to locate psychosis in early modern German history, came up with surprisingly few instances, although as he points out, psychosis slips through the historical record. The most authoritative account of psychiatric illness is typically presented in Kaplan and Sadock's *Comprehensive Textbook of Psychiatry,* which is where I would direct readers interested in schizophrenia (Sadock, Sadock, and Ruiz 2009). A shorter and more contemporary argument is Freedman 2010.

25. Glicksohn and Barrett 2003.

26. Augustine 2001 [1963]: 8.10.177; 8.12.29.

27. Acts 9:3–4.

28. Fox 1976 [1694]:82.

29. Harris 1999:69.

30. Christian 1998:109. The anthropologist William Christian discovered the delight people took in visions in the rural Spanish valley in which he did his ethnography, and he has since done the most complete study we have to date on the nature and frequency (to the extent which this can be judged by the historical record) of these unusual experiences. His work makes two compelling points: first, that visions and other sensory experiences are common and a source of intense satisfaction; and second, that what we know about visions and their visionaries is strictly controlled by prevailing notions about who can be believed and what can be seen and heard (1998:107). He also observes that in the Spanish area where he first worked, apparitions and

shrines gravitated to village boundaries, as if to mark off the territory (1989 [1972]:73).

31. See, for example, the Czech documentary *Ivetka and the Mountain* (2008).

32. Zimdars-Swartz 1991:17–18. When a similar apparition was prophesied for a shrine in Knock, Ireland, it caused a significant increase in hospital cases of solar retinopathy. See Pamela Duncan, "Hospital Sees Increase in Eye Condition After Knock 'Visions,'" *Irish Times,* December 2, 2009.

33. Seeingtherebbe.wordpress.com. The account has been edited slightly for length and clarity. This report appears also in Chabad-Lubavitch Network 2007:124–25. The title of the account, "Between the Refrigerator and the Sink," conveys the domestic nature of the apparition. The anthropologist Yorum Bilu and his student Michal Kraval-Tovi (e.g., Kraval-Tovi 2009, Kraval-Tovi and Bilu 2008) have begun to chronicle the ways in which the community has made the absent rebbe present, through replicating his image in cards, rings, and magazines, on many surfaces—traditionally, a most un-Hasidic style of veneration—and by proselytizing with remarkable outreach, even to Gentiles and even in Nepal. The process is eerily like explosion of proselytizing activity in the aftermath of failed prophecy described in Festinger, Riecken, and Schachter 2008 [1956].

34. Newman 2005.

35. This story is told well in Acocella 2007; Smith 2007; and Sackville-West 1936. See also Barstow 1985 and Wheeler and Wood 1996.

36. Taves 2009a.

37. Bentall 2003:511; see also Smith 2007.

38. Claridge 1997.

39. Newport 2005.

40. The first was *Michelle Remembers,* which was published in 1980—it may actually have been responsible for the Satanic Ritual Abuse panic. It recounts the six hundred hours of therapy in which a Catholic psychiatrist, Lawrence Pazder, used hypnosis to enable his Catholic patient, Michelle Smith, to recover memories of horrific abuse at the hands of a Satanic cult. She had been tortured, raped, locked in cages, and rubbed with the blood of murdered babies in rituals that summoned the devil and involved the timely intervention of Jesus, Mary, and the Archangel Michael, who supernaturally removed the many scars she had received. Another influential book is Francis MacNutt's *Deliverance from Evil Spirits.*

41. Kraft 1992:214.

42. Cunningham 1984:16.

43. Cunningham 1984:86.

44. This sounds like a classic account of an incubus: an evil spirit that seeks to have sex with a female human. The phenomenological experience, probably best described as sleep paralysis, has been reported for centuries.

CHAPTER NINE. DARKNESS

1. Job 30:20; Ecclesiastes 1:14.
2. One of the classic books discussing these responses is Bowker 1970.
3. *Cognitive dissonance* is the name given to the experience of having two conflicting mental commitments or beliefs, such as knowing that smoking is bad for you and knowing that you smoke by choice. The most compelling example in the literature, Festinger, Riecken, and Schnatcher 2008 [1956], is an account of a group that believed that the world would end on a specific day: and what they did when the day passed without incident. Alison Lurie retells the story with verve in *Imaginary Friends.*
4. The ethnography best known for addressing the problem of logical contradiction is Evans-Pritchard 1937 and its many interlocutors. The ethnography really explains why the Azande don't notice that magic does not work. He lists twenty-two reasons. In Luhrmann 1989, I take this problem to modern London and explain the way people's interpretations drift so that they do not notice contradictions that seem glaring to others.
5. The wish not to tempt fate is not restricted to mainstream Christian but in fact can be demonstrated in people of all persuasions. See Risen and Gilovich 2008.
6. For example; in "Moved by compassion, Jesus touched their eyes. Immediately they regained their sight and followed him" (Matthew 20:34); and "So his fame spread throughout all Syria, and they brought to him all the sick, those who were afflicted with various diseases and pains, demoniacs, epileptics and paralytics, and he cured them. And great crowds followed him from Galilee, the Decapolis, Jerusalem, Judea and from the Jordan." (Matthew 4:24–25).
7. John 20:29.
8. In Bellah et al. 1996, the authors see individual choice in religious belief and practice as profoundly American, and indeed there is a great deal of evidence to suggest that Americans pick and choose when it comes to religion, as Wolfe 2003; Wuthnow 1998; and the Pew Research Center 2008 suggest. At the same time, this sense of individuality does not spring out fully formed. Joel Robbins makes this point in a perceptive review of Courtney Bender's *The New Metaphysicals* (Robbins 2010). These practitioners go to a great deal of work, he points out, to be unique.
9. Durkheim 1915.
10. Krista heard this voice—but it was inside her head, not-me but not-outside. "It was very, very vivid, and very, very clear. I wish I could describe it better: but it was as if it came across my brain, for want of a better description, and it stopped me, because it wasn't where I was headed."
11. John 20:19.
12. Hill 2001:133.
13. Feinberg 2005:107.

14. "The Lord said to Moses, 'Gather the people together and I will give them water'" (Numbers 21:16); "Ho, everyone who thirsts, come to the waters" (Isaiah 55:1).
15. John 4:14.
16. Job 31:6, 38:4, 38:18.
17. Merton 1963.
18. Yancey 1988:193, 263.
19. There is a rich theological discussion in what is called "Kingdom" theology, initially presented by Fuller's George Eldon Ladd, or the "now/not yet." See also Willard 1998.
20. *American Psychologist* published a series of meta-analyses in 2003: by Powell, Shahabi and Thoresen; Seeman, Dubin, and Seeman; and Miller and Thoresen.
21. This work is reported in a series of scientific articles: Woods et al. 1999; Banthia et al. 2007; Bradshaw, Ellison, and Flannelly 2008; Campbell, Yoon, and Johnstone 2010; Reiner et al. 2010; Horton et al. 2010; Homan and Boyatzis 2010. The sociologist Christopher Ellison has been involved in a variety of these studies and continues to work on the relationship between religion and health.
22. Inzlicht and Tullett 2010; see also Pargament 1997: 290; Hood et al. 1996; and Paloutzian and Park 2005.
23. Micklethwait and Wooldridge 2009:147; Pew Research Center 2006a. Forty-three percent of white Protestant evangelicals report being very happy; only 33 percent of white mainstream Protestants do. Admittedly, evangelicals sometimes feel that they have a responsibility to report being happy.
24. Copyright Lynn G. Underwood. Permission to use and reproduce the scale at www.dsescale.org. Two additional items are not listed here.
25. Underwood 2006; Underwood 2011; and Underwood and Teresi 2002.
26. The spiritual questionnaire is the Daily Spiritual Experiences (DSE) Questionnaire (Underwood and Teresi 2002); the UCLA Loneliness Scale (Russell, Peplau, and Ferguson 1978); the Perceived Stress Scale (Cohen, Kamarck, and Mermelstein 1983); and the Satisfaction with Life Scale (Diener et al. 1985). For the first fourteen DSE questions in the first session: UCLA loneliness $r(111)=-0.216$, $p=0.023$; Stress $r(111)=-0.268$, $p=0.004$; Diener $r(111)=0.350$, $p<.001$; for "I feel God's love, directly," UCLA loneliness $r(111)=-0.313$, $p=0.001$; Stress $-r(111)=-0.293$, $p<.001$; Diener $r(111)=0.422$, $p<.001$.
27. On this point, in addition to the work already discussed in this book, one might consult the following scientific articles: Granqvist, Mikulincer, and Shaver 2010; Cassibba et al. 2008; Kirkpatrick and Shaver 1990; Rowatt and Kirkpatrick 2002; Ross 2007; Birgegard and Granqvist 2004. Some of this material is summarized and discussed from a more theological perspective in Davis and Badenoch 2009.
28. John 6:68.

29. Lear 2003. The argument draws its inspiration from a famous article by Hans Loewald.
30. Lester 2005.
31. Hebrews 11:1.

CHAPTER TEN. BRIDGING THE GAP

1. See for a discussion Zamova and Faris 1995.; Maria Balfer first drew my attention to the term *magical realism* as a way to describe the current spiritual experience.
2. As Peter Berger put it, "subjectively, the man in the street tends to be uncertain about religious matters. Objectively the man in the street is confronted with a wide variety of religious and other reality-defining agencies that compete for his allegiance or at least attention, and none of which is in a position to coerce him into allegiance." Berger 1967:127.
3. Pew Research Center 2006b makes this clear, as does Jenkins 2002; see also Miller and Yamamori 2007. The basic claim has been supported by many sources.
4. Larson 1997 usefully discusses the differences between the pre- and post-Darwinian interpretations of evolution by Christians.
5. Roger Finke and Rodney Stark give the numbers as 17 percent and 32 percent respectively (2006: 121–22). These numbers are conservative. Some historians place the estimate far higher, basing their figures on the sheer number of immigrants themselves. As Finke and Stark point out, many of those immigrants were not, in fact, Catholic—many of the incoming Irish were Protestant. By any measure, however, by the century's end no American could ignore the presence of this very different Christianity.
6. Frazer 2002 [1922]:827.
7. The great folklorist Andrew Laing, for example, went to some lengths to demonstrate that Zoroastrianism was an ancient monotheism, in order to argue that monotheism did not, in fact, evolve from magic in the neat sequence Frazer and others outlined.
8. The seventeenth-century British philosopher Thomas Hobbes was arguably the first to suggest that Moses had not written the majority of the Pentateuch, basing his inference on inconsistent facts and phrases (like "to this day") that seemed inconsistent with a text supposedly written as an eyewitness account. Hobbes was followed by other scholars—Isaac de La Peyrère, Spinoza—but the scholarly evidence that built a definitive alternative to Mosaic authorship came out of nineteenth-century Germany and from the meticulous linguistic, textual, and historical analysis that characterized scholars willing to argue from evidence, not from tradition. For a general account of the construction of the Hebrew Bible, see Friedman 1987.
9. Armstrong 2007 gives a good account.

10. Armstrong 2007:198, 199.
11. Taves 1999:345.
12. These are quite fascinating and are still available (Torrey, Dixon, et al. 2003 [1917]). They were originally issued as a four-volume edition from the Bible Institute of Los Angles in 1917.
13. Theologians at the famous conservative Presbyterian seminary at Princeton codified a five-point declaration of essential doctrine: (1) the absolute accuracy and divine inspiration of scripture; (2) the virgin birth of Christ; (3) salvation only through Christ's sacrifice; (4) bodily resurrection; (5) the authenticity of biblical miracles.
14. Benjamin Warfield quoted in Dayton 1987:25.
15. Acts 2:1–4. Pentecost marks fifty days after the ascension of Jesus into heaven. The date is also related to the Jewish harvest festival of Shavuot, which commemorates God's giving of the Commandments to Moses fifty days after the Exodus from Egypt.
16. At least, tongues appear to have been rare until the early twentieth century. See Samarin 1972.
17. See Martin Marty's foreword to Dayton 1987:10.
18. See the discussions in Marsden 1987 and Marsden 2006.
19. *New York Times,* July 21, 1925, p. 1, quoted in Larson 1997:189–90.
20. Marsden 1987:7.
21. See Wacker 2001, chapter 13.
22. Marsden 1987:13.
23. Marsden 1987:62.
24. That is the King James. In the New Standard Revised, it is, "Come out from them, and be separate from them."
25. Cited from letter in Marsden 1987:66.
26. The early Fuller faculty took their intellectual project to be to build a theological structure in which political and social action could be conceptualized as a spiritually worthy goal. In one of the best efforts, Carl Henry's *An Uneasy Conscience,* this became the defining impulse of what made Fuller different: "The new evangelicalism embraces the full orthodoxy of fundamentalism in doctrine but manifests a social consciousness and responsibility which was strikingly absent from fundamentalism." See Marsden 1987:146.
27. "Statement of Faith of Fuller," *Bulletin of Fuller Theological Seminary,* 1950–51, cited in Marsden 1987:113. The usual scriptural reference from which this commitment is inferred is 2 Timothy 3:16, "All scripture is inspired by God."
28. By 1958, Billy Graham was asked to join the board of trustees as a symbol of the new evangelism. Graham was already famous and already under attack by strict fundamentalists. He did not see the Bible as a reliable source of scientific knowledge, and he was eager to shed the image of the anti-intellectualism associated with fundamentalism. "The one badge of Chris-

tian discipleship," he asserted in his new journal, *Christianity Today,* "is not orthodoxy, but love." Marsden 1987:158–67, quotation at 165.

29. Marsden 1987:305.

30. By contrast, only 3 percent said that they did so to be part of a community.

31. Again, this is supported by Pew Research Center 2006b, which found that 23 percent of all Americans either attended a Pentecostal church; called themselves Pentecostal; called themselves charismatic; or spoke in tongues at least several times a year. Even if one casts doubt on these specific figures, the *Newsweek* polls about religious experience and the reason for church membership, and the popularity of books like *The Purpose Driven Life,* suggest that many, many Christians seek to experience God in personal relationship.

32. "Trends in Large U.S. Church Membership from 1960," http://demographia .com/db-religlarge.htm. The data were calculated from *World Almanac* and the *Yearbook of American Churches.* Rates are per 1,000 U.S. population.

33. There is a hint of a suggestion that people may be able to experience more unusual experiences in recent years. One set of researchers has found that the mean score of the Stanford Hypnotic Susceptibility Scale is increasing in the population (Benham, Smith, and Nash 2002); another group has found that the external locus of control—the sense that circumstances, rather than onself, control one's destiny in various ways—is also increasing in the population (Twenge, Zhang, and Im 2004). The external locus of control is associated with seeing patterns in unpatterned images (Whitson and Galinksy 2008). I have found that an external locus of control, measured with the common scale, is associated in my undergraduates with reports of unusual experience.

34. He is also quoting from Paul's letter to the Corinthians in this context: "We are fools for the sake of Christ" (1 Corinthians 3:10).

35. In context:

I was in my prayer group, in a small group, and I remember just sitting there quietly. I heard this little voice, not out loud . . . I knew it was God. I remember telling people the story. But I figured out very quickly that you didn't talk about this.

I was in high school. A pastor—he wasn't charismatic—came over to our house. We had a small service, and the pastor was praying for me, and I just started praying in tongues. It was kind of weird. My sisters were a little spooked. At the time it never struck me how weird I may have been looking to my family.

I feel like every day I talk to God. It's not like talking to my husband, when I get a response right back. Yet I certainly have had moments in my life when I pretty much tell God, "Talk to me now." And he's responded. Absolutely. [Then she hesitated and looked aside.] I know it's true, but it sounds just off the wall.

36. Springer and Wimber 1988:xiv.
37. Springer and Wimber 1988:xviii.
38. Wimber 1985:95–96.
39. I heard many evangelical Christians comment enviously about the strength of belief in the supernatural in Africa and in other non-Western settings. They repeatedly said that there was less skepticism and more faith. "It's just *easier* there," a pastor said one morning.
40. This is something I really believe to be true, but one could generate a serious academic argument about it. Many anthropologists would resist the idea that the supernatural is always interpreted as different from the natural. But cognitive evidence increasingly suggests that people do make such a distinction, and that the work of culture is often an attempt to override the distinction. Astuti 2001 lays out the issues well.
41. Justice 2008:13.
42. Evans-Pritchard 1956:316.
43. J. Barrett 2004:116.
44. Edwards and Sutch 2008.
45. Taylor 2007. This quotation comes from a posting on the Immanent Frame, http://blogs.ssrc.org/tif/. See also Asad 2003.
46. Smith 1998:44. Also, "The English 'belief,' which used to be the verbal sign designating allegiance, loyalty, integrity, love, commitment, trust and entrusting, and the capacity to perceive and to respond to transcendent qualities in oneself and one's environment—in short, faith; the Christian form of God's most momentous gift to each person—had come to be the term by which we designate rather a series of dubious, or at best problematic, propositions" (Smith 1998:69).
47. And perhaps that is why the God of the Vineyard is so much like the Jesus of the Gospel of Mark, which was written in a time of great doubt, likely around A.D. 70, just after the second and final fall of the great temple of Rome. It would have been clear to any observer that the Jewish messiah who had died some forty years ago had failed. The temple was gone, the revolt had been crushed, and the faithful had been decimated. Yet the faith lived on. In the first written account of the messiah, Christ is very human and very supernatural, both absolutely of the everyday world—and utterly different. To be sure, this Christ is less playful than the Christ of *Godspell* or of the Vineyard. Yet he is hyperreal, and he forces you to suspend your disbelief and to use your imagination to choose the world in which you want to live. The author of Mark repeatedly insists that the disciples don't understand Jesus'

parables and that nobody recognizes him: but he has Christ say repeatedly, "Follow me."

Meeks 1984 argues it was the intimacy of the Christian groups themselves that drew adherents—that the early Christian community was populated by urban dwellers who felt alienation over status inconsistency: women and freedmen and lowly traders and craftsmen with wealth.

48. Bell 2011:171, 147.

49. Eliot, *The Lifted Veil*, 80.

50. There are many specific exceptions to this general claim. The Roman elite, for example, had leisure time, and their children played with toys that had nothing to do with production. But it does seem to be the case, from an anthropological perspective, that the encouragement of play, and the content of play, vary across time and space. All children play, but in traditional agricultural communities, parents encourage children's play only to the extent that such play encourages participation in productive activity. In these villages, the lives of adults and children are still structured around traditional patterns of household work. In this agricultural world, children's play is seen by adults to serve little purpose. Mothers do not approve of children making more work for them by getting dirty. And fantasy play in particular is not encouraged. Within many such communities—the Yucatec Maya, for example, or many Melanesian communities—adults feel that people should not speak untruths even in jest, and they do not value fiction, written or oral. These values tend not to support children's pretend play. Work is highly valued, and children's play is tolerated when it mimics work. When children do engage in pretend play, it is never their dominant form of play, and play in all its dimensions takes up relatively little time in the child's life over the age of six. See Gaskins, in press. Gaskins, Haight, and Lancy 2007 call this "culturally curtailed play."

51. Haight and Miller 1992; Haight et al. 1999.

52. *The Golden Ass* would be an example; Don Quixote is early seventeenth century; there is of course chivalric romance literature; but by definition, novels reach a literate audience.

53. See, for example, Hansen 2000 and Turkle 2011.

54. Putnam 2000. This perspective is supported by data reported out of the General Social Survey, which suggests that Americans have fewer intimate friends than before. Between 1985 and 2004, the number of people reporting that there was no one with whom they discussed important matters nearly tripled, and the mean network size decreased from 2.94 people to 2.08. The modal respondent in 1985 had three confidants; the modal respondent in 2004 had none (McPherson, Smith-Lovin, and Brashears 2006). This finding has, however, come under a good deal of criticism. Indeed, the loss of community has been bemoaned in American sociology since the 1930s. Granovetter 1973 (a classic paper, "The Strength of Weak Ties") argues that

when communities change, they reform in other ways that sociologists often miss and offers a way to think about this. Yet the basic question of whether we have become more lonely since the mid-twentieth century is haunting, and the data are strong enough to take the possibility seriously. As John Cacioppo demonstrates, if that is true, it is costly. Loneliness adversely impacts almost everything our body does, from cognition to cardiac function. See Cacioppo and Patrick 2008; Olds and Schwartz 2010. The data about the increase in living alone comes from Wright 1995, which associates an increase in social isolation with an increase in depression, a connection Putnam also makes.

BIBLIOGRAPHIC NOTES

THE RESEARCH PROCESS

I participated primarily in two church settings: a Vineyard in Chicago and another Vineyard on the San Francisco peninsula. Each is one of many Vineyards in its geographical area. I attended each church regularly for two years and irregularly for longer periods. In addition, I attended a variety of local, regional, and national events. The pastors were aware of my presence as a researcher and supported the project and the work. Indeed, both churches were remarkably warm and supportive environments in which to ask questions, and they graciously welcomed me. Most of the remarks reported in this book were made in digitally recorded sessions. The people quoted agreed to be interviewed and to have their interviews used as part of the research. Many agreed to be interviewed more than once. Moreover, they talked to me about what I was observing, answered my sometimes blundering questions, and helped me to sharpen my observations. I also participated in one house group in Chicago for a year. I introduced myself to this group as an anthropologist who was interested in attending to understand the house group experience that is so important for members of these churches. At the California Vineyard, I participated in the Ignatian spiritual exercises over a nine-month period, and then the next year I participated in a prayer group among women who had also completed the exercises. In these groups, I was interested in exploring the nature of the prayer experience itself, and although members of the group knew that I was writing a book about the experience of God, I did not treat remarks made within the group as part of my research data. Prayer groups are intensely personal and intensely private. I have not shared any comments made in the group except with the permission of the woman who told the story, although several did agree to be interviewed outside the prayer group context, and I have treated those interviews and the stories told in them as part of my research data. I interviewed well over fifty people with a digital recorder, and I have well over a hundred hours of interviews and many, many notes, without counting the work I did in the Spiritual Disciplines Project. In most cases I corrected the transcripts myself by listening to the interviews again, and I read them obsessively again and again. All names are pseudonyms, and in some cases, identifying details have been changed.

The experiment I ran at Stanford is described in Chapter Seven.

I received Human Subjects approval for all work from the universities with which I was affiliated.

PREFACE

Evolutionary psychology is one of the most interesting and original approaches to religion in many years. Despite the name, many of its founders have been anthropologists. They developed the approach through applying evolutionary theory to the mind with the credo, as the pioneers John Tooby and Leda Cosmides neatly put it, that the modern skull houses a stone age brain. One of the central ideas of the approach is that some habits of interpretation are so basic to human evolution that they must be understood as preadapted representational domains (complex neuronal structures in the brain), which become activated when an individual encounters a suitable stimulus. Domain-specific innate knowledge is a well-established area of research in developmental psychology. Scholars like Susan Carey, Elizabeth Spelke, and Frank Keil, for example, have demonstrated the presence of apparently innate representational structures concerning number, objects, geometry, living beings, and people. That is, very young children appear to reason with concepts that have emerged with very little actual experience.

The cluster of anthropologists and psychologists associated with evolutionary theory use aspects of this approach to look at the way adults reason about religion in many different cultures, and to infer from those patterns of reasoning the kinds of representational models that could explain the common patterns that serve some adaptive end. For example, in *Religion Explained,* Pascal Boyer argues that the tendency to see intentional agents where there are none is so deeply ingrained, it is as if part of the psyche is exquisitely attuned to seek them out. He calls this an "agency detection module," a specialized explanatory device or inference system that evolved to protect our ancestors from predators and that becomes immediately engaged when we hear ambiguous noises and that automatically suggests explanations for the sounds. In *Faces in the Clouds,* Stewart Guthrie describes the process at the heart of religion as anthropomorphism, an approach that is gaining followers in social psychology like John Cacioppo and Nicholas Epley. Justin Barrett's *Why Would Anyone Believe in God?* provides a brief, clear overview of the arguments; Daniel Dennett's *Breaking the Spell* does likewise, though with a quite different ultimate motive. Scott Atran's *In Gods We Trust* evaluates the different arguments with a fireworks display of erudition. Other notable scholars include Harvey Whitehouse, Ilkka Pyysiainen, Joseph Bulbilia, Dmitris Xygalatas, Jesper Sorensen, and Lee McCorkle.

CHAPTER ONE. THE INVITATION

There are many narrative accounts of the dominant shift in American spiritual experience since the 1960s and its meaning. Wade Clark Roof's *Generation of Seekers* argues that the shift is the response of a generation that rebelled, fled their parents' churches, and when they returned, wanted a more engaged spirituality; Mark Noll's *The Old Religion in a New World* emphasizes the Americanization of the religions that earlier generations brought from Europe; and Robert Fogel's *The Fourth Great Awakening* argues that religious foment is a response to technological change and the drive for egalitarian reform. Roger Finke and Rodney Stark suggest in *The Churching of America, 1776–2005* that the lack of marketplace-driven innovation crippled the mainline churches. Martin Marty's synoptic *Modern American Religion* provides a powerful overview of twentieth-century American religion before the 1960s, and his Fundamentalisms Project offers one of the clearest explanations from the rise of conservative religion around the globe: that people want the fruits of modernity without its morals. (Marty and Appleby, *The Glory and the Power,* is a good overview of this perspective.) Some of the best data on these changes are laid out by Christian Smith (*Christian America?: What Evangelicals Really Want; American Evangelicalism: Embattled and Thriving*); Robert Wuthnow (for example, *After Heaven* and *The Restructuring of American Religion*); Alan Wolfe (*One Nation, After All* and *The Transformation of American Religion*); Philip Jenkins's many contributions, among them *The Next Christendom: The Coming of Global Christianity;* and of course, the remarkably useful surveys and books published out of the Gallup Organization and the Barna group. Bethony Moreton's *To Serve God and Wal-mart* thoughtfully captures the spirit of the conservative Christian world. A book that captures the zeitgeist of the 1960s, though it has very little overtly to do with Christianity, is Jeffrey Kripal's *Esalen.*

This ethnographic account has been made far richer by the anthropologists and sociologists who have begun in recent years to turn their attention to evangelical Christianity. The classic description of a new paradigm church is Donald Miller's *Reinventing American Protestantism,* a sympathetic and well-researched account of the Vineyard, Calvary Chapel, and Hope Chapel that centers on the new use of emotional and bodily experience by mainstream, white, and middle-class congregations. Other good sociological and anthropological ethnographies of this new evangelical American Christianity include Margeret Poloma's *Main Street Mystics,* James Bielo's *Words upon the Word* and *The Social Life of Scriptures,* Omri Elisha's *Moral Ambition,* Randall Balmer's *Mine Eyes Have Seen the Glory,* and—although their churches are less experiential—Nancy Ammerman's *Bible Believers,* Susan Harding's *The Book of Jerry Falwell,* Vincent Crapanzano's *Serving the Word,* and, with a lighter scholarly touch and a sure sense of story, Hanna Rosin's *God's Harvard.*

The story of the Jesus People has not yet been fully told, although some fifty popular books were written at the time, along with thousands of articles. (In the meantime, Larry Eskridge's dissertation is terrific.) Glenn Kittler's *The Jesus Kids* is one of the better and better-known of these books. These popular books and articles are chronicled with zealous bibliophilia in David di Sabatino's *The Jesus People Movement*. In *Hippies of the Religious Right*, Preston Shires has written an excellent historical account of the confluence of the hippie Christians with the Pentecostals who eventually mutated into conservative Christians. Steven Tipton's *Getting Saved from the Sixties* covered the ground first from a more sociological perspective. Good histories of Pentecostalism itself and of the period out of which it sprang include Robert Anderson's *Vision of the Disinherited;* Grant Wacker's *Heaven Below;* Edward Larson's *Summer for the Gods;* Harvey Cox's *Fire from Heaven;* Vinson Synan's *The Holiness-Pentecostal Tradition;* Walter Hollenwenger's *Pentecostalism;* and Donald Drayton's *Theological Roots of Pentecostalism.* Simon Coleman, *The Globalization of Charismatic Christianity,* places the spread of spirit-filled Christianity in an anthropological framework, as does Joel Robbins, "The Globalization of Pentecostal and Charismatic Christianity," while Jennifer Cole's *Sex and Salvation* illustrates why Pentecostalism in Madagascar appeals to youth who arrive in the city from their rural birthplace. William Samarin's *Tongues of Men and Angels* also has a rich historical frame.

One of the best accounts of the transformation of American fundamentalism from a backwater separatist movement to a mainstream practice is George Marsden's *Reforming Fundamentalism,* a historical account of the birth pangs of Fuller Theological Seminary. The book seems at first glace to be a tedious, published-at-the-request-of history of the founding of a school. But the book describes the decision, on the part of a group of conservative Christians, to bring fundamentalism out of the backwaters of the culture and into the mainstream, the choices that had to be made to enable that shift, and the consequence of those choices—and the story is compelling, even gripping.

The story of the Vineyard is richly told by its participants. Bill Jackson's *The Quest for the Radical Middle* is a detail-filled account of the birthing process of the group. John Wimber's own most important text was *Power Evangelism,* although interested readers might want to consult *The Way In Is the Way On* and the writings of other influential Vineyard theologians, among them Derek Morphew's *Breakthrough,* Don Williams's *Signs, Wonders and the Kingdom of God,* Rich Nathan and Ken Wilson's *Empowered Evangelicals,* and Carol Wimber's memoir, *John Wimber: The Way It Was.* Wimber's theology has to be set in the context of a theologian at Fuller named George Eldon Ladd: the "already-not yet" theology was unfolded in a remarkable text entitled *The Presence of the Future.* Continuing this story, there is a beguiling set of papers and original documents on the Toronto Blessing and its impact in England entitled *"Toronto" in Perspective* (edited by David Hilborn). These papers reflect the work of smart, competent, and skeptical evangelical observers of the phenomenon: many of them seem to want to believe that these phenomena were the outpouring of the Holy Spirit but just find it difficult to do so.

Jon Bialecki is a sharp young anthropologist who began his research into the

Vineyard around the time I did. He has written a series of articles, among them "Angels and Grass" and "Disjuncture, Continental Philosophy's New 'Political Paul,'" and the "Question of Progressive Christianity in a Southern Californian Third Wave Church." There is a book in progress.

The great achievement of cultural histories of Jesus (in addition to Prothero's *American Jesus*, see Richard Fox's *Jesus in America* and Stephen Nichols's *Jesus: Made in America*) is to underscore how specific Jesus becomes to those who interpret him. Because the idea of God as eternal and unchangeable is central to the meaning of the very concept of God within a Judeo-Christian culture, it can come as a surprise to realize that the God and Christ whom Thomas Jefferson encountered were quite different from the God and Christ embraced by Jonathan Edwards, and that God and Jesus changed character—to some extent—with every decade. Arguably, the concept of unconditional love is new to this late-twentieth-century style of Christian, or was at any rate not emphasized to this degree before. "God is love" appears in the Bible twice, both in 1 John.

In reading the Gospels and thinking about the way Jesus is portrayed, I have been greatly helped by Luke Timothy Johnson's prodigious scholarship. I began with his excellent lectures for the Teaching Company, *Jesus and the Gospels*, and went on to his published work, in particular *Religious Experience in Earliest Christianity* and *Brother of Jesus, Friend of God*. Jaroslav Pelikan's *Whose Bible Is It?* is another deeply learned account of the many ways in which the Bible can be read, as is Karen Armstrong's *The Bible*.

CHAPTER TWO. IS THAT YOU, GOD?

"Theory of mind" is a well-established construct in developmental psychology. (See, for example, Alison Gopnik and Andrew Meltzoff's *Words, Thoughts and Theories*.) It is clear that around the world, toddlers develop the awareness that other people's behavior can be explained by their ideas or beliefs, which are not necessarily shared by others. Anthropologists have begun to explore the ways this inferred theory of mind is both universal and culturally particular. On the one hand, local ideas about mind and spirit and language shape the ways in which children and also adults begin to draw these inferences. On the other hand, local culture can override developmental milestones only to a limited degree. (Angeline Lillard discusses these issues from a psychological perspective in "Ethnopsychologies: Cultural Variations in Theories of Mind"; see also work by David Premack and Henry Wellman.) For example, some cultures, among them Melanesians and some Mayans, explicitly disregard some mental states, as the work of anthropologists Eve Danziger ("The Thought that Counts"), Joel Robbins, Bambi Schieffelin, and Alan Rumsey points out; a special issue of *Anthropological Quarterly* (Spring 2008) edited by Rumsey and Robbins and a collection edited by Lawrence Rosen, *Other Intentions*, focus on this theme. The authors argue that whatever inferences a child draws about other minds arise both out of evolved capacities and from learned (but largely unconscious) beliefs about the nature of mind, language, and the universe. Rita Astuti's work ("Are We Natural Dualists?" and *Constraints on Conceptual Development*) offers a particularly rich account of the interaction between developmental achievement and cultural commitment. The Malagasy Vezo deny the concept of biological inheritance and insist that children become Vezo by living with Vezo. When you ask Vezo directly whether the children inherit biologically from their parents, they deny that they do. And yet when Astuti asked them in other ways, it was clear that they grasped and used the concept of biological inheritance. The cultural commitments override the developmental achievement—but the Vezo have to work hard to maintain the commitment.

It is quite possible that the task of learning to pick out God's voice from one's own thoughts is easier if one grows up in a church where this is taken for granted, but the congregants I knew who did grow up in such churches still struggled with the question of what was God and what was themselves when they reached high school, the period—as Piaget tells us—when humans develop the capacity for abstract logical thought. Some of the children whom Robert Coles describes in The *Spiritual Life of Children* report being confident that they hear God in their thoughts, and the way they distinguish between their own thoughts and God seems very much like the way the Vineyard congregants make the distinction. "It's my voice, but it's not my usual voice: it's different, it says different things, and it even sounds different!" (1990:79). Younger children seem to regard God as person-like, as David Heller (1986) discovered when he carefully interviewed a series of children from different cultures (although even very young Hindus seem to hold simultaneously more personlike and more abstract forcelike models of God). They are also aware that God must have extraordinary qualities: as Justin Barrett demonstrated (2001), five- and six-year-old children, when asked about the contents of a closed box, say that their mothers cannot see inside it, but God can. Yet the human understanding of the ordinarily impossible does seem to alter with age: as the developmental psychologist Paul Harris explains: "As children get older and expand their causal understanding, the number of impossible or 'magical' phenomena that they observe in their everyday life declines, and when they do observe such a phenomenon, they are likely to regard it as a trick or as an illusion. At the same time, the number of impossible phenomena that they can conceive of increases" (2000:166). That is the learning challenge for adults at the Vineyard: they understand intellectually that God is speaking to them in their minds, but they still experience those thoughts as internally generated.

Part of the process of learning to hear God is in fact remarkably like learning physics. Andrea diSessa (diSessa and Sherin 1998; diSessa and Wagner 2005) describes a process of conceptual change that involves shifting proximal sensorial strategies—where people look or how they listen—and then shifting what they infer from what they sensorially experience. He suggests that the major change in acquiring physics knowledge is this shifting sensorial attention, which enables a student to infer the same phenomenon in multiple contexts. This shift of proximal sensorial strategies becomes crucial to the experience of identifying God. More generally, the ways in which metaphors, frames, and categories affect the learning process has been explored by Lera Boroditsky, George Lakoff, Frank Keil, Doug Medin, Dedre Gentner, and many others; the nature and impact of shared schemas—anthropologists call them "cultural models"—has been at the heart of work in cognitive anthropology, as represented by Roy D'Andrade, Naomi Quinn, Claudia Strauss, Jean Lave, and other scholars.

There are many, many evangelical books about how to know God through prayer. They include: C. S. Lewis, *Mere Christianity;* Rick Warren, *The Purpose Driven Life;* Dallas Willard, *Hearing God* and *Renovation of the Heart;* Richard Foster, *Celebration of Discipline* and *Life with God;* Henry Blackaby and Claude King, *Experiencing God;* Bruce Bickel and Stan Jantz, *Talking with God* and *Guide to God;* James Goll, *The Beginner's Guide to Hearing God;* Mark and Patti Virkler, *Dialogue with God;* Loren Cunningham, *Is that Really You, God?;* Cynthia Heald, *Becoming a Woman of Grace;* Edward Bounds, *The Reality of Prayer;* Margaret Feinberg, *God Whispers;* S. J. Hill, *Enjoying God;* Ken Wilson, *Mystically Wired;* Bill Hybels, *Too Busy Not to Pray;* Stormie Omartian, *The Power of Praying;* and a classic beloved in the evangelical world, Brother Lawrence, *The Practice of the Presence of God.*

The classic article on discernment is by Joseph Lienhardt, "On 'Discernment of Spirits' in the Early Church." The challenge of discernment has not altered since then: experiences attributable to God may also be attributable to demons, madness, or human vanity (or folly). But in early centuries, the burden of discernment was weightier. Two books that illustrate the complexity of this process and the ambiguity of the signs that demanded discernment in the medieval period are Nancy Caciola's *Discerning Spirits* and Dyan Elliott's *Proving Women;* also see Barbara Newman's *Gods and Goddesses.*

The debate over literacy is one of the most fascinating at the borders of anthropology and psychology. What is the consequence for the mind of the capacity to write, and the use of reading, writing, print media, and so forth? The discussion in some sense begins with Lucien Lévy-Bruhl and James Frazer, but more modern participants include Jack Goody, *The Domestication of the Savage Mind;* Brian Stock, *The Implications of Literacy;* Brian Street, *Literacy in Theory and Practice;* Sylvia Scribner and Michael Cole, *The Psychology of Literacy;* Walter Ong, *Orality and Literacy;* Eric Havelock, *Preface to Plato;* and James Collins and Richard Blot, *Literacy and Literacies.*

CHAPTER THREE. LET'S PRETEND

The great works on play include Johan Huizinga, *Homo Ludens;* Roger Callois, *Man, Play and Games;* Virginia Axline, *Dibs and Play Therapy;* D.W. Winnicott, *Playing and Reality* and *Psychoanalytic Explorations;* and Gregory Bateson, *Steps Towards an Ecology of Mind.* The anthropologist Helen Schwartzman provides a broad overview in *Transformations: The Anthropology of Children's Play*. Brian Sutton-Smith's *The Ambiguity of Play* is a more recent and masterful survey. Paul Harris's *Work of the Imagination* is one of the most serious explorations of children's imagination within psychology. Margery Taylor's *Imaginary Companions* is perhaps the best work on the imaginary friends of childhood, and Mary Watkins, *Invisible Guests,* on imaginal dialogues. Artin Göncü and Susanne Gaskins (editors of *Play and Development*), David Lancy (*Playing on the Motherground*), Peter Stromberg (*Caught in Play*), and Wendy Haight and Peggy Miller (*Pretending at Home*) are among those anthropologists and psychologists who have been developing the empirical account of the way play varies across cultures. The classic philosophical statement of the value of the fictional, or non-real, is Vaihinger's *The Philosophy of "As If"*: "What I wanted to say, namely that 'as if' i.e. appearance, the consciously false, plays an enormous part in science, in world-philosophies and in life" (1925:xli).

What makes the imaginative richness of this style of Christian spirituality so compelling is the deliberate attempt to make what must be imagined seem real. Children seem mostly clear on the difference between the imagined and the real, as Harris and Taylor point out, although we still know little about the details of their growing understandings of the differences between magic, science, and religion. (One way to enter this scholarly conversation among psychologists is through a collection on *Imagining the Impossible,* edited by Karl Rosengren, Carl Johnson, and Paul Harris.) Adults, however, learn to experience some playlike experiences as real—prayer above all. That is true in many faiths, and as Jacquie Woolley points out in the collection just mentioned, children seem to grasp the nature of prayer at just about the time when they cease to believe that wishing has physical consequences.

I think evangelical Christians are using play to evoke a sense of interaction with an invisible being. The more we look at human interactions, the more complicated they become. Work by anthropologists and psychologists has begun to map out the rich interactive context within which human communication emerges. For instance, a mother with an infant uses face, hands, sounds, even her whole body, and she mimics the child while breaking the rhythm of the behaviors in surprising ways to make the child shriek with laughter: gotcha, gotcha, GOTCHA, as developmental psychologist Daniel Stern tells the story (*The Interpersonal World of the Infant*). This interactive context is profoundly human and arises out of our evolutionary inheritance, but it is also deeply specific to its culture. Suzanne Gaskins, a cultural psychologist with extensive fieldwork among the Yucatec Mayans, points out that even these initial interactions are quite variable: Mayans hold infants more and verbalize to them less than Euro-Americans, and they respond more to negative than positive cues; these differences reflect subtly different ideas about mind and appropriate emotion ("Cultural perspectives on infant-caregiver interaction"). In *The Roots of Human Sociality,* the anthropologist and psychologist Stephen Levinson describes what he calls the human "interaction engine": the distinctive ensemble of interactional signals that are in varying degrees potential in a newborn and that are engaged within a particular social context. He points out that humans respond to intentions as well as behaviors; that they infer what an interlocutor knows and interact on the basis of that knowledge; that they interact often on the basis of expectation rather than rule; that they have immensely sophisticated faces and make rapid interpretations of those faces; and so forth. I think a personal relationship with God becomes possible when an individual's God-concept becomes rich enough, and external enough, to evoke these interactional patterns; and the imagined interaction triggers an interpersonal response.

CHAPTER FOUR. DEVELOPING YOUR HEART

I take the idea of emotional practices from Jean Briggs (although she did not call them that), who described the Arctic-dwelling Inuit behaviors around children in *Inuit Morality Play*. She recounts the way adults relentlessly prod young children in ways that seem cruel to Americans ("Your mother's going to die—look, she cut her finger—do you want to come live with me?") Yet the Inuit love their children intensely, and the teasing is done with warm affection. Briggs thought that the teasing trained children to control their emotional expression, a capacity the Intuit value highly, and possibly that it helped to prepare them for life in a dangerous, unpredictable climate. The questioning begins when the child becomes a toddler but then stops a few years later, when the child is able to contain his or her anxiety and no longer reacts.

This observational approach to identifying patterns of emotional behavior, in the tradition of Margaret Mead, is at the heart of psychological anthropology. Other exemplars include: Robert Levy, *Tahitians;* Catherine Lutz, *Unnatural Emotions;* Theresa O'Nell, *Disciplined Hearts;* Steven Parish, *Hierarchy and Its Discontents;* Margaret Trawick, *Notes on Love in a Tamil Family.* Arlie Hochschild is one of the best-known sociologists who does this sort of work (*The Managed Heart*); Jack Katz (*How Emotions Work*) is another. Richard Shweder is one of the most prominent anthropological theorists of emotion (*Thinking Through Cultures*). Most anthropologists and psychologists who think about the emotions have concluded that emotions are complex but structured. This is often framed as "componential": that emotions emerge out of a set of factors, some of which are more culturally sensitive and others less culturally sensitive, to use Ann Taves's useful phrase. I have summarized this work in an essay entitled "Subjectivity."

Why does psychotherapy work (when it works)? At the beginning of his work, Freud thought that psychoanalysis worked because it enabled people to experience insight, to know something new. At its end, he was not so sure. Now psychoanalysts emphasize the power of a reparative relationship, the experience of describing hurt in the presence of a loving, attentive therapist. Among my favorite discussions of this rich question are Glen Gabbard's *Psychodynamic Psychiatry;* Roy Schafer's *Analytic Attitude;* and Jonathan Lear's *Therapeutic Action.* Janet Malcolm's work, for example *Psychoanalysis: The Impossible Profession,* remains refreshingly insightful. Jerome Frank's *Persuasion and Healing* is the classic comparison of psychoanalysis and other forms of spiritual healing. Meanwhile, I discuss some of the science of psychotherapy in my book *Of Two Minds.* One of my favorite evangelical discussions of the goal of psychotherapy was a sermon delivered by a pastor one Sunday morning. He contrasted the lives of Freud and of C. S. Lewis. Both had similar ideas, he explained, but Lewis died happy.

The more general question of why engaging with practices that are not part of Western psychotherapy might nonetheless be therapeutic is identified in anthropology as the question of "symbolic healing." Every known society has healing practices in which people use words and gestures and nonbiogenic substances to heal. These medical interventions with no known medical efficacy nonetheless appear to have impact. In the Christian setting, one might attribute the efficacy to God. In the social science setting, anthropologists have suggested that the basic structure of symbolic (or spiritual) healing, beyond the mobilization of hope (the simple placebo response), involves the subject's ability to externalize the source of distress and then to experience some degree of control over it. They have pointed out that the process often involves the following components: narrative (Claude Lévi-Strauss; "The Efficacy of Symbols"; Gananath Obeyesekere, *The Work of Culture*); altered attention (Bambi Chapin, "Transforming Possession: Josephine and the Work of Culture"); and social support (Victor Turner, *The Ritual Process*). In *The Sacred Self,* Thomas Csordas describes the way all of these work in concert in charismatic Catholicism.

Finally: a comment on Lewis and Tolkien. *The Lion, the Witch and the Wardrobe* and its successors are richly enough imagined that you can enter their world indifferent to the wellspring of Christian theology that feeds them. At any rate, you can remain indifferent until the last book, where the eschatology becomes as heavy-handed as the story of the Grail. When I came to *The Last Battle* as a schoolgirl, never having noticed the Christian underpinnings of the previous volumes, I felt affronted, as if I had been hoodwinked. It never occurred to me back then that Tolkien's Middle-earth was also fundamentally Christian in its inspiration. Now when I read it, the signs are clear. As his quest draws to a close, Frodo becomes more and more Christ-like. He will not hold a sword; he heals; he is transformed by a suffering he did not choose and did not deserve but bore willingly for the sake of others. Gandalf looks at Frodo after the perilous flight from Weathertop and thinks that he may become, in the end, like a clear glass filled with light, for all to see. Yet the tale is so self-contained, so complete in its creation of a mythic past, that it does not call out for an interpretive key. *The Lord of the Rings* sold poorly when it first appeared soon after the Second World War. When its fame exploded in the countercultural 1960s, few of those who read it thought of it as Christian.

But it is. I have always wondered whether it is possible that C. S. Lewis, whom Tolkien met and converted when his narrative was being created, might not have been the kernel for the basic character of hobbits.

CHAPTER FIVE. LEARNING FROM THE EXPERTS

The approach I have taken here is relatively unusual for anthropologists. I use the ethnographic method to identify a process that seems to be psychological. That is, I am not just describing what Bourdieu would call "habitus" and Mauss "the techniques of the body"—the ways culture shapes profoundly the way we are in the world. Rather, I am identifying the consequences of those practices that seem to have something to do with the way brains and bodies are built.

I do have colleagues forging a similar sort of path between anthropology (or history) and psychology, using ethnographic or historical data to identify a psychological phenomenon. One is Harvey Whitehouse, who argues in *Modes of Religiosity* that different kinds of religious rituals have profoundly different implications for the way people remember details about their religion. Another is David Hufford, a folklorist who pursued a curious piece of folklore, began interviewing people, and discovered that they were reporting a real psychological phenomenon: sleep paralysis. *The Terror that Comes in the Night* is a remarkable example of this kind of method. Hufford now holds a position in a medical school. Ann Taves is another intellectual soulmate. Trained as a historian, she wrote a book on reported religious experiences in eighteenth- and nineteenth-century America. Not content only to look at the ways those experiences were imagined, she then set out to understand their psychological features. In *Religious Experience Reconsidered,* she sets out a new approach to phenomenology.

The idea that there are constrained patterns in what is deemed religious is most famously associated with William James's *Varieties of Religious Experience.* He was not sui generis: at the time, other scholars like Edwin Starbuck, James Leuba, and George Coe shared his ambitions. Rudolf Otto, *The Idea of the Holy* sets out on a similar path. More recent contributions include Alister Hardy's *The Spiritual Nature of Man,* a fascinating categorization of the thousands of reports people sent in response to newspaper solicitations for the spiritual experiences of ordinary people. *The Varieties of Anomalous Experience,* edited by Etzel Cardeña, Steven Jay Lynn, and Stanley Krippner, is another quite interesting example, summarizing what we know about the frequency and consistency of mystical states, out-of-body phenomena, near-death experiences, and so forth. Wayne Proudfoot's *Religious Experience* reminds us how cautious we must be in interpreting these claims.

I myself, based on my fieldwork and my reading, would go so far as to suggest that there are three kinds of intense spiritual phenomena that appear around the world in different faiths:

a. Spiritual seizures: dramatic, transformative events like mystical experiences, near-death experiences, and out-of-body phenomena. These events are consistent with some kind of electrical storm in the brain, although each kind of event has its own phenomenological shape and no doubt its own neural circuitry. The near-death experience usually involves the experience of time slowed to a crawl, as if attention expands to observe every instant of remaining time; life's trajectory unfolds like a string of pearls; and in the West, at any rate, a great white light pulsates beyond a tunnel. Out-of-body experiences take the subject above their body, often hovering in a corner during surgery, looking down. Out-of-body events are typically richer than mere hallucinations. They often involve a sense of travel and transformation, a visceral experience of change.

b. Sensory overrides: sensory perceptions of that which is not materially present; hallucinations. These events sometimes appear with dramatic electrical storms. They are typically brief, spontaneous, unpredictable, pleasant, and often prosaic, and they are advisory rather than commanding. They may be the result of perceptual breaks corrected to represent something that is not physically perceptible. They seem to be related to the reality monitoring system.

c. Intense absorption/trance phenomena: practices like channeling, spirit possession, some prayer practice, and—in many instances—speaking in tongues. Individuals lose a sense of agency in these events. Events seem to happen to them, rather than occurring at their will, and they feel set apart from the everyday world. Time slows or alters. These experiences are associated with the capacity for absorption and for hypnosis and dissociation. Unlike the others, they can be deliberately learned, and deliberately entered into, and they make both sensory overrides and spiritual seizures more likely.

This list is not exhaustive. There are other remarkable phenomenological events: a sense of presence, or Holy Spirit experiences. Nor are these categories mutually exclusive: out-of-body experiences, for example, include sensory overrides. But the point of distinguishing between kinds of experiences is to remind us that spirituality is patterned in distinct and predictable ways.

In thinking about the personal encounter with God, I have read many autobiographies and other similar reflections. Some of my favorites not mentioned in the text are: Simone Weil, *Waiting for God;* Martin Buber *I and Thou;* Anne Lamott, *Traveling Mercies* (the conversion experience is so—so something); Phyllis Tickle, *The Shaping of a Life;* and Emily Benedek, *Through the Unknown, Remembered Gate.*

CHAPTER SIX. LORD, TEACH US TO PRAY

Marcel Mauss raised a really interesting question in his unfinished dissertation on prayer (*On Prayer*). He suggested that prayer has a history (as he later suggested so fruitfully for the concept of the person): that as the person becomes more individualized, so too does prayer practice, and the understanding of what acts in prayer shifts inward from the exactness of the liturgy to the intention of the one who enacts. He argued too that prayer is a social practice: that it enacts a relationship, whose meaning changes with the historical context. Relatively few anthropologists since have written about prayer, although that is changing. (Godfrey Lienhardt and E. E. Evans-Pritchard are notable exceptions.) More contemporary anthropologists have drawn attention to the structured form prayer has as a linguistic performance (Lisa Capps and Elinor Ochs, "Cultivating Prayer"); that it is a special kind of language, intended for special ends (Robin Shoaps, "Pray Earnestly," Webb Keane, "Religious Language," Patricia Baquedano-Lopez, "Prayer"); that it becomes a way of encountering modernity (Joel Robbins, "God Is Nothing But Talk,"); and there are unintended political consequences from its use by colonizers (William Hanks, *Converting Words;* Jean Comaroff, *Body of Power, Spirit of Resistance*). Younger scholars like Anna Corwin and Greg Simon are beginning to contribute to the discussion. Shane Sharp (not an anthropologist by training) has just published a splendid account of the way prayer helps people to manage negative emotion, in "How Does Prayer Help to Manage Emotion?"

There is now an active discussion on the training of spiritual disciplines. Joanna Cook's *Meditation in Modern Buddhism,* Anna Gade's *Perfection Makes Practice,* David Berliner and Ramon Sarró's *Learning Religion,* and Vlad Namasceau and Arnold Halloy's *Learning Possession* are among the more recent voices; Richard Noll's "Mental Imagery Cultivation as a Cultural Phenomenon" and Michael Winkleman's "Trance State" are among the classic ones. They join a larger anthropological discussion about learning in religion, in the work of Charles Hirschkind, *The Ethical Soundscape,* Saba Mahmood, *The Politics of Piety,* Rebecca Lester, *Jesus in Our Wombs,* and Thomas Csordas, *The Sacred Self.* The rich *Prayer: A History* by Philip and Carol Zaleski offers an overview of prayer across time and space, and Margaret Poloma and George Gallup's *Varieties of Prayer* provides arguably our best survey to date.

Historians have begun to narrow in on the kind of mental training involved in spiritual practices. Mary Carruthers's *The Craft of Thought* is a magisterial work; see also Rachel Fulton's *From Judgment to Passion* and in particular her current work. Jonathan Garb, author of *The Chosen Will Become Herds* and *Shamanic Trance in Modern Kabbalah,* is a historian of Jewish mysticism now beginning to train his sights on the psychological experience of the practice, along with anthropologists Yoram Bilu and Michel Kravel-Tovi. See also Elliot Wolfson, *Through a Speculum that Shines.* Francis Yates was the pioneer in describing the structure of these spiritual practices, which she found in Renaissance magic and associated with memory

(*The Art of Memory; The Rosicrucian Enlightenment*); more texts can be found in volumes such as Clare Fanger, ed. *Conjuring Spirits.* The best book I know about Tibetan practices is Stephen Beyer, *The Cult of Tara.* The Ignatian exercises have their own literature, as in Dean Brackley *The Call to Discernment;* William Barry, *Finding God in All Things;* Margaret Silf, *Inner Compass;* and drawing on the tradition more broadly, Gordon Smith, *The Voice of Jesus.* Those interested in centering prayer and Thomas Merton might consult not only *The Seven Storey Mountain* but also *Contemplative Prayer.* Some evangelicals have begun focusing directly on the classic disciplines. Richard Foster's *Celebration of Disciplines* is an example, and so too is Ken Wilson, who in *Mystically Wired* sets out a series of specific practices for people to connect to God.

There is also an emerging discussion on the anthropology and history of the senses. Here the suggestion is that different cultures emphasize different sensory modes. Anthropological contributors include Michael Jackson, "Knowledge of the Body"; Stephen Tyler, "The Vision Quest in the West"; Constance Classen, "Foundations for an Anthropology of the Senses"; David Howes, *The Varieties of Sensory Experience;* Paul Stoller, *The Taste of Ethnographic Things;* Katherine Geurts, *Culture and the Senses;* Robert Desjarlais, *Sensory Biographies;* Nadia Seremetakis, ed., *The Senses Still;* and the recent work by Asifa Majid and Stephen Levinson. Among historians, see William Dyrness, *Reformed Theology and Visual Culture* and *Senses of the Soul;* Leigh Schmidt, *Hearing Things;* Walter Ong, *Orality and Literacy;* and Mark Smith, *Sensing the Past.* A special double issue of *Visual Resources,* edited by Lisa Bitel, looks at the visual history of religious visions. Behind them all lies the great book that sought to give no less than a history of the way reality is understood in Western literature, Erich Auerbach's *Mimesis.*

The literature on shamanism is vast. The work that I have found most useful on the structure of training is Jon Christopher Crocker's *Vital Souls* and Gerardo Reichel-Dolmatoff's *The Shaman and the Jaguar.*

Meanwhile, one of the most interesting books on medieval magic is Frank Klaassen's *The Transformations of Magic;* and on the medieval imagination, Michelle Karnes's *Imagination, Meditation, and Cognition in the Middle Ages.* Both books focus on the mental practices that were thought to produce changes in the world.

Those wishing to explore the Ignatian exercises more practically could do no better than the sessions offered at El Retiro, the Jesuit Retreat Center in Los Altos, California, and at the Mercy Center, in Burlingame.

CHAPTER SEVEN. THE SKILL OF PRAYER

The observation that we select what we attend to (that we pay attention to only some of the vast amount of stimuli available to our senses) and that we interpret what we do attend to (that we fill in, reorganize, and in general override what "raw" stimuli we do take in) is the central observation in cognitive science. Some of the classic texts that spell out these claims are Jerome Bruner, Jacqueline Good-now, and George Austin's *A Study of Thinking*; Jerome Bruner's *Beyond the Information Given*; and Ulrich Neisser's *Cognition and Reality*. Cultural psychologists like Hazel Markus, Shinobu Kitayama, Richard Nisbet, Michael Cole, and Lera Boroditsky have been able to demonstrate that different kinds of cultural invitations (for example, imagining a self as deeply involved with and dependent upon others, as in Japan, as compared to an imagination of the self as set apart from others, as Clifford Geertz described the independent American self) shape the process of selection and of interpretation (for example, see Markus and Kitayama, "Culture and the Self"). The prayer process is an example of this kind of training. It focuses the content of attention on Christ and the scriptures; it focuses the process of attention on inner mental activity.

The first study, done at the University of Chicago, was published as "The Absorption Hypothesis," with myself, Howard Nusbaum, and Ron Thisted as coauthors.

The second study was done at Stanford University, where I was ably assisted by Christina Drymon, who conducted the interviews, entered the data, and kept the process organized, a herculean task. She was replaced in time by Rachel Morgain, who listened to all four hundred or so hours of our interviews and coded them. We worked closely together during this process. In addition, nine undergraduates coded the sensory overrides or hallucination-like spiritual experiences reported in the interviews. That allowed us to look back to see how differently Rachel had coded them (not very). I also independently coded these hallucination-like phenomena while blind to the discipline the subjects had randomly chosen. In addition, my two postdoctoral fellows, Julia Cassaniti and Jocelyn Marrow, coded them while also blind to the disciplines chosen. Julia, Jocelyn, Rachel, and I met as a group to discuss disagreement, and came to a consensus, while still remaining blinded to subject conditions.

I strongly encourage readers to listen to Luke Timothy Johnson's lectures on the Gospels, and indeed all of his Teaching Company courses. He speaks from neither a secular nor a religious perspective. (He was a Benedictine monk for nine years.) He now serves as the R.W. Woodruff Professor of New Testament and Christian Origins at the Candler School of Theology at Emory University.

Relatively little work has been done with the Absorption Scale, although interested readers might pursue the papers cited in the endnotes. The original article by Auke Tellegen and Gilbert Atkinson, "Openness to Absorbing and Self-altering Experiences," is still compelling. John Kihlstrom, a Berkeley psychologist, has a useful website. Winifred Gallagher goes over some of this territory in *Rapt* and captures the essence of the claim "Your ability to focus on this and suppress that is the key to controlling your experience and, ultimately, your well-being." (2009:2).

Reality monitoring, now sometimes called source monitoring, was first described in a series of articles by Marcia Johnson and her colleagues: "Reality Monitoring" (with Carol Raye), "Source Monitoring" (with Shahin Hashtroudi and D. Stephen Lindsay), and "Source Monitoring Fifteen Years Later" (with Karen Mitchell). The concept has proved increasingly useful in understanding psychiatric illness. People with psychosis are more likely to make reality monitoring errors, and giving people conditions in which they are unable to remember hearing their own voice will increase the chance that they will misremember whether they have spoken (as in a paper by Eriko Sugimori and colleagues, "Sense of Agency over Speech and Proneness to Auditory Hallucinations," and by Simon Jones and Charles Fernyhough, "Neural Correlates of Inner Speech and Auditory Verbal Hallucinations"). That seems like a story about an impaired attentional process, and it appeals to many scientists, but it still leaves problems unexplained. For instance, people with schizophrenia continue to experience inner thought and can even carry on a conversation with a hallucinated voice—so why is only half the conversation hallucinated? How is half the conversation hallucinated, given that reality monitoring seems to describe spontaneous, surprising misattributions? (See Joseph Pierre, "Letter.")

Reality monitoring is even more interesting as a normal human process that is, to some degree, learned. How do children come to report what they have imagined and what they have observed or learned from other people? Why do some people hear a voice and dismiss it, while others take it seriously? Why are spontaneous thoughts treated as more "other" than other kinds of inner speech, and when does culture make a difference? These are all questions about "metacognition," the human ability to evaluate one's own mental process—a capacity that to some extent we trick when we get drawn into a good book. John Dunlosky and Janet Metcalfe provide an entry into this discussion in *Metacognition.* From a literary perspective, see Blakey Vermeule's *Why Do We Care About Literary Characters?* A still different perspective might suggest that these are questions about the way the imagined experience of the body becomes real: embodiment. Embodiment is taken up in a most fascinating way by Shaun Gallagher in *How the Body Shapes the Mind,* and by Raymond Gibbs, *Embodiment and Cognitive Science.*

People come to faith not just because they make an intellectual choice—they commit to a proposition—but because they have feelings and experiences: that has been observed by other anthropologists, among them Jon Mitchell, in "A Moment with Christ." The basic argument is that these experiences create what Peter Berger called a "plausibility structure" for propositional commitment. In my own previous scholarly work, I described the complex learning process in which someone came to experience the divine as "metakinesis" (2004). *Metakinesis* is a term used in dance criticism to depict the way emotional experience is carried within the body so that the dancer conveys the emotion to the observer, yet makes the expressive gesture uniquely his or her own. I suggested that there were different kinds of learning that were psychologically distinct: linguistic/cognitive knowledge; emotional and altered states; and relationship practices. Together they enable the new believer to do something quite remarkable—to construct, out of everyday psychological experience, the profound sense that they have a really real relationship with a being that cannot be seen, heard, or touched, and that this relationship is unique and personal.

CHAPTER EIGHT. BUT ARE THEY CRAZY?

Considering how fascinating hallucinations are, the literature is remarkably thin. At the turn of the nineteenth century, in addition to the 1894 Census of Hallucinations, there was Francis Galton's *Inquiry in Human Faculty and Its Development* (1883), which emphasized the continuity between ordinary mental imagery and full hallucination; and Andrew Lang's *The Making of Religion* 2011 [1898]. None of these start with the presumption that hallucinations are a sign of illness. In fact, Lang sees hallucinations and like phenomena as the root of all religion. Recent literature takes for granted that the reader will treat hallucinations as associated with mental illness, and in recent years a small flurry of research has argued that much voice-hearing experience is not, in fact, pathological. Among them are Daniel Smith's compelling *Muses, Madmen and Prophets;* John Watkins's *Hearing Voices;* the publications of Marius Rome and Sandra Escher such as *Accepting Voices;* and Ivan Leudar and Philip Thomas's *Voices of Reason, Voices of Insanity.* Richard Bentall's *Madness Explained* and Andre Aleman and Frank Laroi's *Hallucinations* are excellent sources that focus on psychotic hallucinations (about which we know so much more) but emphasize the nonpathological dimension of the hallucination experience. Benny Shanon's *The Antipodes of the Mind* is an account of ayahuasca-induced experience.

The Origin of Consciousness in the Breakdown of the Bicameral Mind, by Julian Jaynes, is remarkable. Jaynes argued that the archaic Greeks did not have a category for inner speech and that as a result, when they thought thoughts with strong emotions, they actually experienced those thoughts as external to them: as hallucinations. He had a theory about brain development that supported this claim, but the part of his theory that I find most compelling is the suggestion that the way we imagine our mind (as, for example, containing inner thoughts or not) has real consequences for our mental experience.

The anthropological evidence about hallucination-like phenomena suggests that within bodily or temperamental constraints, what we might call the "cultural invitation" shapes a good deal about whether people experience hallucinations and the way they experience them. We have known for a long time that the conditions under which someone is expected to experience a vision are socially specific (Ruth Benedict, "The Vision in Plains Culture"). More recent research suggests that expectation actually generates the nonpathological unusual sensory phenomena I am calling sensory overrides. The work by Yorum Bilu and his student Michal Kravel-Tovi on the new visions of Menachem Schneerson, discussed in the text, certainly supports this idea. So too does the fine work of William Christian (for example, *Apparitions in Late Medieval and Renaissance Spain; Visionaries*) and that of Robert Orsi (*Thank You, St. Jude,* although his subjects resist describing their experiences of the saint they brought into their lives as sensory). One of the bluntest examples of the way expectation generates sensory overrides is that unusual sensory experience is more common in shamanism, where the ideology presents the shaman as leaving his or her body to explore other worlds, than it is in possession (Erika Bourguignon's *Possession*). A collection of anthropological and historical studies in *The "Vision" Thing,* edited by William Christian and Gabor Klaniczay, suggests that visions are more likely to be seen where expected, when expected, and in the form expected, even though the actual moment of the vision is unwilled and spontaneous. In early work, Ari Kiev (*Magic, Faith, and Healing*) captured culture's impact by describing hallucinations as "pathoplastic": hallucinations were biological sequelae of psychological process, shaped by the cultural expectations of the mind.

In fact, I believe that we can develop this general claim about cultural invitation into a specific theory: that the particular dimensions of the way mind is imagined in any society—its "theory of mind"—will shape the incidence and modality of sensory overrides and psychotic hallucinations (see my essay "Hallucinations and Sensory Overrides"). Ethnographic data suggests that at least three dimensions of the local theory of mind shape unusual sensory experience: sensorium (different cultures ascribe meaning to the senses in different ways); boundedness (the degree to which presence external to the mind can be understood to participate within the mind); and interiority (the way inner thought and sensation is given significance). One of the most fascinating examples comes from anthropological work in Borneo. In the West, those who are psychotic sometimes experience what is technically called "thought insertion" and "thought withdrawal," the sense that some external force has placed thoughts in one's mind or taken them out. Thought insertion and withdrawal are standard items in symptoms checklists. But when Robert Barrett ("Kurt Schneider in Borneo") attempted to translate the items in Borneo, he could not. The Iban do not have an elaborated idea of the mind as a container, and so the idea that someone could experience external thoughts as placed with it or removed from it was simply not available to them.

Meanwhile, there is a rich literature on demons in evangelical Christianity. Along with Charles Kraft's *Defeating Dark Angels,* Francis MacNutt's *Deliverance From Evil Spirits* is a classic. Others include Neil Anderson's, *The Bondage Breaker* (over a million sold) and *The Bondage Breaker (Study Guide)*. I picked up T. C. Mather's *Prophetic Deliverance* at a conference on experiencing God. For nonmodern demons, Richard Kieckhefer is one of the foremost scholars on the ritual treatment of demons in medieval Europe. *Forbidden Rites* is his edition of a fifteenth-century necromancer's manual. One of the most interesting recent accounts of demons and the role they played in early modern witch trials is by Laura Stokes, *Demons of Urban Reform.*

CHAPTER NINE. DARKNESS

The question of how it is that people believe in magic and prayer despite their apparent failure is arguably the deep question on which anthropology was founded: the problem of other minds. How can sensible people hold a belief that the observer believes to be false? The early theorists (Sir James George Frazer, Edward Tylor, and other authors of magnificent Edwardian tomes) argued that those who believed in magic were not as evolved as those who did not. Frazer even set up a kind of ladder of cultural evolution: first magic, then religion, and finally a scientific worldview. A more sophisticated version of this argument— exploring the difference between a magical and a scientific worldview—was carried out in one of the great ethnographies of anthropology, *Witchcraft, Oracles and Magic among the Azande*, by E. E. Evans-Pritchard, which was engaged to great effect by Robin Horton, Peter Winch, Ernest Gellner, and others. Evans-Pritchard argued that the Azande thought as logically as his colleagues in the West—they used the idea of witchcraft to describe what Westerners would call bad luck. (The man died because the granary fell on him, but why was he sitting under it when it fell? Witchcraft.) But they did not recognize the contradictions in their ideas about witchcraft because while they thought logically, they did not think scientifically. The debate still continues in the philosophy and history of science, where the scholars are acutely aware of the difference between everyday thought and the structure of science. (The classic debates spring out of Karl Popper, Thomas Kuhn, and Imre Lakatos.) It also continues in anthropology. My first book, *Persuasions of the Witch's Craft*, described well-educated modern people who practiced magic. I argued that they came to believe in magic not because they deliberately chose to believe but because of the ways that their interpretation of reality shifted through their practice of magic. I called this "interpretive drift."

Another early (and still compelling) approach to the problem was to speak of different "modes" of thought, one more instrumental, the other more mystical. Lucien Lévy-Bruhl began this discussion by speaking of a primitive "pre-logical" mentality but soon shifted his perspective to seeing French Catholicism as mystical in the same way as the spiritual beliefs of Amazonian rainforest dwellers. Bronislaw Malinowksi made much the same point in *Magic, Science and Religion*. More recent work in cognitive science has given us a sharp awareness that humans, no matter how highly educated, reach for cognitive frames that are salient to the topic at hand: and those frames are not necessarily consistent with each other.

The emphasis on relationship within the renewalist church should prompt us to ask whether religion is fundamentally about attachment, not explanation. This question is unanswerable, but it does reframe the traditional puzzle of irrational belief. It has not been much pursued in anthropology except implicitly, in the large literature on spirit possession, where in many cases it is clear that people are deeply—and often tempestuously—attached to the spirits who possess them or whom they marry (for example, Vincent Crapanzano's, *Tuhami*, Michael Lambek's, *Human Spirits*, and Janice Boddy's, *Wombs and Alien Spirits*). Freud certainly thought that religion was about the projection of a parental figure, but for Freud, relationship was not life's fundamental goal. It was the object relations theorists and their intellectual heirs (Melanie Klein, Ronald Fairbairn, D. W. Winnicott, Heinz Kohut, John Bowlby) who argued that the basic human drive was toward attachment. This literature and its scientific expansion in developmental psychology is magisterially summarized in Robert Karen's *Becoming Attached.* Beyond Ana-Maria Rizzuto, one of the authors who has developed this approach is John McDargh, in *Psychoanalytic Object Relations Theory and the Study of Religion.*

The endnotes cite many scientific articles on the relationship between religion and health. Those who wish to read further might consider Harold Koenig's *The Healing Power of Faith; Medicine, Religion and Health;* and the collection he edited with Harvey Jay Cohen, *The Link Between Religion and Health. Invisible Forces and Powerful Beliefs,* by the Chicago Social Brain Network, has a series of accessible essays by leading scientists, many of which are about the protective consequences of religious involvement. (Disclaimer: I have an essay in this collection.)

CHAPTER TEN. BRIDGING THE GAP

The question of how to understand modern American Christianity has gripped many thinkers. In *The Stillborn God,* Mark Lilla argues that Christianity's complexity—its deity both present and absent in the world—is inherently unstable. That instability allowed the emergence of a liberal theology in which God was separate from politics but was ultimately unsatisfying; and whose replacement is far more fiery, passionate, and dangerous. *Habits of the Heart,* by Robert Bellah, Richard Madsen, William Sullivan, Ann Swidler, and Steve Tipton, pins the problem on modern individualism; Charles Taylor's *A Secular Age* and Talal Asad's *The Formations of the Secular,* on the social acceptance of nonbelief. All see plainly a world in which the liberal Christian God has failed. In *American Grace,* Robert Putnam and David Campbell see a more complex picture in which there are great tensions between religious imaginations—and great tolerance.

It is here that the contrast to Christianities in other societies becomes so interesting. I take the self-conscious use of play to manage doubt to be characteristic of modern neo-Pentecostal spirituality and quite lacking in never-secular Christianities. Such societies do, of course, face the problem of whether the Christian God exists, but the ethnographic literature presents the challenge in never-secular societies as one of shifting from one spirituality to another, rather than the problem of living with the constant awareness of the possibilities of disbelief in the supernatural itself as an ontological reality.

In *Becoming Sinners,* for example, Joel Robbins presents a vivid account of a Melanesian community who chose to adopt Pentecostal Christianity. Robbins focuses upon what he calls the "moral torment" experienced by the Urapmin. This moral torment was created when a society with a pre-Christian model of intention (or will) as public, in which private thoughts are not regarded as knowable or relevant, adopted a model of the mind in which all deviant ("willful") thoughts, let alone public ones, are known by God and are damnable. The drama of the ethnography is the utter despair that these Urapmins feel when they know themselves to have failed, and the intense ritual activity they use to counteract their failure. This is not a society in which doubt about supernatural ontology is the primary problem.

This lack of doubt about the supernatural as a category can be see in other accounts of never-secular societies. Birgit Meyer's *Translating the Devil* describes the never-secularized Ghanaian Ewe as a social world in which the traditional pre-Christian faith is still alive, but in which the spirits of the traditional faith are understood, by Christians, to be demons. In Meyer's ethnographic picture, the Ewe live in a world in which atheism is not a constant presence. This is true of other recent, compelling ethnographies: the Christians whom Webb Keane describes in Indonesian East Sumba (*Christian Moderns*) also struggle between religious worlds because for them, too, the words that summon the pagan spirits are still powerful; and in Matthew Engelke's account, a Zimbabwean church (*The Problem of Presence*) takes so seriously the limitations of trusting language to grasp God adequately that they refuse to read the Bible at all. Other important ethnographies of Christianity outside the West include Jean and John Comaroff's *Of Revelation and Revolution;* Jennifer Cole's *Sex and Salvation;* and Eva Keller's, *The Road to Clarity;* as well as the work of Brian Howell, Fenella Cannell, Danilyn Rutherford, David Mosse, Peter Gow, and many others. Jean Comaroff's recent work about Christianity in Africa gives a vivid picture of the way the occult becomes politically charged.

In these never-secular societies (a term I take from a conversation with Joel Robbins), where the reality of the supernatural as a category has not been profoundly questioned, doubt is focused on specific supernatural claims—the reality of non-Christian spirits, the validity of spiritually charged mechanisms, the efficacy of particular payers. In never-secular societies, congregants do not need help to persuade themselves to take the entire enterprise seriously in the first place. And in none of these societies do we find an interest in an explicitly as-if engagement that helps to place the spiritual in an epistemological space that is neither straightforwardly real nor transparently fictional.

The characteristically self-conscious, playful, and deliberately paradoxical orientation of the experiential evangelical world has been identified as a secular style in a scholarly collection edited by Joshua Landy and Michael Saler, *The Re-enchantment of the World*. Readers might also be interested in a remarkable book by a Pentecostal philosopher: *Thinking in Tongues*, by James K. Smith. Smith argues that enchantment is central to the Pentecostal construal of the world, that at its heart lies a deep sense of expectation and an openness to surprise.

More broadly still, readers who wish to explore the ways in which culture shapes thought should read Geoffrey Lloyd's *Cognitive Variations*, and the work of Michael Cole, including his now-dated but still wonderful book with Sylvia

Scriber, *Culture and Thought.* The question of how people hold supernatural beliefs in never-secular societies is explored in Paul Veyne's *Did the Greeks Believe Their Myths?* and in recent essays by Stephen Justice.

The last paragraph of Chapter Ten evokes one of the most delightful books inspired by Christianity: Elizabeth Goudge's *The Little White Horse.*

BIBLIOGRAPHY

Acocella, Joan. 2007. *Twenty-eight Artists and Two Saints.* New York: Vintage.

à Kempis, Thomas. 1947. *The Imitation of Christ.* Mount Vernon, N.Y.: Peter Pauper Press.

Agamben, Giorgio. 2005. *The Time That Remains.* Stanford: Stanford University Press.

Albright, Carol Rausch, and James B. Ashbrook. 2001. *Where God Lives in the Human Brain.* Naperville, Ill.: Sourcebooks.

Aleman, A., and F. Laroi. 2008. *Hallucinations.* Washington, D.C.: American Psychological Association.

Al-Issa, I. 1977. "Social and Cultural Aspects of Hallucinations." *Psychological Bulletin* 84:570–87.

———. 1995. "The Illusion of Reality or the Reality of Illusion." *British Journal of Psychiatry* 166:368–73.

American Psychiatric Association. 2000. *Diagnostic and Statistical Manual of Mental Disorders,* 4th ed. Washington, D.C.: American Psychiatric Association Press.

Ammerman, Nancy. 1987. *Bible Believers.* New Brunswick, N.J.: Rutgers University Press.

Anderson, Neil. 2000a. *The Bondage Breaker.* Eugene, Ore.: Harvest House.

———. 2000b. *The Bondage Breaker Study Guide.* Eugene, Ore.: Harvest House.

Anderson, Robert. 1979. *Vision of the Disinherited.* New York: Oxford University Press.

Andrews, Jerry. 1997. "The Father's Discipline: Religious Ideas and Social Roles in Clement of Alexandria." Ph.D. diss., University of Chicago.

Antony and the Desert Fathers: Extreme Faith in the Early Church. 1999. *Christian History* 64 (4). Carol Stream, Ill.: Christianity Today.

Armstrong, Karen. 2007. *The Bible.* New York: Grove.

Arthur, H. M., C. Patterson, and J. A. Stone. 2006. "The Role of Complementary and Alternative Therapies in Cardiac Rehabilitation: A Systematic Evaluation." *European Journal of Cardiovascular Prevention and Rehabilitation* 13 (1):3–9.

Asad, Talal. 1993. *Genealogies of Religion*. Baltimore: Johns Hopkins University Press.

———. 2003 *Formations of the Secular*. Stanford, Calif.: Stanford University.

Astuti, Rita. 2001. "Are We All Natural Dualists?" *Journal of the Royal Anthropological Institute* 7:429–47.

Astuti, Rita, Gregg Solomon, and Susan Carey. 2004. "Constraints on Conceptual Development: A Case Study of the Acquisition of Folkbiological and Folksociological Knowledge in Madagascar." *Monographs of the Society for Research in Child Development* 69 (3):1–135.

Atran, Scott. 2002. *In Gods We Trust*. New York: Oxford, University Press.

Auerbach, Erich. 1953. *Mimesis: The Representation of Reality in Western Literature*. Translated by Willard R. Trask. Princeton: Princeton University Press.

Augustine. 2001 [1963]. *The Confessions of Saint Augustine*. Translated by Rex Warner. New York: New American Library.

Austin, J. H. 1999. *Zen and the Brain: Toward an Understanding of Meditation and Consciousness*. Cambridge, Mass.: MIT Press.

Austin, J. L. 1962. *How to Do Things with Words*. Cambridge, Mass.: Harvard University Press.

Axline, Virginia. 1964. *Dibs in Search of Self*. New York: Ballantine.

———. 1989 [1974]. *Play Therapy*. London: Churchill Livingstone.

Bachner-Melman, Rachel, Dina Christian, Ada Zohar, Naama Constantini, Elad Lerer, Sarah Hoch, Sarah Sella, Lubov Nemanov, Inga Gritsenko, Pesach Lichtenberg, Roni Granot, and Richard Ebstein. 2005. "AVPR1 and SLC6A4 Gene Polymorphisms Are Associated with Creative Dance Performance." *PLoS Genetics* 1 (3):394–403.

Badiou, Alain. 2003. *Saint Paul*. Stanford, Calif.: Stanford University Press.

Balmer, Randall. 1989. *Mine Eyes Have Seen the Glory: A Journey into the Evangelical Subculture in America*. Oxford: Oxford University Press.

Banthia, Rajni, Judith Tedlie Moskowitz, Michael Acree, and Susan Folkman. 2007. "Socioeconomic Differences in the Effects of Prayer on Physical Symptoms and Quality of Life." *Journal of Health Psychology* 12 (2):249–60.

Baquedano-Lopez, Patricia. 1999. "The Pragmatics of Reading Prayers." *Text and Talk* 28 (5):582–602.

———. 2008. "Prayer." *Journal of Linguistic Anthropology* 9 (1–2):197–200.

Barber, T. X., and D. S. Calverey. 1964. "An Experimental Study of Hypnotic (Auditory and Visual) Hallucination." *Journal of Abnormal and Social Psychology* 68:13–20.

Barker, Dave, and Lee Jord. 2004. *Pray Give Go Do: Extreme Faith in an Awesome God*. Grand Rapids, Mich.: Kregel Publications.

Barrett, Justin. 2004. *Why Would Anyone Believe in God?* Walnut Creek, Calif.: Alta Mira.

Barrett, Justin, and Frank Keil. 1996. "Conceptualizing a Non-natural Entity: Anthropomorphism in God Concepts." *Cognitive Psychology* 31:219–47.

Barrett, Robert. 2004. "Kurt Schneider in Borneo: Do First Rank Symptoms Apply to the Iban?" In *Schizophrenia, Culture and Subjectivity,* edited by Janet Jenkins and Robert Barrett, pp. 87–109. New York: Cambridge University Press.

Barry, William A. 1991. *Finding God in All Things: A Companion to "The Spiritual Exercises of St. Ignatius."* Notre Dame, Ind.: Ave Maria Press.

Barstow, Anne Llewellyn. 1985. "Joan of Arc and Female Mysticism." *Journal of Feminist Studies in Religion* 1 (2):29–42.

Bartlett, Frederic. 1932. *Remembering: A Study in Experimental and Social Psychology.* New York: Macmillan.

Bateson, Gregory. 1972. *Steps Towards an Ecology of Mind.* Chicago: University of Chicago Press.

Bauer, Susanne, Hans Schanda, Hanna Karakula, Luiza Olajossy-Hilkesberger, Palmira Rudaleviciene, Nino Okribelashvili, Haroon R. Chaudhry, Sunday E. Idemudia, Sharon Gscheider, Kristina Ritter, and Thomas Stomp. 2011. "Culture and the Prevalence of Hallucinations in Schizophrenia." *Comprehensive Psychiatry* 52:319–35.

Bebbington, David. 2000. *Holiness in Nineteenth-Century England.* Carlisle, U.K.: Paternoster.

Beecher, Henry Ward. 1871. *Life of Jesus, the Christ.* London: Nelson.

Bell, Rob. 2011. *Love Wins.* New York: HarperCollins.

Bellah, Robert, Richard Madsen, William Sullivan, Ann Swidler, and Steve Tipton. 1996. *Habits of the Heart.* Berkeley: University of California Press.

Benedek, Emily. 2001. *Through the Unknown, Remembered Gate.* New York: Schocken.

Benedict, Ruth. 1922. "The Vision in Plains Culture." *American Anthropologist* 24 (1):1–23.

Benham, Grant, Norris Smith, and Michel Nash. 2002. "Hypnotic Susceptibility Scales: Are the Mean Scores Increasing?" *International Journal of Clinical and Experimental Hypnosis* 50 (1):5–16.

Benson, Herbert. 1975. *The Relaxation Response.* New York: William Morrow.

Bentall, Richard. 1990. "The Illusion of Reality: A Review and Integration of Psychological Work on Hallucinations." *Psychological Bulletin* 107 (1):82–95.

———. 2003. *Madness Explained.* London: Penguin.

Berger, Peter. 1967. *The Sacred Canopy.* New York: Anchor.

Berliner, David, and Ramon Sarró, eds. 2007. *Learning Religion: Anthropological Approaches.* New York: Berghahn Books.

Berlinski, Mischa. 2007. *Fieldwork.* New York: Picador.

Bernstein, E., and F Putnam. 1986. "Development, Reliability and Validity of a Dissociation Scale." *Journal of Nervous and Mental Disease* 174:727–35.

Best, Gary. 2005. *Naturally Supernatural.* Cape Town, South Africa: Vineyard International.

Beyer, Stephen. 1978. *The Cult of Tara.* Berkeley: University of California Press.

Bialecki, Jon. 2009. "Disjuncture, Continental Philosophy's New 'Political Paul,' and the Question of Progressive Christianity in a Southern Californian Third Wave Church." *American Ethnologist* 36 (1):110–23.

———. 2010. "Angels and Grass: Church, Revival and the Neo-Pauline turn." *South Atlantic Quarterly* 109 (4):695–717.

Bialecki, Jon, Naomi Haynes, and Joel Robbins. 2008. "The Anthropology of Christianity." *Religion Compass* 2 (6):1139–58.

Bickel, Bruce, and Stan Jantz. 1996. *Bruce & Stan's Pocket Guide to Talking with God.* Eugene, Ore.: Harvest House.

———. 1997. *Guide to God.* Eugene, Ore.: Harvest House.

Bielo, James. 2009a. *Words upon the Word.* New York: New York University Press.

———, ed. 2009b. *The Social Life of Scriptures.* New Brunswick, N.J.: Rutgers University Press.

Biema, David van. 2005. "Religion: Beyond the Wardrobe." *Time.* October 30.

Birgegard, Andreas, and Pehr Granqvist. 2004. "The Correspondence Between Attachment to Parents and God." *Personality and Social Psychology Bulletin* 30 (9):1122–35.

Bitel, Lisa, ed. 2009. *Visual Resources,* special issue, "Visualizing the Invisible."

Blackaby, Henry, and Claude King. 2004. *Experiencing God.* Nashville, Tenn.: Broadman and Holman.

Blanke, Olaf, Stéphanie Ortigue, Theodor Landis, and Margitta Seeck. 2002. "Stimulating Illusory Own-body Perceptions." *Nature* 419 (19):269.

Bloch, Maurice. 2008. "Why Religion Is Nothing Special But Is Central." *Philosophical Transactions of the Royal Society* 365:2055–61.

Boddy, Janice. 1989. *Wombs and Alien Spirits: Women, Men, and the Zar Cult in Northern Sudan.* Madison: University of Wisconsin, Press.

Boroditsky, Lera, and Michael Ramscar. 2002. "The Roles of Body and Mind in Abstract Thought." *Psychological Science* 13 (2):185–89.

Bounds, Edward. 2007. *The Reality of Prayer.* Shippensburg, Penn.: Destiny Books.

Bourguignon, Erika. 1976. *Possession.* San Francisco: Chandler and Sharp.

Bowen, Elenore Smith. 1964. *Return to Laughter.* New York: Doubleday.

Bower, Gordon. 1970a. "Analysis of a Mnemonic Device." *American Scientist* 58:496–510.

———. 1970b. "Mental Imagery and Associative Learning." In *Cognition in Learning and Memory,* edited by L. W. Gregg, pp. 51–96. New York: Wiley.

Bowers, K. S. 1993. "The Waterloo-Stanford Group C (WSGC) Scale of Hypnotic Susceptibility: Normative and Comparative Data." *International Journal of Clinical and Experimental Hypnosis* 41:35–46.

———. 1998. "Waterloo-Stanford Group Scale of Hypnotic Susceptibility, Form C: Manual and Response Booklet." *International Journal of Clinical and Experimental Hypnosis* 46 (3):250–68.

Bowker, John. 1970. *Problems of Suffering in the Religion of the World.* Cambridge, U.K.: Cambridge University Press.

Boyer, Pascal. 2001. *Religion Explained.* New York: Basic Books.

Brackley, Dean. 2004. *The Call to Discernment in Troubled Times: New Perspectives on the Transformative Wisdom of Ignatius of Loyola.* New York: Crossroad.

Bradshaw, Matt, Christopher G. Ellison, and Kevin Flannery. 2008. "Prayer, God Imagery and Symptoms of Psychopathology." *Journal for the Scientific Study of Religion* 47 (4):644–59.

Briggs, Jean. 1998. *Inuit Morality Play.* New Haven: Yale University Press.

Brooks, David. 2008. "The Neural Buddhists." *New York Times.* May 13.

Brown, Michael. 1999. *The Channeling Zone.* Cambridge, Mass.: Harvard University Press.

Brown, Peter. 1988. *The Body and Society.* New York: Columbia University Press.

Brune, Martin. 2005. "'Theory of Mind' in Schizophrenia: A Review of the Literature." *Schizophrenia Bulletin* 31 (1):21–42.

Bruner, Jerome. 1973. *Beyond the Information Given: Studies in the Psychology of Knowing.* New York: Norton.

Bruner, Jerome, Jacqueline Goodnow, and George Austin. 1956. *A Study of Thinking.* New York: Wiley.

Buber, Martin. 1958. *I and Thou,* 2nd ed. New York: Scribner.

Buechner, Frederick. 1977. *Telling the Truth: The Gospel as Tragedy, Comedy, and Fairy Tale.* New York: HarperCollins.

Bufford, Rodger, Raymond Paloutzian, and Craig Ellison. 1991. "Norms for the Spiritual Well-being Scale." *Journal of Psychology and Theology* 19 (1):56–70.

Burgess, Stanley. 2005. "Introduction." *Encyclopedia of Pentecostal and Charismatic Christianity.* New York: Routledge.

Burnham, Sophy. 2002. *The Path of Prayer: Reflections on Prayer and True Stories of How It Affects Our Lives.* New York: Viking.

Burton-Christie, Douglas. 1993. *The Word in the Desert: Scripture and the Quest for Holiness in Early Christian Monasticism.* New York: Oxford University Press.

Butler, Lisa. 2006. "Normative Dissociation." *Psychiatric Clinics of North America* 29:45–62.

Caciola, Nancy. 2003. *Discerning Spirits.* Ithaca, N.Y.: Cornell University Press.

Cacioppo, John, and William Patrick. 2008. *Loneliness.* New York: Norton.

Cahn, B. R., and J. Polich. 2006. "Meditation States and Traits: EEG, ERP, and Neuroimaging Studies." *Psychological Bulletin* 132:180–211.

Callois, Roger. 1960. *Man and the Sacred.* New York: Free Press.

———. 1961. *Man, Play and Games.* Glencoe, Ill.: Free Press.

Campbell, James D., Dong Phil Yoon, and Brick Johnstone. 2010. "Determining Relationships Between Physical Health and Religious Experience, Religious Practices, and Congregational Support in a Heterogeneous Medical Sample." *Journal of Religion and Health* 49:3–17.

Campbell, Ted. 2000. *The Religion of the Heart.* Eugene, Ore.: Wipf and Stock.

Cannell, Fenella, ed. 2006. *The Anthropology of Christianity.* Chapel Hill: Duke University Press.

Capps, Lisa, and Elinor Ochs. 2002. "Cultivating Prayer." In *The Language of Turn and Sequences,* edited by E. Ford, B. Fox, and S. Thompson, pp. 39–55. New York: Oxford University Press.

Cardeña, Etzel, Steven J. Lynn, and Stanley Krippner, eds. 2000. *Varieties of Anomalous Experience: Examining the Scientific Evidence.* Washington, D.C.: American Psychological Association.

Carpenter, Humphrey. 1978. *The Inklings.* London: George Allen and Unwin.

Carruthers, Mary. 1998. *The Craft of Thought.* Cambridge, U.K.: Cambridge University Press.

Carruthers, Mary, and Jan Ziolkowski. 2002. *The Medieval Craft of Memory: An Anthology of Texts and Pictures.* Philadelphia: University of Pennsylvania Press.

Cassibba, R., P. Granqvist, A. Constantini, and S. Gatto. 2008. "Attachment and God." *Developmental Psychology* 44 (6):1753–63.

Chabad-Lubavitch Network. 2007. *Lifko'ah et Ha-yeina'im (Open Your Eyes).* Brooklyn, N.Y.: Chabad-Lubavitch Network.

Chapin, Bambi. 2008. "Transforming Possession: Josephine and the Work of Culture." *Ethos* 36 (2):220–45.

Chicago Brain Network. 2010. *Invisible Forces and Powerful Beliefs: Gravity, Gods and Minds.* Upper Saddle River, N.J.: Pearson Scientific (FT Press).

Chiu, Leo P. W. 1989. "Differential Diagnosis and Management of Hallucinations." *Journal of the Hong Kong Medical Association* 41 (3):292–97.

Christian, William. 1981. *Apparitions in Late Medieval and Renaissance Spain.* Princeton: Princeton University Press.

———. 1989 [1972]. *Person and God in a Spanish Valley.* Princeton: Princeton University Press.

———. 1996. *Visionaries.* Berkeley: University of California Press.

———. 1998. "Six Hundred Years of Visionaries in Spain: Those Believed and Those Ignored." In *Challenging Authority,* edited by M. Hanagan, L. P. Moch, and W. Brake, pp. 107–19. Minneapolis: University of Minnesota Press.

Christian, William, and Gabor Klaniczay, eds. 2008. *The "Vision" Thing.* Budapest: Collegium Budapest Workshop Series No. 18.

Clancy, Susan. 2006. *Abducted.* Cambridge, Mass: Harvard University Press.

Claridge, Gordon, ed. 1997. *Schizotypy.* Oxford, U.K.: Oxford University Press.

Classen, Constance. 1997. "Foundations for an Anthropology of the Senses." *International Social Science Journal* 49 (153):401–12.

Cohen, S., T. Kamarck, and R. Mermelstein. 1983. "A Global Measure of Perceived Stress." *Journal of Health and Social Behavior* 24:385–96.

Cole, Jennifer. 2010. *Sex and Salvation.* Chicago: University of Chicago Press.

Cole, Michael, and Sylvia Scriber. 1974. *Culture and Thought.* New York: John Wiley.

Coleman, Simon. 2000. *The Globalization of Charismatic Christianity.* Cambridge, U.K.: Cambridge University Press.

Coles, Robert. 1990. *The Spiritual Life of Children.* Boston: Houghton Mifflin.

Collins, James, and Richard Blot. 2003. *Literacy and Literacies.* Cambridge, U.K.: Cambridge University Press.

Comaroff, Jean. 1985. *Body of Power, Spirit of Resistance: The Culture and History of a South African People.* Chicago: University of Chicago Press.

Comaroff, Jean, and John Comaroff. 1991. *Of Revelation and Revolution.* Chicago: University of Chicago Press.

Cook, Joanna. 2010. *Meditation in Modern Buddhism: Renunciation and Change in Thai Monastic Life.* Cambridge, U.K.: Cambridge University Press.

Covington, Dennis. 1995. *Salvation on Sand Mountain: Snake Handling and Redemption in Southern Appalachia.* New York: Penguin.

Cox, Harvey. 1995. *Fire from Heaven: The Rise of Pentecostal Spirituality and the Reshaping of Religion in the Twenty-first Century.* Cambridge, Mass.: Da Capo.

Crapanzano, Vincent. 1985. *Tuhami.* Chicago: University of Chicago Press.

———. 2000. *Serving the Word.* New York: New Press.

Crawford, H.J. 1982. "Hypnotizability, Daydreaming Styles, Imagery Vividness, and Absorption: A Multidimensional Study." *Journal of Personality and Social Psychology* 42:915–26.

Crocker, Jon Christopher. 1985. *Vital Souls.* Tucson: University of Arizona Press.

Csikszentmihalyi, Mihaly. 1991. *Flow: The Psychology of Optimal Experience.* New York: HarperPerennial.

Csordas, Thomas. 1993. "The Somatic Mode of Attention." *Cultural Anthropology* 8:135–56.

———. 1994. *The Sacred Self.* Berkeley: University of California Press.

Cunningham, Loren. 1984. *Is That Really You, God?* Seattle: YWAM.

Curtis, Brent, and John Eldredge. 1997. *The Sacred Romance.* Nashville, Tenn.: Thomas Nelson.

Dalai Lama. 2002. *How to Practice.* Translated and edited by Jeffrey Hopkins. New York: Atria Books.

Danzinger, Eve. 2006. "The Thought That Counts." In *Roots of Human Sociality,* edited by Nick Enfield and Stephen Levinson, pp. 259–78. New York: Berg.

Davidson, Richard, Jon Kabat-Zinn, Jessica Shumacher, Melissa Rosenkranz, Daniel Muller, Saki Santorelli, Ferris Urbanowski, Anne Harrington, Katherine Bonus, and John Sheridan. 2003. "Alterations in Brain and Immune Function Produced by Mindfulness Meditation." *Psychosomatic Medicine* 65:64–70.

Davis, Edward, and Bonnie Badenoch. 2009. "Storying God Images." *Connections and Reflections.* Winter: 14–38.

Davis, M. H. 1980. "A Multidimensional Approach to Individual Differences in Empathy." *JSAS Catalog of Selected Documents in Psychology* 10:85.

———. 1983. "Measuring Individual Differences in Empathy: Evidence for a Multidimensional Approach." *Journal of Personality and Social Psychology* 44:113–26.

Davis, Martin, Murray Griffin, and Sue Vice. 2001. "Affective Reactions to Auditory Hallucinations in Psychotic, Evangelical and Control Groups." *British Journal of Clinical Psychology* 40:361–70.

Dawkins, Richard. 2006. *The God Delusion.* New York: Bantam.

Dayton, Donald. 1987. *Theological Roots of Pentecostalism.* Grand Rapids, Mich.: Baker.

Dean, Graham, and Peter Morris. 2003. "The Relationship Between Self Reports of Imagery and Spatial Ability." *British Journal of Psychology* 94:245–73.

Dee, John. 1975 [1564]. *Monas Hieroglyphica* [published as *The Hieroglyphic Monad*]. York Beach, Me.: Weiser Books.

Dein, Simon, and Roland Littlewood. 2007. "The Voice of God." *Anthropology and Medicine* 14 (2):213–28.

Dennett, Daniel. 2006. *Breaking the Spell.* New York: Viking.

Descola, Phillipe, and Gísli Pálsson, eds. 1996. *Nature and Society.* London: Routledge.

Desjarlais Robert. 2003. *Sensory Biographies.* Berkeley: University of California Press.

Devereux, George. 2000 [1956]. "Normal and Abnormal." In *Cultural Psychiatry and Medical Anthropology,* edited by Roland Littlewood and Simon Dein, pp. 213–89. New Brunswick, N.J.: Athlone.

Didi-Huberman, Georges. 1995. *Fra Angelico: Dissemblance and Figuration.* Chicago: University of Chicago Press.

Diener, E., R. Emmons, J. Larsen, and S. Griffin. 1985. "The Satisfaction with Life Scale." *Journal of Personality Assessment* 49 (1):71–75.

Dionysius the Areopagite. 1940. *The Divine Names and the Mystical Theology.* Translated by Clarence E. Rolt. New York: Macmillan.

Di Sabatino, David. 1999. *The Jesus People Movement.* Westport, Conn.: Greenwood.

diSessa, Andrea, and Bruce Sherin. 1998. "What Changes in Conceptual Change?" *International Journal of Science Education* 20 (10):1155–91.

diSessa, Andrea, and Joseph Wagner. 2005. "What Coordination Has to Say About Transfer." In *Transfer of Learning,* edited by J. Mestre, pp. 121–54. Greenwich, Conn.: Information Age.

Dunlosky, John, and Janet Metcalfe. 2009. *Metacognition.* Los Angeles: Sage.

Durkheim, Emile. 1995 [1915]. *Elementary Forms of the Religious Life.* New York: Free Press.

Dyrness, W. 2004. *Reformed Theology and Visual Culture.* Cambridge, U.K.: Cambridge University Press.

———. 2008. *Senses of the Soul.* Eugene, Ore.: Cascade.

Edwards, Kathyrn, and Susie Speakman Such. 2008. *Leonarde's Ghost.* Kirksville, Mo.: Truman State University.

Eliot, George. 1994 [1874]. *Middlemarch.* London: Penguin.

———. 2006 [1859]. *The Lifted Veil.* Hoboken, N.J.: Melville House.

Elisha, Omri. 2011. *Moral Ambition: Mobilization and Social Outreach in Evangelical Megachurches.* Berkeley: University of California Press.

Elliott, Dyan. 2004. *Proving Women.* Princeton: Princeton University Press.

Enfield, Nicholas, and Stephen Levinson, eds. 2006. *Roots of Human Sociality.* Oxford, U.K.: Berg.

Engelke, Matthew. 2007. *A Problem of Presence.* Berkeley: University of California Press.

Epley, Nicholas, Scott Akalis, Adam Waytz, and John Cacioppo. 2008. "Creating Social Connection Through Inferential Reproduction." *Psychological Science* 19 (2):114–20.

Eskridge, Larry. 2005. "God's Forever Family." Ph.D. diss., Stirling University.

Evans-Pritchard, E. E. 1937. *Witchcraft, Oracles and Magic Among the Azande.* Oxford, U.K.: Oxford University University Press.

———. 1956. *Nuer Religion.* Oxford, U.K.: Oxford University Press.

Fanger, Claire, ed. 1998. *Conjuring Spirits.* University Park: Penn State University Press.

Feinberg, Margery. 2005. *God Whispers.* Orlando, Fla.: Relevant Books.

Festinger, Leon, Henry Riecken, and Stanley Schachter. 2008 [1956]. *When Prophecy Fails: A Social and Psychological Study of a Modern Group That Predicted the Destruction of the World.* London: Pinter and Martin.

Finke, R.A. 1989. *Principles of Mental Imagery.* Cambridge, Mass.: MIT Press.

Finke, Roger, and Rodney Starke. 2006. *The Churching of America, 1776–2005: Winnders and Losers in Our Religious Economy.* New Brunswick, N.J.: Rutgers University Press.

Finney, Charles. 1875. *Memoirs.* New York: A. S. Barnes & Co.

Flavell, J., H. Shipstead, and K. Croft. 1980. "What Young Children Think You See When Their Eyes Are Closed." *Cognition* 8:369–87.

Fogel, Robert. 2000. The *Fourth Great Awakening and the Future of Egalitarianism.* Chicago: University of Chicago Press.

Foster, Richard. 1998 [1978]. *Celebration of Discipline: The Path to Spiritual Growth.* New York: HarperSanFrancisco.

———. 2008. *Life with God.* New York: HarperCollins.

Fox, George. 1976 [1694]. *The Journal of George Fox.* Richmond, Ind.: Friends United.

Fox, Richard. 2004. *Jesus in America.* New York: HarperSanFrancisco.

Fox, Robin Lane. 1986. *Pagans and Christians.* New York: Knopf.

Frank, Jerome. 1973. *Persuasion and Healing: A Comparative Study of Psychotherapy.* Baltimore: Johns Hopkins University Press.

Frazer, George James. 2002 [1922]. *The Golden Bough.* New York: Dover.

Freedman, Robert. 2010. *The Madness Within Us: Schizophrenia as a Neuronal Process.* Oxford, U.K.: Oxford University Press.

Freud, Sigmund. 1910. *Leonardo da Vinci; A Psychosexual Study of an Infantile Reminiscence.* New York: Moffat, Yard & Co.

———. 1961 [1927]. *The Future of an Illusion.* New York: Norton.

Friedman, Richard. 1987. *Who Wrote the Bible?* New York: HarperCollins.

Frisbee: The Life and Death of a Hippie Preacher. 2005. Produced by Jester Media in co-production with KQED.

Fromm, Erika, and Stephen Katz. 1990. *Self-Hypnosis.* New York: Guilford.

Fulton, Rachel. 2002. *From Judgment to Passion: Devotion to Christ and the Virgin Mary, 800–1200.* New York: Columbia University Press.

Gabbard, Glen. 2005. *Psychodynamic Psychiatry in Clinical Practice.* Arlington, Va.: American Psychiatric Publishing.

Gade, Anna. 2004. *Perfection Makes Practice.* Honolulu: University of Hawaii Press.

Gallagher, Shaun. 2005. *How the Body Shapes the Mind.* Oxford, U.K.: Clarendon.

Gallagher, Winifred. 2009. *Rapt: Attention and the Focused Life.* New York: Penguin.

Galton, Francis. 1883. *Inquiry into Human Faculty and Its Development.* London: Macmillan.

Gallup, George, Jr., and D. Michael Lindsay. 1999. *Surveying the Religious Landscape.* Harrisburg, Penn.: Morehouse.

Garb, Jonathan. 2009. *The Chosen Will Become Herds: Studies in Twentieth-Century Kabbalah.* New Haven: Yale University Press.

———. 2011. *Shamanic Trance in Modern Kabbalah.* Chicago: University of Chicago Press.

Gaskins, Suzanne. In press. "Pretend Play as Culturally Constructed Activity." In *Oxford Handbook on The Development of Imagination,* edited by Marjorie Taylor. Oxford, U.K.: Oxford University Press.

Gaskins, Suzanne, Wendy Haight, and David Lancy. 2007. "The Cultural Construction of Play." In *Play and Development: Evolutionary, Sociocultural and Functional Perspectives,* edited by Artin Göncü and Suzanne Gaskins, pp. 179–202. Mahwah, N.J.: Lawrence Erlbaum.

Geurts, Kathyrn. 2002. *Culture and the Senses.* Berkeley: University of California Press.

Gibbs, Raymond. 2005. *Embodiment and Cognitive Science.* Cambridge, U.K.: Cambridge University.

Gills, James. 2004. *Imaginations.* Lake Mary, Fla.: Creation House.

Glicksohn, J., and T. R. Barrett. 2003. "Absorption and Hallucinatory Experience." *Applied Cognitive Psychology* 17:833–49.

Glisky, Martha, and John Kihlstrom. 1993. "Hypnotizability and Facets of Openness." *International Journal of Clinical and Experimental Hypnosis* 41 (2):112–13.

Glisky, Martha, Douglas Tataryn, Betsy Tobias, John Kihlstron, and Kevin McConkey. 1991. "Absorption, Openness to Experience and Hypnotizability." *Journal of Personality and Social Psychology* 60 (2):263–72.

Goll, James. 2004. *The Beginner's Guide to Hearing God.* Ventura, Calif.: Regal.

Göncü, Artin, and Suzanne Gaskins, eds. 2006. *Play and Development: Evolutionary, Sociocultural, and Functional Perspectives.* Mahwah, N.J.: Lawrence Erlbaum.

———. 2011. "Comparing and Extending Piaget's and Vygotsky's Understandings of Play: Symbolic Play as Individual, Sociocultural, and Educational Interpretation." In *Oxford Handbook of the Development of Play,* edited by A. D. Pellegrini. Oxford, U.K.: Oxford University Press.

Goodman, Yehuda. 2009. "'You Look, Thank God, Quite Good on the Outside': Imitating the Ideal Self in a Jewish Ultra-Orthodox Rehabilitation Site." *Medical Anthropology Quarterly* 23 (2):122–41.

Goody, Esther. 1995. *Social Intelligence and Interaction: Expressions and Implications of the Social Bias in Human Intelligence.* Cambridge, U.K.: Cambridge University Press.

Goody, Jack. 1977. *The Domestication of the Savage Mind.* Cambridge, U.K.: Cambridge University Press.

Gottesman, Irving. 1991. *Schizophrenia Genesis.* New York: W. H. Freeman.

Goudge, Elizabeth. 2001 [1946]. *The Little White Horse.* New York: Puffin.

Gould, L. 1949. "Auditory Hallucinations and Subvocal Speech." *Journal of Nervous and Mental Disease* 109:418–27.

———. 1950. "Verbal Hallucinations and Automatic Speech." *American Journal of Psychiatry* 107:1010–19.

Grainger, Brett. 2008. *In the World But Not of It: One Family's Militant Faith and the History of Fundamentalism in America.* New York: Walker.

Granqvist, P. M. Mikulincer, and P. R. Shaver. 2010. "Religion as Attachment." *Personality and Social Psychology Review* 14 (1):49–59.

Granovetter, Mark. 1973. "The Strength of Weak Ties." *American Journal of Sociology* 78 (6):1360–80.

Graybeal, Lynda, and Julia Roller. 2006. *Connecting with God.* New York: Harper-Collins.

Grimby, A. 1993. "Bereavement Among Elderly People: Grief Reactions, Post-Bereavement Hallucinations and Quality of Life." *Acta Psychiatrica Scandinavica* 87:72–80.

Gritzalis, Nicoletta, Marc Oster, and Edward J. Frischholz. 2009. "A Concurrent Validity Study Between the Hypnotic Induction Profile (HIP) and the Stanford Hypnotic Clinical Scale for Adults (SHCS:A) in an Inpatient Sample." *American Journal of Clinical Hypnosis* 52 (2):89–93.

Gross, J. J., and O. P. John. 1997. "Revealing Feelings: Facets of Emotional Expressivity in Self-reports, Peer Ratings, and Behavior." *Journal of Personality and Social Psychology* 72:435–48.

Guthrie, Stewart. 1993. *Faces in the Clouds.* Oxford, U.K.: Oxford University Press.

Haight, Wendy, and Peggy Miller. 1992. *Pretending at Home: Development in Sociocultural Context.* Albany: State University of New York Press.

Haight, Wendy, X. Wang, H. Fung, K. Williams, and J. Minz. 1999. "Universal, Developmental and Variable Aspects of Children's Play: A Cross-cultural Comparison of Pretending at Home." *Child Development* 70:1477–88.

Hanks, William. 2010. *Converting Words: Maya in the Age of the Cross.* Berkeley: University of California Press.

Hansen, Mark. 2000. *Embodying Technesis: Technology Beyond Writing.* Ann Arbor: University of Michigan Press.

Happold, F. C. 1990 [1963]. *Mysticism: A Study and Anthology,* rev. ed. Harmondsworth, U.K.: Penguin.

Harding, Susan. 1987. "Convicted by the Holy Spirit: The Rhetoric of Fundamental Baptist Conversion." *American Ethnologist* 14 (1):167–81.

———. 2000. *The Book of Jerry Falwell.* Princeton: Princeton University Press.

Hardy, Alister. 1979. *The Spiritual Nature of Man.* Oxford: Oxford University Press.

Harner, M. 1971. *The Jivaro.* Garden City, N.Y.: Doubleday/Natural History.

Harrington-Watt, David. 1991. "The Private Hopes of American Fundamentalists and Evangelicals, 1925–1975." *Religion and American Culture: A Journal of Interpretation* 1 (2):155–75.

Harris, Paul. 2000. *The Work of the Imagination.* Oxford, U.K.: Blackwell.

Harris, Ruth. 1999. *Lourdes.* New York: Viking.

Harrison, Glyn, Andy Thompson, Jeremy Horwood, Dieter Wolke, and Chris Hollis. 2004. "PLIKS [Psychotic-like symptoms] Interview Schedule." Unpublished ms.

Harvey, Susan. 2006. *Scenting Salvation: Ancient Christianity and the Olfactory Imagination.* Berkeley: University of California Press.

Hatch, Nathan. 1989. *The Democratization of American Christianity.* New Haven: Yale University Press.

Havelock, Eric. 1982. *Preface to Plato.* Cambridge, Mass.: Harvard University Press.

Heald, Cynthia. 1998. *Becoming a Woman of Grace.* Nashville, Tenn.: Thomas Nelson.

Heller, David. 1986. *The Children's God.* Chicago: University of Chicago Press.

Hilborn, David, ed. 2001. *"Toronto" in Perspective.* Carlisle, Cumbria, U.K.: Paternoster Press.

Hilgard, E. R. 1981. "Imagery and Imagination in American Psychology." *Journal of Mental Imagery* 5 (1):5–66.

Hill, S. J. 2001. *Enjoying God.* Orlando, Fla.: Relevant Media.

Hirschkind, Charles. 2006. *The Ethical Soundscape.* New York: Columbia University Press.

Hochschild, Arlie. 1979. "Emotion Work, Feeling Rules and Social Structure." *American Journal of Sociology* 85 (3):551–75.

———. 1983. *The Managed Heart: The Commercialization of Human Feeling.* Berkeley: University of California Press.

Hodge, Archibald, and Benjamin Warfield. 1881. "Inspiration." *Presbyterian Review* 6:225–60.

Hoffman R. 1986. "Verbal Hallucination and Language Production Processes in Schizophrenia." *Behavioral and Brain Sciences* 9:503–48.

Hollenwenger, Walter. 2005. *Pentecostalism: Origins and Developments Worldwide.* Peabody, Mass.: Henricksen.

Homan, K. J., and C. J. Boyatzis. 2010. "The Protective Role of Attachment to God Against Eating Disorder Risk Factors." *Eating Disorders* 18 (3):239–58.

Hood, Ralph, Bernard Spilka, Bruce Hunsberger, and Richard Gorsuch. 1996. *The Psychology of Religion.* New York: Guilford.

Hood, William. 1986. "Saint Dominic's Manner of Praying: Gestures in Fra Angelico's Cell Frescoes at S. Marco." *Art Bulletin* 68 (2):195–206.

Horton, K. D., C. G. Ellison, A. Loukas, D. L. Downey, and J. B. Barrett. 2010. "Examining Attachment to God and Health Risk-taking Behaviors in College Students." *Journal of Religion and Health.* Published online, July 15.

Horwood, Jeremy, Giovanni Salvi, Kate Thomas, Larisa Duffy, David Gunnell, Chris Hollis, Glyn Lewis, Paulo Menezes, Andrew Thompson, Dieter Wolke, Stanley Zammit, and Glynn Harrison. 2008. "IQ and Non-Clinical Psychotic Symptoms in 12-Year-Olds." *British Journal of Psychiatry* 193:185–91.

Howes, David. 1991. *The Varieties of Sensory Experience: A Sourcebook in the Anthropology of the Senses.* Toronto: University of Toronto Press.

———, ed. 2005. *The Empire of the Senses.* Oxford, U.K.: Berg.

Hoyt, Irene, Robert Nadon, Patricia Register, Joseph Chorny, William Fleeson, Ellen Grigorian, Laura Otto, and John Kihlstrom. 1989. "Daydreaming, Absorption and Hypnotizability." *International Journal of Clinical and Experimental Hypnosis* 37 (4):332–42.

Hufford, David. 1982. *The Terror that Comes in the Night.* Philadelphia: University of Pennsylvania Press.

Huizinga, Johan. 1949. *Homo Ludens.* London: Routledge and Kegan Paul.

Hybels, Bill. 1998 [1988]. *Too Busy Not to Pray.* Downers Grove, Ill.: InterVarsity.

Inzlicht, Michael, and Alexa Tullett. 2010. "Reflecting on God: Religious Primes Can Reduce Neurophysiological Response to Errors." *Psychological Science* 2 (8):1184–90.

Jackson, Bill. 1999. *The Quest for the Radical Middle.* Cape Town, South Africa: Vineyard International.

Jackson, Michael. 1983. "Knowledge of the Body." *Man* 18 (2):327–45.

James, William. 1961 [1902]. *The Varieties of Religious Experience: A Study in Human Nature.* New York: Macmillan.

Jaynes, Julian. 1979. *The Origin of Consciousness in the Breakdown of the Bicameral Mind.* Boston: Houghton Mifflin.

Jenkins, Philip. 2002. *The Next Christendom: The Coming of Global Christianity.* Oxford, U.K.: Oxford University Press.

Johns, Louise, James Nazroo, Paul Bebbington, and Elizabeth Kuipers. 2002. "Occurrence of Hallucinatory Experiences in a Community Sample and Ethnic Variations." *British Journal of Psychiatry* 180:174–78.

Johns, Louise, and Jim van Os. 2001. "The Continuity of Psychotic Experiences in the General Population." *Clinical Psychology Review* 21 (8):1125–41.

Johnson, Marcia, Shahin Hashtroudi, and D. Stephen Lindsay. 1993. "Source Monitoring." *Psychological Bulletin* 144 (1):3–28.

Johnson, Marcia, and Carol Raye. 1981. "Reality Monitoring." *Psychological Review* 88 (1):67–85.

Johnson, Luke Timothy. 1998. *Religious Experience in Earliest Christianity.* Minneapolis: Fortress.

———. 2004a. *Brother of Jesus, Friend of God: Studies in the Letter of James.* Grand Rapids, Mich.: Eerdmans.

———. 2004b. *Jesus and The Gospels.* The Teaching Company.

Johnston, William, ed. 1973. *The Cloud of Unknowing.* New York: Doubleday.

Jones, Simon, and Charles Fernyhough. 2007. "Neural Correlates of Inner Speech and Auditory Verbal Hallucinations: A Critical Review and Theoretical Integration." *Clinical Psychology Review* 27 (2):140–54.

———. 2009. "Caffeine, Stress, and Proneness to Psychosis-like Experiences: A Preliminary Investigation." *Personality and Individual Differences* 46:562–64.

Joyce, James. 1916. *Portrait of the Artist as a Young Man.* New York: Huebsch.

Justice, Steven. 2008. "Did the Middle Ages Believe in Their Miracles?" *Representations* 103:1–29.

Karen, Robert. 1998. *Becoming Attached.* Oxford, U.K.: Oxford University Press.

Karnes, Michelle. 2011. *Imagination, Meditation and Cognition in the Middle Ages.* Chicago: University of Chicago Press.

Katz, Jack. 1999. *How Emotions Work.* Chicago: University of Chicago Press.

Keane, Webb. 1997. "Religious Language." *Annual Review of Anthropology* 26:47–71.

———. 2007. *Christian Moderns.* Berkeley: University of California Press.

Keller, Eva. 2005. *The Road to Clarity.* New York: Palgrave.

Kent, G., and S. Wahass. 1996. "The Content and Characteristics of Auditory Hallucinations in Saudi Arabia and the U.K: A Cross Cultural Comparison." *Acta Psychiatrica Scandinavica* 94:433–37.

Kessler, Ron, G. Andrews, L. J. Colpe, E. Hiripi, D. K. Mroczek, S.-L. T. Normand, E. Walters, and A. M. Zazlavsky. 2002. "Short Screening Scales to Monitor Population Prevalences and Trends in Non-specific Psychological Distress." *Psychological Medicine* 32:959–76

Kieckhefer, Richard. 1997. *Forbidden Rites.* University Park: Penn State University Press.

Kierkegaard, Søren. 1986 [1843]. *Fear and Trembling.* New York: Penguin.

Kiev, Ari, ed. 1964. *Magic, Faith and Healing.* New York: Free Press.

Kirkpatrick, Lee, and Phillip Shaver. 1990. "Attachment Theory and Religion." *Journal for the Scientific Study of Religion* 29 (3):315–34.

Kirkpatrick, Lee, Daniel Shillito, and Susan Kellas. 1999. "Loneliness, Social Support and Perceived Relationships with God." *Journal of Social and Personal Relationships* 16 (4):513–22.

Kittler, Glenn. 1972. *The Jesus Kids*. New York: Warner Books.

Koenig, Harold. 1999. *The Healing Power of Faith*. New York: Simon and Schuster.

Koenig, Harold, and Harvey Jay Cohen, eds. 2002. *The Link Between Religion and Health: Psychoneuroimmunology and the Faith Factor*. New York: Oxford University Press.

Kohut, Heinz. 1971. *Analysis of the Self*. New York: International Universities.

Kosmin, B., and A. Keysar. 2008. *American Religious Identification Survey*. Trinity College, Hartford, Conn.

Kraft, Charles. 1992. *Defeating Dark Angels*. Ventura, Calif.: Gospel Light.

Krakauer, Jon. 2003. *Under the Banner of Heaven*. New York: Doubleday.

Kravel-Tovi, Michal. 2009. "To See the Invisible Messiah: Messianic Socialization in the Way of a Failed Prophecy in Chabad." *Religion* 39 (3):248–60.

Kravel-Tovi, Michal, and Yoram Bilu. 2008. "The Work of the Present." *American Ethnologist* 35 (1):64–80.

Kremen, A. M., and J. Block. 2002. "Absorption: Construct Explication by Q-sort Assessments of Personality." *Journal of Research in Personality* 36 (3):252–59.

Kripal, Jeffrey. 2007. *Esalen: America and the Religion of No Religion*. Chicago: University of Chicago Press.

Lambek, Michael. 1981. *Human Spirits*. Cambridge, U.K.: Cambridge University Press.

Lambert, Frank. 1999. *Inventing the "Great Awakening."* Princeton: Princeton University Press.

Lamott, Anne. 1999. *Traveling Mercies*. New York: Anchor.

Landy, Joshua, and Michael Saler, eds. 2009. *The Re-enchantment of the World*. Stanford, Calif.: Stanford University Press.

Lang, Andrew. 2011 [1898]. *The Making of Religion*. Charleston, S.C.: BiblioBazaar.

Laroi, Frank, M. Van der Linden, and P. Marczewski. 2004. "The Effects of Emotional Salience, Cognitive Effort and Metacognitive Beliefs on a Reality Monitoring Task in Hallucination-prone Subjects." *British Journal of Clinical Psychology* 43:221–33.

Larson, Edward. 1997. *Summer for the Gods*. Cambridge, Mass.: Harvard University Press.

Launay, G., and P. Slade. 1981. "The Measurement of Hallucinatory Predisposition in Male and Female Prisoners." *Personality and Individual Differences* 2:221–34.

Lawrence, Brother. 1982, *The Practice of the Presence of God*. New Kensington, Penn.: Whitaker House.

Lear, Jonathan. 2003. *Therapeutic Action: An Earnest Plea for Irony*. New York: Other Press.

Lester, Rebecca. 2005. *Jesus in Our Wombs*. Berkeley: University of California Press.

Leudar, Ivan, and Philip Thomas. 2000. *Voices of Reason, Voices of Insanity*. London: Routledge.

Levy, Robert. 1975. *Tahitians*. Chicago: University of Chicago Press.

Lewis, C. S. 1955. *Surprised by Joy: The Shape of My Early Life.* New York: Harcourt Brace Jovanovich.

———. 1956. *Till We Have Faces.* New York: Harcourt Brace.

——— 1980 [1952]. *Mere Christianity.* New York: Penguin.

Lienhardt, Godfrey. 1961. *Divinity and Experience: The Religion of the Dinka.* Oxford, U.K.: Clarendon.

Lilla, Mark. 2007. *The Stillborn God.* New York: Knopf.

Lillard, Angela. 1998. "Ethnopsychologies: Cultural Variations in Theories of Mind." *Psychological Bulletin* 123 (1):3–32.

Lindsey, Hal, and Carole Carlson. 1970. *The Late Great Planet Earth.* Grand Rapids, Mich.: Zondervan.

Lloyd, G. E. R. 2007. *Cognitive Variations.* Oxford, U.K.: Oxford University Press.

Loyola, Ignatius. 1963. *The Spiritual Exercises of Ignatius Loyola.* Translated by Thomas Corbishley. Whethampstead, Hertfordshire, U.K.: Anthony Clarke.

———. 1992a. *The Spiritual Exercises.* Translated by Joseph Tetlow. New York: Crossroads.

———. 1992b. *The Spiritual Exercises.* Translated by George Ganss. Chicago: Loyola.

Luhrmann, T. M. 1986. "An Interpretation of the Fama Fraternitatis with Respect to Dee's *Monas Hieroglyphica.*" *Ambix* (*Journal for the Society for the History of Chemistry and Alchemy*) 33 (1):1–10.

———. 1989. *Persuasions of the Witch's Craft.* Cambridge, Mass.: Harvard University Press.

———. 1998. "Partial Failure: The Attempt to Deal with Uncertainty in Psychoanalytic Psychotherapy and in Anthropology." *Psychoanalytic Quarterly* 67:449–73.

———. 2000. *Of Two Minds: The Growing Disorder in American Psychiatry.* New York: Knopf.

———. 2004. "Metakinesis: How God Becomes Intimate in Contemporary U.S. Christianity." *American Anthropologist* 106 (3):518–28.

———. 2010. "Down and Out in Chicago." *Raritan.* Winter.

———. 2011. "Hallucinations." *Annual Review of Anthropology* 40:71–85.

Luhrmann, T. M., Howard Nusbaum, and Ronald Thisted. 2010. "The Absorption Hypothesis." *American Anthropologist* 112 (1):66–78.

Luhrmann, T. M., Howard Nusbaum, and Ronald Thisted. Forthcoming. "Prayer Practice Affects Cognitive Processing."

Lurie, Alison. 1967. *Imaginary Friends.* New York: Coward-McCann.

Luskin, F. M. 2004. "Optimal Healing Environments: Transformative Practices for Integrating Mind, Body and Spirit." *Journal of Complementary and Alternative Medicine* 10 (Supplement 1):15–25.

Lutz, Antonine, Heleen Slagter, Nancy Rawlings, Andrew Francis, Lawrence Greischar, and Richard Davidson. 2009. "Mental Training Enhances Attentional Stability: Neural and Behavioral Evidence." *Journal of Neuroscience* 29 (42):12418–3427.

Lutz, Catherine. 1988. *Unnatural Emotions.* Chicago: University of Chicago Press.

Lynn, Steven Jay, and Judith Rhue. 1986. "The Fantasy Prone Person: Hypnosis, Imagination and Creativity." *Journal of Personality and Social Psychology* 51:404–8.

———. 1991. *Theories of Hypnosis: Current Models and Perspectives.* New York: Guilford.

MacLean, K. A., E. Ferrer, S. R. Aichele, D. A. Bridwell, A. P. Zanesco, T. L. Jacobs, B. G. King, E. L. Rosenberg, B. K. Sahdra, P. R. Shaver, B. A. Wallace, G. R. Mangun, and C. D. Saron. 2010. "Intensive Meditation Training Leads to Improvements in Perceptual Discrimination and Sustained Attention." *Psychological Science* 6:829–39.

MacNutt, Francis. 1995. *Deliverance from Evil Spirits.* Grand Rapids, Mich.: Baker.

Mahmood, Saba. 2005. *Politics of Piety.* Princeton: Princeton University Press.

Malcolm, Janet. 1982. *Psychoanalysis, the Impossible Profession.* New York: Knopf.

Malinowski, Bronislaw. 1948. *Magic, Science and Religion.* New York: Free Press.

———. 1989. *A Diary in the Strict Sense of the Term.* Stanford, Calif.: Stanford University Press.

Marks, David. 1973. "Visual Imagery Differences in the Recall of Pictures." *British Journal of Psychology* 64 (1):17–24.

Markus, Hazel Rose, and Shinobu Kitayama. 1991. "Culture and the Self: Implications for Cognition, Emotion, and Motivation." *Psychological Review* 98 (2):224–53.

Marsden, George. 1987. *Reforming Fundamentalism: Fuller Seminary and the New Evangelicalism.* Grand Rapids, Mich.: Eerdmans.

———. 1991. *Understanding Fundamentalism and Evangelicalism.* Grand Rapids, Mich.: Eerdmans.

———. 2003. *Jonathan Edwards: A Life.* New Haven: Yale University Press.

———. 2006. *Fundamentalism and American Culture.* Oxford, U.K.: Oxford University Press.

Marty, Martin. 1986–96. *Modern American Religion,* vols. 1–3. Chicago: University of Chicago Press.

Marty, Martin, and R. Scott Appleby. 1992. *The Glory and the Power.* Boston: Beacon Press.

Mather, T. C. 2000. *Prophetic Deliverance.* Tulsa, Okla.: Insight.

Mauss, Marcel. 2003. *On Prayer,* edited and with an introduction by W. S. F. Pickering. Oxford, U.K.: Berghahn Books.

McDargh, John. 1983. *Psychoanalytic Object Relations and the Study of Religion.* Lanham, Md.: University Press of America.

McDermott, Gerald. 1995. *Seeing God.* Downers Grove, Ill.: InterVarsity.

McKelvie, Stuart. 1995. "Vividness of Visual Imagery." *Journal of Mental Imagery* Fall/Winter: 1–252.

McLoughlin, William. 1978. *Revivals, Awakenings and Reform.* Chicago: University of Chicago Press.

McNally, Richard, Susan Clancy, D. Schnacter, and R. Pitman. 2000. "Personality Profiles, Dissociation and Absorption in Women Reporting Repressed, Recovered or Continuous Memories of Childhood Sexual Abuse." *Journal of Consulting and Clinical Psychology* 68 (6):1033–37.

McNamara, William. 2006. *Wild and Robust.* Cambridge, U.K.: Cowley.

McPherson, Miller, Lynn Smith-Lovin, and Matthew Brashears. 2006. "Social Isolation in America: Changes in Core Discussion Networks over Two Decades." *American Sociological Review* 71 (3):353–75.

Meeks, Wayne. 1984. *The First Urban Christians.* New Haven: Yale University Press.

Meissner, W. W. 2002. *Ignatius of Loyola: The Psychology of a Saint.* New Haven: Yale University Press.

Menzies, Victoria, Ann Gill, and Cheryl Bourguignon. 2008. "Absorption: An Individual Difference to Consider in Mind-body Interventions." *Journal of Holistic Nursing* 26 (4):297–302.

Merton, Thomas. 1948. *The Seven Storey Mountain.* Orlando, Fla.: Harcourt.

———. 1963. *The New Man.* New York: New American Library.

———. 1969. *Contemplative Prayer.* New York: Herder and Herder.

Meyer, Beyer. 1999. *Translating the Devil.* Trenton, N.J.: Africa World.

Micklethwait, John, and Adrian Wooldridge. 2009. *God Is Back.* New York: Penguin.

Midelfort, Erik. 2000. *A History of Madness in Sixteenth-Century Germany.* Stanford, Calif.: Stanford University Press.

Miles, Jack. 1995. *God: A Biography.* New York: Knopf.

Miller, Donald. 1997. *Reinventing American Protestantism.* Berkeley: University of California Press.

Miller, Donald, and Tetsunao Yamamori. 2007. *Global Pentecostalism.* Berkeley: University of California Press.

Miller, Perry. 1949. *Jonathan Edwards.* New York: William Sloane Associates.

Miller, William, and Carl Thoresen. 2003. "Spirituality, Religion and Health." *American Psychologist* 58 (1):24–35.

Mitchell, Karen, and Marcia Johnson. 2009. "Source Monitoring 15 Years Later." *Psychological Bulletin* 135 (4):638–77.

Mitchell, Jon. 1997. "The Importance of Feelings in the Analysis of Belief." *Journal of the Royal Anthropological Institute* 3 (1):79–94.

Moreton, Bethany. 2009. *To Serve God and Wal-Mart: The Making of Christian Free Enterprise.* Cambridge, Mass.: Harvard University Press.

Morewedge, Carey, and Michael Norton. 2009. "When Dreaming Is Believing: The (Motivated) Interpretation of Dreams." *Journal of Personality and Social Psychology* 96 (2):249–64.

Morgain, Rachel, and T. M. Luhrmann. Forthcoming. "Prayer as Inner Sense Cultivation." *Ethos.*

Morphew, Derek. 1991. *Breakthrough*. Cape Town, South Africa: Vineyard International.

Nadon, R., I. Hoyt, P. Register, and J. Kihlstrom. 1991. "Absorption and Hypnotizability." *Journal of Personality and Social Psychology* 60:144–53.

Namasceau, Vlad, and Arnold Halloy. In press. *Ethos,* special issue, "Learning Possession."

Nathan, Rich, and Ken Wilson. 1995. *Empowered Evangelicals*. Westerville, Ohio: Vineyard Church of Columbus.

Neisser, Ulrich. 1976. *Cognition and Reality: Principles and Implications of Cognitive Psychology*. San Francisco: W. H. Freeman.

Newberg, Andrew, Eugene D'Aquili, and Vince Rause. 2001. *Why God Won't Go Away: Brain Science and the Biology of Belief*. New York: Random House.

Newberg, Andrew, and Mark Robert Waldman. 2009. *What God Does to Your Brain*. New York: Ballantine.

Newberg, Andrew, Nancy Winteringa, Donna Morgan, and Mark Waldman. 2006. "The Measurement of Regional Cerebral Blood Flow During Glossolalia: A Preliminary SPECT Study." *Psychiatry Research: Neuroimaging* 148:67–71.

Newman, Barbara. 2005. "What Did It Mean to Say 'I Saw'?" *Speculum* 80 (1):1–43.

Newport, J. Carrol. 2005. "Another Look at Evangelicals in America Today." Gallup News Service.

Nichols, Stephen. 2008. *Jesus: Made in America*. Downers Grove, Ill.: InterVarsity.

Noll, Mark. 1994. *The Scandal of the Evangelical Mind*. Grand Rapids, Mich.: Eerdmans.

———. 2002. *The Old Religion in a New World*. Grand Rapids, Mich.: Eerdmans.

Noll, Richard. 1985. "Mental Imagery Cultivation as a Cultural Phenomenon, with Commentary." *Current Anthropology* 26 (4):443–61.

Nouwen, Henri. 1981. *The Way of the Heart: Desert Spirituality and Contemporary Ministry*. New York: HarperCollins.

Ohayon, M., R. Priest, M. Caulet, and C. Guilleminault. 1996. "Hynagogic and Hynapompic Hallucinations: Pathological Phenomena?" *British Journal of Psychiatry* 169:459–67.

Okulate, G. T., and O. B. Jones. 2003. "Auditory Hallucinations in Schizophrenic and Affective Disorder Nigerian Patients: Phenomenological Comparison." *Transcultural Psychiatry* 40 (4):531–41.

Olds, Jacqueline, and Richard Schwartz. 2010. *The Lonely American*. Boston: Beacon Press.

Omartian, Stormie. 2004. *The Power of Praying*. Eugene, Ore.: Harvest House.

O'Nell, Theresa. 1998. *Disciplined Hearts*. Berkeley: University of California Press.

Ong, Walter. 1982. *Orality and Literacy*. London: Routledge.

Orsi, Robert. 1996. *Thank You, St. Jude*. New Haven: Yale University Press.

Ostling, Richard. 1993. "The Church Search," *Time*. April 5.

Otto, Rudolf. 1923. *The Idea of the Holy: An Inquiry into the Non-Rational Factor in the Idea of the Divine and Its Relation to the Rational.* London: Oxford University Press.

Owen, Alex. 1990. *The Darkened Room.* Philadelphia: University of Pennsylvania Press.

Pagels, Elaine. 1995. *The Origin of Satan.* New York: Random House.

Paloutzian, Raymond, and Craig Ellison. 1982. "Loneliness, Spiritual Well-being and the Quality of Life." In *Loneliness,* edited by L. A. Peplau and D. Perlman, pp. 224–37. New York: Wiley.

Paloutzian, Raymond, and Crystal Park, eds. 2005. *Handbook of the Psychology of Religion and Spirituality.* New York: Guilford.

Pargament, Kenneth. 1997. *The Psychology of Religion and Coping.* New York: Guilford.

Parish, Steven. 1996. *Hierarchy and Its Discontents.* Philadelphia: University of Pennsylvania Press.

Pazder, Lawrence, and Michelle Smith. 1980. *Michelle Remembers.* New York: Pocket.

Pekala, R. J., C. F. Wenger, and R. L. Levine. 1985. "Individual Differences in Phenomenological Experience: States of Consciousness as a Function of Absorption." *Journal of Personality and Social Psychology* 48:125–32.

Pelikan, Jaroslav. 2005. *Whose Bible Is It?* New York: Viking.

Pennington, M. Basil. 1980. *Centering Prayer: Renewing an Ancient Christian Prayer Form.* New York: Doubleday

Perky, C.W. 1910. "An Experimental Study of Imagination." *American Journal of Psychology* 21:422–52.

Pew Research Center. 2006a. *Are We Happy Yet?* Washington, D.C.: Pew Research Center.

———. 2006b. *Spirit and Power: A Ten Country Survey of Pentecostals.* Washington, D.C.: Pew Research Center.

———. 2008. *U.S. Religious Landscape Survey.* Washington, D.C.: Pew Forum on Religious and Public Life.

Pierre, Joseph. 2009. "Letter to the Editor: Naming Names." *Psychological Medicine* 39:1578–80.

Poloma, Margaret. 2003. *Main Street Mystics: The Toronto Blessing and Reviving Pentecostalism.* Walnut Creek, Calif.: Alta Mira.

Poloma, Margaret, and George Gallup. 1991. *Varieties of Prayer.* Philadelphia: Trinity Press International.

Posey, Thomas, and Mary Losch. 1983. "Auditory Hallucinations of Hearing Voices in 375 Normal Subjects." *Imagination, Cognition and Personality* 3 (2):99–113.

Powdermaker, Hortense. 1966. *Stranger and Friend: The Way of an Anthropologist.* New York: W. W. Norton.

Powell, Lynda, Leila Shahabi, and Carl Thoresen. 2003. "Religion and Spirituality: Linkages to Physical Health." *American Psychologist* 58 (1):36–52.

Prothero, Stephen. 2003. *American Jesus.* New York: Farrar, Straus and Giroux.

Proudfoot, Wayne. 1985. *Religious Experience.* Berkeley: University of California Press.

Putnam, Robert. 2000. *Bowling Alone.* New York: Simon and Schuster.

Putnam, Robert, and David Campbell. 2010. *American Grace.* New York: Simon and Schuster.

Radway, Janice. 1984. *Reading the Romance.* Chapel Hill: University of North Carolina Press.

Rambo, Lewis. 1993. *Understanding Religious Conversion.* New Haven: Yale University Press.

Ramsay, David, and Joel Robbins, eds. 2008. *Anthropological Quarterly,* special edition, "Theory of Mind."

Ratzinger, Joseph. 1989. "Letter to the Bishops of the Catholic Church on Some Aspects of Christian Meditation." Issued by the Congregation for the Doctrine of Faith, October 15.

Reichel-Dolmatoff, Gerardo. 1975. *The Shaman and the Jaguar.* Philadelphia: Temple University Press.

Reiner, Sarah R., Tamara Anderson, M. Elizabeth Lewis Hall, and Todd W. Hall. 2010. "Adult Attachment, God Attachment and Gender in Relation to Perceived to Stress." *Journal of Psychology and Theology* 38 (3):175–85.

Ridder, Dirk de, Koen van Laere, Patrick Dupont, Tomas Menovsky, and Paul van de Heyning. 2007. "Visualizing Out-of-Body Experience in the Brain." *New England Journal of Medicine* 357 (18):1829–33.

Risen, Jane, and Thomas Gilavich. 2008. "Why People Are Reluctant to Tempt Fate." *Journal of Personality and Social Psychology* 95 (2):293–307.

Rizzuto, Ana-Maria. 1979. *The Birth of the Living God: A Psychoanalytic Study.* Chicago: University of Chicago Press.

———. 2007. "God in the Mind." *Annual of Psychoanalysis* 35:25–46.

Robbins, Joel. 2001. "God Is Nothing But Talk." *American Anthropologist* 103 (4):901–12.

———. 2004a. *Becoming Sinners.* Berkeley: University of California Press.

———. 2004b. "The Globalization of Pentecostal and Charismatic Christianity." *Annual Reviews in Anthropology* 33:117–43.

———. 2007. "Continuity Thinking and Christian Belief." *Current Anthropology* 48 (1):5–48.

———. 2010. "Working on Individualism." Immanent Frame (SSRC blog). http://blogs.ssrc.org/tif/2010/07/06/working-on-individualism.

Roche, S., and K. McConkey. 1990. "Absorption: Nature, Assessment, Correlates." *Journal of Personality and Social Psychology* 59:91–101.

Romme, Marius, and Alexandra Escher. 1989. "Hearing Voices." *Schizophrenia Bulletin* 15 (2):209–16.

———. 1993. *Accepting Voices.* London: Mind.

Roof, Wade Clark. 1993. *A Generation of Seekers.* San Francisco: HarperSan Francisco.

Rosengren, Karl, Carl Johnson, and Paul Harris, eds. 2000. *Imagining the Impossible: Magical, Scientific, and Religious Thinking in Children.* Cambridge, U.K.: Cambridge University Press.

Rosin, Hanna. 2007. *God's Harvard: A Christian College on a Mission to Save America.* Orlando, Fla.: Harcourt.

Ross, Thomas. 2007. "Attachment and Religious Beliefs—Attachment Styles in Evangelical Christians." *Journal of Religion and Health* 46 (1):75–84.

Rowatt, Wade, and Lee Kirkpatrick. 2002. "Two Dimensions of Attachment to God and Their Relation to Affect, Religiosity and Personality Constructs." *Journal for the Scientific Study of Religion* 41 (4):637–51.

Rush, Norman. 1992. *Mating.* New York: Vintage.

Russell, Dan, Letitia Peplau, and M. Ferguson. 1978. "Developing a Measure of Loneliness." *Journal of Personality Assessment* 42:290–94.

Sackville-West, Vita. 1936. *Saint Joan of Arc.* New York: Grove.

Sadeh, Avi, Shai Hen-Gal, and Liat Tikotsky. 2007. "Young Children's Reaction to War-related Stress: A Survey-assessment of an Innovative Intervention." *Pediatrics* 121 (1):46–53.

Sadock, Benjamin, Virginia Sadock, and Pedro Ruiz, eds. 2009. *Kaplan and Sadock's Comprehensive Textbook of Psychiatry.* Philadelphia: Wolters Kulwer Heath/ Lippincott Williams and Wilkins.

Samarin, William. 1972. *Tongues of Men and Angels.* New York: Macmillan.

San Francisco Oracle. 1966–68.

Schaeffer, Frank. 2009. *Patience with God.* Cambridge, Mass.: Da Capo.

Schafer, Roy. 1993. *The Analytic Attitude.* London: Karnac Books.

Schaff, Philip, and Henry Wace, eds. 1892. *A Select Library of Nicene and Post Nicene Fathers of the Christian Church,* 2nd series, vol. 4. New York: Scribners.

Schieffelin, Bambi. 2002. "Marking Time." *Current Anthropology* 43 (4):5–17.

Schjoedt, Uffe, Hans Stødkilde-Jørgensen, Armin W. Geertz, and Andreas Roepstorff. 2009. "Highly Religious Participants Recruit Areas of Social Cognition in Personal Prayer." *Social Cognitive and Affective Neuroscience* 4:199–207.

Schmidt, Leigh. 2000. *Hearing Things: Religion, Illusion, and the American Enlightenment.* Cambridge, Mass.: Harvard University Press.

Scholem, Gershom. 1974. *Kabbalah.* New York: Quadrangle.

Schwab, R., and K. Peterson. 1990. "Religiousness: Its Relationship to Loneliness, Neuroticism, and Subjective Well-being." *Journal for the Scientific Study of Religion* 29:335–45.

Schwartzman, Helen. 1978. *Transformations.* New York: Plenum.

Scott J. D. Chant, G. Andrews, and J. McGrath. 2005. "Psychotic-like Experience in the General Community." *Psychological Medicine* 36:231–38.

Seeman, Teresa, Linda Fagan Dubin, and Melvin Seeman. 2003. "Religiosity/Spirituality and Health: A Critical Review of the Evidence for Biological Pathways." *American Psychologist* 58 (1):53–63.

Seligman, Rebecca, and Laurence Kirmayer. 2008. "Dissociative Experience and Cultural Neuroscience." *Culture, Medicine and Psychiatry* 32 (1):31–64.

Seremetakis, C. Nadia., ed. 1994. *The Senses Still.* Chicago: University of Chicago Press.

Shanon, Benny. 2002. *The Antipodes of the Mind.* Oxford, U.K.: Oxford University Press.

Shapiro, Kimron L., Jane E. Raymond, and Karen M. Arnell. 1994. "Attention to Visual Pattern Information Produces the Attentional Blink in Rapid Serial Visual Presentation." *Journal of Experimental Psychology: Human Perception and Performance* 20 (2):357–71

Shires, Preston. 2007. *Hippies of the Religious Right.* Houston: Baylor.

Shoaps, Robin. 2002. "Pray Earnestly." *Journal of Linguistic Anthropology* 12 (1):34–71.

Shweder, Richard. 1991. *Thinking Through Cultures: Expeditions in Cultural Psychology.* Cambridge, Mass.: Harvard University Press.

———. 2003. *Why Do Men Barbecue?: Recipes for Cultural Psychology.* Cambridge, Mass.: Harvard University Press.

Sidgwick H., A. Johnson, F. W. H. Myers, F. Podmore, and E. M. Sidgwick. 1894. "Report on the Census of Hallucinations." *Proceedings of the Society for Psychical Research* 34:25–394.

Siegel, Ron. 1984. "Hostage Hallucinations: Visual Imagery Induced by Isolation and Life-threatening Stress." *Journal of Nervous and Mental Disease* 172 (5):264–72.

Silf, Margaret. 1998. *The Inner Compass: An Invitation to Ignatian Spirituality.* Chicago: Loyola University Press.

Silverstein, Michael, and Greg Urban, eds. 1996. *Natural Histories of Discourse.* Chicago: University of Chicago Press.

Slade, Peter, and Richard Bentall. 1988. *Sensory Deception: A Scientific Analysis of Hallucination.* London: Croom Helm

Smietana, Bob. 2005. "C. S. Lewis Superstar." *Christianity Today.* November 23.

Smith, Christian. 1998. *American Evangelicalism.* Chicago: University of Chicago Press.

———. 2000. *Christian America?* Berkeley: University of California Press.

Smith, Chuck. 1992. *Charisma Versus Charismania.* Costa Mesa, Calif.: Word for Today.

Smith, Daniel. 2007. *Muses, Madmen, and Prophets.* New York: Penguin.

Smith, Gordon. 2003. *The Voice of Jesus: Discernment, Prayer and the Witness of the Spirit.* Downers Grove, Ill.: InterVarsity.

Smith, James K. 2010. *Thinking in Tongues.* Grand Rapids, Mich.: Eerdmans.

Smith, Jonathan. 2005. *Relaxation, Meditation, and Mindfulness.* New York: Springer.

Smith, Michael. 2007. *Sensing the Past.* Berkeley: University of California Press.

Smith, Wilfred Cantwell. 1977. *Believing—An Historical Perspective.* Oxford, U.K.: Oneworld.

Spiegel, Herbert, and David Spiegel. 2004 [1978]. *Trance and Treatment.* New York: Basic Books.

Springer, Kevin, and John Wimber, eds. 1988. *Power Encounters Among Christians in the Western World.* San Francisco: HarperCollins.

Stein, H. L. 1981. "Book Review: Birth of the Living God." *Psychoanalytic Quarterly* 50:125–30.

Stern, Daniel. 1985. *The Interpersonal World of the Infant: A View from Psychoanalysis and Developmental Psychology.* New York: Basic Books.

Stokes, Laura. 2011. *Demons of Urban Reform.* New York: Palgrave.

Stromberg, Peter. 1993. *Language and Self-Transformation: A Study of the Christian Conversion Narrative.* Cambridge, U.K.: Cambridge University Press.

———. 2009. *Caught in Play.* Stanford, Calif.: Stanford University Press.

Sugimori, Eriko, Tomohisa Asai, and Yoshihiko Tanno. 2011. "Sense of Agency over Speech and Proneness to Auditory Hallucinations." *Quarterly Journal of Experimental Psychology* 64 (1):169–85.

Suhail, K, and R. Cochrane. 2002. "Effect of Culture and Environment on the Phenomenology of Delusions and Hallucinations." *International Journal of Social Psychiatry* 48 (2):126–38.

Sutton-Smith, Brian. 1997. *The Ambiguity of Play.* Cambridge, Mass.: Harvard University Press.

Svendsen, Margaret. 1934. "Children's Imaginary Companions." *Archives of Neurology and Psychiatry* 32 (5):985–99.

Synan, Vinson. 1971. *The Holiness-Pentecostal Movement.* Grand Rapids, Mich.: Eerdmans.

Taves, Ann. 1999. *Fits, Trances and Visions: Experiencing Religion and Explaining Experience from Wesley to James.* Princeton: Princeton University Press.

———. 2009a. "Channeled Apparitions: On Visions That Morph and Categories That Slip." *Visual Resources* 25 (1–2):137–52.

———. 2009b. *Religious Experience Reconsidered.* Princeton: Princeton University Press.

Taylor, Charles. 2007. *A Secular Age.* Cambridge, Mass.: Harvard University Press.

———. 2008. "Buffered and Porous Selves." *Immanent Frame.* September 2.

Taylor, Marjorie. 1999. *Imaginary Companions and the Children Who Create Them.* Oxford, U.K.: Oxford University Press.

Tedlock, Barbara, ed. 1987. *Dreaming: Anthropological and Psychological Interpretations.* Cambridge, U.K.: Cambridge University Press.

Tellegen, Auke. 1981. "Practicing the Two Disciplines for Relaxation and Enlightenment." *Journal of Experimental Psychology: General* 110 (2):217–26.

Tellegen, Auke, and Gilbert Atkinson. 1974. "Openness to Absorbing and Self-Altering Experiences ('Absorption'), a Trait Related to Hypnotic Susceptibility." *Journal of Abnormal Psychology* 83 (3):268–77.

Teresa of Ávila. 1960. *The Life of Teresa of Jesus: The Autobiography of St. Teresa of Ávila.* Translated by E. Allison Peers. Garden City, N.Y.: Image Books.

Tickle, Phyllis. 2003. *The Shaping of a Life.* New York: Doubleday.

Tien, A. Y. 1991. "Distribution of Hallucinations in the Population." *Social Psychiatry and Psychiatric Epidemiology* 26:287–92.

Tipton, Steven. 1982. *Getting Saved from the Sixties: Moral Meaning in Conversion and Cultural Change.* Berkeley: University of California Press.

Torrey, R. A., A. C. Dixon, and others. 2003 [1917]. *The Fundamentals.* Grand Rapids, Mich.: Baker Books.

Trawick, Margaret. 1990. *Notes on Love in a Tamil Family.* Berkeley: University of California Press.

Turkle, Sherry. 2011. *Alone Together.* New York: Basic Books.

Turner, Denys. 1995. *The Darkness of God.* Cambridge, U.K.: Cambridge University Press.

Turner, Frank Miller. 1974. *Between Science and Religion.* New Haven: Yale University Press.

Turner, Victor. 1969. *The Ritual Process: Structure and Anti-Structure.* Chicago: Aldine.

Twenge, Jean, Liqing Zhang, and Charles Im. 2004. "'It's Beyond My Control': A Cross-Temporal Meta-Analysis of Increasing Externality in Locus of Control, 1960–2002." *Personality and Social Psychology Review* 8 (3):308–19.

Tyler, Stephen. 1984. "The Vision Quest in the West, or What the Mind's Eye Sees." *Journal of Anthropological Research* 40 (1):23–40.

Underwood, Lynn. 2006. "Ordinary Spiritual Experience: Qualitative Research, Interpretive Guidelines, and Population Distribution for the Daily Spiritual Experience Scale." *Archive for the Psychology of Religion* 28 (1):181–218.

———. 2011. "The Daily Spiritual Experience Scale: Overview and Results." *Religions* 2 (1):29–50.

Underwood, Lynn, and Jeanne Teresi. 2002. "The Daily Spiritual Experience Scale: Development, Theoretical Description, Reliability, Exploratory Factor Analysis, and Preliminary Construct Validity Using Health-Related Data." *Annals of Behavioral Medicine* 24 (1):22–33.

Vaihinger, H. 1925. *The Philosophy of "As If."* London: Routledge Kegan and Paul.

Vermeule, Blakey. 2010. *Why Do We Care About Literary Characters?* Baltimore: Johns Hopkins University Press.

Veyne, Paul. 1988. *Did the Greeks Believe Their Myths?* Chicago: University of Chicago Press.

Virkler, Mark, and Patti Virkler. 1986. *Dialogue with God.* Gainesville, Fla.: Bridge-Logos.

Vitale, Maria. 2002. "The Sound of Divine Inspiration." http://peopleoffaith.com/christian-article-two.htm.

Wacker, Grant. 2001. *Heaven Below.* Cambridge, Mass.: Harvard University Press.

Waddell, Helen. 1936. *The Desert Fathers.* London: Constable.

Wakefield, James. 2006. *Sacred Listening: Discovering the Spiritual Exercises of Ignatius Loyola.* Grand Rapids, Mich.: Baker Books.

Waller, Niels, Frank Putnam, And Eve Carlson. 1996. "Types of Dissociation and Dissociative Types: A Taxometric Analysis of Dissociative Experiences." *Psychological Methods* 1 (3):300–21.

Walton, K., R. Schneider, and S. Nidich. 2004. "Review of Controlled Research on the Transcendental Meditation Program and Cardiovascular Disease: Risk Factors, Morbidity and Mortality." *Cardiology in Review* 12:261–66.

Walton, K., R. Schneider, S. Nidich, J. Salerno, C. Nordstrom, and C. Bairey Merz. 2002. "Psychosocial Stress and Cardiovascular Disease, Part 2: Effectiveness of the Transcendental Meditation Program in Treatment and Prevention." *Behavioral Medicine* 28 (3):106–23.

Warren, Rick. 2002. *The Purpose Driven Life.* Grand Rapids, Mich.: Zondervan.

Watkins, John. 2008. *Hearing Voices.* South Yarra, Australia: Michelle Anderson.

Watkins, Mary. 1986. *Invisible Guests: The Development of Imaginal Dialogues.* New York: Analytic.

Weil, Simone. 1951. *Waiting for God.* New York: Putnam.

Weitzenhoffer, A. M., and E. R. Hilgard. 1959. *Stanford Hypnotic Susceptibility Scale, Forms A and B.* Palo Alto, Calif.: Consulting Psychologists.

———. 1962. *Stanford Hypnotic Susceptibility Scale, Form C.* Palo Alto, Calif.: Consulting Psychologists.

West, D. J. 1948. "A Mass Observation Questionnaire on Hallucinations." *Journal of the Society for Psychical Research* 34:187–95.

Whalen, J., and M. Nash. 1996. "Hypnosis and Dissociation: Theoretical, Empirical and Clinical Perspectives." In *Handbook of Dissociation,* edited by L. Michelson and W. Ryan, pp. 191–206. New York: Plenum.

Wheeler, Bonnie, and Charles Wood, eds. 1996. *Fresh Verdicts on Joan of Arc.* New York: Garland.

Whitehouse, Harvey. 2004. *Modes of Religiosity.* Walnut Creek, Calif.: Alta Mira.

Whitson, J. A., and A. D. Galinsky. 2008. "Lacking Control Increases Illusory Pattern Perception." *Science* 322:115–17.

Wickramasekara, Ian, and Janet Szlyk. 2003. "Could Empathy Be a Predictor of Hypnotic Ability?" *International Journal of Clinical and Experimental Hypnosis* 51 (4):390–99.

Wicks, Jared. 1983. *Luther and his Spiritual Legacy.* Wilmington, Del.: Michael Glazier.

Wild, T. Cameron, Don Kuiken, and Don Schopflocher. 1995. "The Role of Absorption in Experiential Involvement." *Journal of Personality and Social Psychology* 69 (3):569–79.

Willard, Dallas. 1998. *The Divine Conspiracy: Rediscovering Our Hidden Life in God.* New York: HarperCollins.

———. 1999. *Hearing God: Developing a Conversational Relationship with God.* Downers Grove, Ill.: InterVarsity.

———. 2002. *Renovation of the Heart.* Colorado Springs, Colo.; NavPress.

Williams, Don. 1989. *Signs, Wonders and the Kingdom of God.* La Jolla, Calif.: Vine Books.

Wilson, Ken. 2009. *Mystically Wired.* Nashville, Tenn.: Thomas Nelson.

Wimber, Carol. 1999. *John Wimber: The Way It Was.* London: Hodder and Stoughton.

Wimber, John. 1985. *Power Evangelism.* Anaheim, Calif.: Vineyard Doin' the Stuff.

———. 2006. *The Way In Is the Way On.* Atlanta, Ga.: Ampelon.

Winkelman, Michael. 1986. "Trance State: A Theoretical Model and Cross-Cultural Analysis." *Ethos* 14 (2):174–203.

Winnicott, D.W. 1971. *Playing and Reality.* London: Tavistock.

Wolfe, Alan. 2003. *The Transformation of American Religion.* Chicago: University of Chicago Press.

———. 2008 [1998]. *One Nation, After All.* New York: Penguin.

Wolfson, Elliot. 1994. *Through a Speculum that Shines: Vision and Imagination in Medieval Jewish Mysticism.* Princeton: Princeton University Press.

Woods, Teresa, Michael Antoni, Gail Ironson, and David Kling. 1999. "Religiosity Is Associated with Affective and Immune Status in Symptomatic HIV-Infected Gay Men." *Journal of Psychosomatic Research* 46 (2):165–76.

Wright, Robert. 1995. "The Evolution of Despair." *Time.* August 28.

Wuthnow, Robert. 1988. *The Restructuring of American Religion.* Princeton: Princeton University Press.

———. 1996. *Sharing the Journey.* New York: Free Press.

———. 1998. *After Heaven: Spirituality in America Since the 1950s.* Berkeley: University of California Press.

Yancey, Philip. 1988. *Disappointment with God.* Grand Rapids, Mich.: Zondervan.

Yates, Francis. 1972. *The Rosicrucian Enlightenment.* London: Routledge and Kegan Paul.

Young, William. 2007. *The Shack.* Newberry Park, Calif.: Windblown Media.

Zaleski, Philip, and Carol Zaleski. 2005. *Prayer: A History.* New York: Houghton Mifflin.

Zamova, L. P, and W. B. Faris, eds. 1995. *Magical Realism.* Durham, N.C.: Duke University.

Zimdars-Swartz, Sandra. 1991. *Encountering Mary.* Princeton: Princeton University Press.

INDEX

Abraham, 336–7n56
absorption
  defined, 200–1
  and focus, 195, 349n4
  intense phenomena of, 378
  as personality trait, 199, 202
  prayer as practice of, 202, 208
  similarity to self-hypnosis, 351n21
  and spirituality, 201–2
  training of, 221
absorption scale
  correlation with sensory experiences,
    195, 197
  development of, 198–9
  and experience of God as a person,
    195–6
  focus experiences and, 195
  literature on, 381
ACTS (Adoration, Confession,
  Thanksgiving, Supplication), 157
Acts, Book of, 23–4
addiction as sin, 104
Agamben, Giorgio, 330n8
Aisha (Vineyard congregant), 287–8
  prayer expert, 149–52
  on prayer team, 51
Alcher of Clairvaux, 171
Alice (Vineyard congregant)
  and absorption scale, 196
  on Bible coming alive in Bible study, 92
  on spontaneous thoughts coming
    from God, 52

  on unwanted sensory experiences,
    153–4
alive, God as, 125
Allende, Isabel, 301
Alpha course, 144–5
Amanda. *See* Peter and Amanda
Anglican churches and revival, 336n53
Anselm, Saint, 103
Anthony, Saint
  and apophatic prayer, 162
  and kataphatic prayer, 169
anthropological attitude, xxiv
anxiety
  about beliefs and experiences, 316
  created by sensory experiences, 143
apophatic practice, 161, 162–8. *See also*
  centering prayer
  compared to kataphatic practice, 187
  development of tradition of, 344n13
  studied in Spiritual Disciplines Project,
    206, 207–8, 213–15
Armstrong, Karen, 334n25
Arnobius, 170
Arnold (pastor of Vineyard church)
  on behaving with God as with
    imaginary friend, 74
  conversion narrative, 7–8
  on faith as taking risks, 84–5
  founding of church, 6, 8–9
  and mendicant, love-centered life, 118
arts, enjoyment of, and absorption, 199
Athanasius of Alexandria, 162, 169

PERMISSIONS ACKNOWLEDGMENTS

Grateful acknowledgment is made to the following for permission to reprint previously published material:

David di Sabatino: Excerpt from the documentary film *Frisbee: The Life and Death of a Hippie Preacher,* directed by David di Sabatino, copyright © 2006. Used by permission of David di Sabatino.

Doubleday: Excerpt from *The Cloud of Unknowing and the Book of Privy Counseling* by William Johnston, copyright © 1973 by William Johnston. Used by permission of Doubleday, a division of Random House, Inc.

Lorita Moffat: Excerpt from a meditation from the Ignatian exercises by Sister Lorita Moffat. Used by permission of Lorita Moffat, RSM staff person at Mercy Center.

Thomas Nelson Inc.: Excerpt from *The Sacred Romance* by Brent Curtin and John Eldredge, copyright © 1997 by Thomas Nelson Inc. All rights reserved. Used by permission of Thomas Nelson, Inc., Nashville, Tennessee.

Lynn Underwood: Items from the Daily Spiritual Experiences, copyright © Lynn G. Underwood. Used by permission of Lynn Underwood, www.dsescale.org.

The University of Minnesota Press: Abbreviated items from the Tellegen Absorption Scale. MPQ™ Booklet of Abbreviated Items, copyright © 2011 by the Regents of the University of Minnesota. All rights reserved. Used by permission of the University of Minnesota Press.

Vineyard Music: Excerpt from "Full Attention" by Jeremy Riddle. Used by permission of Vineyard Music, www.vineyardmusic.com.

A NOTE ABOUT THE AUTHOR

T. M. Luhrmann is a psychological anthropologist and the Watkins University Professor in the Department of Anthropology (and Psychology, by courtesy) at Stanford University. She received her education from Harvard and Cambridge Universities, and was elected as a fellow in the American Academy of Arts and Sciences in 2003. In 2007 she was awarded a Guggenheim Fellowship.

A NOTE ON THE TYPE

This book was set in Minion, a typeface produced by the Adobe Corporation specifically for the Macintosh personal computer and released in 1990. Designed by Robert Slimbach, Minion combines the classic characteristics of old-style faces with the full complement of weights required for modern typesetting.

Typeset by Scribe, Philadelphia, Pennsylvania
Printed and bound by Berryville Graphics, Berryville, Virginia
Book design by Robert C. Olsson